INNOVATION POLICY IN THE KNOWLEDGE-BASED ECONOMY

Economics of Science, Technology and Innovation

VOLUME 23

INNOVATION POLICY IN THE KNOWLEDGE-BASED ECONOMY

Edited by

Maryann P. Feldman
John Hopkins University

Albert N. Link
University of North Carolina at Greensboro

KLUWER ACADEMIC PUBLISHERS
Boston / Dordrecht / London

Distributors for North, Central and South America:
Kluwer Academic Publishers
101 Philip Drive
Assinippi Park
Norwell, Massachusetts 02061 USA
Telephone (781) 871-6600
Fax (781) 871-6528
E-Mail <kluwer@wkap.com>

Distributors for all other countries:
Kluwer Academic Publishers Group
Distribution Centre
Post Office Box 322
3300 AH Dordrecht, THE NETHERLANDS
Telephone 31 78 6392 392
Fax 31 78 6546 474
E-Mail <services@wkap.nl>

 Electronic Services <http://www.wkap.nl>

Library of Congress Cataloging-in-Publication Data

Innovation policy in the knowledge-based economy / edited by Maryann P. Feldman, Albert N. Link.
    p. cm . -- (Economics of science, technology, and innovation ; v.23)
    A collection of 18 papers based on sessions held at the 1999 APPAM annual meeting.
    Includes bibliographical references and index.
    ISBN 0-7923-7296-4 (alk. paper)
    1. Information technology--Economic aspects--Congresses. 2. Information Technology--Government policy--Congresses. I. Feldman, Maryann P. II. Link, Albert N. III. Association for Public Policy Analysis and Management (U.S.). Conference (1999) IV. Series.

HC79.155 15624 2001
338.9'26--dc21
                                                           00-069645

Printed on acid-free paper. Printed in the United States of America

Contents

vi

Acknowledgements

The editors would like to thank Erik Devereux, Executive Director of the Association of Public Policy and Management (APPAM), Mario Bane of Harvard University and Sam Meyers of the University of Minnesota for their help and encouragement in organizing the sessions for the 1999 APPAM annual meetings that form the basis for this volume.

We appreciate the commitment from the scholars in the science and technology community, academics as well as policy makers who contributed to this work. Discussants at the APPAM sessions included David Audretsch of Indiana University, Ronald Cooper of the Small Business Administration, Susan Cozzens of Georgia Tech University, Rosalie Ruegg of the National Institutes of Standards and Technology, Wendy Schacht of the Congressional Research Service, Al Teich of the American Association for the Advancement of Science, and Chuck Wessner of the National Academy of Sciences.

We would like to thank Ranik Jasani, Zachary Rolnik and Thomas Randall of Kluwer Publishers. Ranik was there at the conceptual and early stages of this project while Thomas saw this project through to completion. Finally, we would like to thank Merry Perry for her dedicated editorial and production work in putting together this manuscript. The frantic late night but essential contributions of Frank Baldwin, Susan Conner, Pierre Desrochers, Bryan Flynn and Morris Hunt are greatly appreciated.

Chapter 1

Innovation Policy in the Knowledge-Based Economy
A Preface to the Volume

MARYANN P. FELDMAN
Johns Hopkins University

ALBERT N. LINK
University of North Carolina at Greensboro

1.   INTRODUCTION

In 1987, the National Science Foundation sponsored a workshop entitled *An Agenda for Science Policy Research*. That event was a hallmark in science and technology planning. The participants evaluated the existing knowledge base for science and technology policy planning. They also set forth an agenda of questions that need to be addressed and the policy implications of the answers to those questions for the policy community. Topics discussed included the social importance of basic research; the value of the linear model (ala Vannevar Bush) for policy planning in the current science and technology environment; and a host of competitive issues, such as collaborative research relationships, that were expected to be related to the ever present competitive pressures from global markets. Subsequently, scholars investigated many of the recommended issues, and their research influenced legislative initiatives (e.g., the 1993 amendment to the National Cooperative Research Act) during the following decade.

Since that time, scholars in the science and technology field have not collectively questioned, much less proposed an agenda, for policy makers. It is an appropriate time for such an undertaking. First, there is a growing belief that the U.S. national R&D system, like that of many industrial nations, is changing due to global competitive pressures and advancements in information technology/electronic commerce. Second, industry's R&D relationship with the academic research community is changing not only because of the global competition but also because of alterations in the government's funding of fundamental research in industry and in universities. As a result, it is expected that policy makers will need to re-think their approaches to science and technology issues.

This volume is a collection of essays by eminent scholars about innovation policy in the knowledge-based economy. We expect that the reader will at first question this title by asking, Is innovation policy different in a non-knowledge based economy? We would respond, yes. By knowledge-based economy we mean one for which defined economic growth is based on the creation, distribution, and use of technology embodies in physical and human capital. As such, innovation policy in such an economy must enrich the creation, distribution, and use of knowledge that leads to the creation, distribution, and use of technology. By this definition, the essays contained herein view innovation policy as a dynamic rather than as a static event; any adopted policy has first-order effects as well as second-order effects on the creation of new policies both in the adopting economy and in others.

This volume is divided into four sections:

- Elements of an innovation policy;

- Innovation policy and academic research;

- Innovation policy in electronic commerce; and

- Innovation policy and globalization issues.

These sections were created by the general topics defined in the assigned essays with full understanding that all of the topics discussed in each essay are related. Many of the elements of innovation policy, ranging from tax incentives for research and development (R&D) to infrastructure policy to enhance the overall innovative environment in which firms operate, are affected by the health of the academic community and the means by which knowledge flows among innovative units that are globally dispersed. It was our goal when assembling these essays, that the reader find both the general themes associated with current and future policy as well as the specifics about specific initiatives and events that have and will continue to influence innovation.

ELEMENTS OF AN INNOVATION POLICY

PART ONE

Chapter 2

A Brief Data-Informed History of Science and Technology Policy

JOHN E. JANKOWSKI
National Science Foundation

1. ESTABLISHING A FRAMEWORK FOR SCIENCE POLICY

The history of modern science and technology policy is replete with examples of how data can both inform policy as well as reflect policy. In fact, the critical supporting role of data and measurement has been evident since the earliest formulation of post-war policies for science.[1]

Prior to World War II, the federal government's role in the science system of the United States was relatively minor and its funding for research and development (R&D) was generally small. However, successful wartime experiences demonstrated the potential for productive partnerships among the federal, industrial, and academic research sectors might be extended to peacetime needs as well. As a result of these changing perceptions, President Roosevelt requested in November 1944 — even before the close of the war—that Vannevar Bush, Director of the wartime Office of Scientific Research and Development and *de facto* science advisor, outline how lessons learned from the wartime organization of science and engineering could be applied in times of peace. Roosevelt specifically asked for responses to questions dealing with (1) the declassification of secret wartime research results, (2) the need to develop a program to support health-related research, (3) conditions through which the government could provide aid to research activities in public and private organizations, and (4) the feasibility of creating a program for developing scientific talent. Less than one year later, responses to these questions were summarized in the report *Science—the Endless Frontier* (Bush 1945), which highlighted the importance of scientific progress to the nation's health, prosperity, and security. The importance of government financial support to basic medical research and to military research in peacetime was emphasized, as well as was the importance of providing federal basic research support to universities and colleges. Noting the past wise federal investment in agricultural sciences, Bush recommended that similar support be extended to all science and engineering fields. The Bush report highlighted the need for government sponsorship of undergraduate scholarships and graduate fellowships to help develop scientific talent, and for the provision of federal incentives to industry to conduct R&D with their own funds.

The report also recommended that a National Research Foundation be created to assist and encourage research in the public interest by the disbursement of federal dollars for such purposes. Until then, few people had given serious thought to the need for a continuing government role in the science enterprise during a postwar period; however, the obviously increasing importance of federal government in science policy and its impact on academic research and industrial activities was broadly changing that view. In pressing the case for these several recommendations, Bush was not particularly data-reliant, although appendices to the report did contain a fair amount of pre-war quantitative information. It would appear that very few resources were devoted to the collection of statistical data during the war, and those data that were available were oftentimes classified.

Accordingly, in 1946 President Truman created a Scientific Review Board (SRB), chaired by John Steelman and charged to review current and proposed R&D activities both within and outside of the federal government. The result of that review was a five-volume report, the first of which was titled *Science and Public Policy* (and more commonly referred to as the Steelman Report 1947). Unlike *Endless Frontier*, the Steelman Report included a large amount of supporting data, much of which was compiled specifically to inform the SRB in its deliberations. Both reports included a number of policy recommendations for which objective measures and indicators would be needed.

Steelman argued that the U.S. must continually strengthen and expand its domestic economy and foreign trade through the constant expansion of scientific knowledge and the consequent steady improvement of technology. Further, he observed that most major nations already fully recognized the essential importance of science and were expanding their own R&D budgets. The Steelman Report highlighted the contribution of R&D to national prosperity, international progress, and national security. Consequently, the report included a specific recommendation that by 1957 the United States should devote at least one percent of the national income to research and development. It argued that a heavier emphasis needed to be assigned to basic research activities in general and to medical research in particular. Hence, the report recommended that the federal government support basic research in universities and nonprofit research institutions at a progressively increasing rate, that a federal program of assistance to undergraduate and graduate students in the sciences be established, and that a program of federal assistance to universities and colleges be developed in support of laboratory facilities. The Steelman Report also recommended the creation of a National Science Foundation that would be authorized to spend $50 million in support of basic research in its first year, and considerably more in subsequent years. Together, *Science—the Endless Frontier* and *Science and Public Policy* became *ex officio* blueprints for science policy for perhaps the next fifty years.

The National Science Foundation (NSF) was signed into existence on May 10, 1950 "to promote the progress of science; to advance the national health, prosperity, and welfare; and for other purposes."[2] The presumption that NSF programs should be based on sound quantifiable information was widely shared and eventually codified in its statutory authority. Specifically, NSF was directed to "provide a central clearinghouse for the collection, interpretation, and analysis of data on scientific and engineering resources and to provide a source of information for policy formulation by other agencies of the federal government." With this mandate in place explicitly highlighting the critical role of statistical measurement in formulating science policy, the NSF has since been involved in developing and improving an evolving set of science and technology (S&T) indicators. The underlying premise for defining what are good indicators is that they should (1) reflect past trends and circumstances, (2) contribute to understanding the current environment, and (3) guide the development of future policies.

2. PERSISTENT ISSUES IN FEDERAL SCIENCE & TECHNOLOGY POLICY: A FAST FORWARD

The set of available S&T indicators should, by definition, reflect the most important themes and circumstances that drive S&T policy. Such circumstances, however, change and evolve, and thereby challenge those responsible to identify and maintain a useful and enduring set of indicators. Furthermore, even when the S&T circumstances appear somewhat stable, the policies themselves can alter radically over short periods when there are changing priorities of new administrations and legislatures.

Nonetheless, a number of enduring federal S&T themes that have dominated policy discussions, and consequently the development of indicators over the decades. Table 1 identifies the focus of S&T themes from policy documents and presidential statements (most notably the Bush 1945 and Steelman 1947 reports and more recent documents outlining the importance of science and technology in the Clinton/Gore administration policies—Clinton and Gore 1994 and 1996).

*Table 1:*Enduring Federal Science & Technology Themes

Theme	Related Policy Concerns
Coordination of federal research policies and programs	Absence of a consolidated R&D or S&T budget
Importance of science and engineering to national security	Contentious balance between R&D funds for defense and non-defense purposes
Budget support for health-related research	National needs versus fiscal austerity and support for other social goals
Major federal responsibility for supporting university basic research	Issues of balance among S&E fields and across geographic regions, and linkage between research and education
Adequacy of academic research facilities	Small federal role and pork-barrel politics
Importance of R&D, especially industrial R&D, to economic growth	Issues of the proper federal government role, from tax and patent policies to promoting S&T partnerships within and across sectors
Importance of elementary and secondary education	Measurement of student achievement and teacher preparation
Need for trained scientists and engineers	Issues of shortages and diversity of goals
Importance of foreign students in universities	Issues of their contributions versus crowding out of domestic students
Importance of public understanding of science	Issues of public support for S&T initiatives and funding
Global character of science research and technology	Growing importance in issues of competition and cooperation

Both Presidents Truman and Clinton identified many of these specific themes in public addresses before annual meetings of the American Association for the Advancement of Science in 1948 and 1998, respectively. According to Blanpied (2000), these are the only two times that a sitting president addressed the public with the principal objective of outlining his science and technology policy priorities. President Truman highlighted the need to double national R&D spending, increasing the R&D/Gross Domestic Product (GDP) ratio from 0.4 percent to 1.0 percent); provide greater emphasis on basic research and medical research; establish a National Science Foundation; provide more aid to universities in the form of scholarships and research facilities; and better coordinate federal research agencies. He also noted that fundamental research serves national defense needs; the S&T system should receive adequate R&D funds and facilities; the pursuit of science should be free from political concerns; new knowledge encompasses all science and engineering disciplines; and there is a need for greater public awareness about the importance of research.

Fifty years later, President Clinton stressed the need for a "Research Fund for America" in order to provide stable S&T funding and an expanded commitment to discovery (i.e., basic research). He emphasized that health research depends on progress in many science and engineering fields; and that R&D furthers growth in the economy, improvement in the environment, and benefits the nation's overall quality of life. He outlined his reasons for strengthening partnerships between science and other national sectors; improving primary and secondary education; fostering information technology as an S&T enabler; and increasing public understanding of science.

It is immediately apparent that some of the themes are more amenable to data collection and measurement than are others, and that not all of the issues are readily amenable to policy directives. The two sets (those for which data can be collected and those for which policies are readily formulated) are not independent. In broad terms, there are issues of budget and issues of human resources development. Not surprisingly, the historical focus of federal intervention efforts has been accomplished primarily through the purse.

Since the early 1950s, the federal government has spent $1.5 *trillion* on research and development activities.[3] The decomposition of this funding reflects well the changing focus of government priorities in addressing the evolving S&T concerns of the day.

3.   SNAPSHOTS OF FEDERAL R&D SUPPORT

3.1   A National Perspective

The earliest systematic data collection efforts reflect the budgetary prominence in S&T information needs and statistics. During the early 1950s, R&D surveys were established for each of the major S&T sectors: industry, the federal government, universities, and other nonprofit organizations (Table 2). Collectively from these surveys, it is estimated that the country spent $6.3 billion on R&D in 1955, 57 percent of which came from federal agencies (Figure 1). Total R&D equaled about 1.5 percent of the economy's total output (gross domestic product). These amounts represented major increases from levels reported before the national call for peacetime increases in S&T support. Data cobbled together from a variety of sources indicate that only about $345 million had been spent on R&D nationwide in 1940, of which the federal government was the source of just $67 million (19 percent of the total). Most of the Federal money came from defense agencies. Industry provided an estimated $234 million (68 percent) of the national 1940 R&D total (Bush 1945; Bureau of the Census undated).

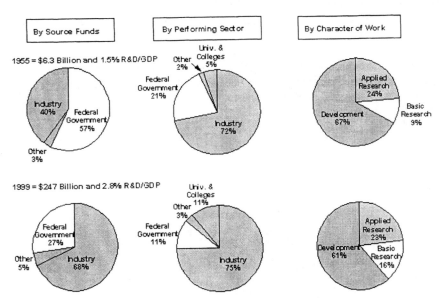

Figure 1: National R&D Expenditures[4]
Source: National Science Foundation (2000a).

Table 2: Meeting *Science* and Technology Data Needs

Decade	Survey	Year
1950s	National Register of Science & Engineering Personnel (NRSEP)	1952
	Survey of Federal Funds for R&D	1953
	Survey of Industrial R&D	1953
	Occasional Survey of Academic R&D	1953
	Occasional Survey of Nonprofit R&D	1954
	Doctorate Records Project	1957
1960s	Post-census Manpower Survey	1962
	Biennial Survey of Academic R&D	1964
	Integrated Post-secondary Education Data System	1966
	Survey of Graduate Students and Post-doctorates	1966
	Occasional Survey of State and Local Government R&D	1967
	National Patterns of R&D Resources Report	1967
	Survey of Federal Support to Universities and Nonprofits	1968
	Trend Data on Immigrant Scientists and Engineers	1968
1970s	Last NRSEP (1970) replaced by	
	Manpower survey	1972
	Survey of Doctorate Recipients	1973
	Survey of New Entrants	1974
	Science Indicators mandated report	1972
	Annual Survey of Academic R&D	1972
	Last R&D Survey on Nonprofit Organizations	1973
	Occupational Employment Survey, including Scientists and Engineers	1977
	Survey of Public Attitudes	1979
1980s	Post-census Survey of Scientists and Engineers	1982
	Survey of Academic Research Instruments	1983
	Women and Minorities in Science & Engineering mandated report	1984
	Biennial Academic Science & Engineering Research Facilities	1986
	Science & Engineering Indicators report name change	1987
1990s	Integrated Scientists and Engineers Statistical Data (SESTAT) System	1992
	Pilot Survey on Industrial Innovation	1994
	Survey of Nonprofit Institutions R&D	1998
	Survey of Innovation in Information Technologies	1999

Source: Derived from National Research Council (2000).

In terms of where the R&D is performed, the federal government including its federally funded R&D centers (then consisting primarily of work at its atomic weapons laboratories) accounted for 21 percent of the national 1955 R&D total, with industrial firms accounting for most of the rest. Overall, about nine percent ($600 million) was devoted to fundamental basic research activities (Figure 1). Over the next 45 years, national R&D spending increased forty-fold to $247 billion in 1999 (or an eight-fold increase in inflation-adjusted dollars, from 25 billion 1992 dollars in 1955 to $200 billion in 1999). Of this 1999 total, 16 percent is now used on basic research projects. Concurrent with industry remaining the dominant R&D performing sector in the country (at 75 percent of total), it also has become the primary source of R&D funds (accounting for 68 percent of the 1999 total). The federal government's funding share has dropped from 57 percent in 1955 to 27 percent in 1999, and its lab activities now account for just 11 percent of the national R&D performance total. Particularly during the past decade or so, federal R&D funding has remained flat (in inflation-adjusted terms); reflecting the pressure of fiscal constraints imposed on all parts of the budget, not specifically R&D programs. Meanwhile, industrial financing of R&D activities has grown on average by more than nine percent per year in each of the past five years. As a result of these disparate trends, there has been a mirror reversal in sources of R&D funding from that which existed forty years prior: the relative funding shares from industry and the federal government have switched (Figures 2 through 4).

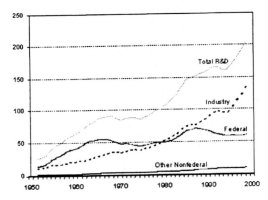

Figure 2: National R&D Funding by Source: Total R&D (Billions 1992 Dollars)
Source: National Science Foundation (2000a).

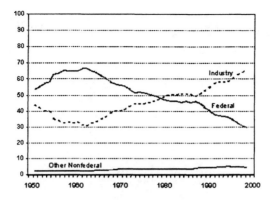

Figure 3: National R&D Funding by Source: Percent of Total R&D
Source: National Science Foundation (2000a).

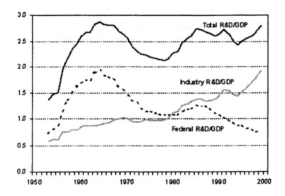

Figure 4: National R&D Funding by Source: R&D as a Percentage of GDP
Source: National Science Foundation (2000a).

3.2   A Budgetary Perspective

Despite the apparent *relative* decline in federal R&D funding during the past 50 years, there actually has been broad bipartisan support for such activities throughout the period. With few exceptions, this circumstance has been the case in both periods of growth as well as times of severe fiscal austerity. The relative and continuing importance of R&D in the federal portfolio is notably evident by comparison with all programmatic spending, both "mandatory" and "discretionary." Certain expenditures, including those for Social Security, Medicare, Medicaid, and interest on the national debt, are considered mandatory items in the federal budget. That is, the government is already committed to financing those programs at certain levels and cannot cut them without a change in the law. In contrast, discretionary items, including both defense and non-defense R&D programs, do not enjoy the same level of protection from budget-cutting proposals; and the federal government generally is not committed by law to finance such programs at particular levels. In terms of the overall federal budget, the discretionary component has been a declining share of total for decades.

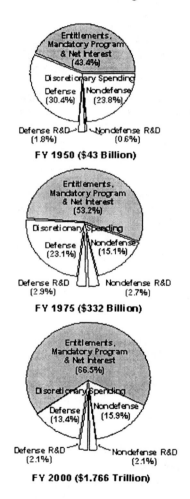

Figure 5: The R&D Share of the Federal Budget
Source: Office of Management and Budget (2000); American Association for the Advancement of Science (1999).

In 1950, discretionary funds accounted for 57 percent of the total budget: R&D funding accounted for 2.4 percent of the total budget and about 4 percent of discretionary funds (Figure 5). During the next 25 years, there were two distinctively different periods in terms of federal R&D funding trends. Between 1950 and 1967, federal R&D expenditures grew at a real rate of about 11 percent per year. Such funds were provided to support a variety of public objectives. For nearly a decade thereafter, however, R&D funding failed to keep up with either inflation or general increases in economic output, reflecting government's general de-emphasis on research programs. Federal R&D outlays fell 20 percent in real terms, a decrease that was felt in both defense and civilian R&D programs. Nonetheless, by 1975—at which point mandatory program spending then exceeded half of the budget—the relative share devoted to R&D was still higher than it had been in 1950: R&D funding accounted for 5.6 percent of the total budget and for 11 percent of all discretionary funds. Finally, following several years of first budgetary growth and subsequently fiscal austerity, R&D now accounts for more than 12 percent of the discretionary budget even while mandatory spending consumes approximately two-thirds of all federal outlays.

4.   MAJOR FEDERAL R&D FUNDING TRENDS

The above discussion, however, may be a bit misleading. Although federal support for R&D is indeed allocated annually through the budget process, there is no federal R&D budget *per se*. Funding for R&D priorities, similar to the federal budget as a whole, is never enacted as a single piece of legislation. Rather, in keeping with the decentralized character of the U.S. government generally, budget decisions on individual parts of the federal R&D portfolio are made through dozens of pieces of legislation each year largely independent of one another with few opportunities for coordination or system-wide priority-setting. Further, where there are opportunities for programmatic trade-offs in the budget-setting process, they are not usually among the merits of competing science and technology activities. Rather, the budget allocation system is such that R&D programs and non-R&D programs alike are judged against their potential contributions toward agencies' missions. Because agency budgets are written independently of one another, budgets for R&D programs are also considered independently form one another (except for some coordination in planning multi-agency cross-cutting S&T projects).[5] Further undermining the likelihood of coordinated R&D funding decisions, agency' budget proposals seldom are based on solicited input from the industry and university performers who actually perform much of the federal R&D work.

4.1   Socio-economic Objectives

Government support for science and technology historically has been driven by "grand challenges" that invigorate the nation and expand scientific boundaries. In many cases, such investments have resulted in a fall-out of unanticipated and unintended technological and economic benefits unrelated to the crisis or challenge at hand. Undoubtedly the most consistent and enduring driver in U.S. S&T policies has been the need to strengthen national security, which—as Vannevar Bush described it—is best grounded in scientific progress. Only twice during the entire post-war period (1966 and 1978-79) has the defense share of the federal R&D total dipped below 50 percent, and in both instances other "national challenges" were in the forefront of funding concerns.

In the aftermath of the war, federal defense-related R&D continued to expand and dominate the total federal R&D funding picture. Having been spurred on by both Korean hot war demands and Soviet Cold War concerns, defense-related funding accounted for approximately 85 percent of the total federal R&D effort as late as 1957 (upper half, Figure 6). At that point, however, R&D priorities shifted markedly toward the space program largely as a response to the launch of Sputnik in 1957 (lower half, Figure 6). Driven by the National Aeronautics and Space Administration's (NASA) goal to put a man on the moon by the end of the 1960s, space R&D came to dominate the federal civilian R&D total, peaking in 1966, at which point NASA was second only to the Department of Defense (DOD) in terms of federal R&D funding. After the success of the Apollo moon landings, however, R&D support for space declined in both relative and absolute terms.

During in the 1970s, the oil embargoes of 1973 and 1979 fostered the new national challenge resulting in an upward spike in the government's support for energy R&D (especially nuclear energy R&D) that is noticeable in the aggregate statistics of Figure 6. At that point, defense R&D spending was slightly less than federal R&D spending for all other purposes. This circumstance changed rapidly, however, with the Carter Administration decision to rebuild the country's defense capabilities, including an infusion of new R&D funds. Defense R&D funding expanded considerably in the early- and mid-1980s as a result of the Reagan Administration's decision to continue the military build-up by increasing reliance on technological superiority and large programmatic R&D support budgeted for the Strategic Defense Initiative, more commonly known as Star Wars. By 1986, the defense share of the federal R&D total reached a local peak of 69 percent. Since then, and as a result of an explicit Clinton Administration policy to affect such change, the fiscal year 2000 defense/non-defense R&D funding shares are once again almost equal.

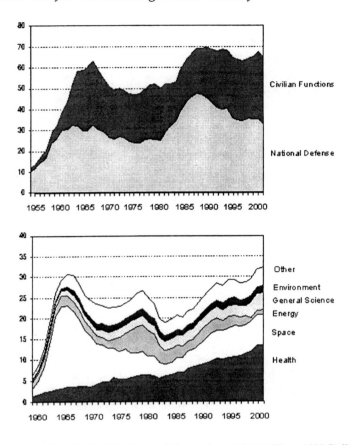

Figure 6: Trends in Federal Defense and Non-defense R&D (Billions 1992 Dollars)
Source: National Science Foundation (2000b).

Concurrent with these various federal R&D trends of the past decades has been the constant growth in federal health R&D—in both dollar terms and, more recently, as a share of the total. Health accounted for about 3 percent of the federal R&D total in the 1950s (ten percent of the non-defense component), rising steadily to 20 percent of all federal R&D in the year 2000 (and 40 percent of the non-defense share). The government's long-standing support for health and medical research can be traced back to the earliest pronouncements in the Bush and Steelman reports. In *Science—the Endless Frontier*, health concerns alone among the various governmental objectives warranted a full chapter, in which was noted "[p]rogress in combating disease depends upon an expanding body of new scientific knowledge." Medical research continues to be a funding priority today. In the early 1970s, most of the health R&D growth stemmed from the nation's launch of the war on cancer. In the 1980s, AIDS research was the new catalyst for health-related research growth. Both diseases continue to receive the largest R&D budgetary shares of the National Institutes of Health (NIH). More recently, however, the rapid rise in federal support for health research reflects the widespread view that there are major opportunities for a host of medical breakthroughs stemming from potential advances in biotechnology-based sciences.

4.2   Federal R&D Support to the Industrial Sector

Most of the R&D funds provided by the federal government are *not* used in federal labs. Rather, more than 30 agencies provide R&D funding to thousands of organizations in both the private and public sector through contracts, grants, and other formal arrangements. The industrial sector historically has been the far largest recipient of federal R&D dollars, received most commonly to undertake work needed by mission agencies such as the Department of Defense, NASA and the Department of Energy (DoE). During the past 50 years, industry annually has received more R&D money than has any of the other performing sectors and during several periods of particularly active military buildup, firms were funded at levels practically equivalent to that provided all other sectors combined.[6] Indeed the double-hump bulges in federally financed industrial R&D exhibited in Figure 7 reflect the military buildups stemming from the Vietnam hot and cold war priorities of the 1960s and from the Star Wars spending spree in the 1980s. Not surprisingly then, given these military catalysts for funding, firms located in the aircraft and missiles industry have received the dominant share of these federal dollars for decades (Figure 8). Even with recent shifts in the federal funding focus (including a diminished emphasis on defense R&D), such firms continue to receive close to half of the federal R&D provided all of industry. Indeed, approximately two-thirds of total federal R&D dollars flowing to the private sector came from defense agencies as recently as 1998. Similarly, federal agency—particularly defense agency—funding has accounted for 60 to 80 percent of all R&D performed by firms in the missiles and aircraft industry. In any other industry sector, federal funds seldom exceed 30 percent of the total R&D funds used.

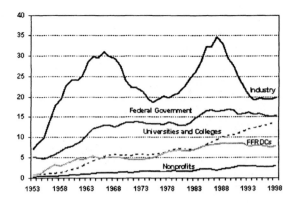

Figure 7: Federal R&D Support to Performing Sectors (Billions 1992 Dollars)
Source: National Science Foundation (2000a).

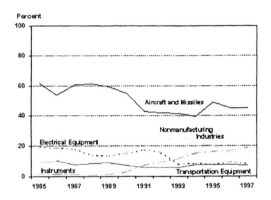

Figure 8: Industry Shares of Total Federal R&D Support to all Industry Sectors
Source: National Science Foundation (1999a).

The defense focus notwithstanding, federal funding in support of non-defense industrial R&D purposes is also well established, especially via programs located at the Departments of Transportation and Commerce and the National Institutes of Health. Indeed, dating back at least to the Bush report, it has been a long-standing federal presumption that the nation's economic and technological prosperity depends critically on industry's R&D efforts. That the government has a major role in fostering these activities, however, is a view that has been much less widely shared. Nonetheless, over time Congress has put into place several government-wide programs specifically designed to support the industrial R&D effort. Most notable among them is undoubtedly the *Small Business Innovation Research*

Program (SBIR*)*, created in 1982 specifically to strengthen the role of small firms in federal R&D competitions. That such direct preferential support is warranted reflects a widely held assumption that small business is a significant source of innovation and engine of economic growth. SBIR is the country's largest merit-based competitive grants program through which R&D funds are available to thousands of qualified small high-technology businesses. Under this program, an agency must set aside 2.5 percent of its external R&D obligations (that is, other than for in-house R&D programs) for SBIR projects. To obtain grant funding, a company's proposed project must meet an agency's research needs and have commercial potential. Ten federal agencies participated in the SBIR Program in 1997, making awards totaling $1.1 billion (Figure 9)—an amount equivalent to 1.6 percent of all government R&D obligations (3.5 percent of federally funded R&D received by industrial firms). DOD, mirroring this agency's share of the federal R&D funding total, provided approximately 51 percent of all SBIR obligations. More than one-fourth of all SBIR awards made during 1983–97 were electronics-related and roughly one-sixth involved computers. Computer- and electronics-related projects received more than 70 percent of their support from DOD and NASA. One-seventh of all SBIR awards went to life sciences research; the U.S. Department of Health & Human Services (HHS) provided the bulk of this funding (SBA 1999; NSB 2000).

The U.S. government has tried various policy instruments in addition to direct financial R&D support to indirectly stimulate corporate research spending. Proponents of such measures note that, especially as direct federal discretionary spending for R&D is squeezed, incentives must be used to invigorate U.S. investment in private-sector innovation and to expand U.S. global leadership in high technology. Among the earliest incentives were *tax credits on incremental research* and experimentation (R&E) expenditures. The credit, first put in place in 1981, provides for a 20 percent credit for a company's qualified R&D amount that exceeds a certain threshold. According to a report prepared for the Joint Economic Committee of the U.S. Congress (based on information from the Internal Revenue Service Statistics of Income publications), more than 12,000 firms use the tax credit annually (Whang 1998). Large manufacturers—especially pharmaceuticals, motor vehicles, aircraft, electronics and computer firms, claim the largest credits. Companies with more than $250 million in assets account for three-quarters of the dollar value of all credit claims. On the other hand, three-quarters of credit claimants have assets of $25 million or less, and medium-sized manufacturers and service providers file many claims. Between fiscal years 1981 and 1999, more than $34.2 billion was provided to industry through this indirect means. For FY 1998 alone, the credit was worth about $3.3 billion to industry, an amount equivalent to almost five percent of all federal R&D outlays (Figure 9) or ten percent of federal direct R&D support to industry alone.

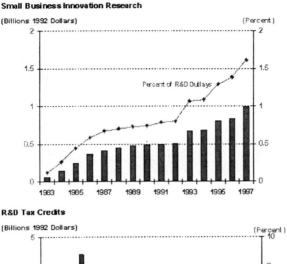

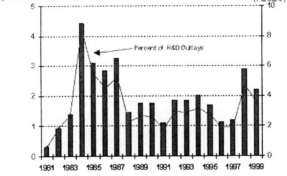

Figure 9: Outlay Value of Federal R&D Programs
Source: Office of Management and Budget (1999); Small Business Administration (1998).

4.3   Federal R&D Support to the Academic Sector

Since early in the post-war period, and continuing through the present, federal funding of basic fundamental research and of university performed research in particular, has been a bipartisan constant in federal policies and priorities. Federal R&D support to universities and colleges has grown rather steadily throughout the past fifty years and now exceeds $15 billion annually (Figure 7). Since at least the early 1950s, universities have come to rely on 60 percent or more of their R&D funding from federal agencies. Although the available data are somewhat spotty, it would appear that initially much of the federal academic research support was provided by the Public Health Service and to a lesser extent DOD, USDA, and the Atomic Energy Commission (one of several predecessor agencies to the Department of Energy) (Bureau of the Census undated; Rowberg 1999). Towards the end of the 1950s, the importance of National Science Foundation funding of university research increased substantially. (NSF is the only agency to fund basic research in all science and engineering fields simply for the sake of creating new knowledge, rather than for fulfilling a specific agency mission need.) Indeed, during the early 1960s, growth in NSF funding particularly contributed to the federal share of university R&D support reaching about 75 percent of their total (Figure 10). Reflecting their preference for high levels of federal support, advocates have coined this period to be the Golden Age of Science. In hindsight, such high academic reliance on federal funds is unlikely to reoccur given today's fiscal realities.

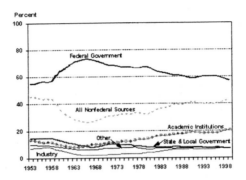

Figure 10: Sources of Academic R&D Funding
Source: National Science Foundation (1999b).

Although many federal agencies support R&D activities on our Nation's campuses, just three agencies are responsible for most of these federal obligations (approximately 83 percent in 1999). The National Institutes of Health accounted for 58 percent of all federal academic R&D financing; NSF for 15 percent; and the Department of Defense for ten percent. There are notable differences in such support from these agencies: NIH and NSF place greater emphasis on research, biomedical and all other science and engineering fields, respectively, while DOD places greater emphasis on development funding.

In addition to providing academic research support in general, it has been a long-standing federal concern that such funding be available to universities throughout the Nation. Indeed the Organic NSF Act of 1950 actually charges the Foundation to "strengthen research and education in the sciences and engineering... throughout the United States, and to avoid undue concentration of such research and education." For years, this base broadening was one of the implicit goals of federal academic research funding. However, it was only in 1978—responding to widespread Congressional concerns about the extent of geographical concentration in federal R&D funding—that NSF put in place a preferential grants program, the *Experimental Program to Stimulate Competitive Research* (EPSCoR). An EPSCoR premise is that university research can potentially influence a state's development in the 21st century much in the same way that agricultural, industrial, and natural resources did in the 20th century (Chapter 6 in NSB 2000). Eligibility for EPSCoR participation was limited to those states (and Puerto Rico) that historically had received lesser amounts of federal R&D funding but had demonstrated a commitment to develop their university research bases. Since 1979, other federal agencies have adopted their own EPSCoR or EPSCoR-like programs: DOD, DOE, the Environmental Protection Agency (EPA), NASA, NIH, and USDA. In 1998, these seven agencies spent $89 million on EPSCoR or EPSCoR-like programs.

Outside of the specific support generated by EPSCoR programs, the number of academic institutions receiving federal support for their R&D activities has increased generally over the past three decades. Between 1971 and 1997, the number of institutions receiving support increased almost 50 percent, from less than 600 to more than 800 (Figure 11). Since most institutions designated as research and doctorate-granting institutions were already receiving federal support in 1971, most of the increase has occurred among the group containing comprehensive; liberal arts; two-year community, junior, and technical; and professional and other specialized schools (NSB 2000).

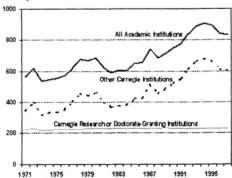

Figure 11: Academic Institutions Receiving Federal R&D Support
Source: National Science Foundation (1999c).

4.4   Federal Basic Research Support

Most (66 percent in 1999) of the R&D conducted at universities and colleges is basic research and most (52 percent) of the nation's basic research (including that performed by universities and all other types of institutions) is financed by federal agencies.[7] Most of the federal support for basic research comes from relatively few agencies. NIH accounts for the largest agency share (47 percent in 1999) of total basic research financing from government. Four agencies, NIH combined with NSF (14 percent), DOE (13 percent), and NASA (13 percent) account for 87 percent of all federal basic research dollars (Figure 12). Collectively, federal agency support for basic research climbed almost 90 percent—even after adjusting for inflation—during the past 20 years. These support levels compare most favorable with those for federal R&D overall, which grew by roughly only 20 percent in real terms between 1979 and 1999.

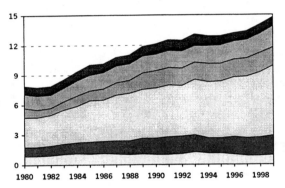

Figure 12: Basic Research Obligations by Agency (Billions 1992 Dollars)
Source: National Science Foundation (1999d).

In terms of overall support, the federal government has historically provided the majority of funds used for basic research (Figure 13). As a percentage of all basic research funding, the federal share peaked at 72 percent in 1967—the pinnacle of the Golden Age of Science. It remained near 70 percent throughout most of the 1970s, before dropping 18 percentage points—from 70 percent to 52 percent—between 1980 and 1999. This decline in the federal share, however, does not reflect a decrease in the actual amount of federal basic research support, which grew by more than three percent per year in real terms during the 1980-99 period. Rather, it reflects a growing tendency for basic research funding to come from other sectors. This broad-based support for basic research has resulted in significant shifts in the composition of the national R&D effort: In 1955, basic research accounted for nine percent of the national R&D total. In 1999 support for basic fundamental research represented 16 percent of all R&D expenditures (Figure 1). By comparison, over the past decade federal applied research and development support has been level or declining (in real terms). In 1999, federal support accounted for less than 30 percent of total dollars spent on each of such activities in the nation, compared with federal funding shares reaching well over 50 percent in the 1960s.

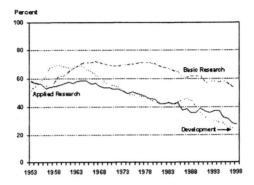

Figure 13: The Federal Share of U.S. Funding of Basic Research, Applied Research and Development
Source: National Science Foundation (2000a).

5.   FEDERAL TECHNOLOGY DEVELOPMENT POLICIES

Although the importance of research and technology in fostering economic growth and prosperity was acknowledged in the earliest documents on science policy, the road to enacting direct federal support mechanisms has been a bumpy one at best. Indeed, in speaking to the importance of industrial research, Vannevar Bush wrote: "The simplest and most effective way in which government can strengthen industrial research is to support basic research and to develop scientific talent." The only other concerns specifically addressed in the "Industrial Research" section of *Science—the Endless Frontier* dealt with the need to improve the patent system and to enact and clarify tax provisions that would help foster industry R&D investments.

A willingness to reconsider the more-or-less "hands-off" federal role in technology promotion changed considerably in the late 1970s and early 1980s. At the end of the war and for several decades thereafter, the United States was by far the economic and technological world leader. Productivity soared, real wages grew steadily, and U.S. business dominated many if not most industry sector markets. Of course, American economic hegemony was neither sustainable nor even necessarily desirable. Not surprisingly, except perhaps to some legislators and policymakers, this situation slowly changed. Perhaps one of the most telling manifestations of official concern was the establishment of a Presidential Commission on Industrial Competitiveness in 1983. Premised on the observation that "America's competitive preeminence in world commerce has eroded over the past decade... [and that] sustaining America's competitiveness is important for maintaining our standard of living, our foreign policy aims, and our national security" the Commission was tasked

- To identify the problems and opportunities for the private sector to transform new knowledge and innovations into commercial products, services, and manufacturing processes; and

- To recommend policy changes at all levels of government to improve the private sector's ability to compete in the international marketplace.

Against this backdrop, a multitude of legislation was enacted in the 1980s and early 1990s with the goal to further science- and technology-based economic growth and productivity. Several laws were put in place that provided direct federal R&D assistance, such as the SBIR program discussed earlier. Other steps were taken to provide indirect financial inducements for expanding the Nation's research investments, such as the R&E tax credit also described earlier. Particularly new and more prevalent, however, were laws intended (i) to promote the commercial use of research results by sectors previously uninvolved in such activities and (ii) to foster R&D partnerships, collaborations, and technology sharing within and across each of the three major R&D-performing sectors--industry, academia and the federal laboratories (Table 3).[8]

5.1   University-Related Federal Policies

Throughout the post-war period and continuing to this day, the primary focus of federal science policy toward the academic sector has been support in the form of research dollars. Universities traditionally performed much of the fundamental research that is integral to technological advances, but had little involvement in direct university-industry collaboration or in the commercialization of their research results. Consequently, the federal government, particularly the NSF, has helped fund a number of centers programs that serve to link industry and university researchers in order to help shape priorities and build relationships. The earliest such effort was the Industry/University Cooperative Research Centers program established 1973. Subsequently, in the mid-1980s and early 1990s a variety of collaborative programs were put in place, including NSF's Engineering Research Centers (1985); Science & Technology Centers (1987); Centers of Research Excellence in Science and Technology (1987); and the State/Industry/University Cooperative Research Centers program (1990).

Table 3: Federal Legislation Supporting Technology Growth

Act	Year	Purpose
Stevenson-Wydler Technology Innovation Act	1980	Required federal laboratories to facilitate the transfer of federally owned and originated technology to the private sector.
Bayh-Dole University and Small Business Patent Act	1980	Encouraged universities to retain title to inventions and to license inventions to industry.
Research and Experimentation Tax Credit	1981	Used the tax code to encourage industry funding of more R&D.
Small Business Innovation Development Act	1982	Established the Small Business Innovation Research (SBIR) Program to increase government funding of research with commercialization potential in the small high-technology company sector.
National Cooperative Research Act	1984	Reduced antitrust exposure to encourage firms to form joint research venture collaborations.
Federal Technology Transfer Act	1986	Authorized cooperative research and development agreements (CRADAs) between federal laboratories and other entities.
Omnibus Trade and Competitiveness Act	1988	Created programs to enhance industrial competitiveness: Advanced Technology Program and the Manufacturing Technology Centers in NIST.
National Competitiveness Technology Transfer Act	1989	Allowed government-owned, contractor-operated laboratories to enter into CRADAs.
Defense Conversion, Reinvestment & Transition Assistance Act	1992	Initiated Technology Reinvestment Project to facilitate technology development and deployment with both defense and commercial applications.
National Cooperative Research and Production Act	1993	Extended limitation of antitrust exposure to encourage firms to form joint production collaborations.

Source: Office of Technology Policy (2000) and National Science Board (2000).

To foster the commercialization of university research, Congress passed the Bayh-Dole Act in 1980, which permitted government grantees to retain title to federally-funded inventions and encouraged universities to license inventions to industry. As with the various Centers programs, the Act was designed to foster interactions between academia and the business community and to speed the dissemination of academic research into commercial applications. As one indicator of this Act's possible influence, Figure 14 tracks trends in *academic patenting.* The U.S. Patent and

Trademark Office (USPTO) assigns property rights in the form of patents for inventions deemed to be new, useful, and non-obvious in order to foster inventive activity that may have important economic benefits. The bulk of academic R&D is basic research, that is, not undertaken to yield or contribute to immediate practical applications. However, academic patenting data show that universities are giving increased attention to potential economic benefits inherent in even their most basic research—and that the USPTO grants patents based on such basic work, especially in the life sciences (NSB 2000).

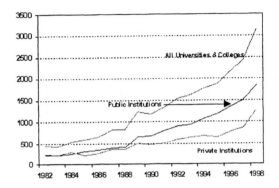

Figure 14. Academic Patents Granted
Source: U.S. Patent and Trademark Office (1999).

After slow growth in the 1970s, the number of academic institutions applying for, and receiving, patents increased rapidly in the 1980s from about 75 early in the decade to double that by 1990 and more than 170 by the late 1990s. Comparable to research funding trends described above (Figure 11), the number of institutions outside the ranks of the largest research universities with patent awards increased at a rapid pace starting in the early 1980s. The nation's largest research universities represented 64 percent of all academic institutions receiving patents in 1985; their number had fallen to half by 1996 (NSB 2000). Much of the base broadening of patenting institutions occurred among public universities and colleges. In terms of the number of patents granted to universities, there were fewer than 500 issued in 1982. By 1992, the number of academic patents had more than tripled to more than 1,500 and the number granted approximately doubled again to 3151 in 1998 (Figure 14).

5.2   Federal Policies to Encourage Industry Collaborations

As is the case with defense-related R&D, the federal government historically has funded industrial R&D projects to meet mission requirements: the results of the R&D tended to be in areas where the government was the primary user. A major focus of legislative efforts since the early 1980s has been to encourage companies to undertake cooperative R&D arrangements with the goal of improving U.S. firms' international competitiveness. Declining trade balances led many legislators to conclude that existing U.S. antitrust laws and penalties were too restrictive and could be impeding the ability of U.S. companies to compete in the global marketplace. U.S. companies were at a disadvantage compared to their foreign counterparts, because of an outdated antitrust environment—designed to preserve domestic competition—that prohibited them from collaborating on most activities, including R&D. Therefore, in 1984, restrictions on multi-firm cooperative research relationships were lifted with the passage of the National Cooperative Research Act (NSB 2000). The law was enacted to encourage U.S. firms to collaborate on generic, pre-competitive research that might not otherwise be undertaken because it was too long-term, risky, and expensive for a single company. To gain protection from antitrust litigation, NCRA requires firms engaging in *research joint ventures* (RJVs) to register them with the U.S. Department of Justice. In 1993, Congress again relaxed restrictions—this time on cooperative production activities—by passing the National Cooperative Research and Production Act, which enables participants to work together to apply technologies developed by their RJVs. By the end of 1999, 791 RJVs had been registered (Figure 15).

Firms in the electronics industry registered the largest number of RJVs from 1985 to 1999 (140 of the 791 total) (Link 2000). Communication services were a close second with 134, followed by transportation equipment with 122. In terms of their cross-sector collaborative impact, the data indicate that only ten percent of all RJVs included federal laboratories as research members, but that 16 percent of all RJVs included university research members. About 29 percent of RJVs had foreign affiliates. Fifty percent of RJVs (393 of the 791 total) had research that was process-focused; 42 percent had research that was product-focused; and the remaining eight percent had research that included both.

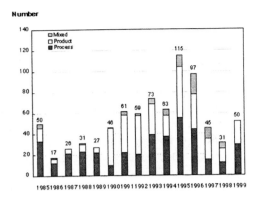

Figure 15: Growth in R&D Consortia Registered Under the National Cooperative Research and Production Act

Source: A. N. Link (2000).

Further, there have been instances where direct federal R&D funding of specific technologies has been coupled with these regulatory efforts to foster industrial research partnerships. The most notable example of this dual approach involved the Department of Defense funding of SEMATECH, an RJV initially consisting of 14 large companies (when registered in 1988) whose stated objectives related to R&D in advanced semiconductor manufacturing techniques (Heizer 1991). DOD provided annual funding of about $100 million between 1988 and 1996. It is generally believed that SEMATECH's activities helped U.S. industries regain leadership in global markets for this particular high-tech product. Other federal initiatives in support of specific technological goals include the Partnership for a New Generation of Vehicles, inaugurated in 1995 and now funded at more than $200 million annually, a cost-sharing partnership with industry which aims to produce environment-friendly, fuel efficient vehicles (OMB 1999).

5.3   Technology Transfers from Federal Laboratories

The term "technology transfer" can cover a wide spectrum of activities, from informal exchanges of ideas between visiting researchers to contractually structured research collaboration involving the joint use of facilities and equipment. As is the circumstance with federally-financed R&D that is contracted out, however, most of the R&D work undertaken in federal laboratories is designed with only the mission needs of the "agency as customer" in mind. Although some agencies had long shared their research with the private sector (e.g., USDA's Agricultural Research Experiment Stations and NASA's civilian aeronautics programs), most of the R&D traditionally was performed without any intention to commercialize—or transfer to the marketplace—the research results.

Government-wide policies formally changed early in the 1980s when several laws were passed (notably, the Stevenson-Wydler Technology Innovation Act of 1980) to specifically encourage such sharing of federal technologies with the private sector. As were other policy initiatives of the time, technology transfer was regarded as a means of addressing federal concerns about U.S. industrial strength and world competitiveness. Only since the late 1980s, however, has technology transfer become an important mission component of some federal labs, particularly several of the government defense labs that were seeking alternatives to their declining defense work. In addition to technology-sharing incentives, several laws encourage federal agencies to work cooperatively with industry partners and to commercialize their research results. The Federal Technology Transfer Act of 1986 authorized government-owned and-operated laboratories to enter into cooperative R&D agreements (CRADAs) with private industry, and the 1989 passage of the National Competitiveness Technology Transfer Act allowed contractor-operated labs (including DOE's FFRDCs) to also enter into CRADAs.

According to most available indicators, federal efforts to facilitate private-sector commercialization of federal technology have made considerable progress since 1987 (Figure 16). The number of CRADAs entered into by federal laboratories has grown geometrically, from 34 in 1987 to 3,688 in 1996--an average growth rate of more than 68 percent per year. Between 1996 and 1998, however, the number of active CRADAs declined, to 3,201. Invention disclosures increased rapidly at first, from 2,662 in 1987 to 4,213 in 1991--a 58 percent increase in only four years. Over the succeeding seven years (to 1998), however, that level was not reached again. The annual number of invention disclosures since 1991 seem to be random, averaging 3,815, but still remaining above 3,500 each year. Patent applications have had a similar history. They rose in number from 848 in 1987 to an all time-high of 1,900 in 1991--a 124 percent increase. Policy changes of the 1980s had a particularly positive impact on patenting activities of Department of Energy laboratories. Before this period, such facilities had considerably fewer patents per R&D dollar than the average university had; now they are about equal. After 1991, patent applications from all agencies averaged 1,765, with no apparent trend. The number of licenses granted rose steadily between 1987 and 1998, from 128 to 510. These results indicate probable success in policies designed to advance the dissemination of federal R&D products to the private sector.

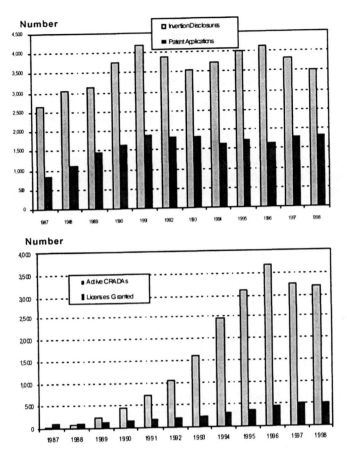

Figure 16: Federal Technology Transfer Indicators
Source: Office of Technology Policy (2000).

6.   SUMMARY OBSERVATIONS

Much is revealed about federal science and technology priorities and policies from the available S&T statistics and indicators. Throughout the post-war period, the federal government has continually provided extensive direct funding support for scientific and technological advancements. In many instances, the purpose was to advance specific agency mission goals that historically were the responsibility of government. R&D funding for defense purposes remain paramount among such goals. However, as national and international circumstances evolved, priorities have somewhat shifted with the result that other national goals are now commanding a growing share of the federal R&D effort, notably health-related activities.

The perceived importance of support for fundamental university-based research is documented in the earliest pronouncements on the appropriate federal role in the S&T enterprise. Recognized as the bedrock foundation underpinning technological growth and societal well being, university research funding has grown steadily during the past fifty years. Federal funds for basic research—performed in academia and other sectors—have also increased uninterruptedly during the entire period for which data exist. Conversely, federal funding for applied research and development activities, and to industrial performers in particular, have tended to reflect the "grand challenges" of the time.

Since the mid-1980s, available indicators reflect a more willing governmental role in providing support for commercially oriented R&D than had been the case previously. Although there are numerous examples of direct funding for such activities, federal technology policies indicate a preference for indirect mechanisms. In most cases, such legislation was explicitly designed to foster research partnerships and collaborations in order to create a more globally competitive nation. All sectors of the economy have been identified as potential contributors to S&T-based economic growth. Consequently, each of the R&D-performing sectors has benefited from specific research-promoting legislative and regulatory mechanisms.

ACKNOWLEDGEMENTS

John Jankowski is the director of the Research & Development Statistics Program in the Division of Science Resources Studies of the National Science Foundation. The views expressed here are strictly those of the author and do not necessarily reflect the views of the National Science Foundation.

REFERENCES

American Association for the Advancement of Science (AAAS). (1999). *Research and Development: FY AAAS Report XXIV: Research and Development FY 2000*. Washington, DC: AAAS

Blanpied, W. A. (2000). "Science and Technology in Times of Transition: the 1940s and 1990s" in National Science Board, *Science & Engineering Indicators: 2000*. Arlington, VA: U.S. Government Printing Office.

Bureau of the Census. (undated). *Historical Statistics of the United States: Colonial Times to 1957*. Reprint. Washington, DC: U.S. Department of Commerce.

Bush, V. (1945). *Science—the Endless Frontier: A Report to the President on a Program for Postwar Scientific Research*. Reprinted 1990. Washington, DC: National Science Foundation.

Clinton, W. J. (1998). "Address to the 150th Anniversary AAAS Annual Meeting." in A. H. Teich, S. D. Nelson, C. McEnaney, and T. M. Drake, eds., *AAAS Science and Technology Policy Yearbook 1999*. Washington, DC: American Association for the Advancement of Science.

Clinton, W. J., and A. Gore, Jr. (1994). *Science in the National Interest*. Washington, DC: Office of Science and Technology Policy.

Clinton, W. J., and A. Gore, Jr. (1996). *Technology in the National Interest*. Washington, DC: Office of Science and Technology Policy.

Heizer, J. (1991). *Research and Development Consortia Registered Under the National Cooperative Research Act of 1984*. (unpublished). Washington, DC: Department of Commerce/Technology Administration

Link, A. N. (2000). "Federal Register Filing: The 1998 Update of the CORE Database." Report submitted to National Science Foundation, Division of Science Resources Studies, R&D Statistics Program.

National Research Council. (NRC). (2000). *Measuring the Science and Engineering Enterprise: Priorities for the Division of Science Resources Studies*, Washington, DC: National Academy Press.

National Science Board (NSB). (2000). *Science & Engineering Indicators—1991*. NSB 00-1. Arlington VA: U.S. Government Printing Office.

National Science Foundation (NSF). (1999a). *Research and Development in Industry: 1997*. Detailed Statistical Tables. NSF 99-358. Arlington, VA: NSF.

National Science Foundation. (1999b). *Academic Research and Development Expenditures: Fiscal Year 1997*. Detailed Statistical Tables. NSF 99-336. Arlington, VA: NSF.

National Science Foundation. (1999c). *Federal Support to Universities, Colleges, and Nonprofit Institutions: Fiscal Year 1997*. Detailed Statistical Tables. NSF 99-331. Arlington, VA: NSF.

National Science Foundation. (1999d). *Federal Funds for Research and Development: Fiscal Years 1997, 1998, and 1999*. Detailed Statistical Tables. NSF 99-333. Arlington, VA: NSF.

National Science Foundation. (2000a). *National Patterns of R&D Resources* (annual series), by S. Payson. Arlington, VA: NSF.

National Science Foundation. (2000b). *Federal R&D Funding by Budget Function: Fiscal Years 1998–2000*. NSF 00-303. Arlington, VA: NSF.

Office of Management and Budget (OMB). (1999). "Promoting Research." *Budget of the United States Government: Fiscal Year 2000*. Washington, DC: U.S. Government Printing Office.

Office of Technology Policy. (2000). *Tech Transfer 2000: Making Partnerships Work*. Washington, DC: Department of Commerce, Technology Administration.

President's Commission on Industrial Competitiveness. (1985). *Global Competition: The New Reality*. Washington, DC: U.S. Government Printing Office.

Rowberg, R. (1998). *Federal R&D Funding: A Concise History*. Washington, DC: Congressional Research Service.

Schacht, W. (2000). *Cooperative R&D: Federal Efforts to Promote Industrial Competitiveness*. Washington, DC: Congressional Research Service.

Shapley, W. (1992). *The Budget Process and R&D*. New York: Carnegie Commission on Science, Technology, and Government.

Small Business Administration (SBA). (annual). *Small Business Innovation Research Program (SBIR): Annual Report*. Washington, DC: Small Business Administration.

Steelman, J. R. (1947). *Science and Public Policy*. Washington, DC: U.S. Government Printing Office. Reprinted 1980. New York: Arno Press.

Truman, H. S (1948). "Address to the Centennial Anniversary AAAS Annual Meeting." in A. H. Teich, S. D. Nelson, C. McEnaney, and T. M. Drake, eds., *AAAS Science and Technology Policy Yearbook 1999*. Washington, DC: American Association for the Advancement of Science.

U.S. Patent and Trademark Office. (1999). *Technology Assessment and Forecast Report, U.S. Universities and Colleges, 1969–98*. Washington, DC: USPTO.

Whang, K. (1998). "A Guide to the Research Tax Credit." Working Paper Series offered to Joint Economic Committee Minority.

---

[1] For a truly wonderful summary of these post-war science policy developments, see the "Science and Technology in Times of Transition: the 1940s and 1990s" chapter prepared by William Blanpied in NSB (2000). The opening section presented here draws heavily on that summary. A brief historical overview on federal R&D funding is found in Rowberg (1998).

[2] These words are included in the National Science Foundation Organic Act of 1950.

[3] In constant 1992 dollars, the figure is closer to $2.4 trillion.

[4] Federal performers include all Federally Funded Research and Development Centers (FFRDCs)

[4] Federal performers include all Federally Funded Research and Development Centers (FFRDCs)

[5] For an excellent overview of complexities in the R&D budget process, see Shapley (1992).

[6] Federal laboratories are the second largest type of performer using federal funds. They include most notably activities at DOD, NASA, Energy, and U.S. Department of Agriculture labs. Adding in the work at Federally Funded Research and Development Centers (FFRDCs) and the federal sector is itself the largest recipient of federal R&D dollars. FFRDCs are organizations that perform R&D exclusively or substantially financed by the federal government in order to meet a particular R&D objective of the funding mission agency. FFRDCs are often government owned but administered and operated by an industrial firm, university, university consortia or another nonprofit institution under contract. The earliest predecessor labs of the FFRDCs were the atomic weapons labs established during World War II.

[7] The objective of basic research is to gain comprehensive knowledge or understanding of a subject under study, without specific applications in mind. In industry, basic research is defined as research that advances scientific knowledge but does not have specific immediate commercial objectives, although it may be in fields of present or potential commercial interest. Applied research is aimed at gaining the knowledge or understanding to meet a specific, recognized need. Development is the systematic use of the knowledge or understanding gained from research directed toward the production of useful materials, devices, systems, or methods, including the design and development of prototypes and processes.

[8] In addition, see Schacht (2000) for a more extensive listing of technology related legislation.

Chapter 3

R&D Policy Models and Data Needs

GREGORY TASSEY
National Institute of Standards and Technology Strategic Planning and Economic Analysis Group

1.   NEEDED: A TECHNOLOGY-BASED ECONOMIC POLICY MODEL

From a policy perspective, the "S" portion of Science and Technology (S&T) is relatively easy to deal with. Basic science is widely recognized as close to a pure public good, which means that massive under investment occurs without government support. This premise has been understood and incorporated into policy since the end of World War II.

The "T" portion is another matter. Unlike basic science, technology is a "mixed" good, containing both private and public elements. The resulting complexity of market failure mechanisms and subsequent under investment patterns leads to poorly defined roles for industry, universities, and especially government, leaving endless debates over different classes of possible policy responses.

Most S&T analyses gloss over the economics of Research and Development (R&D) investment and the associated market failure mechanisms, jumping to a set of poorly defined policy recommendations. For example, support for some form of "collaboration," "cooperation," or "partnering" appears in most policy documents. Yet, few specifics are available regarding what technologies, what point in their life cycles (e.g., what phase of R&D), and what number and combination of institutions—public and private—should receive support.

As discussed later, a varied set of factors can and does thwart private sector investment in certain types of essential R&D. These sources of emerging technologies and supporting infrastructures. The number and complexity of these market failures have caused the Federal government's role in supporting industrial R&D to be poorly understood and therefore inefficiently funded and managed.

More specifically, inadequate R&D policy analysis is due to the absence of the following three elements:

1. The R&D policy process needs a conceptual model for assessing government roles in support of technology development, based on the idea of a national innovation system. This includes the concept of networks as the basic structure of a modern, effective R&D establishment. That is, the typical industrial technology consists of a set of distinctly different technology elements requiring the combined efforts of both private and public entities. This premise distinguishes the required policy model from 50 years of simplistic concepts where science is a pure public good and technology is viewed as a homogeneous, purely private good. Under the latter, government provides purely public science goods and purely private technology goods are provided by industry. As a result, government roles in supporting technology development have either been undeservedly rejected or poorly conceived and implemented.

2. An effective policy model must be grounded in an economic context that provides clear descriptions of the mechanisms by which technology drives productivity and economic growth. Policy studies typically make the general statement that "technology is essential for economic growth" and move on. While this characterization engenders little dissent, it also is woefully inadequate for defining issues relating to technology development and diffusion. In particular, the competitive dynamics of technology-based economic activity need to be represented in a way that allows incisive analyses of the factors determining under investment at critical stages in a technology's evolution.

3. More data from a variety of sources need to be collected and analyzed to fully identify, characterize, and assess government roles in supporting industry's R&D investment. Most S&T policy studies not only fail to provide a robust conceptual model and its economic underpinnings, but they offer little or no data to either elucidate the relevant policy issues or identify and construct policy responses that efficiently remove the market failure.

2. LIFE CYCLE MODELS OF TECHNOLOGY DEVELOPMENT

As increasing numbers and types of technology permeate the global economy, and as the number of technology-based competitors grows, the dynamics of global markets will become more volatile. Technology (and hence R&D) life cycles will continue to shorten, industry structures and employment opportunities will evolve more rapidly, and employment opportunities will evolve more rapidly. To deal effectively with this complexity, decision makers need a realistic and policy-relevant economic framework of investment and performance over the technology life cycle and, equally important, the transition between life cycles.

Drucker (1998) simply but accurately summed up the nature of technology-based progress:

> Knowledge-based innovations differ from all others in the time they take, in their casualty rates, and in their predictability, as well as in the challenges they pose to entrepreneurs... They have, for instance, the longest lead times of all innovations. There is a protracted span between the emergence of new knowledge and its distillation into usable technology. Then there is another long period before this new technology appears in the marketplace in products, processes, or services... To become effective, innovation of this sort demands not one kind of knowledge but many.

Drucker argues that major technology life cycles have persistently taken about 50 years from the initiation of significant basic research to the emergence of market applications. Simple numbers—the increasing resources around the world devoted to scientific and technology research—argue for a reduction in this time frame in the future.

Within these long-term cycles, national economies will undoubtedly vary in how they absorb scientific advances and demonstrate economic potential through technological proof of concept. This fact raises a critical issue from a national economic growth perspective: How can a domestic industry gain early access to both the basic science and the generic technology based on that science?

The technology assessment literature identifies three distinct cycles. The shortest and least controversial is the "product life cycle," which is simply the time from concept or initiation of product development through market penetration and eventual decline. A number of product life cycles are typically derived from the same underlying generic or fundamental technology, which collectively forms a "generic technology life cycle." The generic technology is not static but evolves during its life cycle. However, this evolution is not of major significance compared with differences from the previous generic technology that drove product development for the same market functions before being replaced by the current technology. Finally, several generations of generic technology life cycles typically evolve from the same underlying set of basic scientific principles. Eventually, a major new science base appears, allowing a transition to a new long-term "major technology life cycle" or "wave."[1]

Over the typical generic technology life cycle, product technologies become progressively more stable. As opportunities to apply the underlying or generic technology decline, design volatility decreases and an industry's product structure takes on a commodity character (electric power transmission is an example). Competition shifts to efficiency in production processes and hence to price and service as increasingly important determinants of market performance. Over such a life cycle, this evolutionary pattern of technology-based competition increasingly favors less advanced and low-cost economies. They can acquire the now maturing technology and combine it with cheap labor and incremental improvements in process technology. Even within industries viewed as high-tech, this pattern occurs. Certain classes of semiconductors, computers, and many types of software are examples of maturing phases of this life cycle pattern and the resulting competitive convergence.

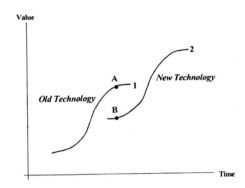

Figure 1: Transition Between Two Technology Life Cycles
Source: Tassey (1997: 60).

The transition between two generic technology life cycles presents a different set of competitive threats. Such a transition typically demands multidisciplinary skills needed to conduct the research for the new technology life cycle, skills that existing firms do not fully possess. Hence, they assign higher technical and market risk values to the prospective research program. A company considering undertaking the risk of investing in the new technology faces a value (performance per dollar) curve, such as curve 2 in Figure 1. The expected market value of the new technology initially will be below the existing or "defender" technology (represented by curve 1) and may remain so for some time. This situation can persist due to typical early performance problems associated with certain product attributes and inadequate process technology. In spite of superior potential performance, these two factors combine to yield performance-cost ratios that are too low, at least to overcome perceived risk by buyers associated with new technologies.

Therefore, two key policy issues based on this technology life cycle concept are

1. *Within* a generic technology life cycle the amount and speed of advance achieved by the domestic industry is critical because these performance variables determine the economic return realized on the total investment over successive product life cycles. A broad technology development and utilization capability is required by the domestic industry.

2. Transitioning *across* technology life cycles is an even more difficult issue for the policy process to address. A number of high-tech companies manage transitions among successive product life cycles quite effectively. However, the majority, if any, of firms applying the defender technology, seldom achieves the transition between two generic technology life cycles, especially to a radically new generic technology. Most of these companies lose out to new industries—either domestic or foreign. Thus, a cycle transition capability is required.

Under a Vannevar Bush-type of model, government can rationalize funding years, even decades, of basic research. At some point, enough knowledge is accumulated to allow judgments of risk associated with potential market applications of a new technology based on the underlying science. In an oversimplified extension of this model, industry should more or less automatically initiate applied technology research and a new technology life cycle is started.

However, a major problem for R&D policy arises at this transition from basic research to technology research. Here, for the first time, market risk assessments must be added to estimates of technical risk. Combining technical and market risk complicates corporate R&D decisions way beyond what is involved in allocating government funds for basic research.

Figure 2 indicates that technology research, with its ultimate objective of market applications, encounters an initial major increase in total risk because the scientific principles presented must now be proven capable of conversion into specific technological forms with specific performance attributes that meet specific market needs. This additional risk, RR', is incurred once the technology development portion of the R&D life cycle is initiated. It can and does act as a substantial barrier to private investment in technology research. Understanding the evolution of and the interaction between technical and market risk and the consequent impacts on private-sector investment are the key elements for effective R&D policy analysis.

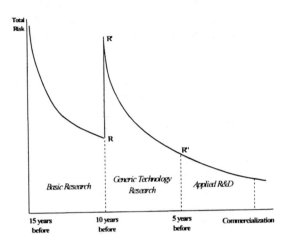

*Figure 2:*Risk Reduction over an R&D Life Cycle
Source: Tassey (1997: 76).

The last phase of a major technology life cycle is characterized by increasingly intense competition, shrinking profit margins, and structural unemployment or underemployment—all of which have been observed in major industry groups within industrialized nations during the 1990s. Certainly, economic growth policy must help ease transition costs, but it also must facilitate adaptation to new technology life cycles.

During the last phases of a given life cycle, the new technologies that will drive the next life cycle already exist, but with small market shares (Freeman 1979). Thus, opportunities for adaptation are available, but attempts to take advantage of them usually do not occur until economic conditions have become significantly distressed. By the time that policy makers recognize these conditions, first mover advantage has been lost and catch-up potential is limited.

3.   THE DUAL VALUE OF AN R&D CAPABILITY

R&D has two strategically critical roles in the knowledge-based economy: (1) implementing internal innovation strategies, and (2) providing the capability to absorb technology from external sources.

Given the growing importance of these functions, many firms have increased the amount of R&D expenditures. In 1997 and 1998, Hewlett-Packard (HP) spent more on R&D than on plant and equipment ($3.1B versus $2.3B and $3.4B versus $2.0B, respectively), and more than one-half of HP's sales now come from products the company developed within the previous two years. To some extent, such relative increases in R&D spending are because high-tech firms such as HP are contracting out more of their manufacturing requirements than in the past, which reduces capital expenditures. However, such strategies only accentuate the evolution of these companies toward a focus on knowledge-based competitive advantage.

HP exemplifies the dual R&D strategy. The company is recognized as one of the world's leading innovators, but one of HP's most successful products in recent years, the ink-jet printer is the result of successful imitation and improvement upon the innovating firm, Canon. Canon had the patents on early ink-jet designs but made a strategic error by choosing to attempt a complex implementation that ultimately set it years behind.

This is but one example of the fact that R&D at the company level cannot exist in a vacuum. Corporations increasingly require access to R&D conducted by other firms in their supply chains and to the broader technology infrastructure provided by a national innovation system. The overall health of the entire R&D network, in turn, determines the breadth and depth of national competitiveness.[2]

4.   TRANSITION TO A LIFE-CYCLE BASED ECONOMIC MODEL

The essence of technology-based economic growth is that a body of scientific knowledge is drawn upon for the development of technologies, which, to varying degrees and in various forms, eventually result in markets that contribute to the gross domestic product of the economy. This value added is therefore the end point for economic growth policy, and the factors determining its growth over time constitute the critical elements of policy analysis.

An effective economic model of technology-based growth will incorporate four basic elements:

1. The early phases of technology development encounter considerable technical and market risks that are often beyond the capabilities and hence the investment criteria of individual firms or even groups of firms.
2. Efficient development of technology by industry requires a complex set of supporting technical infrastructures to evolve along with the technology itself.
3. Transactions in technology-based markets involve sophisticated products and services, which require equally sophisticated infrastructure support.
4. R&D investment patterns and the consequent success or failure of domestic industries in global markets is time dependent; that is, the *technology life cycle* should be the dominant framework for the critical analysis of how different R&D investments are made—including the early investments that initiate the cycle across supply chains.

Corporate managers, business analysts, and economists have argued over how to best represent all four elements in a conceptual economic model. So-called linear models capture the time dimension to a degree but have been appropriately rejected as too narrow in scope and overly simplistic. However, no consensus on a more comprehensive policy-relevant replacement has emerged. Other concepts, such as feedback loops and chain-link or cross-fertilization among several areas of science and technology, represent different dimensions of R&D investment patterns. Each of these concepts enables a characterization of specific factors in the evolution of technology at various phases in the R&D life cycle.

While each concept has its limitations, they are not mutually contradictory. In fact, they embody complementary elements of the needed economic policy model. The feedback loop seems to be an attractive concept for R&D managers, referring to the integration of the three phases of economic activity—R&D, production, and marketing. Market experiences feed back to R&D and production, resulting in adjustments to product design and process technologies. Companies consciously compress certain feedback loops—in particular, the interactions between products and process R&D that reduces manufacturing problems. This phenomenon is most prominent in shorter product life cycles. The existence of information feedback creates a concept of technological change that is more dynamic and even circular, in which the phases of R&D and subsequent market use change almost simultaneously.

Academic researchers, who are interested in a broad representation of the innovation process itself, have proposed more complicated frameworks such as the chain link model.[3] Such models not only embody interactive relationships among stages in the development and commercialization of technology, but also include complementary roles of several distinctly different technologies. Here, the pattern of technological progress is ascribed more to a mating of complementary technology assets, independent of any evolutionary process. In fact, some proponents purport to show how "technological breakthroughs are just as likely to precede, as to stem from, basic research" (National Science Board 1996: 4-10).

The chain link effect occurs most prominently in the mid-length or generic technology life cycles. That is, when new generic technologies are being developed and applied for the first time, cross-fertilization often occurs among previously separate areas of technology.

For example, HIV protease inhibitors were synthesized by chemists in the pharmaceutical industry based on understanding the structure of HIV protease as determined by biologists using physicists' x-ray diffraction techniques. Two drug companies finalized their formulations using the ultra-powerful x-ray beams from synchrotron radiation sources normally used for nuclear physics research. Today, about 35 percent of the running time on the Department of Energy's synchrotron radiation sources is used for this kind of structural biology. Conversely, the development of neural network computing algorithms to efficiently sort complex multi-dimensional data sets has it origins in neurobiologists' attempts to develop an understanding of the brain's structure (Richter 1998).

Applying Alternative Models—Biotechnology

One frequently used example of the non-linearity of technological progress is Pasteur's development of the first vaccine, where both basic and applied research is characterized as being conducted at the same time. That is, Pasteur set out to solve a problem—the need to cure a disease—but at the same time he discovered some basic principles of microbiology.

However, such historical examples do not reflect the status of the majority of research and development as a process. Today, R&D is more structured and sequential out of necessity. Scientists or engineers use somewhat specialized tools and techniques for each research phase with unique skills for that type of research. Moreover, technology R&D today seldom progresses very far unless it can draw on a reservoir of scientific knowledge.

Medicine is, in fact, a good example of this evolutionary pattern. Through NIH, the U.S. government sponsored basic research over a thirty-year period before the science of molecular biology evolved to the point at which a biotechnology industry could begin to evolve. It is hard to imagine that the genetically engineered drugs that are appearing with increasing frequency could have been developed by a modern-day Pasteur using trial and error methods (which is basically the way drugs were developed from Pasteur's time until the past fifteen years of biotechnology R&D).

The example of biotechnology (text box) does not mean that technology evolves in a purely linear process. Obviously, areas of science such as molecular biology continue to advance and thereby make possible new technological applications. Moreover, the basic research producing these advancements often is influenced by the success or failure of past technological applications. As the HIV protease example shows, chain-link phenomena are real and important. Feedback loops have been accentuated in recent years by corporate strategies such as concurrent engineering, rapid prototyping, and, more recently, quality function deployment approaches to managing technology development and commercialization.

In general, neither increases in scientific knowledge nor technological progress are particularly steady. Major advancements occur and feed a host of applications for a period. The process of developing these applications for the marketplace creates knowledge, which feeds back to stimulate a more orderly evolution of the initial breakthrough. Demand pressures and technological opportunities promote linking across previously separate areas of technologies.

However, the example of molecular biology and other important areas of science, such as solid-state physics, demonstrate that a linear evolution of knowledge still takes place as the technology life cycle progresses.[4] The knowledge gained feeds back into the existing life cycle *and* eventually contributes to the subsequent technology life cycle.

Thus, the debate over whether to use a linear model or to adopt one of the more sophisticated variants is somewhat artificial. In some cases, those who use a linear model typically do so for simplicity's sake. The policy analysis to be undertaken does not require a more complex representation, only acceptance of a net progression of knowledge to successively more applied levels. Most users of such linear models acknowledge that reality is more complicated. Moreover, another distinction is that the two conceptual approaches address two different steps in long-term technological change. The linear model typically represents a higher level of aggregation of technology than does the chain-link framework, which focuses on single technologies.

5. ELEMENTS OF AN ECONOMIC POLICY MODEL OF R&D

Any sound policy approach to understanding technology-based growth must satisfy two basic requirements.
1. The first requirement is the need to define a set of elements that comprise the typical industrial technology. These elements are distinguished primarily by differences in private sector incentives to invest in them.
2. A second requirement is that the relevant investment behavior be depicted over time because of the existence of multiple cycles that characterize private-sector investment in technology research.

With these two requirements satisfied, a more accurate and policy-relevant analysis of specific market failure mechanisms is possible. Equally, important, appropriate government policy responses can be constructed and matched to these market failures, thereby greatly increasing the efficiency of R&D policy.

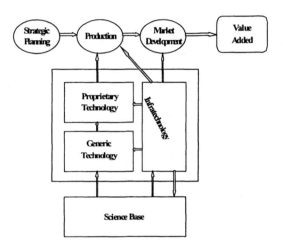

Figure 3: Economic Model of a Technology-Based Industry
Source: Tassey (1997).

The major elements of the typical industrial technology relevant for R&D policy are depicted in Figure 3. The relevance of these elements derives from the fact that each needs a unique set of R&D skills, facilities, and supporting infrastructures. Each one also requires a different research time frame (especially relative to each other) within the R&D cycle. Finally, each element displays a markedly different degree or type of public good content. Thus, the sources of and processes for the development of each technology element are significantly different.[5]

5.1   Generic Technology

A particular science base evolves over several decades and eventually reaches a critical mass, at which point industry begins to apply this knowledge to develop commercially relevant technology. Typically, before large amounts of private-sector funds can be committed to developing market applications of the technology, the generic technical concept must be demonstrated. This *generic technology research* provides evidence that the general technology may work in specific market applications. For many technologies, proof of concept can be a laboratory prototype. Each generation of digital electronic technology (transistor, integrated circuit, multifunction chip) was first demonstrated in the laboratory and then further developed to yield market applications over many product life cycles.

The existence of a demonstrated generic technology as a necessary condition for huge amounts of follow-on private sector investment was originally identified by Nelson (1987, 1992), but policy models have only vaguely recognized its critical importance. In essence, generic technology provides general inferences about how the technology works, identifies the attributes that determine the performance of the technology, demonstrates how these attributes combine to realize overall performance, and indicates initial ranges of variation for each attribute.

The broader and deeper the generic technology is, the greater the amount of R&D stimulated and the larger the number of market applications eventually produced. Equally important for R&D policy is the fact that generic technology diffuses more than the applied versions of the technology. Such spillovers mean that generic technology is simultaneously drawn upon by competing companies in developing market applications and therefore has some infrastructure characteristics.

Biotechnology provides an excellent example of how generic technologies arise out of the science base, but ahead of specific market applications. The biotechnology industry is, in fact, typical of the existence of multiple technology elements and the complex relationships among them. As shown in Table 1, multiple areas of science have had to advance before a larger set of generic product and process technologies could evolve. Supported by a number of infratechnologies, these generic technologies have advanced over the past 20 years and are just now beginning to yield significant numbers of proprietary market applications.

Table 1. Elements Driving the Biotechnology Life Cycle

Basic Research	Generic Technologies			Products
	Product	**Process**	**Infratechnologies**	**Products**
■ Molecular and cellular biology ■ Microbiology/ virology ■ Immunology ■ Neuroscience ■ Physiology ■ Pharmacology ■ Genomics ■ Proteomics	■ biomaterials ■ bioelectronics ■ gene testing ■ gene therapy ■ gene delivery systems ■ gene expression systems ■ antisense ■ apoptosis ■ antiangiogenesis ■ stem-cell ■ functional genomics ■ pharmacogenomics ■ biosensors ■ tissue engineering	■ recombinant DNA/genetic engineering ■ nucleic acid amplification ■ gene transfer ■ transgenic animals ■ cell culture ■ separation technologies ■ immunoassays ■ monoclonal antibodies ■ cell encapsulation ■ implantable delivery systems ■ DNA arrays/chips	■ biospectroscopy ■ combinatorial chemistry ■ DNA chemistry, sequencing, and profiling ■ Protein structure modeling/analysis techniques ■ nucleic acid diagnostics ■ thermodynamics of protein-nucleic acid interactions ■ gene expression analysis ■ bioinformatics	■ protease inhibitors ■ hormone restorations ■ DNA probes ■ neuroactive steroids ■ neuro-transmitter inhibitors ■ vaccines ■ coagulation inhibitors ■ inflammation inhibitors

5.2   Infratechnology

The other category of industrial technology with significant public good content is infratechnology. Infratechnologies are a varied set of technical tools that perform a wide range of measurement, integration, and other infrastructure functions. These functions include:

- Measurement and test methods;
- Artifacts such as standard reference materials that allow these methods to be used efficiently;
- Scientific and engineering databases;
- Process models; and
- Technical bases for both physical and functional interfaces between components of systems technologies, such as factory automation and communications systems (Tassey 1997).

Table 2: Uses of Infratechnologies by Stage of Economic Activity

R&D	PRODUCTION	MARKET DEVELOPMENT
Timing & Efficiency	**Process & Quality Control**	**Transaction Cost Reduction**
• Materials Characterization • Measurement Methods • Techniques (design for manufacturing, rapid prototyping)	• Process Modeling • Measurement and Test Methods • Process and Quality Control Techniques	• Acceptance Test Methods • Interface Standards • Compatibility/ Conformance Test Facilities

Source: Tassey (1997: 158).

As Table 2 indicates, these technical tools are ubiquitous in the technology-based economic growth process. They affect the efficiency of R&D, production, and marketing. Because individual infratechnologies typically have a focused application and impact (e.g., measurement and test methods are applied to specific steps in a production process), their economic importance has been overlooked. However, the complexity of technology-based economic activity and the demands by users of technology for accuracy and high levels of quality have reached levels that a large number of diverse research-intensive infratechnologies are required—even within single industries. The resulting aggregate economic impact of these infrastructural technologies is substantial.[6] Examples of infratechnologies supporting a specific industry (biotechnology) are shown in Table 1.

One indication of the pervasive and substantial impact of measurement infratechnologies has been provided by a NIST study of the semiconductor industry's investment in measurement equipment. This industry invested about $2.5 billion in measurement equipment in 1996, triple the amount spent in 1990. This expenditure is expected to continue growing at least 15 percent per year, reaching between $3.5 billion and $5.5 billion in 2001.[7] Thus, the cost of not having needed infratechnologies and associated standards in place to support this investment can be substantial. Another NIST study of interoperability in the U.S. automotive supply chain found that the lack of standard formats for transferring electronic product design data between suppliers and automobile manufacturers is costing that industry approximately $1 billion per year (Research Triangle Institute 1999).

The range and technical sophistication of infratechnologies support a varied and complex standards infrastructure. Infratechnologies are a necessary basis for standardization at all levels in the modern manufacturing process: individual equipment, the process systems level, and even at the customer/vendor interface. In service industries, infratechnologies help define output, interoperability, security protocols, and intellectual property.

Infratechnologies also could include the various techniques, methods, and procedures that are necessary to implement the firm's product and process strategies. Methods such as total quality management can be differentiated upon implementation within a firm. However, they must be traceable to a set of generic underlying principles if customers are to accept claims of product quality. Hence, they have an infrastructural or public good character.

6. MARKET FAILURE AND UNDERINVESTMENT

The concept of technology life cycles is particularly important for R&D policy because it implies a time order or evolutionary character—including both a beginning and an end—for various market failures that appear at different points in the typical life cycle. Hence, this concept helps determine appropriate policy responses within life cycles as well as the critical transitions between cycles.

In general, four basic categories of under investment can and do occur:

1. Aggregate under investment by an industry (e.g., insufficient total R&D);
2. Under investment in applied R&D in new firms (e.g., insufficient venture capital);

3. Under investment in new generations of existing technology or in radically new technology (e.g., insufficient generic technology research); and

4. Under investment in supporting technology infrastructures (e.g., insufficient infratechnology R&D).[8]

Because the process of technology development evolves cyclically, under-investment due to market failure tends to repeat. Moreover, distinctly different types of market failure exist and therefore require different government or industry/government response modes. In each case of market failure, the particular barrier increases the probability that the project is risk-adjusted and time-discounted expected rate of return will not exceed a company's hurdle rate. In such cases, where the social or aggregate economic rate of return is high (above society's hurdle rate), under investment occurs and economic growth is reduced below its potential (Tassey 1997).

6.1   Important Sources of Market Failure

The following are the major types of market failure that can and frequently do occur over the typical technology life cycle.

1. *Technology is inherently complex.* A certain amount of risk is reasonable given the considerable expected rewards from technology investment. However, the more radical or complex the attempted technical advance (technical risk), or the longer the time period needed to conduct the R&D during which demand can shift or competitors can commercialize the technology first (market risk), the greater the probability of an inadequate rate of return being realized.

2. *Increased global competition shortens R&D and product life cycles.* The shortening of time available for making decisions to enter new markets, conduct R&D, scale up for efficient production, and attain target market shares leads firms to apply higher discount rates to investment options and hence choose less radical or discontinuous innovation opportunities.

3. *The benefits from technology tend to diffuse or leak to firms beyond the originator (innovator).* Such spillovers are of two major types: price and knowledge.

  (a) *Price spillovers* occur when the market price does not fully capture the additional benefits from the new technology. That is, the user (buyer) in effect receives some of the benefits free. Up to a point, the existence of such spillovers is desirable because, if the new technology were fully priced, the buyer would be indifferent between the old and the new technologies. Market forces determine the actual distribution of benefits. The supplier (innovator) must simply capture enough of the benefits to meet or exceed the investment hurdle rate applied to the original R&D investment decision. For most technologies and competitive structures, a sufficient rate of return cannot be projected when significant price spillovers occur.

(b) *Knowledge spillovers* refer to leakage of the innovator's new technical knowledge horizontally to competing suppliers. This type of spillover is good for the economy as a whole, but it decreases the expected returns for potential innovators. To the extent that rates of return fall below the private hurdle rate, investment by potential innovators will not occur.

4. *Market Structure can reduce expected rewards from technology investment.* An increasing number of technologies are systems. System components must interface seamlessly with other components to work effectively. That is, they must interact in a fully functional manner with minimal effort by the user (system integrator). Otherwise, the cost and flexibility advantages from having choices among suppliers of individual components (as opposed to buying turnkey systems from a single supplier) are eroded.

Interfaces between complex components frequently are just as complex as the components themselves and hence are far from seamless. Achieving compatibility or interoperability can thus result in significant additional costs, raising total system costs and lowering the expected rate of return to both the suppliers and users of the components. These costs are particularly high (and, in fact, interoperability is usually not achieved) when competing private interests attempt to provide this type of infrastructure independently. The higher cost of non-interoperable systems, coupled with reduced functionality, lowers the technology's rate of market penetration.

This segmentation of markets for systems technologies can last for long periods and therefore result in significant economic loss.[9]

5. *Corporate strategies often are narrower in scope than a new technology's market potential.* Some new technologies (advanced ceramics, for example) have applications in a number of markets previously served by very different technologies and hence industries. Companies in the existing industries typically do not have the strategic profile or the production and marketing knowledge to target all the potential applications (i.e., to capture economies of scope). Thus, the

expected rate of return to each company is lowered relative to the risk of developing the generic technology which applies to all potential applications (economies of scope).

6. *Increasingly dominant "systems" technologies require complex infrastructure.* Automated production systems and technology-based services such as finance, communications, and entertainment all require sophisticated information infrastructures. Significant private investment in applications only occurs after the infrastructure is developed and implemented (for example, several decades of government support for the Internet were required before private investment in applications using it took off).

7. *Market segmentation is an increasing problem for production technologies.* Sophisticated customers demand customized versions of the technology which require highly complex and flexible productions systems. To the extent significant economies of scale exist, profit potential can be constrained.

In addition to price and knowledge spillovers, network externalities frequently are labeled as a third type of spillover (Arthur 1996). However, this phenomenon does not cause a redistribution of benefits from the innovating firm to other firms. Rather, it usually results in increased benefits for all market participants. The expanding market for the network increases the value for individual network participants and therefore most likely for the original supplier (innovator). The market failure risk here is the potential for network externalities to generate increasing returns to scale to the extent that the innovator could become a monopoly and bar entry by other firms, possibly restraining innovation for some period of time.[10]

In summary, the scope of market failure mechanisms affecting technology-based investment is broad. Spillovers are the most frequent (and sometimes are the only) reason cited for private sector under investment in R&D. However, as the above analysis indicates, spillovers are only one characteristic of technology-based competition that can lead to inadequate investment.

6.2   Transitions Between Technology Life Cycles

One of the main factors causing shifts in market share leadership across companies, industries, and countries is the phenomenon of transitions between successive generic or major technology life cycles that serve the same market function (e.g., computing or communications). New technologies often have very different characteristics from the old or defender technologies that they seek to replace. Hence, strategies, R&D

capabilities, and organizational characteristics that work well in one life cycle are not effective in the next cycle.

An example is computing. The first life cycle's generic technology was manifested in the mainframe computer. Processing power was a scarce resource and hence everything was optimized to maximize the productivity of the processor. A single, huge machine was housed in an air-conditioned room, operated by technicians who strictly allocated users' access. In the second life cycle, the personal computer reversed the control of the system. The user now owned the highly dispersed processing power. Now, a third technology life cycle is emerging in which the Internet offers the prospect of a reversion to a centralized computing system. In each of these three periods, the nature of the technology, the organizations supplying it, and the interface with the user varies significantly.

Within each life cycle, technology evolves according to conventional market dynamics. Efficiency can be achieved *within* short-term product life cycles largely by the private sector, with modest infratechnology support from government. However, significant market share shifts can occur across national economies, if the original generic technology is not improved over its life cycle. Even greater shifts in competitive position can occur *between* generic and major life cycles. Failure to prepare domestic industries for the transition by demonstrating potential applications of the science base (i.e., by advancing new generic technologies) typically causes major losses in sales, profits, and jobs to foreign competition.

7.   THE TENUOUS NATURE OF COMPETITIVE ADVANTAGE

Even when industry has access to a rich generic technology base for applied R&D, market success can be fleeting or never achieved. The past several decades are littered with U.S. firms and entire industries that failed to conduct enough R&D or the right type of R&D to create and sustain competitive advantage. Too many instances exist of important a technology whose development was initiated in the United States but were taken over by industries in other nations to the substantial benefit of those other nations' economies.

7.1   Examples of Technology-Based Markets Lost to Foreign Competition

The following are just a few examples of technology-based economic growth opportunities that have been lost by U.S. industry for a variety of reasons:

- **Semiconductor production equipment: Steppers.** The stepper was invented in the United States, but the Japanese now hold the largest market share. The loss of competitive position in semiconductor manufacturing equipment not only reduces the contribution to domestic economic growth in the electronics supply chain, but it also may reduce the productivity of other levels in that supply chain (particularly, U.S. semiconductor manufacturers). These manufacturers can find themselves at a competitive disadvantage relative to their competitors in Japan, who are more closely linked to the Japanese equipment suppliers. (Solving this vertical integration problem has been the primary objective of SEMATECH.)

- **Flat panel displays.** RCA invented the liquid crystal display, but had too narrow a view of its applications and essentially gave the technology to the Japanese. The Japanese now own 95 percent of a world market that is growing rapidly and driving downstream equipment/product markets.

- **Advanced Ceramics.** The current revolution in wireless communications would not have been possible without the discovery and development of oxide ceramics. The ceramic requirements of microwave applications (e.g., filters, oscillators, resonators) are critical and these components collectively represent a majority of end-use devices. Every modern commercial wireless communication and detection system in actual use or in advanced development incorporates oxide ceramics. This important compound was discovered and its processing phase diagrams determined in the early 1970s at Bell Labs and the National Institute of Standards and Technology (formerly National Bureau of Standards), respectively. Despite these early and fundamental U.S. advances, Japanese industry today clearly dominates the markets for these ceramics (estimated at $700 million for 1997). For example, only two U.S. companies (Motorola, which serves a captive market, and Trans-Tech, a small company with annual sales of $35 million) produce ceramic components, as compared with six major companies in Japan. Furthermore, control of this technology has stimulated additional Japanese R&D and led to most of the new materials that are enabling dramatic advances in miniaturization and performance of wireless communications equipment.

- **Robotics.** Today's industrial robotics market (worth about $6 billion) is dominated by Japanese companies such as Fanuc, Yaskawa Electric, Kawasaki Robotics, Mitsubishi Electric, and Motoman. U.S. companies—Westinghouse, General Electric, General Motors, and Unimation—first established the industrial robotics market in the 1960s but by the mid-1980s; all had sold their robotics interests to Japanese companies. Today, the largest U.S. robotics manufacturer (Adept Technology, San Jose) employs just 375 people. The only non-Japanese robotics manufacturer of any size is the Swiss-Swedish company ABB Flexible Automation.

- **Videocassette recorder.** Ampex and RCA developed the video tape recorder (VTR) in the 1950s. By the 1980s, its descendent, the videocassette recorder (VCR), was in one-half of American homes, with virtually all of these VCRs made by Japanese firms.

- **Semiconductor memory devices.** The United States invented the transistor and the integrated circuit. Yet, between 1979 and 1986 U.S.-based firms saw their world-market share decline from 75 percent to 27 percent. After that, U.S.-based firms recovered some of this loss. However, the persistently weak U.S. position is indicated by the fact that only two of the top ten firms worldwide in the major memory circuit markets (DRAM and SRAM) are based in the United States.

- **Digital watches.** The first electronic digital watch was introduced in 1971 by a U.S. company, Time Computer, which held all the patents. The semiconductor chip that ran the watch was purchased from RCA. Today, the Japanese dominate both the component and watch markets. Even though a number of U.S. electronics companies (such as Motorola, National Semiconductor, and Texas Instruments) made significant improvements and cost reductions early in the technology life cycle, the Japanese relentlessly improved the technology and reduced its cost, thereby taking over this market.

- **Interactive electronic games.** In 1972, Magnavox developed the first interactive game designed to be played on the screen of a TV. Two years later, Atari, Inc., was formed and led the market for a number of years. Now Japanese firms control that market.

Many argue that competitive failures such as the above examples are the fault of poor industry strategy and that the inherent efficiency of the market place demands no government interference. This view has considerable merit with respect to market applications within a single technology life cycle that result largely from applied R&D. However, if applied R&D needs no stimulus at all from government, various tax incentives such as the R&E tax credit are not good policy. Moreover, data cited below suggest that industry is increasingly under investing in two critical areas:

- Next generation technology (the generic technology base for the next technology life cycle), and
- Extremely varied sets of technical tools (infratechnologies) which are used to conduct R&D, control production processes, and execute the sale of complex technology-based goods and services.

7.2   Under Investment in Generic Technology Research

Universities are the primary source of a nation's basic science. Scientific knowledge diffuses in part through contact with industry and certain types of collaboration, but mainly through new graduates in science and engineering. The next step—proving the generic technological concept, so that corporate R&D managers can make the technical and market risk assessments necessary for follow-on applied R&D investments—is much more complex. This early-phase generic technology research does not absorb a large portion of total R&D spending in most areas of technology, as indicated in Table 3. However, its critical position in the R&D cycle means it has the potential to leverage much greater amounts of follow-on applied R&D.

Table 3: Fraction of R&D in Central Research Lab, 1999

Company	Company-Funded R&D As % of Revenues		Ratio
	Total Company	Central Lab	
Nokia	12.2%	1.2%	10.0%
Rockwell	5.0	0.5	10.0
United Technologies	5.1	0.3	6.5
Hughes	2.0	0.3	14.0
Raytheon	3.0	0.1	2.8

Source: HRL Laboratories, 2000.

As the next section describes, various combinations of industry, government, and universities fund or conduct generic technology research through a variety of organizational arrangements. These partnerships are attempts to deal with the quasi-public good nature of generic technologies and the consequent set of market failures that result from the mismatches between their characteristics and private-sector risk tolerances, R&D capabilities, and market strategies.

Case studies have shown that long-term, high-risk corporate research is declining.[11] In Table 4, Industrial Research Institute data for "directed basic research" spending plans by industry during the 1990s supports the case studies.[12] Moreover, this research has a discontinuous character, thereby stretching out the R&D life cycle and making the eventual market applications highly uncertain. From 11 case studies of radical innovation efforts within major corporations, a team from Rensselaer Polytechnic Institute concluded, "the life cycle of a discontinuous innovation project is profoundly different from a continuous improvement project". The 11 projects exhibited many of the types of market failure described earlier. In eight of the 11 case studies, the researchers found that government was a major source of funds after the project was formalized. For the most part, these funds were used to extend, expand, or accelerate projects. Collaborating with other firms (large and small), universities, and government laboratories was a common approach.[13]

Table 4: IRI R&D Trends Forecast for Industry-Funded Directed Basic Research, 1991-2000

Survey	Percent of Respondents Increasing Directed Basic Research	Percent of Respondents Decreasing Directed Basic Research
1991-1995	8–14 %	23–38 %
1996	17 %	5 %
1997	15 %	13 %
1998	14 %	28 %
1999	14 %	37 %
2000	17 %	4 %

Source: Industrial Research Institute.

The critical point for R&D policy is that major technological advances take more time and entail more risk than do incremental change and improvements. R&D that is more radical often is contracted out or accomplished through partnering to access needed R&D resources and pool risk. However, both options lengthen R&D cycle time and therefore encounter the same excessive discounting, as does internal long-term research. Yet, as a study by Kim and Mauborgne (see Figure 4) clearly indicates, longer-term and more radical R&D projects are more profitable.

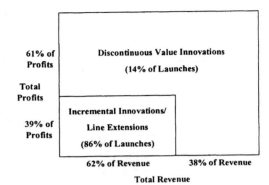

Figure 4: Profit Differentials from Major and Incremental Innovations
Source: Kim and Mauborgne (1997).

7.3   Under Investment in Infratechnology Research

Support for infratechnology research also has been generally inadequate. For example, the budget for the NIST laboratories has grown only 2.0 percent per year in real terms in the last 24 years, 1973-97, compared with an average annual real growth rate of 8.9 percent for industry-funded R&D. Over such an extended period, this shortfall implies a significant reduction in the capability of NIST's measurement-related infratechnology research to carry out its mandate to support the productivity of industry's R&D investments. The markedly different growth rates have resulted in the NIST laboratory research budget declining by one half relative to industry R&D spending during this period.

The NIST labs provide a wide range of measurement-related infratechnologies to industry. As described earlier, these infratechnologies—either directly or through incorporation in industry standards—are pervasive in terms of their economic impacts. They leverage the productivity of R&D, enhance quality and process control, and facilitate efficient marketplace transactions for complex, technology-based products and services (Tassey 1997). Because of the large number of infratechnologies required by a single technologically advanced industry, the collective economic impact is large. However, their infrastructural and hard-to-visualize character along with the diffuse nature of their impacts creates difficulties for policy makers.

8.   POLICY IMPLICATIONS

Corporate R&D investment decisions do not take place in a vacuum. They are driven by "the invisible hand"—perceived technological and market opportunities—as well as by "the hidden foot"—the threat of competition. In addition to these factors, investment decisions are also strongly influenced by the breadth and depth of a supporting technological infrastructure.

8.1   The Relative Size and Impacts of Government-Funded Research

Figure 5 (supported by data such as that in Table 3) indicates that amounts spent on generic technology research and infratechnology research between the 10th and 5th years before commercialization is relatively small. However, significant risk reduction in terms of advancing the generic technology to at least proof of concept or laboratory prototype often is essential to stimulate the much larger applied R&D investment by individual companies that eventually brings products, processes, and services to market. The availability of appropriate infratechnologies makes this process more efficient and, in some cases, is necessary for it to occur at all. The subsequent acceleration of industry R&D spending over the average R&D life cycle is pronounced. Industry spends 4.4 times as much on applied research as on basic research and 2.7 times as much on development as on basic research and 2.7 times as much on development as on applied research.[14]

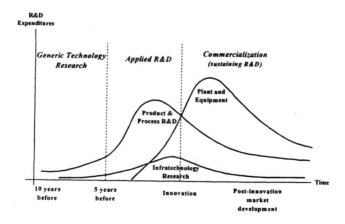

Figure 5. Relative Expenditures by Phase of R&D over Technology Life
Source: Tassey (1997: 74).

8.2   Matching Market Failure and Policy Response

Four major categories of under investment were identified in Section 6.0. Each requires a very different policy response:

1. *Aggregate under investment by an industry—insufficient total R&D.* This problem is the result of either excessive risk avoidance due to adverse macroeconomic conditions or inadequate R&D capability (which raises entry costs and hence risk). Tax incentives can be effective as long as the R&D being targeted is comparable to the type already pursued by industry—that is, as long as the normal corporate R&D investment decision criteria can be applied. In other words, a tax incentive can stimulate more of the same type of R&D already conducted (Tassey 1997: 107-111).

2. *Under investment in the formation of new firms—insufficient venture capital.* Venture capital is plentiful in the United States and available for most areas of technology, once the generic technology is sufficiently advanced to allow the private sector sources of venture funding to make assessments of both technical and market risk. The policy issue is how to get to that point. A government role in advancing generic technology research has been accepted in the United States only in a few situations where an industry structure deemed necessary to achieve a major social objective was either inadequate or not formed at all. That is, if a new technology has potentially large social as well as economic benefits, is not capital intensive (it can be supplied by small firms), and is radical enough to inhibit investment by large firms focused on the existing technology, then R&D policy can consider subsidizing the creation of a new industry structure as a policy objective.

   Biotechnology is an example of a new technology that meets these criteria. The National Institutes of Health (NIH) therefore funds some technology research in small biotech firms. The Small Business Innovation Research (SBIR) Program was created to fund research in new technologies that are both socially and economically important. In such cases, funding R&D by young, development-stage companies can expand both the number and variety of such firms.[15]

3. *Under investment in new generations of existing technology or in radically new technology—insufficient generic technology research.* Because of the highly microeconomic character of technology development, and hence the uniqueness of the sets of market failures that affect individual technologies, broad R&D incentives, such as a tax credit, are generally not effective. Tax expenditures tend to leak to both technologies and phases in the R&D process that do not require government support. Instead, the efficient policy response would

combine direct funding of generic technology research with appropriate joint strategic planning among government, industry, and universities (Tassey 1997).

Early-phase, generic technology research often is conducted through a variety of partnership mechanisms, because this approach allows more effective combinations of research skills and facilities, pools risk, and increases the rate of technology diffusion. All nations with technology-based growth strategies have industry-government programs to cooperatively advance the early phases of a variety of technologies with considerable economic potential.

4. *Under investment in supporting technology infrastructures— insufficient infratechnology R&D.* Infratechnologies not only have common use characteristics (including their use as standards), but they often derive from a different science and generic technology base than does the core technology being applied by industry through its internally funded R&D. The latter fact argues for a strong role by government laboratories in the conduct and diffusion of infratechnology research. Government labs can realize economies of scale and scope from unique research skills and facilities that can be applied to meet the infratechnology needs of a number of industries (Tassey 1997). These labs also can provide neutral third party facilitation of the standards process.

8.3   Responding to Technical and Market Risk Barriers

As described earlier, the intrinsic technical and market risk faced by R&D firms varies over a technology's life cycle. Therefore, both industry and government responses to market failures and resulting under investment in R&D and/or slower market penetration by the new technology also must vary. Figure 6 indicates how a set of policy responses can be used to mitigate market failures over the different phases of an R&D life cycle.

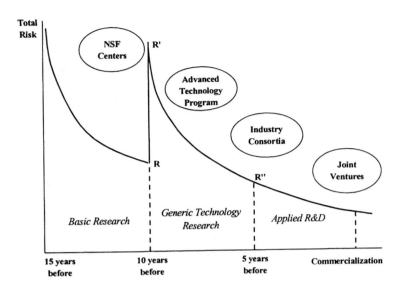

Figure 6. Risk Reduction over an R&D Life Cycle
Source: Tassey (1997).

Specifically, after basic research has gone on for some time, the accumulated level of knowledge begins to spark interest by industry in the possibility of developing technologies based on this science. Diffusion of the basic science and subsequent initial evaluation of its economic potential can be facilitated through graduates of universities and entities such as the National Science Foundation's Science and Technology Centers and Engineering Research Centers, where industry and university researchers can interact. For specific areas of technology, industry-operated entities such as the Semiconductor Research Corporation (SRC) fund research under a similar format. More recently, the Focus Center Research Program (FCRP) was established as a network, including the U.S. semiconductor industry, the U.S. Government, and 14 major universities.

Diffusion of basic scientific knowledge through mechanisms such as the NSF centers and the FCRP can provide industry with an indication of an emerging technology's potential. Nevertheless, the decision process for investing in the early phases of technology research is a difficult one for individual companies to manage effectively. There are several reasons for this difficulty:

• Competitive pressures of fighting for market share in the current technology life cycle consume corporate energies;

- Corporate management applies different decision criteria and metrics to long-term projects compared with the bulk of corporate R&D;

- Recognition of the extremely high technical and market risks associated with a potential technology whose concept has not been proven even in the laboratory; and

- R&D capabilities needed to launch a significant research program in a new technology, especially involving multiple research disciplines and laboratory facilities, are frequently incomplete within individual firms.

Even with new R&D management approaches such as options pricing techniques, these factors can combine to raise overall risk to prohibitive levels.[16] The lack of appropriate R&D capability relative to the skills and facilities required for pursuing development of emerging technologies increases risk substantially beyond the intrinsic risk associated with an immature state of development. This latter factor is especially important when new technological opportunities require combining several previously separate areas of scientific or technical knowledge.

The result is the large jump in overall risk from R to R' in Figure 6. This combined technical and market risk must be reduced to levels that fit within conventional R&D decision criteria—that is, those criteria applied by companies to the majority of candidate R&D projects.

In response, risk pooling is a common strategy for conducting early-phase technology research. Consortia are widely used for this purpose in advanced economies.[17] A number of cooperative organizational forms can be used to share costs and complementary R&D capabilities. National laboratories and research institutes frequently participate in research consortia because they have the time horizons, the multiple disciplinary skills, and the unique research facilities to undertake generic technology research.

Cost-shared research consortia with various combinations of industry, government, and universities as partners are the efficient approach to conducting much early-phase generic technology research in the United States. NIST's Advanced Technology Program (ATP) stimulates investment in generic technology through cost-shared industry/government partnerships. Similar but larger programs include the European Framework Program and, in Japan, the Industrial Science and Technology Frontier Program and the System to Support Development of Creative Technology for New Industries. As portrayed in Figure 6, such programs focus on generic technology research, i.e., early-phase research where economies of scope, long time to expected commercialization, R&D capability mismatches, and other factors inhibit corporate R&D investment decision making.

Once beyond this early-phase, industry can usually apply conventional R&D decision criteria and take on most of the applied research and development required to achieve commercialization of the generic technology. Figure 6 indicates that firms also will use consortia for applied research. However, such industry-led consortia seldom have a life of more than five years, with three to five years being the typical range (Mowery 1998: 39). Scientific research programs are usually at least 10 years long and often span several decades. Proof of concept through generic technology research often begins 5 to 10 years before commercialization. In other words, this period in the R&D life cycle can constitute a funding "gap" between basic research—largely a public good—and applied R&D—largely a private good. The widely discussed Ehlers' report provides a Congressional view of the "widening gap between federally-funded basic research and industry-funded applied research and development".[18] Government programs such as ATP attempt to help fill this gap.

9.   SUMMARY

A number of categories of technology embody significant public good elements:

- **Emerging** technologies that entail high risk and long gestation periods, but create new markets with significant value added;

- **Systems** technologies that provide infrastructure to many product and service technologies and thereby drive growth in major economic sectors;

- **Enabling** or multi-use technologies that benefit multiple segments of an industry or group of industries, but that encounter economies of scope and diffusion investment barriers; and

- **Infratechnologies** that leverage investment in both development and use of proprietary technologies, but that require distinct competencies to develop and common ownership (such as standards) to effectively use.

For these classes of technology, the evolutionary patterns of technical and market risk over the relevant life cycle can and do result in inadequate investment a key points in the life cycle. This under investment results from a much wider set of economic conditions (market failures) than commonly believed. Specifically,

- *Technical complexity:* The unmet requirement for multiple disciplines within one organizational structure needed to conduct R&D;

- *Time:* The negative effect on investment decision making of excessive discounting;

- *Capital intensity:* The negative effect on risk assessment of the capital intensity of many research processes (i.e., of the cost of these processes, especially as a percentage of a firm's R&D portfolio);

- *Economies of scope:* A broad and uncertain scope of potential market applications that extends beyond most firms' market foci;

- *Spillovers:* A tendency for technical knowledge produced by individual companies to "leak" or "spillover" to others that did not contribute to the research;

- *Infratechnologies and standards:* The disincentives for adequate investment due to the public good character, unique science base, and low visibility; and

- *Market segmentation:* The emergence of sophisticated users who demand sets of performance attributes that cannot be provided by industrial R&D capabilities.

Three particularly important negative impacts of these market failures are:

1. *Corporate investment decision dysfunction with respect to longer-term, complex, and multidisciplinary technology research.* Under investment is particularly pronounced in the early phases of the R&D life cycle, which most strongly exhibit investment barriers resulting from the intrinsic *technical* risk of the technology and its mismatches with existing corporate strategies and competencies.

2. *Excessive compression of R&D life cycles with resulting disincentives to undertake long-term, high-payoff research.* Global competition is forcing shorter total product life cycles, which, in turn, are forcing corporate R&D portfolios to overemphasize product-line extensions and incremental process improvements. In general, less *market* risk is assumed by the private sector.

3. *Failure to project access to the markets for increasingly system-based technologies.* Many of today's most important technologies have complex system structures, which require equally complex interfaces to enable market entry by small and medium suppliers and system optimization by users. Without the needed infrastructure, inefficient industry structures evolve.

Given the nature of technology market failures and the significance of rectifying them, the two major R&D policy issues facing the U.S. economy today are

1. *Understanding and providing appropriate policy responses for the early phases of technology research.* Efficiently bridging the valley of death—the widening gap between federally funded basic research and industry-funded applied research and development—does not require large

amounts of federal funding. However, this funding for generic technology research is essential to lowering the substantial technical and market risks typical of early phases in a technology's life cycle and must be available when the window of opportunity is open. All industrialized nations have or participate in industry-government partnerships of various forms to provide this essential category of technology infrastructure.

2. *Identifying and providing technical infrastructures needed by technology-based industries.* The needs for these infrastructures vary over the typical technology life cycle and have strong public good content, thereby requiring effective government support. As with generic technology, research support for the needed range of infratechnologies requires relatively modest amounts of funding. However, this funding must not only be adequate, but it needs to be directed to unique research facilities that can achieve the large economies of scale and scope that characterize this type of technology infrastructure and that can also efficiently diffuse it to industry, standards organizations, and other users.

The major trends and issues discussed here obviously have implications for the amount and type of R&D needed to achieve steady, high rates of economic growth. Equally important, technology trends interact with corporate strategy, industry structure, and government policy (in particular, policies that provide technical infrastructure at the various phases in a technology's life cycle). Technology trends or trajectories, once established, can have dramatic effects on a number of industries or even sectors of the economy in terms of both rate and directions of growth. Hence, early evaluation of the multiple trajectories afforded by the timely development of generic technology and supporting infratechnologies is essential.

REFERENCES

American Electronics Association. (1997). *Cybernation*, Washington, DC: The American Electronics Association.

Arthur, W. B. (1996). "Increasing Returns and the New World of Business." *Harvard Business Review*, July-August, 74: 100–109.

Caracostas, P. and U. Muldur. (1995). "Long Cycles, Technology and Employment: Current Obstacles and Outlook," *STI Review* 15: 75–104.

Cohen, W. and D. Levinthal. (1989). "Innovation and Learning: The Two Faces of R&D." *Economic Journal*, September, pp. 569–596.

Corcoran, E. (1994). "The Changing Role of U.S. Corporate Research Labs." *Research-Technology Management*, July–August, pp. 14–20.

Department of Commerce. (1998). *The Emerging Digital Economy,* Washington, DC: U.S. Department of Commerce, April.

Doremus, P., W. Keller, L. Pauly, and S. Reich. (1998). *The Myth of the Global Corporation,* Princeton, NJ: Princeton University Press.

Drucker, P. (1998). "The Discipline of Innovation." *Harvard Business Review* 76:6, November-December, pp. 149–157 (reprint of his classic 1985 *Harvard Business Review* article).

Duga, J. (1994). "IRI Forecast Reflects Major Change in How U.S. Industry Will Perform R&D." *Research-Technology Management,* May–June, pp. 9–11.

Eidt, C. and R. Cohen. (1997). "Reinventing Industrial Basic Research." *Research-Technology Management,* January–February, pp. 29–36.

Finan, W. (1998). *Metrology-Related Costs in the U.S. Semiconductor Industry, 1990, 1996, and 2001* (NIST Planning Report 98-4), Gaithersburg, MD: National Institute of Standards and Technology, May.

Freeman, C. (1979). "The Kondratiev Long Wave" in *Structural Determinants of Employment and Unemployment,* Paris: Organization for Economic Cooperation and Development.

Geppert, L. (1994). "Industrial R&D: The New Priorities." *IEEE Spectrum,* September, pp. 30–41.

Industrial Research Institute. *R&D Trends Forecast.* Washington, DC: Industrial Research Institute, (annual). 1991 to 2000.

Kim, W. C. and R. Mauborgne. (1997). "Value Innovation: The Strategic Logic of High Growth." *Harvard Business Review* 75: 1, January-February, pp. 102–112.

Klein, S. and N. Rosenberg. (1986). "An Overview of Innovation" in R. Landau and N. Rosenberg, eds., *The Positive Sum Strategy: Harnessing Technology for Economic Growth,* Washington, DC: National Academy Press.

Link, A. N. and J. T. Scott. (1998). *Public Accountability: Evaluating Technology-Based Institutions,* Norwell, MA: Kluwer.

Luehrman, T. (1998). "Strategy as a Portfolio of Real Options." *Harvard Business Review* 76, September–October, pp. 89–99.

Mowery, D. (1998). "Collaborative R&D: How Effective Is It?" *ISSUES in Science and Technology,* Fall, pp. 37-44.

National Science Board. (1996). *Science & Engineering Indicators – 1996.* Arlington, VA: National Science Foundation, NSB 96-1.

National Science Board. (1998). *Science & Engineering Indicators – 1998.* Arlington, VA: National Science Foundation, NSB 98-1.

Nelson, R. (1987). *Understanding Technological Change as an Evolutionary Process*, Amsterdam: North Holland.

Nelson, R. (1992). "What Is 'Commercial' and What Is 'Public' About Technology, and What Should Be?" in N. Rosenberg, R. Landau and D. Mowery, eds., *Technology and the Wealth of Nations*, Stanford, CA: Stanford University Press.

Papaconstantinou, G., N. Sakurai, and A. Wyckoff. (1998). "Domestic and International Product-Embodied R&D Diffusion." *Research Policy* 27: 301–314.

Research Triangle Institute. (1999). *Interoperability Cost Analysis of the U.S. Automotive Supply Chain* (Planning Report 99–3), Gaithersburg, MD: National Institute of Standards and Technology, March.

Rice, M., G. C. O'Conner, L. Peters, and J. Morone. (1998). "Managing Discontinuous Innovation." *Research - Technology Management* 41: 3, May–June, pp. 52–58.

Richter, P. (1998). "Long-Term Research and Its Impact on Society," Address to a Senate Forum on "Research as an Investment," February.

Schumpeter, J. (1939). *Business Cycles: A Theoretical, Historical and Statistical Analysis of the Capitalist Process*, New York: McGraw Hill.

Schumpeter, J. (1950). *Capitalism, Socialism and Democracy* (3rd ed.), New York: Harper and Row.

Tassey, G. (1992). *Technology Infrastructure and Competitive Position*, Norwell, MA: Kluwer.

Tassey, G. (1996). "Choosing Government R&D Policies: Tax Incentives vs. Direct Funding." *Review of Industrial Organization* 11: 579–600.

Tassey, G. (1997). *The Economics of R&D Policy*, Westport, CT: Quorum Books.

Tassey, G. (1999). *R&D Trends in the U.S. Economy: Strategies and Policy Implications* (NIST Planning Report 99-2), Gaithersburg, MD: National Institute of Standards and Technology, March.

Tassey, G. (2000). "Standardization in Technology-Based Markets." *Research Policy* 29: 587–602.

U.S. House of Representatives, Committee on Science. (1998). *Unlocking Our Future: Towards a New National Science Policy*, Report to Congress, Washington, DC.

Vonortas, N. (1997). *Cooperation in Research and Development*, Norwell, MA: Kluwer.

---

[1] Schumpeter (1939, 1950) and Caracostas and Muldur (1995). Several generations of microprocessors are an example of product life cycles "nested" under a generic technology

life cycle (integrated circuits). These generic technology cycles are, in turn, nested under a major technology life cycle (solid-state digital electronics). See Tassey (1997).

[2] The term supply chain as used here refers to the vertical structure of industries that begin with raw materials and eventually serve a final demand. An example of a first level in a supply chain would be silicon and other semiconductor materials. These materials are used to manufacture semiconductor devices, which are combined to form electronic components and equipment. The latter are further combined to form systems, such as an automated factory that manufactures a product or a telecommunications network that provides a service.

[3] See, for example, Klein and Rosenberg (1986).

[4] In the important area of digital electronics, the transistor could never have been invented without prior knowledge of the basic science of solid-state physics, which provided the theoretical basis for thinking that a semiconducting material could be used to construct an electronic switch or amplifier. Once invented, the importance of the transistor stimulated an avalanche of further basic research making possible further generations in digital electronics technology.

[5] Economists distinguish among these elements with the concepts of rival and non-rival goods. One individual cannot consume the former without preventing consumption by others (e.g. toothbrush), while the latter can be collectively consumed (software). Non-rival goods present investment incentive problems because "free riders" consume the good but do not pay for it. However, a second condition—excludability—is necessary to determine private sector investment in non-rival goods. Patents, for example, are a mechanism for excluding free riders from consuming technical knowledge produced by others. Technology infrastructure falls into the non-rival category, but excluding additional consumers of this knowledge is not in the public interest. Thus, technology infrastructure is funded to varying degrees by government in order to compensate for—in fact, to ensure—spillovers.

[6] For summaries of microeconomic studies of infratechnologies and associated methodologies, see Link and Scott (1998) and Tassey (1997, 1999).

[7] Finan (1998). The estimate does not include the labor and overhead required to implement this measurement infrastructure.

[8] These four categories of market failure and the appropriate policy responses are discussed in detail in Tassey (1997).

[9] The role of standards is particularly important here. See Tassey (2000).

[10] This phenomenon was the general economic basis for the Justice Department's antitrust suit against Microsoft.

[11] See, for example, Corcoran (1994), Duga (1994), and Geppert (1994).

[12] This is comparable to generic technology research.

[13] Rice, et al. (1998: 57–58). Also, see Eidt and Cohen (1997).

[14] National Science Board (1998, Appendix Tables A 4-7 and A 4-11).

[15] Small firms now get a lot of NIH funding, both through the SBIR Program and otherwise; but, prior to SBIR they did not. In fact, Congressional hearings in 1978 documented the fact that NIH had no research contracts with small business at that time.

[16] For an overview of these new R&D decision techniques, see Luehrman (1998).

[17] Vonortas (1997) provides a comprehensive overview of cooperative R&D.

[18] See U.S. House of Representatives, Committee on Science (1998).

Chapter 4

Technology Innovation Indicators
A Survey of Historical Development and Current Practice

JOHN A. HANSEN
State University of New York College at Fredonia

1. INTRODUCTION

Government policies with regard to innovation have sometimes played the role of promoter, sometimes regulator, and sometimes referee between competing private interests. To support these functions, a substantial effort has been made to understand the nature of technological innovation and to measure various facets of technological development.

Technological innovation is a concept that is sufficiently complex, multi-dimensional, and impossible to measure directly.[1] Technological innovation is a process that involves the interaction of many different resources. Innovation is also a variety of outputs that cannot be measured along any single-dimensioned scale. Indicators of innovation provide information on various facets of the innovation process, helping us to understand the phenomenon better and assisting those (both in the public and private sectors) whom must formulate policy.

Changes in our understanding of the innovation process over time have resulted in substantial changes in indicators of innovation. Originally, the early work resulted in innovation input indicators and has provided, together with productivity data and patent data, the only long-term time series data related to innovation in the U.S. However, because of its focus on inputs, and the implicit relationship of inputs to a linear model of innovation that largely neglected inter-firm linkages, the earlier work also distorted our understanding of innovation. For example, since a relatively small number of large firms in the U.S. economy accounted for the vast majority of R&D expenditures, it was assumed that they were also responsible for almost all-technological innovation. Thus, these data suggest that innovation policy could be usefully directed at large R&D firms, and not at small- and medium-sized firms, who generally have no central R&D lab. In the heyday of the large corporate R&D lab, this was an easy enough mistake to make, but it became harder to justify this view in the face of the extremely rapid growth of small, technology-based enterprises in the past two decades. Thus, many felt it was essential to look beyond indicators based on innovation inputs toward indicators that were "downstream" from research and development.

Our understanding of the innovation process changed.   For example, innovation was no longer perceived as being a linear process within each firm.   Some innovations occurred without any traditional research at all. Others began at a stage that had been thought of as downstream from research, but then required scientific and engineering expertise later to solve problems related to the commercialization of a new product or process. This view of innovation, popularized by Kline and Rosenberg as the "chain-link model" of innovation, serves a key foundation for most of the recent innovation indicator development (Kline and Rosenberg 1986).

Innovation is also not an activity that occurs wholly within firms. Studies in many countries have confirmed that a significant portion of firms that introduce new products or new production processes have no formal R&D processes at all.   In many cases, firms rely on adapting technologies developed elsewhere or combining technologies to produce improved or completely new products or production techniques.   The importance of backward linkages with supplier firms, at least in some industries, has been understood for a very long time. In the 1970s, largely based upon the work of von Hippel, considerable attention was focused on the role of users and customers in the innovation process as well.   More recently, DeBresson argued that the relationships between firms involved in innovation really consist of complex networks with an array of communications and interactions among firms (DeBresson 1996).

Our understanding of the nature of interactions among firms (whether they are customers, suppliers, or more complex relationships) any examination of the linkage between innovation (as measured by older indicators) and economic performance may be tenuous at best. For example, correlations between firm performance measures such as sales growth or profitability and R&D expenditures have always been difficult because it was nearly impossible to specify the lag structure between innovation investment and improved performance. However, if the underlying R&D that serves as a basis for sales growth due to new products or processes is not even made by the firm that introduced the innovation, then documenting this relationship with traditional innovation indicators will be impossible.

Furthermore, policies that rely on traditional measures to indicate where innovation is occurring maybe fundamentally flawed.

The newer indicators of innovation were designed to paint a more detailed picture of innovation by more directly examining innovative outputs, by collecting data on the structure of innovative activities within firms, and by tracing the linkages between firms that give rise to innovation. While development work on these indicators has been going on for at least two decades, they are "new" in the sense that their collection is only now becoming regularized, and they are not being regularly collected at all in the United States.

2. THE OSLO MANUAL

In 1988, the first multinational study to collect innovation indicators began in Scandinavia, under the aegis of the Nordic Fund for Industrial Development (Nordic Industrial Fund 1991). The questions on this group of surveys revolved many of the same themes that were pursued in the earlier surveys in Europe and the United States. From the beginning, however, it was anticipated that the surveys would be constructed so international comparisons among the participating countries (Norway, Denmark, Finland, and Sweden) would be possible.[2]

The first Oslo Manual did not contain specific questions. Instead, it laid a conceptual framework for developing indicators and discussed data that had been collected by existing surveys. Specific topic areas were recommended for inclusion in future national surveys including firm objectives, sources of innovative ideas, factors that hamper innovation, the proportion of sales and exports due to new products, the structure of R&D, the acquisition and sale of technology and the costs of various innovation activities.

The European Community (EU) sought to design a common questionnaire that would be based on the Oslo Manual and administered in all EU countries.[3] Data collection was completed in Belgium, Germany, Denmark, France, Greece, Italy, Ireland, Luxembourg, the Netherlands, Portugal, the United Kingdom, and Norway. Over 40,000 firms were surveyed in the course of this project (Evangelista, et al. 1996).

A revised version of the Oslo Manual was published in 1997 (hereafter Oslo-2) based on the field survey experience of the first attempt to the manual were in part based upon the field survey experience of the first Community Innovation Survey (CIS-1), but were also driven by fundamental changes in the economy itself. Notably this was the first attempt to draft innovation indicator data that would apply to service industries as well as manufacturing industries. Just as the first version of the Oslo Manual served as a basis for CIS-1, the second version of the Manual laid the underpinnings for the second CIS survey.

In Oslo-2, technological innovation is divided into two categories: Technological Product Innovation and Technological Process Innovation. Product innovations are further subdivided into new products and improved products. The definitions for the three types of innovation are provided as follows:

A technologically new product is a product whose technological characteristics or intended uses differ significantly from those of previously produced products.[4]

A technologically improved product is an existing product whose performance has been significantly enhanced or upgraded.[5]

Technological process innovation is the adoption of technologically new or significantly improved production methods, including methods of product delivery.[6]

A key definitional problem is the specification of the degree of novelty required in order for a product or process to be considered truly "new." To take two extremes, an innovation might be considered new only if it was introduced for the first time anywhere in the world in any industry. Alternatively, it might be considered new if it were used for the first time by the innovating firm even if it had been previously widely used in other firms in the same industry.[7]

While it may be reasonably argued that every application of existing technology in a different setting requires a degree of adaptation and thus innovation, it is also clear that the adoption of existing technology that is widely used elsewhere involves a substantially reduced degree of innovation relative to the creation and first use of new technology. After all, the introduction of a production process that is new to the firm might simply occur because the firm was expanding its product line into a new area that required different equipment based on existing (and possibly quite ancient) technologies.

On the other hand, firms generally know when a product or production process is new to their firm. Often they do not know whether it is also new to their industry, new to their country or region, or new to the world. In fact, in DeBresson's object-based study of innovation in Canada, he found that a rather large number of firms claimed to have developed world first innovations (DeBresson and Murray 1984). In fact, in a number of cases more than one Canadian firm claimed to have been the first in the world to develop a particular innovation.

There is a tension between data helpful from a policy perspective and the data firms are readily able to provide. Survey design is often something of a balancing act between obtaining the best possible data and the most complete response rate.

A key issue that has been a source of some frustration for innovation indicator researchers concerns the proper statistical unit at which to collect the data. If data are collected at the corporate or *enterprise* level, it is easy to merge them with other data including data on R&D. This approach has been attractive to many national statistical offices because they collect data at this level. In addition, the technology strategies of firms may be developed at this level. On the other hand, data can be collected at the *establishment* level where most innovation activities actually occur. However, reaggregating establishment level data to provide information about the enterprise as a whole is difficult.[8]

The major topic areas covered in Oslo-2 are:

- Whether the firm has had any innovation activities within the past three years;
- Whether the firm has introduced any innovations within the past three years;[9]
- General data on the firm: sales, R&D expenditures, R&D employment, exports, employment, and operating margin (if not available from other data sources);
- Firm's innovation objectives;
- Sources of information for firm innovations;
- Factors that hamper firm innovation;
- Percentage of firm sales, over the past three years, subdivided by the proportion that stem from:
    1. technologically new products (disaggregated by new to the firm and new to the world)
    2. technologically improved products (disaggregated by new to the firm and new to the world)
    3. products that are technologically unchanged but produced with changed production methods
    4. products that are technologically unchanged and are produced with unchanged production methods;
- Average length of the firm's product lifecycle;[10]
- Degree to which firms are engaged in custom production;

- Impact of innovation on production inputs: employment, materials consumption, energy usage, and use of fixed capital;
- If innovation has resulted in a reduction in production costs, to what degree has the average cost of production been reduced?
- Main sectors of economic activity of the users of a firm's technologically new or improved products, by sales, in percentage terms;
- Evaluation of the effectiveness of various means for protecting intellectual property rights including patents, design registration, secrecy, complexity of design and lead-time;
- Information on purchases and sales of technology subdivided by domestic and foreign firms; and
- Expenditures on innovation activities by type of activity.

A substantial amount of effort has been spent attempting to develop survey questions that measure the resources devoted to the wide range of innovation activities within firms. Many of these efforts have resulted in data of questionable value. The biggest problem stems from separating expenditures that relate to new and improved products and processes from the part that relates to routine activities.

For example, research and development expenditures are relatively easy to collect because almost all R&D expenditures are directly related to the development of new products or processes.[11] However, expenditures for plant and equipment often cannot be segregated into expenditures for new products and expenditures for expansion of the production. The same thing is true for marketing expenditures. Most survey response analysis has shown that the questions on innovation expenditures are the most difficult for respondents, have the lowest response rates, and produce results of questionable value.[12]

3.   THE COMMUNITY INNOVATION SURVEY

The second Community Innovation Survey (CIS-2) developed a "harmonized" set of questions for the surveying of the European Community. Individual countries were free to modify questions. The questionnaire was developed in early 1997. By the end of 1998, fourteen of the European Union countries and Norway had implemented this survey.

The second community innovation survey is actually two surveys: one designed to cover manufacturing industries and one for the service sector.

The inclusion of the service sector represents a major step forward since each year services account for a larger fraction of most national economies.[13]

One key distinction between the first and second CIS questionnaires is that the first one refers to innovations that were "developed or introduced" in the relevant period while the second refers to innovations that were "introduced onto the market" or "used within a production process". Arundel, et al. (1998) argue that this leads to a confusion of the technology creation process with the diffusion process and suggest rewording this question so that it asks separately about the introduction of innovations that were developed within the firm and the introduction of innovations developed elsewhere. This approach, it is argued, would clarify the interpretation of many of the remaining questions, which seem to apply mostly to the creators of new products rather than those who diffuse the technology.

Firms were asked to specify the main source of information for innovations during the 1994-96 period. The same scale was used as in the objective question and the question was identical on the services and manufacturing questionnaire. The sources included were:

- Sources within the enterprise;
- Other enterprises within the enterprise group;
- Competitors;
- Clients or customers;
- Consultancy enterprises;
- Suppliers of equipment, materials, components, or software;
- Universities and other higher education institutes;
- Government or private non-profit research institutes;
- Patent disclosures;
- Computer based information networks; and
- Fairs, exhibitions.

Firms specified whether they had been involved with any joint R&D or other innovation projects during the 1994-96 period. If they were, they were then asked to specify whether their partners were located in the same country, Europe, the United States, Japan, or elsewhere. The types of partners specified was identical to the sources of information list, except for the obvious deletions of the enterprise itself, patents, information networks, and fairs.

Finally, firms indicated if they had had at least one innovation project seriously delayed, abolished, or aborted. If so, the list of possible reasons that included:

Excessive perceived economic risk;

- Innovation costs too high;
- Lack of appropriate sources of finance;
- Organizational rigidities;
- Lack of qualified personnel;
- Lack of information on technology;
- Lack of information on markets;
- Fulfilling regulations, standards; and
- Lack of customer responsiveness to new products.

It is worth noting, however, that the survey provided no guidance to firms concerning how to separate the twin issues of economic risk and innovation costs.

CIS-2 also recommends that the national surveys ask firms to describe their most important technologically new or improved product or process. The next round of the Community Innovation Survey is scheduled to occur in 2001 with data collected from the year 2000. Plans are currently underway for the revision of the survey instrument.

4.   OTHER RECENT INNOVATION SURVEYS OUTSIDE THE UNITED STATES

Aside from the European Community, the most extensive efforts to collect data on innovation have been conducted in Canada. In addition to conducting surveys based on the Oslo Manual, Canada also significantly expanded that design towards drawing connections between technology developers and technology users. They have performed significant development work in service sector innovation surveys, and have also conducted a couple of industry-specific surveys that shed useful information on future innovation indicator development. The discussion below focuses on areas where the Canadian questions were significantly different from those used elsewhere.

The Canadian surveys are significantly longer than those contemplated in either of the Oslo manuals. In part, this is because Canadian law mandates completion of the survey. This permits the Canadians to survey on a wider range of topics than in other countries. Canadians have the additional advantage of having a single statistical data collection agency for the country. As a result, routine questions about the firm that might have to be duplicated on multiple surveys in other countries can simply be obtained in Canada by linking data sets based on a tax identification number.

Questions that have been added to the survey by the Canadians include the usage of employee development and training programs, employee access to the Internet, and the firm's use of the Internet for selling its products. In addition, there is a rather detailed section on the qualitative impacts of innovation activities on the firm, including its impact on productivity, the quality of service, the range of products offered, the size of the geographic market, and the firm's impact on the environment. Firms are also asked the degree to which new products replaced products that the firm previously offered.

The Canadian survey asked firms to describe their most important innovation. The principal reason the Canadians have focused on the firm's most important innovation is that the Canadian theoretical framework looks at innovation as having three parts: the generation of knowledge, the diffusion of knowledge and the use of knowledge. Very often, these three functions do not occur in the same firm. The direction this theory is moving is to look at clusters of firms that may have complex relationships and information flows. As a result, it is important to pursue, in some detail, the linkages between technology developers and technology users. Therefore, for example, they ask firms to specify the industry or industries and country or countries that were the main suppliers of ideas for the specified innovation as well as the ones who were the main customers for the new product. The idea here is to move beyond questions that, for example, might ask firms to specify the percentage of new ideas obtained from customers, and instead begin to identify networks of firms and industries that produce and use new technology.

In addition, firms evaluated whether the innovation was a world first, a first for Canada, or simply a first for a local market. If it was not a world first, firms were asked where it was developed first and the length of time between its initial development and adoption by the responding firm. Firms are also asked about the effect of this innovation on firm employment and on the skill requirements of the firm's workers.

The Canadians devote a substantial section of their questionnaire to intellectual property rights. They ask both how frequently various mechanisms were used over a three year period and how effective they were in protecting intellectual property (using a threshold question and a five point scale). In this question, they specifically ask about copyrights, patents, industrial designs, trade secrets, trademarks, integrated circuit designs, and plant breeders' rights. They also ask firms about the effectiveness of two additional strategies: being the first to market, and having a complex product design.

Finally, firms are asked to rate the importance of various factors to their overall competitive strategy and to the overall success of their firm. This permits one to assess in a more general way the role of innovation in the firm.

A number of other European countries have built upon the basic structure of the CIS. Surveys have been carried out in at least the following countries: Switzerland, Norway, Poland, the Slovak Republic, Russia, Japan and Australia. These offer some questions that are significantly different from those discussed above.

The Italian survey, for example, asks about the impact of innovation on firm employment, and also adds opinion questions about the impact of innovation on firm performance and about the firm's innovation plans for the future.

The Swiss survey explores a number of interesting new areas. Firms are asked to evaluate, on a 1-5 scale, the technological opportunities available in their industry. The questionnaire also asks firms to evaluate the level of competition (with separate questions for price competition and other kinds of competition) using the same 1-5 scale. Firms are asked to characterize their products as standardized, differentiated, and/or custom built; though the survey does not ask firms to specify the percentage of products that fall in each category. In addition, firms are asked to rate the contribution of external information to the effectiveness of internal innovation development.

Switzerland also conducted a separate survey on the diffusion of basic technology in industry, focusing mainly on the conditions surrounding the adoption of computer-assisted production and the diffusion of microelectronic-based technologies.

The United Kingdom survey asks an interesting question about the degree to which firms have implemented technologically oriented management or organizational changes, specifically about electronic data interchange, just in time planning systems, electronic mail, use of the Internet, investments in people, quality management systems or standards (such as ISO9000), and benchmarking performance against other firms. The UK survey also asks which sources of information were used to actually carry out innovation projects as opposed to just suggesting ideas.

5.   UNITED STATES INNOVATION SURVEYS

Efforts to collect innovation indicator data (other than input indicators) in the United States have been on going for at least twenty-five years. In the mid-70s, NSF sponsored a group of pilot studies that were geared toward measuring the resources devoted to innovation on a project-by-project basis

(Fabricant 1975; Posner and Rosenberg 1974; Roberts 1974; Hildred and Bengstrom 1974). These studies encountered significant problems because it was determined that firms rarely kept records of this sort that attributed specific costs to specific development projects.

In the early 1980s, the focus shifted to collecting data about firms rather than collecting data about specific innovation projects. Hill, et al. (1982) explored the feasibility of a very wide range of potential innovation indicators. These indicators were developed through an exhaustive search of the extant literature on innovation theory and tested by conducting in-depth interviews with potential respondents using a series of trial innovation questionnaires. Some of the questions in CIS-1 and CIS-2 can trace their roots to this indicator development project. This project culminated in the survey of 600 manufacturing firms in 1983-84 (collecting 1982 data) (Hansen, Stein, and Moore 1984). The topics covered in this survey were:

- Number and sources of new products and proportion of firm sales due to them;

- Degree to which R&D was performed centrally in firms or in product divisions;

- Degree to which firms made grants or contracts to universities for research;

- Extent to which firms were involved in various kinds of internal and external technological ventures including venture capital investments and R&D limited partnerships;

- Expenditures for new plant and equipment, production start-up, and marketing for new products and production processes;

- Degree to which firms relied on patents and trade secrets; and

- Amount of royalty and license fees from domestic and foreign firms and the number of firms from which such payments were received.

This survey achieved a response rate in excess of fifty percent. The completion rate for individual questions on the returned surveys was in excess of ninety percent. The survey was repeated in 1986 (collecting 1985 data) by Audits and Surveys, Incorporated. Roughly, two thousand firms were involved in this latter study, but the response rate was substantially lower than with the previous survey. Almost 100 firms were respondents to both surveys. While minor changes were made to a few of the questions, for the most part the data collected were the same in both surveys. In some cases, the same individual answered both questionnaires while in others two different individuals within the same firm answered the questionnaire. One effort to assess the quality of the data consisted of analyzing whether the differences between the survey responses were greater when a different person responded than when the same person completed both surveys (Hansen 1991).

In 1994, the U.S. Census Bureau conducted another pilot survey of 1000 firms to develop innovation indicators in the U.S. covering 1990-1992. The questionnaire contained many of the same topics as the Eurostat surveys:

- Incidence of product and process innovation;

- Objectives of innovation;

- Sources of information for innovation;

- Channels used to obtain new technology and channels for the transfer technology out of firms;

- R&D or innovation partnerships with external entities; and

- Target technologies for R&D (such as new materials, flexible manufacturing systems, software, etc.).

The response rate from this survey was 57 percent. One hundred thirty of the firms were the subjects of intensive follow-up and for these firms a response in excess of 80 percent was achieved.

One of the most interesting results of this survey was the finding that of those firms introducing innovations, 84 percent also were R&D performers (Rausch 1996). This is in stark contrast with most European studies that found a very large number of innovating firms that performed no R&D at all.

In the 1980s Levin, et al. (1987) conducted a survey designed to elicit information concerning the ability of firms to appropriate the results of their own technology development programs. This survey, which came to be known as the Yale survey was later adopted and expanded by Cohen, et al. at Carnegie Mellon University. The second survey (hereafter CMU) is the focus of this section. It is significant for a number of reasons. Most importantly, the reporting unit for this survey is the business unit, rather than the enterprise. As a result, questions that are more detailed are possible.

The sampling frame for this survey was constructed from the Directory of American Research and Technology (Bowker Press 1984) as supplemented by Standard and Poor's Compustat database. The sample was thus limited to R&D labs or units within firms that actually conducted R&D. The focus on firms that perform R&D was driven by the fact that the survey principally concerned the R&D function within the firm rather than the broader range of innovation activities, thus a firm that did not perform R&D would have found little on the survey that pertained to them. The CMU survey did not, however, focus primarily on measuring R&D inputs, but rather looked carefully at research objectives, information sources, and the structure of the environment in which R&D occurred within the firm. As a result, many of the questions are similar to those found on the CIS and MIT questionnaires. In addition, the CMU questionnaire also asked about the competitive environment in which the firm operated and the mechanisms that were used to protect intellectual property rights.

It is useful to focus on those areas of CMU survey that asked questions that were wholly different from those incorporated on previous surveys. For example, in attempting to identify characteristics of the R&D environment in firms, questions were asked about how frequently R&D personnel interacted face to face with personnel in the firm's marketing and production units or in other R&D units. This is an example of the type of question that would be impossible to explore at the enterprise level, but certainly makes sense at the establishment level and seems to work at the business unit level as well. Firms were also asked questions about the relationships between R&D and other firm functions, such as whether personnel were rotated across units or whether teams were constructed drawing on various cross-functional units. They were also asked to specify the percentage of R&D projects that were started at the request of another unit within the firm. All of these questions stem from a more complex, non-linear model of innovation within firms.

While a number of other studies ask about the importance of firm interactions with universities and government labs, the CMU questionnaire was able to ask for more information about the nature of these relationships. For example, in each of three categories (research findings, prototypes and new instruments and techniques) it asked the percentage of R&D projects that used research results from universities or government labs. It also presented a series of scientific fields (biology, chemistry, electrical engineering, etc.) and asked on a four-point scale what the significance of university or government research was to the firm's R&D activities.

The CMU survey also included a section that asked about the relationship between the firm and its competitors. Firms were asked to name the most innovative firms in their industry and to assess their own level of innovation (disaggregated by product and process innovation) relative to other firms in the industry. Then firms were asked to assess the overall rate of product and process innovation in the industry as a whole. Questions aimed at assessing how early in the innovation process firms became aware of their competitor's innovations and what percentages of their innovation projects have the same technical goals as their competitors. Finally, firms were asked to estimate the number of competitors they have by region of the world, and how many were able to introduce competing innovations in time to effectively diminish the profitability of the firm's own innovations.

A significant section of the CMU questionnaire is devoted to assessing the firm's ability to capture the returns from innovation using various mechanisms (patents, trade secrets, etc.). First, firms were asked to specify the percentage of their innovations (disaggregated by product innovations and process innovations) that were effectively protected by secrecy, patents, other legal mechanisms, being first to market, having complementary sales or service, having complementary manufacturing facilities, or by product complexity. A number of questions were then asked about the firm's patenting behavior, including the reasons patent applications are made (to prevent copying by other firms, to measure researcher performance, to obtain revenue, etc.) and the reasons the firm might decide not to patent a new discovery (information disclosure, cost of patent application, difficulty in demonstrating novelty, etc.). In addition, firms were asked how long it took competitors to introduce similar alternatives both in cases where patents had been obtained and in cases where they had not. This question was asked separately for product and process innovations.

6.   CONCLUSION: INNOVATION INDICATOR DEVELOPMENT ISSUES

A careful review of existing surveys of technological innovation reveals a number of key issues that must be resolved by those who would continue this work in the future. These include specification of the reporting unit to be used, the composition of the questionnaire, and sectoral coverage.

6.1   The Reporting Unit

The reporting unit determines the types of questions that can be asked. Detailed questions concerning various types of innovation expenditure cannot be collected at the enterprise level because the data simply are not known. On the other hand, questions about the firm's strategy may be collected at the enterprise level, but not the establishment level. Thus it is important to make a decision about the level at which data will be collected before making final decisions about what data to collect.

Archibugi, et al. (1995) point out that there are really a number of different candidates for the reporting unit:

> *The legally defined enterprise* is a unit that has legal status in a given country. It might have one or several establishments, one or several business units. In several cases, it corresponds to the unit registered for tax purposes. According to this definition, establishments or business units located outside the borders of the nation should not be considered.

> *The economically defined enterprise* is classified according to the ownership or control. It includes all establishments or business units

whom are owned or controlled by the enterprise, located in the same or in a different country from the enterprise's headquarters. Often, large economically defined enterprises are subdivided even within one country, into several legally defined enterprises.

The business unit is part of the enterprise, although a single business unit composes several enterprises. A business unit may have one or more establishments.[14]

The establishment is a geographically specific production unit. Several enterprises, especially among those of smaller size, have a single establishment only. (Archibugi, et al. 1995).

Given the importance of developing national data on innovation, the economically defined enterprise is unlikely to be adopted as the reporting unit. As a result, we will focus on the other three candidates, which will be concisely referred to at the enterprise, the business unit, and the establishment.

Most ongoing innovation indicator studies use the enterprise as the reporting unit (and the statistical unit of analysis). The Oslo Manual specifically makes this recommendation, but adds that diversified firms may be subdivided according to the type of economic activity in which they engage. To date, all of the U.S. National Science Foundation innovation indicator data have been collected from enterprises as well. In the first round of CIS surveys, only two countries used something other than the enterprise as the basis for their survey.

One key reason for relying on the enterprise as the reporting and statistical unit is pragmatic. Other data, notably R&D expenditures, are collected with the enterprise as the reporting unit. Thus, data collectors both have a great deal more experience collecting data from enterprises and have other historical data series that are collected on an enterprise basis.

Policy makers have traditionally wanted firm-level data so that they could link it to other firm-level data sets and so that they could address questions that were inherently firm-level questions, such as the distribution of innovation activities by firm size. Virtually every innovation indicator study has attempted to collect data and report results disaggregated by firm size. This is impossible without firm-level data.

If having firm-level data is important, the only practical way to obtain it is to collect data at the enterprise level. This may be observed by considering the methodology that would be required to collect firm level data at a lower level within the firm. In principle, if the data collected were purely quantitative, it should be possible to collect the data from each of the firm's establishments or business units and then re-aggregate it back to the level of the firm as a whole. This would be possible if either a census was taken of all of the firm's establishments or business units or if some method were established for imputing values for the missing components of the firm. Even if a census were used, however, it is likely that there would be some non-respondents among the firm's establishments, requiring imputation of some missing values in any case. This technique would probably require that each firm be treated as a special case so that the analyst has a list of each of the units within the firm and is able to keep track of which units responded and which did not. The analyst would have to be sufficiently well informed about the firms operations that he or she could intelligently estimate the missing values.

In the case of qualitative data, it is likely to be impossible to reconstruct firm data from data provided by the various establishments or business units. For example, consider the following question from CIS-2:

Between 1994-96, has your firm introduced any technologically new or improved processes? If yes, who developed these processes?

Mainly other enterprises or institutes	o
Your enterprise and other enterprises or institutes	o
Mainly your enterprise	o

Suppose a firm has four establishments or business units. Further, suppose that three of them indicate the first response (mainly other enterprises or institutes) and one indicates the third (mainly your enterprise). How should we re-aggregate this data to the firm level? Should we assume that since this work is done both within and outside the firm, the appropriate response for the firm as a whole is item 2 (even though no entity has checked it)? Should we conclude that the answer should be the first response because three of the four units checked it? Should we weight the responses by sales or R&D expenditure to come up with an average response?

On the other hand, suppose the one establishment that indicated the third choice also contains the firm's central R&D lab. Ought we not to conclude from this that the establishment with the central R&D lab is fundamentally different from the rest of the firm and that no single answer to this question will adequately describe the firm's behavior? This raises fundamental problems with collecting data at the enterprise level. If it is not possible for the data collector to construct a reasonable answer to the question based on information obtained from the various firm establishments (or business units) this may be because a single reasonable answer for the firm, as a whole does not exist.

Another problem with collecting data at the enterprise level is that it makes sector-level analyses rather difficult. Many, if not most, enterprises span more than one industrial sector. The Oslo Manual recommends using

International Standard Industrial Classification (ISIC) codes or NACE codes to classify enterprises by sector. The recommended divisions are only to the two-digit classification level, so the categories tend to be broad.[15] Even at the two-digit level, however, it is extremely difficult to classify even moderately diversified firms. Oslo-2 recommends classification by principal area of economic activity. Thus, for a firm in more than one two digit category, all of its activities will be attributable to its principal category. This creates problems at the two-digit level, but classification of enterprises at any finer level of stratification than two digits is virtually impossible.

If we come to the conclusion that the only practical way to collect data about the enterprise as a whole is to survey at the enterprise level rather than the establishment or business unit level, it has a substantial effect on the type of data that can be collected for two reasons. First, enterprises know less about the activities going on in the business units than the units themselves do, so they are less able to answer detailed questions (especially in areas such as innovation costs) than are business units or establishments. Thus, surveys of enterprises rely heavily on either qualitative data or on rough estimates of quantitative data. Second, asking for qualitative data at the enterprise level does not eliminate the aggregation problem described above; it merely causes it to be dealt with by the firm itself rather than by the data collector. It is still necessary for someone to look at the various behaviors of the business units within the firm and make a judgment about what data should be reported for the firm as a whole. While it is arguable that individuals inside the firm are in a better position to make judgments about how to aggregate qualitative data from disparate business units, it does not mean that it will be possible to report meaningful summary data in situations where no meaningful summary data actually exist.

If it were possible to do without data aggregated on an enterprise-wide basis, it would be possible to collect the data on either the establishment or business unit basis. An establishment represents an entity that is limited to a single geographic area. As a result, respondents at this level generally tend to have more detailed information available than do respondents at the enterprise level. Collecting data at the establishment permits analysis disaggregated by geographic region. Neither enterprise-level data nor business unit data permit tracking the geographic location of innovation activities.

There are a number of problems with the establishment approach, however. There is a much larger population of establishments than of firms. This would represent a very significant increase in cost for those surveys that attempt to conduct a census rather than select a sample. Even for those researchers who only wish to survey a sample of establishments, significant problems will arise in identifying the population from which the sample is to be drawn.

There are particular problems associated with achieving high response rates when surveying establishments. Generally, someone is concerned with innovation at the enterprise level. This person may have a title such as Vice President for Research and Development, Chief Technical Officer, or Director of Technology. This person is likely to have at least some sympathy with the goals of the project and some interest in the underlying concepts. In doing surveys of this type we have found that many of these individuals have a great deal of enthusiasm for the innovation indicators project and have launched their own ongoing internal innovation data collect efforts. It is far less likely that a similar individual will exist at the establishment level. Potential respondents at the establishment level are more likely to find the survey an inconvenience that interferes with the flow of their work. Previous studies have found that one thing that contributes to increasing response rates is that the survey be addressed to an individual within the firm by name. This involves identifying the name of the person within the firm that is the most appropriate individual to fill out the questionnaire. Because establishments generally do not have offices or individuals who are specifically responsible for innovation within the firm, respondent identification will be substantially more difficult than it is for enterprises.

Response rates at the establishment level may also be hampered if respondents do not believe that they have the authority to complete and return the questionnaire. In this case, respondent may forward the questionnaire back to the enterprise level rather than completing it themselves.

An alternative is to collect data at the level of the business unit. A business unit consists of all establishments within an enterprise that are in the same line of business. While the activities of individual establishments may span multiple NACE code categories, all of the activities of an establishment would be attributable to its principal NACE category. Because the activities of establishments are substantially more homogeneous than the activities of enterprises, this problem is significantly less serious than in the case of establishments. As a result, line of business reporting generally can be successfully achieved at a more disaggregated sectoral level than enterprise-based reporting.

There are a number of advantages to this approach. To the extent that it is desirable to analyze innovation on a sector basis, the business unit approach provides data that will most clearly facilitate this analysis. Companies themselves often view business units as natural divisions for record keeping and strategic planning, so it would be easier for them to provide data at this level. However, it is worth noting that there is no particular reason that companies would view the boundaries between business units as being the same as those that were called for by the various standard industrial classification systems.

In addition, since the data are designed to summarize firm behavior, it makes sense to collect these data at a level where the data within each reporting unit are relatively homogeneous and the differences between reporting units are greatest. Because the line of business often dictates the type of technology developed and used and the way it is applied, these categories occur most naturally when the statistical unit is based on business units.

Some of the problems identified in conjunction with collecting data at the establishment level also exist in the case of business unit reporting. Obtaining a population of business units to sample (or to conduct a census) is likely to be even more difficult than obtaining a list of establishments. This is because establishments at least have a relatively unambiguous identifying characteristic (a distinct geographical address) whereas the identifying characteristic of business units is more amorphous. Identifying the appropriate individual within the company to respond to the survey will also be more difficult, but since lines of business are generally a higher level of aggregation within a firm than establishments, there is a better chance that someone is specifically responsible for innovation.

The degree of difficulty posed by these considerations depends on how the firm is organized. If firms are already organized along business unit lines (for example, with divisions that correspond to NACE business units) then locating someone to provide the data and obtaining the data will be relatively easy. If, however, the firm is not internally divided along business unit lines, simply trying to explain to a potential respondent (who may never have heard of SIC, ISIC or NACE codes) what data is being requested will pose an daunting task. It might be useful to discuss this issue in some detail with representatives of the Federal Trade Commission who attempted to collect data along business unit lines in the 1980s. Their perspective on the level of difficulty associated with requesting data from firms might provide some guidance as to whether it is reasonable to expect acceptable response rates if data is collected in this fashion.

The focus until now on collecting data from enterprises is based on the view that innovation is an activity that is firm centric. That is, information flows and new product and process development are activities that occur mostly within firms. As we have begun to understand the degree to which linkages with customers, suppliers and others are important to the innovation process, these linkages have been dealt with as exceptions—important exceptions, it is true, but exceptions nonetheless. Thus, it was considered reasonable to argue that collecting data on an establishment level was problematic because central R&D labs, which would be treated as separate establishments, report R&D but no sales. However, if the R&D that underlay a new product innovation were conducted in a completely different firm for some reason this was not viewed as a reason for abandoning enterprise-based data collection. The situation is made worse because the reporting unit has generally been the legally defined enterprise, not the economically defined enterprise. Thus, R&D performed within the firm, but in a subsidiary that is in a different country, is not counted either.

Recent research results from Statistics Canada cause one to wonder if the problem is not even more serious. In an ongoing data collection effort on the construction industry in Canada, researchers are finding that the very concept of a firm is beginning to disappear. On some projects, "firms" as we think of them have no persistence. The firm is essentially a joint venture of contractors (*not* working as subcontractors for a general contractor) that come together to form a "firm" for the life of a single construction project. This results in economies in the design process and reduces litigation costs if something goes wrong.

Similar behavior can be seen in other industries as well. Firms on a project are contracting out engineering expertise by project basis. In some cases these relationships are with engineering consulting firms, while in others independent contractors are hired. Some of these relationships will persist for long periods while others will relate to just one project. The research capacity of firms using this technique is thus extremely fluid. Perhaps most interesting is the fact that the firms that are consumers of these engineering services are often firms that have almost no internal development capacity of their own. They may regularly introduce new products or new production processes, but have done essentially no development themselves. This model has been observed for quite some time in computer software, where firms with no in-house software development capability would hire outside consultants or firms to create custom software packages, and in the process substantially alter their production processes. The approach is now quite common.

6.2   Questionnaire Composition

A great deal of time has been spent over the past two decades on the development of specific questions that might be included on innovation indicator surveys. It is important to design surveys so that the results will be comparable with previous surveys and with surveys that are conducted in other countries. Thus, it is useful to consider questions that have been included on CIS-2. However, since the field is not likely to stand still, it is also important to not ignore on-going theoretical developments that may result in productive new areas of inquiry.

CIS-2 asks for innovation data in six basic areas: scope and importance of innovation activities, resources devoted to innovation activities, objectives of innovation, sources of information, cooperative innovation ventures, and factors hampering innovation.

Questions on the scope and importance of innovation activities ask whether the firm is involved in the introduction of new products and processes and the extent to which these activities have contributed to firm sales. These questions have now been tested in quite a number of countries over a substantial period. All indications are that firms are able to answer them and that the data produced is reliable (Hansen 1991).

Questions on the resources devoted to innovation have caused significant problems for most studies in which they have been included. Oslo-2 concedes, "Not many enterprises keep separate records of other [non-R&D] technological product and process innovation expenditures", but concludes, "Experience has shown that it is quite possible for them to give acceptable estimates of the non-R&D portion." Later though, the Manual notes that most studies that have attempted to collect this data have found that firms simply do not have it (OECD 1997).

Some work has been done to assess the validity of this indicator. For example, comparisons of data collected in the U.S. in 1982 and 1985 found large unexplainable differences in the responses to this question. They also found that the percentage of total innovation expense accounted for by R&D was much higher than was indicated by previous studies. For example, in 1985, firms reported that on average expenditures for new plant and equipment related to the introduction of new products was only twice as high as their expenditures on R&D. Just three years earlier an admittedly smaller sample of firms reported it was 21 times higher. Other studies have reported similar anomalies. For example, in a survey conducted in the Nordic Countries that was sponsored by the Nordic Industrial Fund, it was found that R&D accounted on average for more than two thirds of all innovation expenditures in Norway (Hansen 1992).

This is not to say that this question has never worked. In a series of annual studies of innovation expenditures in Germany, Scholz found that this data could be collected in a meaningful way. However, it required a substantial amount of close work with the companies involved in the survey. When the survey was first begun, response rates were rather poor. However, as the survey continued over time and firms began to see the value in it, response rates improved, as did the apparent quality of the data. The firms believed the survey had value because as participants they received a sector report that summarized the collected data for their specific industry. Scholz believed that firms became more skilled at preparing these estimates, as they became more experienced with them. He also suggested that experienced firms used a procedure of estimating the change from the preceding survey rather than constructing a wholly new estimate for each year's survey.

Questions on the firm's objectives for innovation, sources of information, and cooperative arrangements with others are answered easily. As discussed above, it is sometimes difficult to know how to interpret the answers to these questions when the response is from an enterprise with many disparate business units. With regard to all survey questions that ask simply whether a firm has a particular activity, relationship or goal, the larger and more diversified the enterprise the more likely it is to answer "yes". Diversified firms simply do more different kinds of things than do smaller, less diversified firms. If the activity, relationship, or goal exists in any of the diversified firm's various units, the answer to the question for the enterprise as a whole will be in the affirmative. However, the total amount of innovation produced by a large firm that does a wide range of things is not necessarily more than the innovation produced by a group of small firms that, if taken together, would have the same range of activities.

The final area on CIS-2 concerned factors that hamper innovation. Questions of this type have appeared on a large number of surveys over the years either as factors that hamper innovation or as obstacles to innovation. The importance of this subject stems from a desire on the part of policy makers to promote innovation in the economy. Policy maker's concerns over the level of innovation stem from two sources. First, early economic studies that pointed out both theoretically and empirically that there is a divergence between the private and social returns to investment in innovation. As an innovation becomes diffused through the economy, the firm that introduced it is will only be able to capture a portion of the benefits that accrue from that innovation. As a result, the incentive to develop innovations in the first place is less than it would be if firms could capture all of the benefits.

Second, the government necessarily has a role in the innovation process. For example, it determines the rules and regulations surrounding firms' use of patents and technology licensing. It finances a significant amount of research either directly through grants and contracts or indirectly through its purchases of goods and services that have new technologies embedded in them. It also establishes environmental (and other) regulations that affect technological development. As a result, it is concerned about the degree to which these policies promote or hamper innovation in private firms.

While recognizing that assessing the degree to which firm innovation is hampered by various factors is important, it may not be that the best way to do this is to ask firms directly. There are a number of reasons for this. It is not clear that firms (or anyone else for that matter) can usefully disaggregate hampering factors that are inherently intertwined. For example, CIS-2 asks firms whether they are hampered by "excessive perceived economic risks," by "innovation costs [being] too high," or by a "lack of appropriate sources of finance." The decision to invest in new product or process development stems from an analysis (albeit sometimes an informal analysis) of the likely return on the investment, adjusted for the perceived risk, and the cost of the investment. Lower risks or higher returns will justify innovation investments with higher costs. It is difficult to see how a firm could look at these three factors one at a time, rather than considering them as a group.

Even when it is possible to disentangle the various hampering factors, it is not clear that the firms actually know the answer to this question. We can find out from a survey how important they perceive these factors to be (or at least what they report this importance to), but it is quite possible that one of the most significant factors hampering innovation is that firms do not have a good understanding of what obstacles they actually face. It is also possible that on a government questionnaire asking whether government regulations or standards hamper innovation, firms may view the survey is an opportunity to alter government policies in this area.

Finally third, there is a substantial bias built into most of the questions of this type. The words used in the question are usually pejorative. Firms are asked if they are "hampered" by "obstacles" or "barriers." They are not asked if they are restrained from making unwise and unprofitable investments in products or processes that have little market potential.

Aside from those questions specifically included on the CIS-2 survey, there are some areas where it might be useful to consider making additions. One area that deserves consideration is the collection of data that will help trace the relationships that are part of an innovation production/diffusion network. The "sources of information" question is designed to move in that direction, but it collects data concerning only one kind of interaction (information exchange) and looks only at very broad categories of firms (customers, suppliers, competitors).

Another approach is that taken by Canada and a few other countries, where firms are asked to identify specifically their most important innovation. Follow-up questions can then be asked about other firms that were involved in either the development or diffusion of this innovation. This provides much more detailed information about the inter-relationships of various firms' innovation activities.

A key problem with this approach is that it generally asks about only one innovation. On the one hand, the firm's "most important" innovation may not be a typical innovation. It may stand out in the mind of a respondent precisely because it was so unusual. On the other hand, it would be rather difficult to ask firms to name a "typical" innovation, since these are likely to be relatively routine and unmemorable. This question is best addressed at the enterprise or business unit level.

An alternative approach has been at least partially explored in the CMU study. Instead of only asking about the importance of sources of information by various categories of firms, the CMU study disaggregates the sources of information question by type of technology (at least when asking about university or government contributions). For example, it asked whether university or government research yielded significant results to the firm in the area of biology, or physics, or chemistry. It is possible to envision extending this to the questions about sources of information from customers and suppliers as well, asking firms to specify the industries that had some relationship to their innovation efforts. This might facilitate identifying the clusters of firm-types that are responsible for innovation.

While it is mentioned in the current Oslo manual, the latest CIS questionnaire does not ask for any information about mechanisms the firm might use to appropriate the benefits of its technology developments. At a minimum, it may be worth considering whether a question or two about the relative importance of various forms of intellectual property protection ought to be included. Such information is, of course, useful on its own, particularly since the legal environment created by government policies has a significant impact on firm's strategic decisions with regard to protecting intellectual property. However, patents themselves have often been collected as intermediate outputs of the innovation process. Understanding how firms view the importance of patents relative to other forms of protection is critical to interpreting the patent data itself.

6.3   Sectoral Coverage

The service sector of the economy continues to grow relative to manufacturing and now accounts for well over half of all employment in the United States. However, until now, innovation indicators in the United States have focused exclusively on manufacturing. Partly the reason for this was pragmatic; it was deemed more difficult to collect meaningful data from the service sector. It was also partly policy driven. Evangelista et al. (1998) point out that innovation policy is almost exclusively directed toward the manufacturing and university sectors. Hence, the need for innovation data for policy purposes was limited to those sectors. However, not only has the service sector become a large portion of our economy, it is also major contributor to technological innovation. In OECD countries, the service sector accounted for nearly a quarter of all business R&D in 1991 (Evangelista and Sirilli 1998). As the importance of the service sector of our economy grows, it is difficult to imagine that the collection of innovation indicator data could be limited to the industrial sector for much longer.

If the decision is made to include service sector firms in innovation indicator data collection projects, it is reasonable to ask what, if anything, about these firms causes them to require any different treatment than manufacturing enterprises. While there are a number of distinctions, the key element cited in most studies is that in the service sector production and consumption occur simultaneously (Miles 1995). From an indicator standpoint, this leads to a general concern about whether it would be possible to treat product and process innovations separately, since the process by which the service is produced is generally also the product. An example of this sort of problem can be found in the introduction of the automatic teller machine (ATM) in the banking industry. The ATM is a production process as the mechanism that delivers banking services to consumers. Consumers, however, view the ATM as the product. A clear distinction here is probably impossible.

Eurostat approached this problem by sponsoring a series of pilot studies of service industry innovation. Initially twenty interviews were conducted in Germany and the Netherlands (ten in each country) to determine whether the definitions in the Oslo manual would have to be changed to accommodate the service sector. Note that the assumption was made that the questionnaire would be pretty much the same for the service sector as for the manufacturing industries, but some changes might be required in the definitions of "new products," "new processes," etc.

A number of significant changes in the definitions were recommended because of the pre-test. Most importantly, separate definitions for product and process innovation are not included. Instead, the final version of CIS-2 is clear that both types of innovation need to be included, but does not ask firms to attempt to separate them

Another major change that came about because of the pre-test was that questions that attempted to assess the significant of innovation by asking about their contribution to sales were dropped. The reason is that firms have trouble identifying the sales that result from a product addition or change. In these industries, services are often bundled together and sold a package. Often the product itself dictates this sales method. Returning to the example of ATM machines, the services provided by these machines are most often packaged with a range of other bank account services. It might be possible to calculate the amount paid by consumers (in fees and foregone interest) for the services associated with a particular type of account (though even this is questionable), but it is impossible to isolate the component of the fee that is related to ATM services.

The inability to develop data for the new product sales indicator is disappointing because in manufacturing, firms have generally been able to provide this data and it provides a quantitative measure on diffusion. Its value as an indicator is demonstrated in part by the quantity and range of surveys on which it has been used.

Yet, few efforts have been made to develop any new indicators of innovation in the service sector that do not have counterparts in the manufacturing sector. It may be that there simply are none. However, when the current crop of indicators was developed, the researchers who developed them clearly had manufacturing in mind. Had they focused on the service sector instead, it is not clear that this same group of indicators would have emerged. As a result, it might be worth considering devoting some resources to taking a fresh look at the service sector from this perspective.

One other item is worth mentioning. None of the work that has been done to assess the feasibility of applying these indicators to the service sector has been performed in the healthcare industry. In fact, this sector is not mentioned in the classification list of service sector enterprises in the Oslo Manual, nor was it treated in the Canadian service sector survey. The reason for this is that in these countries the healthcare industry is generally viewed as a part of the public sector of the economy rather than the private sector. This raises two interesting issues. First, should health care be included in an U.S. survey of innovation in the service sector? Second, should public sector service providers in the U.S. (the U.S. Postal Service, for example, or public universities, as education providers, not R&D providers) be included? As long as innovation data collection was related solely to manufacturing, this issue did not arise, since there is very little public sector manufacturing. As the focus shifts to the service sector, however, it must be addressed.

ACKNOWLEDGEMENTS

The research that underlies this chapter was performed on behalf of SRI, International and funded by the U.S. National Science Foundation Division of Science Resources. The author is grateful to SRI, International and NSF for its support and for comments on earlier drafts. All opinions expressed herein are those of the author and do not necessarily represent the views of SRI, International or the National Science Foundation.

REFERENCES

Archibugi, D., S. Cesaratto, and G. Sirilli. (1991). "Sources of Innovation Activities and Industrial Organization in Italy," *Research Policy*, 20, pp. 299-314.

Archibugi, D., P. Cohendet, A. Kirstensen, and K. Schaffer. (1995). "Evaluation of Community Innovation Survey (CIS) – Phase I: European Innovation Monitoring System (EIMS)," Publication No 11.

Arundel, A., K. Smith, P. Patel, and G. Sirilli. (1998). "The Future of Innovation Measurement in Europe: Concepts, Problems and Practical Directions," Idea Paper Number 3, The Step Group, pp. C-IV to C-VI.

Avveduto, S. and G. Sirilli. (1986). "The Survey on Technological Innovation in Italian Manufacturing Industry: Problems and Perspectives," OECD workshop on Innovations Statistics.

Bowker Press. (1984). *Directory of American Research and Technology New York.* Bowker Press.

DeBresson, Christian. (1996). *Economic Interdependence and Innovation: An Input-Output Analysis.* London: Edward Alger.

DeBresson, Chris and B. Murray. (1984). "Innovation in Canada. A Retrospective Survey: 1945-1978," New Westminster, B.C.: Cooperative Research Unit on Science and Technology.

Evangelista, R., T. Sandven, G. Sirilli, and K. Smith. (1996). "Measuring the Cost of Innovation in European Industry," presented at the International Conference on Innovation Measurement and Policies, May.

Evangelista, R., and G. Sirilli. (1998). "Innovation in the Service Sector: Results from the Italian Survey," IDEA Paper No. 7, The STEP Group, p. 1.

Evangelista, R., G. Sirilli, K. Smith. (1998). "Measuring Innovation in Services," IDEA Paper No. 6, The STEP Group.

Fabricant, S., (1975). "Accounting by Business Firms for Investment in Research and Development," (New York: New York Univ. Dept of Economics NSF/RDA 73-191).

Gellman Research Associates. (1976). "Indicators of International Trends in Technological Innovation," Gellman Research Associates.

Hansen, J. (1991). "New Innovation Indicator Data Validation," Final Report to the National Science Foundation.

Hansen, J. (1992). "New Indicators of Industrial Innovation in Six Countries: A Comparative Analysis," Final Report to the National Science Foundation, June 22.

Hansen, J., J. Stein, and T. Moore. (1984). "Industrial Innovation in the United States: A Survey of Six Hundred Companies," Boston: BU Center for Technology and Policy.

Hildred, W., and L. Bengstom. (1974). "Surveying Investment in Innovation," Denver: Denver Research Institute, NSF/RDA 73-21.

Hill, C., J. Hansen and J. Maxwell. (1982). "Assessing the Feasibility of New Science and Technology Indicators," Cambridge, MA: MIT Center for Policy Alternatives

Kline, S and N. Rosenberg. (1986). "An Overview of Innovation," in Landau, R. and N. Rosenberg, eds. *The Positive Sum Strategy. Harnessing Technology for Economics Growth.* Washington: National Academy Press.

Levin, R., A. Klevorick, R. Nelson and S. Winter. (1987). "Appropriating the Returns from Industrial R&D," *Brookings Papers on Economic Activity.* pp. 783-820.

Miles, I. (1995). "Services Innovation, Statistical and Conceptual Issues," Working Group on Innovation and Technology Policy, OECD (DEST/EAS/STP/NESTI/ (95) 12).

Nordic Industrial Fund. (1991). *Innovation Activities in the Nordic Countries* Oslo: Nordic Industrial Fund.

OECD. (1980). *The Measurement of Scientific and Technical Activities: Frascati Manual.* Paris, OECD.

OECD. (1992). *OECD Proposed Guidelines for Collecting and Interpreting Technological Innovation Data: Oslo Manual.* Paris: OECD 1992.

OECD. (1997). *OSLO Manual: Proposed Guidelines for Collecting and Interpreting Technological Innovation Data.* Paris: OECD.

Pavitt, K. (1983). "Characteristics of Innovation Activities in British Industry," *OMEGA,* 11(2): 113-130.

Pavitt, K., M. Robson, and J. Townsend. (1985). "The Size Distribution of Innovating Firms in the U.K. 1945-1983," Brighton, Science Policy Research Unit, University of Sussex.

Posner, L. and L. Rosenberg (1974). "The Feasibility of Monitoring Expenditures for Technological Innovation," Washington: Practical Concepts Inc.

Rausch, L. (1996). "R&D Continues to be an Important Part of the Innovation Process," NSF *Data Brief,* no. 7, August 7.

Roberts, R. (1974). "Investment in Innovation" Final report prepared by the Midwest Research Institute for the National R&D Assessment Program, National Science Foundation.

Scholz, L. and H. Schmalholz. (1982). "IFO — Innovation Survey. Efforts to Inform Decision-Makers of Innovation Activities in the Federal Republic of Germany," Paper prepared for the OECD Workshop on Patent and Innovation Statistics, June.

Smith, A. (1776). *The Wealth of Nations,* (New York: The Modern Library 1937 1965) p. 9.

Smith, K. (1989). "The Nordic Innovation Indicators Project: Issues for Innovation Analysis and Technology Policy," Oslo: Gruppen for Ressursstudier, April.

Townsend, J., F. Henwood, G. Thomas, K. Pavitt, and S. Wyatt. (1981). "Science Innovations in Britain Since 1945." SPRU Occasional Paper Series N. 16. Brighton, Science Policy Research Unit, University of Sussex.

---

[1] In this sense it is a bit like measuring the health of a human being. There is no single measure of human health, so we must rely on a range of indicators, such as body temperature, skin color, level of pain or discomfort, the levels of various different components of the blood, dark and light areas on x-rays, and so forth. Each of these indicators is based on our fundamental understanding of how the various biological systems in humans work. As our understanding of human physiology improves, so does our capacity to develop better indicators of human health. The underlying system is sufficiently complex and multi-faceted that it is reasonable to conclude that no single measure of human health will ever be developed. Therefore, it is with innovation.

[2] About the same time, the Nordic Industrial Fund also sponsored a series of workshops to move toward a standardized approach to data collection. The initial intent was to provide some input for the ongoing Nordic Survey. The keynote paper for the first set of meetings, developed by Smith of the Resource Policy Group in Oslo, referenced only the Nordic Survey (Smith 1989), but from the beginning the group, which comprised most of the individuals who had developed extant survey instruments (including Sirilli from Italy, Scholz from Germany, DeBresson from Canada, Hansen from the United States, Akerblom from Finland, Keinknechy from the Netherlands, Patel from Britain, and Piatier from France, as well as representatives from the Nordic Countries and the OECD), framed the discussion more generally in terms that could be applied across the OECD. An additional workshop was held the following year and the general framework for a guide to collecting innovation indicator data was in place. Drafting of what (at the suggestion of Kleinknecht) came to be know as "The Oslo Manual" was left to Smith and Akerblom. The first revision of the manual was adopted and published b the OECD in 1992 (OECD 1992).

[3] This project was implemented as a joint venture of Eurostat and the SPRINT/European Innovation Modeling System (EIMS) program of DGXIII. In 1991-92, there was a small-scale pretest of the survey in five countries. The survey instrument was revised in early 1992, and in 1992/93.

[4] Such innovations can involve radically new technologies, can be based on combining existing technologies in new uses, or can be derived from the use of new knowledge.

[5] A simple product may be improved (in terms of better performance or lower costs) through use of higher-performance components or materials, or a complex product that consists of a number of integrated technical sub-systems by partial changes to one of the sub-systems.

[6] These methods may involve changes in equipment, or production organization, or a combination of these changes, and may be derived from the use of new knowledge. The methods may be intended to produce or deliver technologically new or improved products, which cannot be produced or delivered using conventional production methods, or essentially to increase the production or delivery efficiency of existing products.

[7] While it may be reasonably argued that every application of existing technology in a different setting requires a degree of adaptation and, thus, innovation, it is also clear that the adoption of existing technology that is widely used elsewhere involves a substantially reduced degree of innovation relative to the creation and first use of new technology.

After all, the introduction of a production process that is "new to the first" might simply occur because the firm was expanding its product line into a new area that required different equipment based on existing (and possibly quite ancient) technologies. On the other hand, firms generally know when a product or production process is new to their firm. Often they do not know whether it is also new to their industry, new to their country or region, or new to the world. In fact, in DeBresson's object-based study of innovation in Canada, he found that a rather large number of firms claimed to have developed world first innovations (DeBresson and Murray 1984). In fact, in a number of cases more than one Canadian firm claimed to have been the first in the world to develop a particular innovation.

[8] The Second Oslo Manual considered the issue of which level within the firm should provide data and noted a distinction between the reporting unit (which is the part of the firm that was asked to provide the data) and the statistical unit (which is the part of the firm about which the data is collected). The principle difference between the treatment of the statistical unit in the first and second Oslo Manuals is that Oslo-2 seems to have a much greater recognition of the problems involved in selecting any one unit of analysis. Its basic recommendation is that the enterprise-type unit generally is used, but it makes this recommendation "taking into account how innovation activities are usually organized." It also recommends that when enterprises are involved in several industries, a smaller unit like the kind-of-activity unit (KAU) "an enterprise or part of an enterprise which engages in one kind of economic activity without being restricted to the geographic area in which that activity is carried out" may be more appropriate (OECD 1997). The kind-of-activity unit (KAU) groups all the parts of an enterprise contributing to the performance of an activity at class level (four digits) of NACE Rev. 1 and corresponds to one or more operational subdivisions of the enterprise. The enterprise's information system must be capable of indicating or calculating for each KAU at least the value of production, intermediate consumption, manpower costs, the operating surplus and employment and gross fixed capital formation." (Council Regulation (EEC) No 696/93 of 15 March 1993 on the statistical units for the observation and analysis of the production system in the Community, OJ No. L 76, p. I, Section III/F of the Annex). (OECD 1997).

[9] Note that the difference between the first two items is that a firm may have engaged in innovation activities that either were aborted before the introduction of a new product or process or have not yet come to fruition.

[10] Some concern is expressed in the manual that firms with short product lifecycles would naturally have a higher percentage of sales from new products and that it might be useful to separate the effect of large new product sales due to short lifecycles from large new product sales due to other factors.

[11] However, even R&D expenditures may not be trivial to calculate because many firm's research personnel spend a portion of their time working on products that reflect style variations which are not properly viewed as technologically new products. Interviews with the individuals in these firms who are responsible for reporting R&D expenditures reveal that they are only partially successful in separating out R&D expenditures related to technologically new products from those which are not.

[12] Oslo-2 recognizes many of these problems and devotes a substantial section to attempting to hone the definitions to be clear about which items should be included and which should not. Despite this, Oslo-2 clearly sees the problem as "not which data to collect, but how to collect reliable data on innovation expenditures other than R&D expenditure." (OECD 1997) To try to improve the situation, Solo-2 recommends that surveys ask firms to indicate whether the data provided in this area are accurate or are rough estimates only.

The Manual notes that this may result in more firms simply doing rough estimates, but it might also raise response rates. It is worth noting that a high response rate is not always desirable. If the alternatives are high response rates but poor quality data or low response rates but carefully answered questions, the latter may, in fact, be preferable.

[13] Service sector industries that are covered by CIS-2 include electricity, gas and water supply (NACE 40-41), wholesale trade (51), transportation (60-62), telecommunications (64.2), financial intermediation (65-67), computer and related activities (72) and engineering services (74.2 in part). Notable absent is the health care sector.

[14] This unit is intended to be similar to the "line of business" concept in the U.S.

[15] It is interesting to note that the initial Yale study found that a two-digit sector analysis was sufficient to elucidate most of the important inter-industry differences (Levin, et al. 1987).

Chapter 5

Trends in Cooperative Research Activity
Has the National Cooperative Research Act Been Successful?

ANDREW C. BROD AND ALBERT N. LINK
University of North Carolina at Greensboro

1.   INTRODUCTION

The National Cooperative Research Act of 1984, Public Law 98-462, was legislated "to promote research and development, encourage innovation, stimulate trade, and make necessary and appropriate modifications in the operation of the antitrust laws."[1] While the Act sets forth this objective, it does not place it in an historical perspective. Such a perspective is important not only to appreciate the trends in cooperative research activity presented in this paper, but also to provide a backdrop against which the National Cooperative Research Act was passed and against which it can begin to be evaluated.

In the early 1980s, there was growing concern in the United States about the persistent slowdown in productivity growth that first began to plague the U.S. industrial sector in the early 1970s and about industry's apparent loss of its competitive advantage in world markets.[2] As noted in a November 18, 1983 House report about the proposed Research and Development Joint Ventures Act of 1983 (HR 4043):

> A number of indicators strongly suggest that the position of world technology leadership once held by the United States is declining. The United States, only a decade ago, with only five percent of the world's population, was generating about 75 percent of the world's technology. Now, the U.S. share has declined to about 50 percent and in another ten years, without fundamental changes in our Nation's technological policy ... the past trend would suggest that it might be down to only 30 percent.

[In Committee hearings] many distinguished scientific and industry panels had recommended the need for some relaxation of current antitrust laws to encourage the formation of R&D joint ventures.[3] ... The encouragement and fostering of joint research and development ventures are needed responses to the problem of declining U.S. productivity and international competitiveness. According to the Congressional testimony, the legislation will provide for a significant increase in efficiency for firms doing similar research and development and will encourage more effective use of technically trained personnel.

In an April 6, 1984 House report on competing legislation, the Joint Research and Development Act of 1984 (HR 5041), the supposed benefits of joint research and development were for the first time clearly articulated:

Joint research and development, as our foreign competitors have learned, can be procompetitive. It can reduce duplication, promote the efficient use of scarce technical personnel, and help to achieve desirable economies of scale... [W]e must ensure to our U.S. industries the same economic opportunities as our competitors, to engage in joint research and development, if we are to compete in the world market and retain jobs in this country.

The National Cooperative Research Act (NCRA) of 1984, after additional revisions in the enabling legislation, was passed on October 11, 1984 (PL 98-462).[4] The NCRA created a registration process, later expanded by the National Cooperative Research and Production Act (NCRPA) of 1993 (PL 103-42), under which research joint ventures (RJVs) can disclose their research intentions to the Department of Justice.[5] RJVs gain two significant benefits from such voluntary filings: (i) if subjected to criminal or civil action they are evaluated under a rule of reason that determines whether the venture improves social welfare; and (ii) if found to fail a rule-of-reason analysis they are subject to actual rather than treble damages.[6]

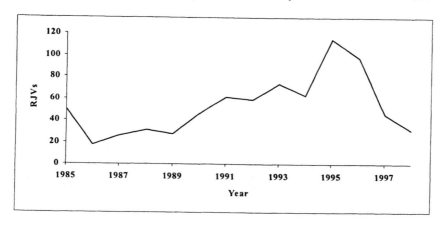

Figure1: Federal Register RJV Filings, by Year

A direct and encompassing evaluation of the success of the NCRA could entail, for example, comparing the behavior of a sample of collaborating firms with a comparable sample of non-collaborating firms in terms of alternative innovation performance criteria. Another alternative would explore counterfactual situations with firms through interviews, perhaps, that did file with the Department of Justice (e.g., asking, in the absence of the NCRA, what would the innovation profile of participants look like?).[7] However, requisite data for such analyses are certainly not available in the public domain, and have not been reported in the survey-based literature as reviewed by Hagedoorn, Link, and Vonortas (2000). This chapter attempts to provide only initial and somewhat indirect insights to answers to these questions; this is done through an econometric analysis of factors correlated with the trend in collaborative activity.

2. INSTITUTIONAL ISSUES RELATED TO *FEDERAL REGISTER* RJV DATA

The annual data on new RJVs filed with the Department of Justice in Figure 1 come from the *CO*operative *RE*search (CORE) database constructed and maintained by Link for the National Science Foundation. The CORE database uses *Federal Register* filing information as its primary information source.[8] While the trend in Figure 1 is revealing, and certainly it motivates the questions posed just above, as well as many more, a more complete understanding of the underlying data may be gleaned from an inspection of monthly as opposed to annual filings, as illustrated in Figure 2.

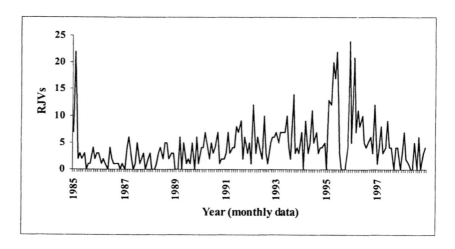

Figure 2: Federal Register RJV Filings, by Month

There are at least two important patterns embedded in Figure 2. First, the number of new RJVs filed in February 1985 was the second most in any month over the entire fourteen-year period. Second, no new RJVs were filed in August, September, and October 1995—the longest stretch of zero filings over this period—followed by four filings in November and then a record 24 filings in December, before the government furlough that began on December 19, 1995, and continued into January 1996.

Perhaps the February 1985 "blip" in filings represents the accumulation of RJVs unrelated to the passage of the NCRA but not registered with the Department of Justice until January 1985 and published in the *Federal Register* in the following month, or perhaps an unusually large number of new RJVs were formed in late 1984 in anticipation of the passage of the NCRA, and then filed in early-1985. We do not have information to support one or the other of these possibilities. However, we know more about the specifics of the 1995 occurrences. Through extensive discussions with the staff in the pre-merger group of the Department of Justice as background for this study, we learned that the group ceased to work on filings, beginning in July 1995, while being reorganized. The large increase in pre-furlough December represents primarily a "catch up" of previous work.

3.   AN ANALYSIS OF TREND

3.1   Specification of the Model

We posit that there are five variables possibly correlated with the number of new RJVs filed in the *Federal Register*, by month, between January 1985 and December 1998.

The first variable, *DevPct*, is the annual percentage of industry-funded R&D allocated to development as opposed to research (either basic or applied research). This variable is included in the analysis to examine the possibility that firms rely on cooperative research relationships as a substitute for their internal research endeavors. First, as even mentioned in the pre-legislative discussions noted above, it is expected that firms would rely on cooperative research arrangements as a means to reduce costs by reducing duplicative research.[9] Second, theory predicts that firms have the greater incentive to join an RJV if the research focus is closer to the basic end of the basic/applied/development spectrum.[10] If such a substitution takes place, we expect there to be a positive correlation between *DevPct* and involvement in new cooperative research ventures, *ceteris paribus*.

The second variable, *GBC*, captures the general business conditions that influence the overall behavior and strategy of firms. When the economy is strong and the level of investments by firms in innovative activity, R&D in particular, is growing, firms may rely less on cooperative research arrangements to generate new technical knowledge than when the economy is weak and internal resources are more constrained. To the extent that such cyclical behavior is revealed in the data, we expect there to be a negative correlation between *GBC* and involvement in new cooperative research ventures, *ceteris paribus*.[11]

The third variable, *WSJ*, represents the legal environment in which the RJV makes decisions about disclosing its collaborative research intentions to the Department of Justice. In an environment in which there is little indication that the Department of Justice is overly concerned about antitrust violations, firms may choose not to disclose their joint research to avoid having it made public through a *Federal Register* filing. However, in a more aggressive legal environment, firms may disclose their actions to the Department of Justice to ensure indemnification. Hence, we expect a positive correlation between the aggressiveness that characterizes the legal environment in which firms operate and their reporting of new joint venture activity, *ceteris paribus*.

The fourth variable, *D-ATP*, is a dummy variable that accounts in time for the creation of the Advanced Technology Program (ATP) within the

National Institute of Standards and Technology and its funding influence on the establishment of RJVs.[12] Absent the joint venture funding by ATP, such joint ventures would not otherwise exist.[13]

The fifth variable is the dummy variable *D-Gov*, which is included in our analysis to account for the following facts: (i) the pre-merger group in the Department of Justice that is responsible for *Federal Register* notices of disclosed RJVs was closed for several months during the summer of 1995; and (ii) government employees were furloughed in December of that year. This accounts for the filing implications of this interruption variable.

Thus, we posit the following regression model in an effort to explore factors correlated with the trend in collaborative research activity illustrated in Figure 2:

$$(1) \qquad RJV_t = f(\mathbf{x}_t) + \varepsilon_t = f\left(DevPct_t, \, GBC_t, \, WSJ_t, \, D\text{-}ATP_t, \, D\text{-}Gov_t\right) + \varepsilon_t$$

3.2   The Data

The monthly data in Figure 2 measure the dependent variable in the model in equation (1).[14] As previously noted, data on *RJV* come from information published in the *Federal Register* as contained in the CORE database. As required under the NCRA, a venture must re-file with the Department of Justice if the membership of the venture changes or if its scope of research changes. Re-filings are not treated as new RJVs; the initial filing and its initial publication date are incorporated in the CORE database.

DevPct is the percentage of industry-funded R&D allocated to development as opposed to research (either basic or applied research). Annual percentages were calculated from data reported in *Science & Engineering Indicators—1998* and from unpublished National Science Foundation data.[15]

GBC is measured as real industrial production changes by the seasonally adjusted industrial production index (1987=100), as reported in the *Federal Reserve Bulletin* (G.17 series).

WSJ represents the legal environment in which the RJVs make decisions about disclosing their collaborative research intentions to the Department of Justice. We quantified the legal environment of RJVs by counting the number of relevant news articles each month in *The Wall Street Journal* related to joint venture and antitrust issues. We did not use as a proxy variable the number of prosecutions or civil suits initiated by the federal government or by other firms because corporate leaders likely have—and act on—more timely information than that. If there is an increase in the number of antitrust actions, those firms that are most likely to engage in collaborative R&D should know about the increase before it is observed in the courts. In the construction of this variable we followed the methodology of Lamont (1995) and chose a proxy more closely associated in time with the information firms are likely to have, namely the number of new articles each month in *The Wall Street Journal* that contain both the phrase "antitrust" and "joint venture."[16]   A larger number of such occurrences or mentions represents greater newsworthiness of antitrust issues within the relevant business community and hence a more aggressive legal environment.[17]

Because we do not know *a priori* either the timing of changes in general business conditions or in the legal environment on firm's incentives to form an RJV and file with the Department of Justice, we employed a distributed lag on each variable out to twelve months. The shortest lag is two months because current institutional information is that at least two months must elapse between a corporate decision to register an RJV and the appearance of the filing in the *Federal Register* (not less than one month to assemble the documentation required to register the RJV and, based on discussions with appropriate individuals with the Justice department, at least another month to publication). For the same reason, the shortest lag of the *GBC* is also two months.

D-ATP is a dummy variable equaling one from August 1991 forward, and zero otherwise, because the first ATP award recipients' filing did not appear in the *Federal Register* until that month.

Finally, *D-Gov* is a dummy variable equaling one for all months other than the twelve-month period beginning with July 1995. Since we know that the pre-merger group ceased to do filing work in July 1995, but since have no *a priori* information about the backlog of filing that resulted from the December 1995 furlough of government employees, we chose to dummy out an entire twelve-month period.

3.3   The Statistical Results

Because RJV_t is a count variable, we considered a Poisson and a negative binomial (NB), or generalized Poisson, specification.[18]   The basic Poisson model as applied to filings is:

$$(2) \qquad \Pr(y_t) = \frac{e^{-\lambda_t}\lambda_t^{y_t}}{y_t!}$$

where $y_t = RJV_t$ and $\log(\lambda_t) = f(x_t)$, the deterministic (linear) function of x_t from equation (1). Estimates of the parameters of $f(\cdot)$ can be obtained by maximizing the log-likelihood function derived from equation (3). The

Poisson distribution implies that $E(y_t) = Var(y_t) = \lambda_t$, conditional on $\mathbf{x}_t$. This restrictive distributional assumption is relaxed in the negative binomial distribution, which allows $Var(y_t) > E(y_t)$, the property known as overdispersion or extra-Poisson variation. The NB specification generalizes λ_t to be distributed as a Gamma random variable with parameters $e^{f(x_t)}$ and a shape parameter α. The resulting likelihood function for y_t is:

$$(3) \qquad \ell(y_t) = \begin{pmatrix} \delta + y_t - 1 \\ y_t \end{pmatrix} p_t^{\delta} (1 - p_t)^{y_t}$$

where $\delta = 1/\alpha$ and $p_t = (1 + \alpha\, e^{f(x_t)})^{-1}$.[19] The Poisson distribution (and hence the property of no overdispersion) corresponds to the special case of $\alpha = 0$.

The results of the negative-binomial (NB) regression based on equation (3) are in Table 1. For comparative purposes, ordinary least squares (OLS) estimates also appear in Table 1. Because of the *a priori* ambiguous meaning of the large number of filings in February 1985, we estimated each model with January and February of 1985 included (in column (A)) and excluded (in column (B)). For the NB regression, we report the χ^2 statistic (with one degree of freedom) for the test of the null hypothesis that $\alpha = 0$, that is that the data are distributed as Poisson (conditional on $\mathbf{x}_t$). The restriction is rejected in each sample (though more strongly in the longer sample), justifying our use of the negative binomial. Only the coefficient on the *GBC* and *WSJ* variables that are significant at the .10 level or greater are reported in the table.[20]

Table 1: Estimated Results of the RJV Filings Models

Variable	Ordinary Least Squares		Negative Binomial	
	(A)	(B)	(A)	(B)
DevPct	0.409	0.352	0.107**	0.092*
	(1.59)	(1.42)	(2.00)	(1.76)
			[1.113]	[1.096]
GBC_{-2}	-0.098***	-0.081**	-0.022**	-0.018**
	(-2.59)	(-2.24)	(-2.88)	(-2.39)
			[0.978]	[0.982]
WSJ_{-4}	0.221	0.214	0.054*	0.052*
	(1.52)	(1.56)	(1.80)	(1.78)
			[1.056]	[1.053]
WSJ_{-8}	0.200	0.206	0.048*	0.051*
	(1.37)	(1.49)	(1.64)	(1.81)
			[1.049]	[1.052]
WSJ_{-9}	0.229	0.222	0.056**	0.055**
	(1.56)	(1.60)	(1.99)	(2.02)
			[1.057]	[1.056]
D-ATP	2.963***	3.137***	0.760***	0.801***
	(3.18)	(3.59)	(4.12)	(4.46)
			[2.139]	[2.227]
D-Gov	1.611	2.335*	0.246	0.377
	(1.14)	(1.72)	(0.93)	(1.45)
Constant	-19.67	-16.754	-5.22	-4.402
	(-1.05)	(-0.94)	(-1.37)	(-1.19)
R^2	0.239	0.257		
Log-ℓ			-402.99	-392.28
χ_1^2 ($\alpha=0$)			122.90	100.82
No. Obs.	168	166	168	166

Key: *** significant at the .01 level or better
       ** significant at the .05 level
       * significant at the .10 level
Values in parentheses are t-statistics for the OLS regressions and z-statistics for the NB models. Values in brackets are incidence rate ratios for statistically significant variables in the NB models

The OLS and NB results are reported in Table 1. The coefficients in a NB regression are not interpreted as partial derivatives, so we also report the corresponding incidence rate ratios (IRRs) for statistically significant NB coefficients.[21]

Focusing on the NB results for the complete (column A, n=168) sample, the estimated coefficient on *DevPct* is positive, as hypothesized, and significant at the .05 level. Thus, this finding suggests that firms do participate in RJVs as a substitute for conducting in-house research. Similarly, the estimated coefficient on *GBC* is negative, as hypothesized, and highly significant. Business cycle forces do have a relatively quick impact on the decision of RJV firms to make public their relationship, and subsequent changes in it, and the nature of the research on which they are collaborating. The only lagged variable that is significant is at two months.[22] Apparently, the cost of such disclosure is perceived to increase the stronger the business climate. This may be interpreted that in periods of slack, firms view the benefits from the cost savings and research efficiency from collaboration to be greater than the costs of disclosure.

As hypothesized, changes in the legal environment of RJVs, as measured by the variable *WSJ*, have an impact on the disclosure decision, and these changes appear to have their greatest impact with a nine-month lag. Looking at the IRRs, it seems that a five-mention increase will raise the number of filings by nearly 30 percent after nine months. This pattern is not present in the OLS results.

The introduction of the ATP program had a significant and positive effect on the number of RJVs that did file in the *Federal Register*. The positive impact of the ATP variable is consistent with case-based information that absent ATP's support the funded joint venture would not have formed and disclosed its intentions.[23]

Finally, controlling for the period of reorganization within the pre-merger group in the Department of Justice and the subsequent government furlough does not have an independent impact on the overall pattern of behavior of RJV activity seen in Figure 2.

4.   CONCLUSIONS

Not only do the results from the statistical models presented in this chapter explain approximately one-fourth of the variation in reported cooperative research activity, but also they provide a basis upon which to begin to address the more important policy question: Has the National Cooperative Research Act been successful? Based on our findings, the answer is "it depends."

Before elaborating on this conclusion, there is a more pressing question to address: why have *Federal Register* filings declined since 1995? We conclude that the observed decline is cyclical: when the economy slows more collaborative activity will be disclosed.

Regarding whether the Act has been successful, our tentative response of "it depends" is not based explicitly on the fact that the number of new filings declined precipitously in the post-1995 period. There is no reason to expect that the Act's success is strictly a function of the positive trend in new RJVs over time. Growth in collaborative activity was not a purpose of the Act. To address whether the NCRA has been successful, one must, in our opinion, reflect on the original purpose of the NCRA and determine if that purpose has been and is still being fulfilled. What was the purpose of the NCRA? The preamble to the Act explicitly states that its purpose is "to promote research and development, encourage innovation, stimulate trade, and make necessary and appropriate modifications in the operation of the antitrust laws." If that explicit statement is the benchmark upon which to measure the success of the NCRA, then the analysis presented in Section 3 above makes a positive first step in the evaluation direction.

Our econometric results suggest that over the business cycle, the favorable availability of cooperation as a research option, as created by the NCRA, facilitates firms continuing their R&D and innovative activity through such a relationship. In addition, holding cyclical effects constant, when firms, through their own strategic calculus, alter the research/development mix of their R&D portfolios away from research toward development, cooperative research provides a favorable alternative venue for maintaining their innovative research involvement. Hence, in that limited regard, the Act has been successful in that it has "promoted research and development and encouraged innovation."

In addition, based on the Act's stated purpose, the NCRA has certainly succeeded in "making necessary and appropriate modifications in the operation of the antitrust laws." All of the discussion surrounding the passage of the Act—some of which was referred to explicitly in Section 1 above—makes clear that although pre-NCRA legislation offered special treatment to collaborative activity involving basic research, it was nonetheless perceived to be legislation and untested legislation. Congressman Sensenbrenner stated his view in the April 6, 1984, House report on the Joint Research and Development Act of 1984:

> If we are to encourage the formation of joint ventures, which is the essential premise of this legislation, we must provide a definite "Safe Harbor," in which businesses are assured that their actions will not subject them to treble damages. The Department of Justice attempted to do so through the issuance in 1981 of its *Antitrust Guide Concerning Research Joint Ventures*, which provided that if the joint venture was properly structured, most research joint ventures are compatible with our antitrust laws. However, lacking the force and effect of law and the ability to control private litigants, these guidelines have not had their intended effect. Thus, only through Congressional enactment of definite guidelines, commonly referred to as "Safe Harbor" provisions, will we provide the required certainty, which is essential if we are to encourage businesses to risk their capital and form research and development joint ventures.

Thus, there appears to be the perception among joint venture participants that the NCRA is an effective "Safe Harbor," otherwise there would not be the observed responsiveness of participants to filing with the Department of Justice as the legal environment (the *WSJ* variable) changes.

Lastly, nothing, however, can be inferred from our econometric analysis about the success or lack of success of the Act with regard to its influence on the ability of firms to "stimulate trade."Still, overall, the evidence is on the positive side. Based on our econometric analysis, albeit exploratory and constrained by data availability, the NCRA appears to be successful in that it is meeting several of its explicit purposes.

ACKNOWLEDGEMENTS

This research was funded, in part, by a grant from the National Science Foundation. Extremely useful comments were received from Susan Cozzens, John Jankowski, Don Siegel, Geoff Shephard, Nick Vonortas, and our colleague Ken Snowden on earlier versions of this chapter.

REFERENCES

Bozeman, B., A. N. Link, and A. Zardkoohi. (1986). "An Economic Analysis of R&D Joint Ventures." *Managerial and Decision Economics*, August, pp. 263-266.

Hagedoorn, J., A. N. Link, and N. S. Vonortas. (2000). "Research Partnerships." *Research Policy* 29: 567-586.

Hausman, J., B. H. Hall, and Z. Griliches. (1984). "Econometric Models for Count Data with an Application to the Patents-R&D Relationship." *Econometrica*, July, pp. 909-938.

Kamien, M., E. Mueller, and I. Zang. (1992). "Research Joint Ventures and R&D Cartels." *American Economic Review*, June, pp. 1293-1306.

Katz, M. (1986). "An Analysis of Cooperative R&D." *Rand Journal of Economics*, Winter, pp. 527-543.

Lamont, O. (1995). "Do 'Shortages' Cause Inflation?" National Bureau of Economic Research Working Paper No. 5402, December.

Link, A. N. (1989). *Technological Change and Productivity Growth*, London: Harwood Academic Publishers.

Link, A. N. (1996). "Research Joint Ventures: Patterns from *Federal Register* Filings." *Review of Industrial Organization*, October, pp. 617-628.

Link, A. N. and L. L. Bauer. (1989). *Cooperative Research in U.S. Manufacturing: Assessing Policy Initiatives and Corporate Strategies*, Lexington, MA: Lexington Books.

Link, A. N. and J. T. Scott. (1998). *Public Accountability: Evaluating Technology-Based Institutions*, Boston: Kluwer Academic Publishers.

National Science Board. (1999). *Science & Engineering Indicators—1998*, Arlington, VA: National Science Foundation.

Scott, J. T. (1989). "Historical and Economic Perspectives of the National Cooperative Research Act." in A. N. Link and G. Tassey, eds., *Cooperative Research and Development: The Industry-University-Government Relationship*, Boston: Kluwer Academic Publishers, pp. 65-84.

U.S. Department of Commerce. (1990). "Emerging Technologies: A Survey of Technical and Economic Opportunities." Washington DC: Technology Administration.

Winkelmann, R. (1994). *Count Data Models: Econometric Theory and an Application to Labor Mobility*, Berlin: Springer-Verlag.

---

[1] This purpose is stated as a preamble to the Act.

[2] The declining U.S. position in the semiconductor industry was well known at this time, but there was widespread concern in other industries although the empirical evidence about the competitive position of the United States in international markets was not complete. However, when the Department of Commerce (1990) released its 1990 report on emerging technologies, it was apparent that the concerns expressed in the early 1980s were valid. A review of the productivity slowdown issues is in Link (1989).

[3] The Committee referred to is the Subcommittee on Investigations and Oversight and the Subcommittee on Science, Research and Technology as assembled on June 29-30, 1983, for hearings on Japanese Technological Advances and Possible United States Responses Using Research Joint Ventures.

[4] The passage of the NCRA culminated a five-year effort to ease the antitrust treatment of collaborative research. For a complete legislative history, see Link and Bauer (1989) and Scott (1989).

[5] We use the term RJV to refer to a collaborative research arrangement through which firms jointly acquire technical knowledge. This usage of the term RJV is more general than employed in the theoretical literature. See, for example, Kamien, Muller, and Zang (1992).

[6] Filing with the Department of Justice is distinct from the decision of whether to form an RJV in the first place. For a theoretical analysis of the formation decision, see, for example, Katz (1986). Economic theory always applies a rule-of-reason approach to antitrust issues. One of the primary focuses of the theoretical literature on cooperative R&D agreements has been to identify the conditions under which an RJV will be welfare enhancing. For a review of this literature, see Hagedoorn, Link and Vonortas (2000). However, the theoretical literature does not address the private decision of whether to file with the Department of Justice, that is to announce publicly the formation of the RJV, and to then have that filing made public through publication in the *Federal Register*.

[7] Other evaluation exercises are certainly possible in an environment without data constraints. The Government Performance and Results Act provides one useful set of guidelines.

[8] A description of the CORE database is in Link (1996); the CORE database is available upon request.

[9] This research is reviewed in Hagedoorn, Link, and Vonortas (2000).

[10] See Bozeman, Link, and Zardkoohi (1986) and Link and Bauer (1989) for a theoretical explanation.

[11] Link and Bauer (1989) provide suggestive evidence that this is in fact the case among manufacturing firms.

[12] The ATP was created as part of the Omnibus Trade and Competitiveness Act of 1988 (PL 104-418) to assist U.S. businesses in refining manufacturing technologies and commercializing new technologies and discoveries. In general, ATP underwrites one-half of the research cost of a funded collaborative research effort, with the remainder being funded by the venture. The first ATP awards were in April 1991. Since 1994, ATP has explicitly stated (but has not enforced) its expectations that funded ventures file as RJVs with the Department of Justice.

[13] See Link and Scott (1998) for case-based evidence that in the absence of ATP funding, the joint venture research would not have occurred.

[14] It is important to note that *Federal Register* data at any level of time aggregation are unweighted observations. They represent nothing more that the count of new RJVs filed with the Department of Justice. They do not reflect the importance of one RJV compared to another in terms of the criticalness of the innovation strategy of the participants, and they do not reflect any resource allocations to the venture. That said, the empirical study of research partnerships, RJVs as a special case, is extremely young, and researchers are fortunate at this early stage to have generalized public domain data from the Department of Justice for initial investigations. In the fall of year 2000, the National Science Foundation will sponsor its first workshop on research partnerships with an eye toward a systematic collection of indicator data.

[15] Although the dependent variable is measured by monthly data, as are the other independent variables, the estimated coefficient on *DevPct* retains all of the classical properties.

[16] Lamont (1995) used the number of new paper occurrences of variants of the word "shortage" as a proxy for the existence of market shortages.

[17] We also considered alternative measures, including the number of articles on the first page of all sections and the number in the first section alone. The former yielded too few occurrences, when specifications with the latter were quite similar to those reported herein. We used some discretion, however, in counting mentions to eliminate spurious occurrences in the search process. For example, we did not count a story in the May 15, 1996, edition, "Heir Freight: How the Strange Life of a DHL Founder Left His Estate a Mess," which told of the legacy of eccentric behavior and paternity suits left after the death of DHL Corporation co-founder Larry Hillblom. One of the other founders of DHL is described in the article as having been an *antitrust* expert in the 1970s, and the story recounts Hillblom's involvement in Continental Airlines' 1985 buy-out of shareholders of its *joint venture* with Air Micronesia.

[18] See Hausman, Hall, and Griliches (1984).

[19] See also Winkelmann (1994).

[20] Results from Poisson regressions, as well as from alternative specifications of equation (1), are available upon request.

[21] If variable x_j (with coefficient β_j) increases by one unit in a NB model, then the estimated incidence rate ratio is e^{β_j}, the estimated percentage increase in the dependent variable.

---

[22] The *GBC* variable and the *WSJ* variable exhibit little or no serial correlation.

[23] This issue of disclosure is less important with ATP-funded joint ventures than with others since ATP makes public on its web site and in research reports the identities of members of funded joint ventures and a more detailed description of their research than appears in the *Federal Register*.

Chapter 6

The Best and Brightest for Science
Is There a Policy Problem Here?

WILLIAM ZUMETA AND JOYCE S. RAVELING
University of Washington

1. INTRODUCTION

Scientific research is exacting work, requiring not only long years of training but also high intellectual ability. Beyond this, one widely subscribed theory holds that within the scientific enterprise it is less the many worker bees than the few genuinely creative minds who make the most critical contributions (Kuhn 1962). In any case, few would argue but that the health of the enterprise requires a steady inflow of top-flight talent.

Since around 1993, graduate enrollments in most fields within the natural sciences and engineering (S/E)[1] have been declining. It can be argued that this is a response to labor market signals and could be offset by recruiting more non-U.S. citizens. However, the enrollment fall-off would be more disturbing if it were found that the numbers of the very best U.S. students embarking on S/E graduate studies were falling faster than the total decline. Moreover, careful observers might say that it is risky to cede away too many of this countries best minds when many other countries' universities and research institutions are becoming increasingly attractive to their own natives. In addition, other countries appear to be competing more actively now than in the past in the international market for top scientific talent.

This chapter presents preliminary evidence of a fall-off in interest in advanced studies in science and engineering by top young U.S. talent.[1] We make some assumptions for purposes of the present discussion about what additional research may show, and then focus on exploring conceptually the broad contours of the policy options available to policymakers and the constraints operating upon these. To preview the conclusions, as with many problems there do not appear to be a set of feasible, low cost, high efficacy options to choose from in this complex policy arena.

First, it is not at all clear that simply facilitating the "natural" operation of the labor market by improving the information available to prospective students, although desirable and probably now technically feasible, will help much with the problem of declining attraction of the "best and brightest." Indeed, it seems likely that it is market signals that are dissuading many in this key group from pursuing advanced S/E studies. Policies designed to work directly on the supply side, such as enhancing fellowship and other graduate student support, would likely have an impact but would also have serious unintended consequences. By themselves, such policies ignore the demand side roots of the problem and indeed are likely to lead to further supply/demand imbalances in the longer run.[2] While we find that certain modest supply side steps are desirable, the major conclusion is that a carefully targeted effort probably should be made on the demand side of the issue. We give some attention then to sketching the design parameters of a feasible policy response that provides some promise of enhancing the attractiveness of advanced studies in S/E to the nation's most talented young college graduates.[3]

2.   A BRIEF HISTORY OF THE UPS AND DOWNS OF THE S/E PHD LABOR MARKET

The essentials of this history are well known.[4] The Cold War, in particular the Sputnik era, the scientific and technical possibilities of the atomic age, and the need to teach the baby boom generation of college students produced a burst of demand for scientists and engineers in the late 1950s and the 1960s, fed in large measure by public R&D and higher education spending. The scientific, technological and career prospects this burst created, along with the graduate fellowships and assistantships it supported, stimulated a large gain in graduate enrollments in the S/E fields. PhDs awarded in the sciences and engineering approximately trebled from 1960 to 1970 (Fechter and Gaddy 1998).

A sharp cutback occurred in the growth rate of R&D spending in the late 1960s and 1970s. Some fields experienced real declines for several years. In addition, in the early 1970s, college and university enrollments stopped growing rapidly as the cohorts associated with the big postwar jump in births passed on through the system. The federal government reduced its support of graduate fellowships quite abruptly (Breneman 1975). In response, PhD awards began to fall off considerably in engineering, mathematics, and the physical science disciplines and leveled off in the biological sciences

(Fechter and Gaddy 1998, National Research Council, annual publication). Fewer graduate students created problems for the academic research economy which needs these relatively low cost apprentice scientists to produce its research products cost-effectively. Hence, partly as a replacement mechanism, the number of non-citizen graduate students in the S/E fields climbed sharply (although there had long been gradual gains in foreign graduate students and PhD recipients at U.S. universities). Such an increase was possible because U.S. science and universities were very attractive to foreign students.

Another noteworthy response to the abrupt downturn in demand developed in the S/E PhD labor market. For decades, a small share of young scientists, in large measure the most promising ones, opted for additional post-PhD training as *postdoctoral appointees* (sometimes called fellows or associates or simply *postdocs*) in academic or occasionally other research laboratories.[5] Postdoctoral appointments are temporary research appointments undertaken by young scientists, usually immediately after obtaining the PhD, ostensibly to deepen and/or broaden their experience in research. The usual pattern is to move to a different university from the one where the young scientist obtains the doctorate in order to maximize new learning and cross-fertilization of ideas. In the past, typically, the young scientist remained in this temporary student/research associate status for a year or two before moving on to a faculty or other career research position (NRC 1969). As late as the 1960s, the proportion of new PhDs taking such immediate postdoctoral research/study appointments was modest, 20-30 percent in chemistry, physics and most of the biosciences, though already around 50 percent in the biomedical disciplines. Historically, those young scientists who chose the postdoctoral route were the cream of the crop, disproportionately those from the best graduate departments, national fellowship winners and the like (NRC 1969, Zumeta 1985).

By the late 1970s, a distinctly different pattern was developing in the postdoctoral ranks. First, the numbers of postdoctoral appointees and their share of the new PhD cohort climbed abruptly in a pattern coinciding closely with measures of the slackness of the PhD labor market (Zumeta 1985: especially pp. 22-26). Second, the typical time spent in the ostensibly temporary postdoctoral status began to grow (NRC 1981), suggesting that young scientists were backing up in a relatively stagnant postdoctoral pool with insufficient outlets. Third, when he examined the self-reported motivations of more recent postdocs (1970s) compared to those of earlier eras, Zumeta found that those of more recent vintage saw themselves not only as becoming or extending their postdoctoral stay in order to await improved market conditions but at the same time were investing further in their human capital, which they felt the market eventually would reward.[6] But Zumeta also found that the big increase in the number of postdoctoral appointees included not just those who, from all indications,[7] were the most promising of the PhD crop as in the past, but also for the first time a substantial number of young scientists who seemed to be less promising and to report that they became postdocs because they had few other options (Zumeta 1985: chapter 3).

Zumeta expressed concern that the disappointing labor market returns to postdoctoral training might be dissuading the most able students from pursuing this training although it showed signs of improving their subsequent research productivity (see note 7). Although market conditions improved (from the standpoint of new PhD scientists) somewhat in the mid- and late 1980s—albeit in part because new PhD output had fallen off considerably in many of the S/E fields—this improvement was short-lived. Even as the economy boomed in the late 1980s, several analytical reports appeared forecasting a strong academic market for additional PhD scientists and engineers by the mid-1990s as colleges and universities saw 1960s era faculty members retire just as the children of the baby boom echo reached college age (Bowen and Sosa 1989, National Science Foundation 1989, 1990).

Graduate student enrollments responded fairly strongly and S/E PhD output again increased (Fechter and Gaddy 1998, Shapiro 1999). On the demand side, the economic setback of the early 1990s intervened and the much longer-lasting sluggishness and caution in university finances (Zumeta 1998). Again, S/E graduate students completing the PhD faced limited permanent job prospects, the pool of postdoctoral appointees reached unprecedented size (Commission Professionals in Science and Technology 1997, Association of American Universities 1998), and the length of postdoctoral stays grew (Regets 1999).[8] Meanwhile, the number of non-U.S. citizen graduate students and new PhDs in the S/E fields leveled off in the early 1990s after growing for many years (Fechter and Gaddy 1998: 358, Sanderson and Dugoni 1999: 18-19).

3.   WHAT IS KNOWN ABOUT THE BEHAVIOR OF TOP STUDENTS

There is little to say about how the top tier of young scientists in particular have responded to these ups and downs for the issue has been little studied. Several single-institution studies have suggested that top baccalaureate graduates (by class rank, etc.) from certain elite institutions have been much less likely in recent years than their earlier counterparts to pursue graduate studies in the arts and sciences compared to professional schools (Goheen 1984, Rosovsky 1990). Reviewing a broader range of literature (but little specifically pertaining to the quality of those who pursue science and engineering studies), Bok (1993) draws a similar conclusion.

The most recent thorough empirical study directly pertinent to the issue was published by Hartnett (1985, 1987). He indicated that a motivation for his investigation was that the diminished prospects for academic careers might have hurt the relative attractiveness to top students of PhD studies in the arts and sciences compared to major professional fields (medicine, law, business). Thus, he sought to compare the quality, as best it could be measured, of then-recent cohorts of professional degree recipients in these fields with comparable cohorts of PhD recipients in eight arts and science disciplines, including chemistry, electrical engineering, mathematics and physics among the S/E fields. Because professional degree seekers and PhD seekers usually do not take the same graduate school tests, Hartnett's procedure was to go back to a comparable national scale that most of them did have in common: the Scholastic Aptitude Test (SAT). After great expense and years of effort, he was able to construct a large sample of degree recipients from several cohorts and identify their SAT scores.[9]

In brief, Hartnett found that in virtually all the arts and sciences fields (including all the natural sciences and engineering disciplines studied), the PhD recipients held a considerable SAT score advantage over the professional degree recipients, and this gap changed little over the degree cohorts he studied: 1966, 1971, 1976, and 1981. The PhD recipients' advantage was approximately 25-35 points on each of the SAT scales (quantitative and verbal) for the three most recent cohorts, for which the data were more complete. In order to get test score data for both the PhDs and professional degree recipients, even his most recent cohort had taken the SAT test in the early 1970s so the data, while interesting, are now so old as to be of essentially historical interest. We are left with the question of how S/E has fared in the decision making of more recent cohorts, ideally of entering graduate students rather than completed degree recipients, since PhD completion takes so many years.

The same year Hartnett's journal article was published, the National Academy of Sciences and its sister organizations convened a steering committee "to examine the issue of whether graduate departments in the sciences, engineering and mathematics are continuing to attract an appropriate share of the brightest students" (National Academy of Sciences, National Academy of Engineering, and Institute of Medicine steering committee report 1988). This group reported that it was quite concerned about the problem but did not have access to enough data or research resources to draw any firm conclusions and simply called for more research "into the nature and causes of the problem" (*ibid.*).

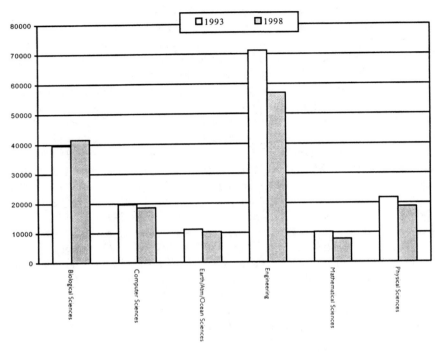

Figure 1. Changes in the Number of Natural Science & Engineering Graduate Students in Doctorate Granting Institutions, by Broad Field. Source: National Science Foundation.

4.   NEW EVIDENCE ABOUT THE BEST AND BRIGHTEST IN SCIENCE AND ENGINEERING

Graduate enrollments in virtually all the natural sciences and engineering fields other than biological sciences have been falling since about 1993.[10] Declines between 1993 and 1998 range from six percent in computer science to over 23 percent in mathematical sciences (see Figure 1). Significantly, these declines are not confined to U.S. citizens in most disciplines although the declines are generally steeper among citizens.[11]   Only in computer science, electrical engineering, and aerospace engineering have there been gains over this period in temporary resident students, and the gain in aerospace engineering did not occur until 1998. Aggregating across all the natural science and engineering fields, the graduate enrollment decline from 1993 to 1998 was 8.6% for U.S. citizens and 3.6% for non-citizens (temporary residents).   The negative trend in temporary resident students may signal a new problem – or simply a fact of life – emerging for the U.S. academic science enterprise: we may no longer be able to count on replacing U.S. citizen graduate students with non-citizens.[12]

Table 1. Mean GRE Scores of U.S. Citizen Examinees, by Intended Field of Graduate Study

Intended Field	Verbal				Quantitative				Analytical			
	89	92	95	98	89	92	95	98	89	92	95	98
Biological Sciences	534	526	515	507	587	588	590	597	583	585	598	590
Math Sciences	537	527	516	511	693	694	686	694	637	628	630	620
Physical Sciences	545	534	518	510	643	631	625	632	604	593	606	595
Computer Science	536	528	519	516	650	643	634	636	610	598	602	590
Engineering	523	515	504	499	687	682	676	681	610	600	613	604
Behavioral Sciences	515	508	492	488	518	517	512	516	543	545	550	537
Social Sciences	497	489	475	473	487	485	480	485	514	516	520	511
Art	509	507	501	499	492	494	501	513	532	532	546	545
Other Humanities	567	561	551	547	530	532	531	537	563	567	577	566
Education	463	459	448	447	472	472	474	483	491	496	503	497
Health Science	484	472	458	455	509	503	507	521	527	522	533	529
Applied Biology	486	479	467	462	528	523	523	536	534	531	542	542
Other	494	499	478	477	500	508	510	520	525	535	544	537
Undecided	506	499	485	491	535	532	528	543	548	548	551	548
No Response	500	495	498	479	514	511	529	514	516	519	548	515
ALL FIELDS	**507**	**500**	**487**	**481**	**532**	**528**	**525**	**531**	**541**	**541**	**548**	**538**

Source: Educational Testing Service.

Within these recent graduate enrollment declines in S/E fields, what can be said about trends in the quality composition of the U.S. citizen group? One piece of indirect evidence is provided by trends in students' test scores. With the cooperation of the Educational Testing Service, we analyzed trends in the scores of all Graduate Record Examination (GRE) General Test examinees for selected years from 1989 through 1998.[13] Each examinee completes a questionnaire at the time he or she registers for the test that includes a question about intended field of graduate study which is the basis for the trend analyses reported here.[14] Of course, no one can claim with great confidence that high GRE scores are a highly valid predictor of unusual scientific talent or creativity but they are an important indicator used by most graduate department admissions committees and there are few alternatives to choose from with broad national coverage across disciplines and a comparable scale.[15]

Among the U.S. citizen examinees indicating intent to pursue S/E graduate studies, there is a general pattern of modest declines in mean GRE scores between 1989 and 1998, on all three of the General Test scales (see Table 1). On the verbal scale, the decline of 20-27 points in mean scores in the S/E fields over this period is quite comparable to the 26-point decline in mean scores of all examinees (bottom row). On the GRE analytical scale, mean scores of all examinees changed only a little over this period (-3 points). Four of the five S/E field categories experienced greater decreases, ranging from a decline of six points among would-be engineers to -9 to -20 points in physical sciences, mathematics, and computer science. However, there was a 7-point *gain* in the mean analytical score of students indicating intent to pursue graduate studies in the biological sciences. The pattern in the quantitative scale scores is similar but less steep: among all examinees mean scores fell just one point over the nine year period, while there were declines in three of the five S/E disciplines ranging from –6 points among would-be engineers to –14 points among prospective computer scientists. There was an 11-point decline among prospective physical scientists, virtually no change among those headed for mathematics, and a 10-point *gain* in mean scores for those seeking to become biological scientists.

Table 2. Proportion of High Scorers (≥700) Among U.S. Citizen GRE Examinees, by Intended Field of Graduate Study

	Verbal				Quantitative				Analytical			
Intended Field	89	92	95	98	89	92	95	98	89	92	95	98
Biological Sciences	7.6	6.0	4.8	4.1	18.1	17.3	17.9	19.5	17.8	17.0	20.4	20.8
Math Sciences	10.6	9.0	8.6	7.2	57.1	57.4	56.1	59.2	35.5	31.8	33.7	34.3
Physical Sciences	9.7	7.9	6.2	4.3	37.4	32.9	30.4	32.8	25.0	21.2	23.6	23.7
Computer Science	11.6	10.4	8.4	7.1	41.2	39.4	37.5	39.7	27.8	24.5	27.2	26.9
Engineering	5.9	4.8	3.4	3.4	53.5	52.3	50.1	53.6	26.3	23.3	27.0	27.6
TOTAL:	8.2	6.7	5.2	4.5	41.6	40.0	35.8	37.2	25.2	22.4	24.8	25.0
Behavioral Sciences	6.4	5.1	3.9	3.6	8.7	7.9	7.3	7.5	11.4	11.1	12.3	12.5
Social Sciences	5.7	4.2	3.4	3.2	5.6	5.0	4.6	5.3	7.3	7.7	8.5	9.2
Art	6.4	5.3	4.5	3.7	5.6	5.6	6.4	7.5	9.3	9.2	12.4	14.6
Other Humanities	14.3	12.0	10.2	9.6	10.0	9.6	9.0	10.2	14.4	14.6	16.5	17.4
Education	2.5	20.	1.6	1.4	4.2	4.3	4.7	4.9	4.7	5.4	6.3	6.7
Health Science	3.0	2.0	1.3	1.1	5.9	4.7	5.0	6.5	7.0	6.3	7.8	9.4
Applied Biology	3.2	2.6	1.7	1.2	7.6	6.0	7.1	8.0	8.2	7.8	10.1	11.2
Other	5.9	5.9	3.7	3.2	7.1	7.5	7.5	8.1	10.0	11.5	12.1	11.9
TOTAL:	5.9	4.8	3.6	3.2	6.8	6.3	6.1	6.8	8.8	9.0	10.1	10.7
Undecided	6.8	5.7	4.3	4.7	14.1	13.0	11.5	14.3	13.8	13.3	13.1	14.8
No Response	7.4	5.6	5.7	4.1	12.1	10.6	12.6	10.3	9.6	9.8	14.0	10.7
ALL EXAMINEES	6.5	5.2	4.1	3.5	13.7	12.4	11.2	11.9	12.2	11.6	12.7	13.0

These changes are not large (only a small fraction of the GRE standard deviation unit of 100 points). Additionally, mean scores could be misleading and may not be reflective of changes at the top end of the distribution with which we are most concerned. Table 2 shows the proportion of U.S. citizen examinees scoring above 700 on each scale.[16] For all examinees, these proportions of high scorers decreased by 2-3 percentage points over the 9-year period on the verbal and quantitative scales but changed little on the analytical scale. The main differences between the would-be natural scientists and engineers and those interested in other fields shows up in the quantitative scale. Here, decreases in proportions of high-scoring physical scientists and computer scientists drive down the composite figure for S/E by more than four percentage points over the period while there is no change in the proportion of high quantitative scorers headed for non-science fields (Total: All Other Fields). Note also that the proportions of high scorers on the quantitative and analytical scales among those headed for biological sciences increased.

Table 3. Proportion of Very High Scorers (≥750) Among U.S. Citizen Examinees, by Intended Field of Graduate Study

Intended Field	Verbal				Quantitative				Analytical			
	89	92	95	98	89	92	95	98	89	92	95	98
Biological	2.4	1.7	1.2	1.0	8.2	6.1	6.3	7.6	8.5	8.1	10.4	8.9
Math Sciences	4.3	3.8	3.0	2.2	35.3	35.2	33.6	37.3	21.1	19.3	21.5	18.9
Physical	3.5	2.7	2.0	1.1	20.5	16.2	15.2	16.3	13.0	11.6	13.2	11.5
Computer	4.6	3.7	3.0	1.9	22.6	20.0	20.5	23.4	15.5	14.4	16.6	14.4
Engineering	1.8	1.4	0.9	0.7	30.7	28.2	25.9	29.4	12.9	12.0	14.8	13.8
TOTAL: NAT SCI & ENG	2.9	2.2	1.6	1.1	23.3	20.8	18.0	19.5	13.0	12.0	13.8	12.1
Behavioral	2.2	1.5	1.1	1.1	3.6	2.9	2.5	2.8	4.9	5.2	5.9	4.9
Social Sciences	2.0	1.3	0.9	0.9	2.1	1.8	1.4	1.8	2.8	3.3	3.9	3.6
Art	2.1	1.5	1.4	1.4	2.3	2.0	2.0	2.9	3.7	4.3	6.0	6.2
Other	53.5	4.2	3.1	3.1	4.0	3.5	2.8	3.7	6.2	6.9	8.2	7.5
Education	0.7	0.5	0.4	0.4	1.7	1.6	1.7	1.8	1.6	2.1	2.7	2.4
Health Science	0.8	0.6	0.3	0.3	1.9	1.4	1.3	1.9	2.6	2.4	3.0	3.2
Applied Biology	0.9	0.9	0.4	0.4	2.9	1.8	1.6	2.1	3.0	3.4	4.2	4.3
Other	2.5	1.9	0.8	0.8	2.9	2.8	2.6	3.2	4.4	5.5	6.1	5.0
TOTAL: ALL OTHER	2.1	1.5	1.0	1.0	2.6	2.2	1.9	2.4	3.5	4.0	4.6	4.1
Undecided	2.3	1.9	1.3	1.3	6.9	5.7	4.7	6.6	6.5	6.5	6.4	6.4
No Response	2.6	1.8	1.7	1.7	5.4	4.8	5.2	4.6	4.4	4.5	7.0	4.3
ALL EXAMINEES	2.3	1.7	1.2	1.2	6.7	5.6	4.7	5.2	5.5	5.5	6.2	5.4

Source: Educational Testing Service.

The broad patterns over the years from 1989 to 1998 are very similar if we narrow the definition of high scorers to focus on those scoring 750 or above (Table 3).[17] The proportion of very high scorers on the verbal scale is very low and declining similarly among both would-be S/Es and those headed for non-science fields. The proportion of very high scorers on the analytical scale changed little overall but declined slightly among S/Es, and the proportion of very high quantitative scorers is down around four percentage points among prospective S/Es but little changed among those headed for other fields. [18]

Table 4. Distribution of High Scoring (≥700) U.S. Citizen GRE Examinees, by Intended Field of Graduate Study

Intended Field	Verbal				Quantitative				Analytical			
	89	92	95	98	89	92	95	98	89	92	95	98
	%	%	%	%	%	%	%	%	%	%	%	%
Biological Sciences	3.9	3.7	4.6	5.3	4.4	4.4	6.2	7.4	4.9	4.7	6.3	7.3
Math Sciences	2.0	2.0	1.9	1.7	5.0	5.4	4.4	4.0	3.5	5.2	2.3	2.1
Physical Sciences	4.5	4.3	4.2	3.6	8.2	7.5	7.4	7.9	6.1	5.2	5.1	5.2
Computer Science	4.5	3.9	2.9	3.6	7.6	6.1	4.8	5.9	5.8	4.1	3.0	3.7
Engineering	5.7	5.5	3.8	4.1	24	25	20	19	13	12	9.6	9.1
TOTAL: NAT SCI & ENGR	20	19	17	18	49	48	43	44	33	29	26	27
Behavioral Sciences	15.	16.	15.	16.	10.	10.	10.	10.	14.	16.	15.	15.
Social Sciences	8.5	7.9	7.0	7.9	4.0	3.9	3.4	3.8	5.8	6.4	5.6	6.0
Art	1.8	1.8	1.6	1.6	0.8	0.8	0.8	0.9	1.4	1.4	1.4	1.7
Other Humanities	20.	24.	22.	24.	6.9	8.0	7.0	7.5	11.	13.	11.	11.
Education	5.8	5.4	5.1	538	4.6	5.0	5.5	5.9	5.9	6.6	6.6	7.4
Health Science	4.8	4.7	5.3	5.9	4.5	4.7	7.1	9.7	6.0	6.7	9.7	12.
Applied Biology	0.9	0.8	0.7	0.6	1.0	0.8	1.1	1.3	1.2	1.1	1.4	1.7
Other	1.1	1.3	1.2	2.6	0.6	0.7	0.9	2.0	1.0	1.2	1.3	2.7
TOTAL: ALL OTHER FIELDS	59	62	59	65	32	34	36	41	47	53	53	59
Undecided/No Response/Other	19	17	23	16	18	16	20	14	19	17	20	13
TOTAL NUMBER >700 SCORERS	14,161	14,531	11,903	8,639	29,894	34,740	32,962	29,435	26,588	32,381	27,312	32,184

Another way to view the data is to ask whether there have been notable changes over time in the distribution among fields of the high (≥700) or very high scorers (≥750). This analysis asks more directly about the relative attractiveness of S/E studies as compared to other fields to evidently high ability students. Again the findings are very similar whichever cutoff point is used (see Tables 4 and 5). In terms of top scorers on any of the three scales, S/E lost some ground over the last nine years. Comparing the 9-year changes in the shares of high scorers headed for S/E fields to those headed for other designated fields, all the S/E fields except biological sciences have lost ground while non-science fields (see Total: All Other Fields) have gained significantly in their attraction (at least to the point of stated intent) of top students.

Table 5. Distribution of Very High Scoring (≥750) U.S. Citizen GRE Examinees, by Intended Field of Graduate Study

Intended Field	Verbal				Quantitative				Analytical			
	89 %	92 %	95 %	98 %	89 %	92 %	95 %	98 %	89 %	92 %	95 %	98 %
Biological Sciences	3.5	3.2	4.1	5.2	4.1	3.5	5.3	6.5	5.2	4.6	6.6	7.4
Math Sciences	2.3	2.6	2.3	2.1	6.4	7.4	6.4	5.7	4.6	4.1	3.1	2.8
Physical Sciences	4.6	4.5	4.7	3.5	9.1	8.2	8.9	8.9	7.1	6.0	5.8	6.1
Computer Science	5.2	4.3	3.7	4.0	8.5	6.9	6.3	7.9	7.1	5.0	3.8	4.7
Engineering	5.1	5.0	3.5	3.6	28.	30.	25.	24	14.	13.	10.	11.
TOTAL: NAT SCI & ENGR	20.	19.	18.	18.	56.	56.	51.	53.	38.	32.	30.	32.
Behavioral Sciences	15.	15.	14.	16.	8.5	9.0	8.7	8.6	14.	16.	15.	14.
Social Sciences	8.6	7.6	6.6	7.1	3.0	3.2	2.6	3.0	4.9	5.8	5.2	5.6
Art	1.7	1.6	1.7	1.6	0.6	0.6	0.6	0.8	1.3	1.4	1.4	1.7
Other Humanities	23.	26.	23.	25.	5.6	6.5	5.4	6.2	10.	13.	11.	12.
Education	4.9	4.4	4.7	4.1	3.8	4.0	4.8	5.0	4.4	5.4	5.6	6.5
Health Science	3.7	4.3	4.5	5.5	3.0	3.0	4.4	6.4	5.0	5.3	7.8	10.
Applied Biology	0.7	0.9	0.6	0.6	0.8	0.5	0.6	0.8	1.0	1.0	1.2	1.5
Other	1.3	1.4	0.9	2.7	0.5	0.6	0.7	1.8	1.0	1.2	1.3	2.7
TOTAL: ALL OTHER FIELDS	59.	62.	57.	63.	25.	27.	27.	32.	42.	49.	49.	55.
Undecided/No Response/Other	19.	18.	24.	17	17.	16.	20.	14.	19.	17.	20.	13.
TOTAL NUMBER >750 SCORERS	4,919	4,648	3,432	2,146	14,640	15,584	13,726	13,012	12,030	15,443	18,234	13,400

Source (Both Tables): Educational Testing Service.

All these proportions and shares are based on the total number of U.S. citizen GRE examinees in a given year. It is important to note also that the number of GRE test-takers has fallen off considerably in the last few years The number of U.S. citizen General Test examines was around 219,000 in 1989, climbed steadily to a peak of 301,000 in 1994, then fell in each succeeding year to a level of around 248,000 in 1998. Numbers of examinees by intended graduate study field for the four years for which detailed data were available for this analysis are shown in Table 6. Interestingly, among these four years, the peak year for total examinees was 1995, with about 293,000 examinees (just 2.6% below the 1994 peak). Interestingly, among these four years, the peak year for total examinees was 1995, with about 293,000 examinees (just 2.6% below the 1994 peak). But, among the available years, the peak for examinees reporting intent to study S/E fields was earlier, in 1992, with the 1998 figure 16% lower and slightly below the figure for 1989. Note that biological sciences again run counter to the S/E trend.

Table 6. Number of U.S. Citizens Taking GRE General Test, by Intended Field of Graduate Study

Intended Field	1989	1992	1995	1998	Change 92 - 98	% Change
Biological Sciences	7,287	8,867	11,516	11,222	2,355	26.6%
Mathematical Sciences	2,641	3,271	2,599	2,007	-1,264	-38.6%
Physical Sciences	6,521	7,928	8,061	7,117	-811	-10.2%
Computer Science	5,501	5,417	4,184	4,393	-1,024	-18.9%
Engineering	13,544	16,687	13,248	10,634	-6,053	-36.3%
TOTAL: NAT SCI & ENGR	*35,494*	*42,170*	*39,608*	*35,373*	*-6,797*	*-16.1%*
Behavioral Sciences	34,686	47,762	48,005	39,802	-7,960	-16.7%
Social Sciences	21,067	27,022	24,693	21,165	-5857	-21.7%
Art	4,094	4,911	4,238	3,692	-1,219	-24.8%
Other Humanities	20,619	29,228	25,930	21,615	-7,613	-26.0%
Education	33,097	40,101	38,633	35,687	-4,414	11.0%
Health Science	22,814	34,342	46,828	44,398	10,056	29.3%
Applied Biology	3,856	4,737	5,028	4,771	34	0.7%
Other	2,608	3,247	3,987	7,157	3,910	120.4%
TOTAL: ALL OTHER FIELDS	*142,841*	*191,350*	*197,342*	*178,287*	*-13,063*	*-6.8%*
Undecided or No Response	75,930	46,177	56,268	34,446	-11,731	-25.4%
TOTAL: U.S. CITIZEN EXAMINEES	*218,771*	*279,697*	*293,218*	*248,106*	*-31,591*	*-11.3%*

Source: Educational Testing Service.

Juxtaposing the decline in numbers of test-takers headed for S/E fields with the earlier-discussed modest fall in proportions of would-be S/Es who scored highly produces a picture of apparent decline in interest in S/E among top students that is more complete and more sobering (see Tables 7 and 8). Compared to the 1992 peak, the number of high scorers on the quantitative scale headed for S/E fields in 1998 is down 21-22% (depending upon whether the 700 or 750 score cutoff is used) while the number of such top students headed for other designated fields (Total: All Other Fields) has been essentially stable over this period.[19] Moreover, the 20%+ declines in top-scorers headed for S/E fields in aggregate is net of a large *gain* in such students headed for the biological sciences. All the other S/E field categories show declines in top scorers, ranging from –4% in number of 750+ scorers headed for graduate computer science programs to declines of more than one-third in both 700+ and 750+ scorers headed for mathematics and engineering. Thus, the declines in top GRE scorers headed for graduate studies in the natural sciences and engineering, biological sciences excepted, appear to be consistent (not likely to be a single-year aberration), sizeable, and disproportionate (i.e., larger than the declines in all GRE examinees and in all those who say they are headed for S/E fields).

Table 7. Number of High Scoring (≥700) U.S. Citizens GRE Quantitative Examinees, by Intended Field of Graduate Study

Intended Field	1989	1992	1995	1998	Change 92 - 93	% Change
Biological Sciences	1.315	1.529	2.044	2.178	649	42.2%
Mathematical Sciences	1,495	1,876	1,450	1,177	-699	-37.5%
Physical Sciences	2,451	2,606	2,439	2,325	-281	-10.8%
Computer Science	2,272	2,119	1,582	1,737	-382	-18.0%
Engineering	7,234	8,720	6,658	5,710	-3,010	-34.5%
TOTAL: NAT SCI & ENGR	14,768	16,849	14,174	13,127	-3,722	-22.0%
Behavioral Sciences	2.989	3.787	3.494	3.002	-785	-20.7%
Social Sciences	1,196	1,355	1,121	1,119	-236	-17.4%
Art	239	278	264	265	13	4.7%
Other Humanities	2,063	2,779	2,307	2208	-571	-20.5%
Education	1,375	1,737	1,813	1,737	0	0.0%
Health Science	1,345	1,633	2,340	2,855	1,222	74.8%
Applied Biology	299	278	363	383	105	37.8%
Other	179	243	297	589	346	142.4%
TOTAL: ALL OTHER FIELDS	9,686	12,090	11,998	12,157	67	0.6%
Undecided or No	5.440	5.801	6.790	4.151	-1.650	-28.4%
TOTAL: U.S. CITIZEN	29,894	34,740	32,962	29,435	-5,305	-15.3%

Source: Educational Testing Service.

5. WHERE ARE THE TOP STUDENTS GOING?

If top students appear to be turning away from graduate studies in the sciences and engineering (other than biological sciences), where are they going instead? This is a very important, but complex, question to answer. A clue about a part of the answer may come from examining the trends in the indicated graduate study fields of top GRE scorers, although able students may pursue professions not requiring the GRE, or may opt to enter the workforce.[20] To begin with GRE data, Tables 7 and 8 show that in the non-science field set, the only specified field with a notable increase in top scorers is health science (ETS terminology).

This field grouping is dominated by applied, master's-level health *professions* and includes few basic science specialities or research-oriented doctoral degrees. Thus, we group it with non-science fields, not the S/E fields. The dominant fields, in terms of numbers of graduate students and recent growth in enrollments, making up the health category are speech/language pathology, physical therapy, nursing, veterinary medicine, and public health. The first two professions accounted for 48% of the total gain over 1989 to 1998 in numbers indicating intent to pursue graduate work in the health sciences category. Table 7 shows that, among 1998 GRE test-takers scoring above 700 on the quantitative scale, more headed for these applied health professions than for the biological sciences, and the increase in high scorers was about twice as large in absolute terms in the health fields. At the 750+ level (Table 8), the numbers of potential biological scientists and health professionals were similar but the health professions experienced more growth.

Table 8. Number of Very High Scoring (≥750) U.S. Citizens GRE Quantitative Examinees, by Intended Field of Graduate Study

Intended Field	1989	1992	1995	1998	Change 92 – 98	% Change
Biological Sciences	586	545	727	846	301	55.2%
Mathematical Sciences	937	1,153	878	742	-411	-35.6%
Physical Sciences	1,332	1,278	1,222	1,158	-120	-9.4%
Computer Science	1,244	1,075	865	1,028	-47	-4.3%
Engineering	4,158	4,706	3,432	3,136	-1,570	-33.4%
TOTAL: NAT SCI & ENGR	*8,257*	*8,757*	*7,124*	*6,909*	*-1,848*	*-21.1%*
Behavioral Sciences	1,244	1,403	1,194	1,119	-284	-20.2%
Social Sciences	439	499	357	390	-109	-21.8%
Art	88	93	82	104	11	11.8%
Other Humanities	820	1,013	741	807	-206	-20.3%
Education	556	623	659	651	28	4.5%
Health Science	439	468	604	833	365	78.0%
Applied Biology	117	78	82	104	26	33.3%
Other	73	94	96	234	140	148.9%
TOTAL: ALL OTHER FIELDS	*3,776*	*4,271*	*3,815*	*4,242*	*-29*	*-0.7%*
Undecided or No Response	2,607	2,556	2,787	1,861	-695	-27.2%
TOTAL: U.S. CITIZEN EXAMINEES	*14,640*	*15,584*	*13,726*	*13,012*	*-2572*	*-16.5%*

Source: Educational Testing Service.

Students headed for medicine, law, and business generally take specialized tests designed for the graduate schools of their profession rather than the GRE.[21] It seems plausible that the decline in GRE test taking might be accompanied by a corresponding rise in numbers of examinees taking these other tests. Ideally, one would want to look at such patterns by age or baccalaureate cohort but the available data are limited to recent trends in numbers of professional school applicants, matriculants, test-takers, and mean scores. From these data, law schools seem unlikely to be attracting many students who might otherwise opt for S/E careers. Between 1992 and 1998 total applicants (unduplicated count of individuals applying) to U.S. law schools dropped by 26,000 (27%) and new matriculants decreased slightly. Mean LSAT scores were virtually unchanged over the period while those for matriculants actually fell by two points.[22]

Such indicators as are available regarding interest in medical school and quality of applicants suggest that some more top students may have headed in this direction in recent years. Generally, numbers of top students and total applicants have tended to move in similar directions in graduate professional fields (Adelman 1985, Bok 1993). This pattern may have changed in medicine recently. Medical school applicants (unduplicated number of individuals applying) jumped from around 37,400 in 1992 to 47,800 in 1996, but fell back to 38,500 in 1999.[23] The numbers of new matriculants remained virtually level, at around 16,200 entering medical students annually between 1992 and 1999. This means that, however much interest there is, educational opportunities in medicine are not growing. Both applicant and matriculant mean scores on the MCAT gradually increased throughout the 1990s, which does not prove that more top students are taking the test but is suggestive. In short, medicine may have attracted the interest in recent years of more of the top students who could have pursued S/E research careers, but it is not clear that they are all being accommodated in the medical schools since enrollments are flat. Perhaps some of these students are spilling over into the non-M.D. health professions mentioned earlier.

There are also mixed signs in the area of graduate business education. The number of U.S. citizen GMAT examinees declined from 154,000 in 1990 to under 129,000 in 1995 before climbing back to over 142,000 in 1997.[25] The numbers of S/E majors taking the GMAT followed a similar pattern with over 31,200 examinees in 1990, 23,200 in 1993, and slightly over 27,650 in 1997. Among the S/E majors, the number of computer science majors taking the GMAT decreased by nearly 33 percent, from roughly 4,200 in 1990 to 2,800 in 1997. This decrease was offset by a near 38 percent increase in the number of biological sciences majors, with about 2,950 taking the GMAT in 1990 compared to 4,100 in 1997. This increase in biological sciences majors may reflect the influence of the perceived employment market in businesses related to biotechnology and similar fields.

Significantly, after relative stability between 1990 to 1992, the average overall GMAT scores climbed by over 30 points on a 500-point scale between 1993 and 1999. Likewise, the annual mean score on the quantitative sub-scale increased, with the mean for S/E majors increasing 4.8% while the mean for non-S/E students increased only 1.1%.

Although the GMAT examinees decreased between 1990 and 1997, the numbers of MBAs conferred increased 27 percent.[26] The number of degrees conferred grew steadily from roughly 73,000 degrees in 1990 to 97,600 in 1997. Together with the renewed growth in GMAT test-takers with S/E backgrounds, and the increasing scores of this group, the data suggest that graduate business schools are likely providing serious competition to S/E graduate programs for the top students.

Table 9. Number of U.S. Citizen Examinees Scoring ≥ 700 on GRE Quantitative Test, by Intended Field of Study and Gender*

Intended Field	1989		1998		Change 1989 -		% Change	
	Male	Female	Male	Female	Male	Female	Male	Female
Biological	752	556	1,219	965	467	409	62.1%	73.6%
Math Sciences	1,002	511	757	434	-245	-77	-	-15.1%
Physical	1,921	511	1,643	683	-278	172	-	33.7%
Computer	1,859	404	1,514	228	-345	-176	-	-43.6%
Engineering	6,056	1,166	4,524	1,150	-	-16	-	-1.4%
TOTAL: NAT SCI & ENGR	11,590	3,148	9,657	3,460	-	312	-	9.9%
TOTAL: ALL OTHER FIELDS	5,701	3,905	6,426	5,673	725	1,768	12.7%	45.3%
Undecided/No Reponse/Other	5,571	1,809	2,400	1,714	-	-95	-	-5.3%
TOTAL: NUMBER > 700	22,862	8,862	18,465	10,847	-	1,985	-	22.4%

*Excludes examinees who did not indicate gender
Source: Educational Testing Service.

6.   GENDER AND RACE/ETHNICITY DIFFERENCES

Significantly, the declines in numbers of high GRE scorers headed for S/E graduate studies are concentrated among males and whites. Between 1989 and 1998, numbers of male U.S. citizens indicating intent to pursue graduate studies in S/E and scoring 700 or greater on the GRE quantitative scale have fallen by 4,000 (-19%), as shown in Table 9. The only S/E field showing an increase in interest among male high scorers was biological sciences. Also, the numbers of high scoring males indicating plans for graduate study in other specified fields (i.e., outside natural sciences and engineering) grew by 725, or nearly 13%, as the number of high scorers interested in S/E declined. The number of high scoring women headed for S/E fields has increased, but fairly modestly, by around 300 individuals per year, or less than 10%, for all the S/E fields combined. There were decreases among both women and men in mathematical sciences, physical sciences, computer science, and engineering (though the change was very small for women in engineering). In sum, increases in high-scoring women have not offset the much larger declines in the number of high scoring men headed for S/E. For both sexes, however, biological sciences is an important exception: it continues to attract healthy increases in top scoring students of both sexes.

Turning to the race/ethnicity categories, the numbers of cases are very small so data for all natural science and engineering fields have been combined (Table 10). There have been healthy percentage increases between 1989 and 1988 in the numbers of high scoring students (≥700 on the GRE quantitative scale) headed for S/E in each race/ethnicity group: Asian-Americans- +22%; African-Americans- +50%; and Hispanic-Americans- +50% (see lower right panel). But the original bases were quite small, so the additional absolute numbers of high scorers are also small: 283 additional Asian-Americans in 1998 compared to 1989, 203 additional African-Americans and Hispanics combined. This total gain of less than 500 minority high scorers is more than offset by a decline of more than 1,700 white high scorers headed for S/E fields. Also rates of increase were greater in high scorers headed for *non*-S/E fields (All Other Fields) than in those headed for S/E among all the race/ethnicity groups.

Table 10. Number of U.S. Citizens Scoring ≥700 on GRE Quantitative Scale, by Intended Broad Area of Graduate Study and Ethnicity,* 1989 and 1998

Broad Field	1989				1998			
	White	Asian	Af	Hisp	White	Asian	Af Am	Hisp
Nat Sci & Engr	11,985	1,279	151	267	10,250	1,562	226	400
All Other Fields	8,346	433	59	150	9,971	1,100	140	275
Undecided/No Response/Other	3,930	292	37	43	3,076	525	47	89
TOTAL NUMBER ≥700 SCORERS	24,261	2,004	247	460	23,297	3,187	413	764

Broad Field	Change between 1989 – 1998				% Change			
	White	Asian	Af	Hisp	White	Asian	Af Am	Hisp
Nat Sci & Engr	-1,735	283	75	133	-	22.1%	49.7%	49.8%
All Other Fields	1,625	667	81	125	19.5%	154.0%	137.3%	83.3%
Undecided/No Response/Other	-854	233	10	46	-	79.8%	27.0%	107.0%
TOTAL NUMBER ≥700 SCORERS	-964	1,183	166	304	-4.0%	59.0%	67.2%	66.1%

*Excludes examinees who indicated ethnicity as Other or did not answer.
Source: Educational Testing Service.

7.   QUALITY TRENDS IN NEWLY-ENROLLED GRADUATE STUDENTS

While these trend data are interesting and suggestive, tracking trends in field designations of GRE test-takers is inherently limited in its ability to identify accurately changes in patterns of graduate enrollment by top students. In addition to the limitations on GRE validity as a predictor of scientific potential, we cannot be sure how precisely examinees' stated intent about graduate field of study matches with who actually enrolls in graduate school. For example, it may be that decreases in quality *potential* students of the magnitude shown are not large enough to affect *enrollments* of highly capable students, given selective admissions.

To begin to address this issue, we secured access to a database containing quality indicators[27] on successive cohorts of newly-enrolled graduate students in leading departments in ten academic disciplines between 1989 and 1996.[28] Designed to study graduate attrition and retention, this data file was developed by the Association of Graduate Schools of the Association of American Universities (AAU), a national organization of leading research universities, and is maintained by the Educational Testing Service. Of the ten academic disciplines, this report will concentrate on the five in natural sciences and engineering: biochemistry, mathematics, physics, chemical engineering and mechanical engineering. Data were not collected on physics and chemical engineering until 1992, so only five year trends are available for these disciplines.

Reporting for individual fields and years is much less than complete so we first eliminated all institutions with substantial reporting gaps that would make meaningful trend analysis not feasible in the fields of interest. The remaining 32 universities were evaluated individually for their GRE score reporting rates in each S/E discipline on both the GRE quantitative and analytical scales.[29]Since the data file was developed for other purposes, this required substantial effort to isolate the variables relevant for a trend analysis of GRE scores of newly-enrolled graduate students by S/E field. Each institution's annual reporting rates for the GRE quantitative and analytical scores were evaluated separately for U.S. citizen plus permanent resident first-year graduate students in each S/E discipline.[30] This yielded ten separate sets of institution-by-institution reporting rates, one for each GRE scale for each of the five S/E disciplines.

Our goal was to insure a high level of comparability across years in the institutions being compared. Thus, to be included in the trend analysis for a discipline, an institution had to achieve high rates of individual GRE score reporting over all years of data collection—1989 through 1996 for biochemistry, mathematics, and mechanical engineering, and 1992 through

1996 for chemical engineering and physics. Institutions were retained if they had roughly a 70% or higher individual reporting rate for all years, although in a very few instances, we included an institution with one year below the 70% reporting threshold when there were high reporting rates in all other years. Low reporting rates in one field or on one GRE scale did not exclude an institution from all analyses, instead it was included for the disciplines for which it passed the reporting rate threshold. Between 17 and 24 institutions qualified for analysis in the five S/E disciplines with a total of 10,155 individual records included on the GRE quantitative scale and 10,077 records on the GRE analytical scale. Appendix A lists the institutions included in the trend analyses, by discipline and GRE scale.

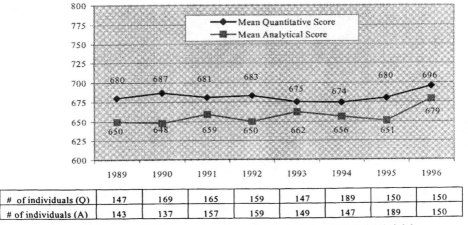

	1989	1990	1991	1992	1993	1994	1995	1996
# of individuals (Q)	147	169	165	159	147	189	150	150
# of individuals (A)	143	137	157	159	149	147	189	150

* Universities meeting our GRE Score reporting rate threshold. See Appendix A for institutions included.

Figure 2: Mean GRE Quantitative and Analytical Scores for Newly Enrolled Graduate Students in **Biochemistry** at 20 Selected AAU Universities,* by Year of Entry
Source: Educational Testing Service.

7.1   Changes in GRE Quantitative and Analytical Scores of Newly-Enrolled S/E Graduate Students

In general, the mean GRE quantitative and analytical scores for newly enrolled U.S. citizen and permanent resident graduate students in the five S/E disciplines do not reveal consistent upward or downward trends, although there are hints that mean analytical scores may be increasing in both chemical and mechanical engineering. Certainly there is no indication of a downward trend in student mean test scores in any of the disciplines.

The GRE quantitative mean score for graduate students enrolled in biochemistry was 16 points higher in 1996 than in 1989 (see Figure 2). The annual mean score changes from 1989 to 1995 were quite small and the 1989 and 1995 mean scores were identical at 680. The 16-point increase actually occurred between 1995 and 1996, and one year clearly does not provide a sufficient basis to draw any conclusion about trend. The mean GRE analytical test scores for biochemistry students mirror the quantitative scores. The mean score was 650 in 1989 and 651 in 1995, but jumped to 679 in 1996. All other yearly score changes were small.

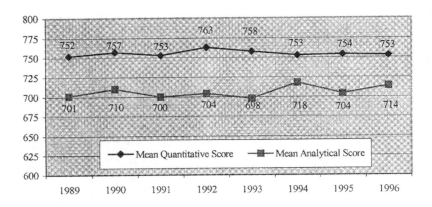

# of individuals (Q)	254	305	279	290	284	267	277	244
# of individuals (A)	249	304	269	289	284	267	276	239

* Universities meeting our GRE Score reporting rate threshold. See Appendix A for institutions included.

Figure 3. Mean GRE Quantitative and Analytical Scores for Newly Enrolled Graduate Students in **Mathematics** at 23 Selected AAU Universities,* by Year of Entry
Source: Educational Testing Service.

The trend-lines for GRE quantitative and analytical mean scores for mathematics graduate students were also largely flat (see Figure 3). The mean quantitative score was 752 in 1989 and 753 in 1996. Changes during the intervening years were small; and even the 10-point increase between 1991 and 1992 was followed by offsetting decreases in succeeding years. The mean GRE analytical score of mathematics students increased 13 points between 1989 and 1996, starting at 701, peaking at 718 in 1994, and ending at 714 in 1996. Again, there is no clear sign of a trend here.

Only five years of data were available for physics graduate students (1992 through 1996) and again clear trends in the mean GRE scores do not emerge (see figure 4). Although the mean quantitative score started at 753 in 1992 and then dropped each year before leveling at 748 in 1995 and 1996, the decrease of only 5 points is insufficient to conclude there is a meaningful downward trend. The mean analytical score for physics students was 688 in

1992 and 700 in 1996. However, there was little movement after the 15-point gain between 1992 and 1993.

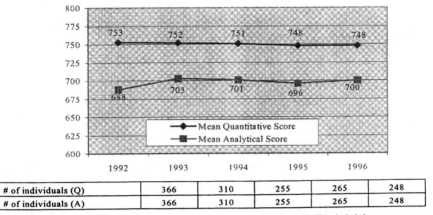

	1992	1993	1994	1995	1996
# of individuals (Q)	366	310	255	265	248
# of individuals (A)	366	310	255	265	248

* Universities meeting our GRE Score reporting rate threshold. See Appendix A for institutions included.

Figure 4. Mean GRE Quantitative and Analytical Scores for Newly Enrolled Graduate Students in **Physics** at 22 Selected AAU Universities,* by Year of Entry
Source: Educational Testing Service.

There were also only five years of GRE data (1992 to 1996) available on new graduate students in chemical engineering. The pattern of the mean GRE quantitative test scores is nearly flat, starting at 736 in 1992 and ending at 740 in 1996 (see Figure 5). Over the five years, the mean analytical scores of chemical engineering graduate students increased 37 points, from 679 in 1992 to 716 in 1996. While the mean scores increased each year, 26 points of the increase occurred between 1995 and 1996. The consistent year-to-year gains and the relatively large five-year change imply a meaningful upward trend in this scale at least.

Finally, the patterns of GRE quantitative and analytical test scores of newly enrolled mechanical engineering graduate students resemble those in chemical engineering (see Figure 6). The mean on the GRE quantitative scale was relatively stable, decreasing only 2 points from 737 to 735 between 1989 and 1996. The peak was 744 in 1992 and the lowest mean score was 730 in 1994. The mean analytical scores in this discipline rose from 659 in 1989 to 675 in 1996. The mean score fell below 659 only once (1990), and scores peaked in 1996. Again, the consistent upward trend in this scale is noteworthy.

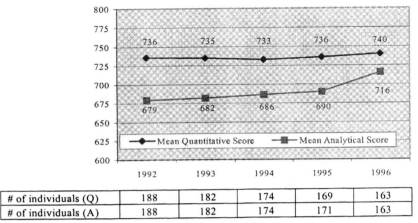

| # of individuals (Q) | 188 | 182 | 174 | 169 | 163 |
| # of individuals (A) | 188 | 182 | 174 | 171 | 163 |

* Universities meeting our GRE Score reporting rate threshold. See Appendix A for institutions included.

Figure 5. Mean GRE Quantitative and Analytical Scores for Newly Enrolled Graduate
Students in **Chemical Engineering** at 19 Selected AAU Universities*, by Year of Entry
Source: Educational Testing Service.

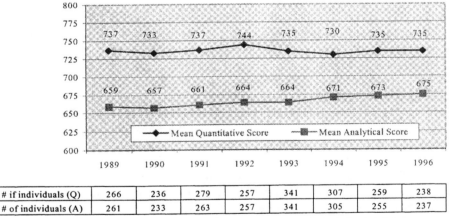

| # if individuals (Q) | 266 | 236 | 279 | 257 | 341 | 307 | 259 | 238 |
| # of individuals (A) | 261 | 233 | 263 | 257 | 341 | 305 | 255 | 237 |

* Universities meeting our GRE Score reporting rate threshold. See Appendix A for institutions included.

Figure 6. Mean GRE Quantitative and Analytical Scores for Newly Enrolled Graduate
Students in **Mechanical Engineering** at 17 Selected AAU Universities, by Year of Entry
Source: Educational Testing Service.

Overall, mean GRE scores of entering U.S. citizen graduate students in
these five S/E disciplines have been fairly stable over the period studied.
Certainly, there is no evidence of a significant decline in this measure of
student quality.

7.2   Numbers of High and Very High GRE Scorers Enrolled in S/E Disciplines

The AGS/AAU data also permits analysis of trend in numbers of high ($\geq$ 700) and very high ($\geq$ 750) scorers among newly-enrolled graduate students in the five S/E disciplines. With one clear exception, these departments are evidently not enrolling fewer top students, at least through 1996.

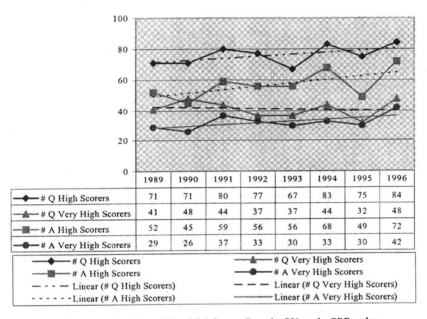

	1989	1990	1991	1992	1993	1994	1995	1996
# Q High Scorers	71	71	80	77	67	83	75	84
# Q Very High Scorers	41	48	44	37	37	44	32	48
# A High Scorers	52	45	59	56	56	68	49	72
# A Very High Scorers	29	26	37	33	30	33	30	42

- # Q High Scorers
- # A High Scorers
- Linear (# Q High Scorers)
- Linear (# A High Scorers)
- # Q Very High Scorers
- # A Very High Scorers
- Linear (# Q Very High Scorers)
- Linear (# A Very High Scorers)

* High Scorers earned $\geq$ 700 and Very High Scorers Earned $\geq$ 750 on the GRE scales

Figure 7. Number of Newly Enrolled Graduate Students in **Biochemistry** Who Earned High and Very High Scores* on the GRE Quantitative and Analytical Scales, by Year of Entry

Source: Educational Testing Service.

There were modest increases in the numbers of top scoring graduate students enrolling in biochemistry (see Figure 7), although the aggregate numbers are so small it is difficult to draw strong conclusions about trends. Consistent with the undulating pattern of mean GRE quantitative and analytical scores of biochemistry students (see Figure 3), the actual numbers of biochemistry students earning high and very high scores on these scales also rose and fell, but the underlying trends were modestly upward. Also consistent with the mean score pattern, the largest increases in numbers of high-scoring students occurred between 1995 and 1996.

The numbers of graduate students in chemical engineering earning high and very high GRE quantitative scores changed little between 1992 and 1996 while the numbers earning high and very high scores on the analytical scale increased by as much as 75 percent for ≥ 700 scorers.

In mathematics, the numbers of new graduate students who had earned high and very high scores on the GRE quantitative and analytical scales were generally stable over the seven years for which data were available. There were 217 high scorers and 170 very high scorers on the quantitative scale in 1989 with 221 high scorers and 169 very high scorers in 1996. On the analytical scale, there were 150 high and 105 very high scorers in 1989, and 163 high and 118 very high scorers in 1996. The annual numbers of top scorers rose or fell slightly each year but no clear increasing or decreasing trends emerged. ..

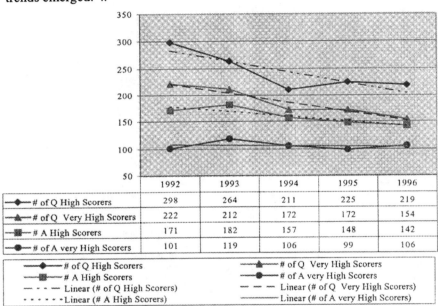

	1992	1993	1994	1995	1996
# of Q High Scorers	298	264	211	225	219
# of Q Very High Scorers	222	212	172	172	154
# A High Scorers	171	182	157	148	142
# of A very High Scorers	101	119	106	99	106

◆ # of Q High Scorers	▲ # of Q Very High Scorers
■ # A High Scorers	● # of A very High Scorers
‐ ‐ ‐ Linear (# of Q High Scorers)	— — — Linear (# of Q Very High Scorers)
· · · · · Linear (# A High Scorers)	—— Linear (# of A very High Scorers)

* High Scorers earned ≥ 700 and Very High Scorers earned ≥ 750 on the GRE scale.

Figure 8. Number of Newly Enrolled **Physics** Graduate Students Who were High and Very High Scorers* on the GRE Analytical Scale, by Year of Entry
Source: Educational Testing Service.

In mechanical engineering, there were 208 newly enrolled graduate students earning high scores and 151 earning very high scores on the GRE quantitative scale in 1989. The numbers of top scorers peaked at 269 in 1993 before falling to 192 and 132 respectively in 1996. Although no clear trend emerged, the numbers of these top scorers on the GRE quantitative scale fell a bit each year between 1993 and 1996. Additional years of data might show this pattern to be indicative of a meaningful trend. On the analytical scale, the numbers of high and very high scorers increased minimally between 1989 and 1996. Of the five S/E fields, only physics showed an appreciable decline in the number of high and very high scorers among the newly enrolled graduate students (see Figure 8). This decline was especially clear for the quantitative scale where there was a 27 percent drop-off in high scorers and a 31 percent decrease in very high scorers over the five years for which data were available. This follows the decreasing trend in total numbers of new physics students enrolling in the AAU departments we examined

Although the data are limited in coverage and the numbers are small, the picture that emerges is broadly consistent with the earlier analysis of trends in high scorers among all U.S. citizen and permanent resident GRE-takers who plan to enroll in these S/E fields. The total enrollments of graduate students in the five fields in the AAU database have declined, but the numbers of top scorers have remained largely stable, except in physics which shows declining enrollment of top students. Biosciences, such as biochemistry, seem to be attracting an increasing number of top scorers. In general, the concern that fewer top GRE-scorers indicating interest in science would mean fewer top students in entering classes is not borne out in the recent trend data from select AAU departments (physics excepted).

Clearly, it would be desirable to have data on more departments in each field, broader field coverage of the S/E fields, and a continuation of the trend data on newly-enrolled students through more recent years to fully understand the emerging patterns. Since graduate students provide a large part of the academic research workforce in these disciplines, decreased enrollments will eventually lead either to reduced research output or to the need to substitute other factors of production for graduate students. Postdoctoral appointees seem the most likely candidates, but other substitutions may also be possible, such as undergraduates, more technicians, perhaps some automation, or possibly different kinds of research problems will be studied. The patterns that emerge will bear close watching.

8.   FURTHER ANALYSES

In order to investigate both recent and longer-term trends in the relative attractiveness of graduate studies in S/E compared to professional schools and other careers more fully than has been done in the past, we have secured access to a series of surveys of the senior (undergraduate) classes of colleges and universities who are members of the elite Consortium on Financing of Higher Education (COFHE). (See Appendix B for a listing of the COHFE institutions.) The surveys with adequate and comparable response rates at the institution level for all years cover the senior classes from 1982, 1984, 1989, 1994, and 1998 from six or seven of the COFHE schools (approximately 4,000 students per year).[31] The surveys ask students from these elite schools about their immediate and ultimate graduate school plans. COFHE has done some follow-up studies of the 1982 and 1984 cohorts and has found that the initial responses about graduate school plans were reasonably valid for these cohorts at least.[32]

Our analyses will focus on shifts in the patterns of graduate school plans of S/E majors and high ability students (measured in this data set by self-reported undergraduate grades) compared to all of these elite school graduates. These analyses should at least broaden the picture as to how the graduate school destinations of top students have changed over the years; in particular those who would be prime candidates for graduate S/E studies. To date, the conventional wisdom about the decline in attractiveness of S/E relative to the professions seems to be based largely on single institution studies comparing two cohorts separated somewhat in time (see earlier discussion).

9.   POLICY ALTERNATIVES

Clearly, the discussion that follows is preliminary for there is much further research and analysis to be done on this issue. But for purposes of policy discussion here, we will assume that the indications of disproportionate declines in the attractiveness of S/E graduate studies to top students are borne out in further studies. Given that assumption, we will now briefly explore the contours of alternative policy responses.

9.1   Let Market Forces Work

Given the predilections of the U.S. policy system, particularly in regard to labor market policies relating to the highly decentralized and prickly world of higher education, public policymakers might well elect to simply let the market work here. If more of the very best U.S. students elect medicine, business or other professions—or no graduate work at all--so be it, at least until conditions in these alternative fields become so congested that S/E research careers begin to look relatively more attractive. Labor markets are inherently cyclical and many possible policy interventions may do more harm than good (Freeman 1971).

The problem with leaving the current system alone is that it may be seriously out of balance. The recent report on *Trends in the Early Careers of Life Scientists* by a committee of the National Research Council's Commission on Life Sciences (1998) and scholars such as Massy and Goldman (1995) have noted that the U.S. academic research and graduate training enterprise employs graduate students in response more to current research and undergraduate teaching needs than to the ultimate demand for the services of finished PhDs in the labor market. Thus, if demand for PhDs in relatively permanent career positions grows only slowly, as it has in recent years, while the training system grows independently in response to the continued growth in academic R&D funds that appears likely to be available, numbers of high quality applicants to S/E graduate school may continue to fall in response to the long-term prospects for PhDs while new graduates may continue to back up in substantial numbers in the temporary postdoctoral pool.[33] These unattractive outcomes would tend to further depress interest in S/E studies among the best students whose career options in business, professions, or information technology, should be the strongest. Such a result, especially if the best U.S. students could not be so readily replaced from abroad as in the past, must eventually affect the quantity and quality of the U.S. research effort, economic competitiveness, and perhaps ultimately the nation's capacity to understand as a society, economy, and polity the essentials of the scientific age.

In such a scenario, the usual suggestion that prospective graduate students be provided more and better information about their career prospects in various fields, while desirable on principle and now more technically feasible than ever, is unlikely to help attract the best students to science and engineering if the tale told by the market data is unattractive. It seems likely that the best students will also have the best alternative prospects in other fields and, in the past, hot fields in terms of general student interest have usually been most attractive to the top cadre of students as well (Adelman 1985, Bok 1993).

In response to decreasing interest from top students, universities might well respond to such clear signs of weakness in the graduate student pool by reallocating discretionary resources to enhance graduate assistantships so as to be more attractive to these top students. This is a logical response for them in the current decentralized decision making regime, but to the extent universities are able to do this, does nothing to help on the demand side in terms of PhD career opportunities in S/E. It might simply increase the logjam problem at the output end of the graduate education pipeline as universities were tempted to increase total enrollments as they received more good applicants in response to improved student support opportunities. Depending upon the extent of market information provided or available to students, such an approach by itself could even be regarded as misleading to them. More or richer graduate fellowships or assistantships also necessarily mean additional resource costs.

9.2   More Government Support for Graduate Fellowships and Assistantships

This step is of course broadly similar to allowing universities to take the initiative but permits federal agencies more control over how (e.g., more competitive fellowships or higher pay for existing research assistants), in which fields, and to what extent enhancements are made. Thus, the system-wide impact might be greater. To limit public costs and ensure some input from academe, some form of matching incentive grant mechanism might be used. The disadvantages are similar to those that apply to the *laissez-faire* approach—more or better graduate student support may well add to supply-demand imbalances at the PhD end of the system as more students (not just top students) are attracted— but the costs in this case are borne more directly by the taxpayer.

9.3   Adjust Immigration Policies to Import More Non-Citizen Graduate Students

Federal immigration policies might be employed to encourage more recruiting of competitive S/E graduate students from other countries. As has sometimes been done in the past (although not with much precision), immigration policies might conceivably be more effectively manipulated to respond to shortfalls of highly qualified potential scientists and engineers.[34]

Such an approach raises the question of whether the U.S. should, as a matter of national policy, raid the young brainpower of the rest of the world, particularly the developing world, primarily to staff its own academic R&D enterprise at low cost. Moreover, signs are emerging that the pool of available non-citizen students may not be as bottomless (or at least as inexpensive) as it once appeared. The direction of scientific capabilities and career prospects in many of the countries that have contributed many S/E graduate students in the past seems to be on the way up, potentially encouraging more students to stay home (Desrusseaux 1998, Lloyd 1998). The recent declines in non-citizen graduate students and PhD recipients in most of the S/E disciplines in U.S. universities already noted may be a warning sign of this. In any case, it seems likely to become a problem in the long run.

Moreover, other developed countries are competing more aggressively for S/E graduate students (e.g., Maslen 1998), which raises the stakes. There are also some potential domestic political problems given perceptions that there are too many foreign graduate students in U.S. universities, especially state universities, being subsidized by public funds (Wilson 1999). While the subsidy claim is dubious, given what these students contribute to the research enterprise and the fact that they have to compete for admission on the basis of quality, the perceptions are real.

9.4   Demand Side Approaches

If market signals are now being correctly read by top students but there is a market failure (positive spillover) in regard to the long-term social benefit of having at least a stable flow of top U.S.-origin talent into advanced S/E training, then it follows that policy should take stimulative steps on the demand side. The federal government could in principle act to permanently increase demand for PhD scientists and engineers, but this is practically difficult for it requires committing additional resources into the future. Yet, no other actor in the system possesses sufficient leverage to materially affect demand for research scientists and engineers.

One hoary suggestion along this line is that the federal government commit to supporting the research program of virtually every PhD scientist trained in a reputable institution and not otherwise employed in R&D. Moving substantially in this direction would no doubt make career prospects for S/E PhDs much more attractive than they are now and should have a corresponding impact on the supply of U.S. students interested in graduate studies, although not necessarily only on the top talent. While some other countries have arrangements more or less like this via government-sponsored research institutes and the like, they can typically bound their commitments by controlling the supply side much more directly than is the case in the U.S. Such a centralized human resource planning approach seems plainly a poor fit in this country.

A more modest and viable approach that more directly targets the young talent issue would focus on the postdoctoral stage. The federal agencies, mainly NIH and NSF as the largest supporters of postdoctoral fellows and associates, could apply some leverage on universities linked to their' funding to upgrade these positions selectively. With the aid of some matching from institutions now extensively supported by federal funds, the idea would be to create a gradually increasing and ultimately significant number of senior research fellow positions open on a competitive basis to postdocs who had proven themselves beyond the PhD, over, say, 2-3 years in the standard postdoctoral track.[35] (In the majority of cases, the standard track implies working as a research associate on a faculty member's grant-supported project. National Research Council 1998).

Candidates for the senior fellow positions would propose a project of their own and need not elect to locate at their current institution. Proposals would be competitive and peer reviewed and positions would be guaranteed for 2-3 years, perhaps renewable once upon submission and review of another proposal. Crucially, the positions would be designed to be competitive with junior faculty positions in terms of salary, benefits and research support. This should be reasonably attractive since a young scientist seeking to build a research record in this type of position would be unencumbered by most of the teaching and other obligations of a faculty member.[36] Some individuals might perceive better long-run prospects for a tenure-track or other career research position arising from such a post than from beginning a career as an assistant professor (particularly if 5-6 years of support were a realistic possibility). More broadly, the idea would be to increase significantly and predictably the number of attractive relatively junior research positions available so as to expand demand for young scientists enough to affect the decisions of very able students considering S/E careers.

Some of the federal funds for such an initiative could come from reallocation from existing research programs in the same fields—which already support many postdoctoral positions—but substantial new resources would surely be needed to have the desired impact on the market. To try to maximize the effect on decisions of U.S. students, policymakers should consider giving preference in the awards to U.S. citizens although this contradicts pure meritocratic values.

Besides new costs, this proposal has other problems of course. For example: How could laboratory space, now at a premium in many S/E fields, be made available to a significant number of additional, relatively autonomous junior scholars and, at the same time, appropriate collegial arrangements facilitated? Would universities offer overwhelming resistance or could enough incentives and facilitating devices be designed in to make them at least willing to participate? Might not such a program have to be extensively adjusted for the peculiarities of research arrangements in different disciplines? Would this make it too complex to administer? Most importantly, could a program of this kind significantly affect the decisions of the best and brightest young people at a feasible net incremental cost? Although it would expand research positions for young scientists and engineers, such a program could not assure that universities, industry and government created any additional more senior positions. So, *ceteris paribus,* the career pyramid in S/E research could become even more peaked than it would be without the program, but hopefully with a larger cadre of highly able candidates.

9.5 Addressing the Decline in Interest in S/E by Whites and Males

Turning back to the supply side of the equation for a moment, the apparent fairly sharp decline in attraction of top-scoring whites and males to S/E, while female and minority numbers of top scorers have generally increased, may need to be addressed. This finding suggests that programs designed to interest young people in S/E may need to be broadened in appeal.[37] Yet, supply-side approaches alone seem destined to fail unless the poor post-PhD prospects facing even the best young research scientists and engineers are improved.

10. CONCLUSION

The data do not yet permit a firm conclusion that the flow of the very best U.S.-origin students into graduate programs in the natural sciences and engineering is declining, but the evidence is accumulating that this group is turning away from S/E careers, at least in physical sciences and related fields. This poses potential problems for the national interest both in the short term and, at least in physical sciences and related fields, the longer run. It is not clear that the nation can (or should) easily replace these top students with their equivalents from other countries. Yet, if they are not replaced, the academic science enterprise will soon face pressures to reduce graduate admission standards, reduce research output, or substantially restructure itself.

The past pattern of explicit human resource policies for PhD-level scientists, to the extent these have existed at all, has been to work mostly on the supply side of the problem by varying graduate fellowship support and at times encouraging the provision of better market information to prospective students. Indeed, when R&D support or forecasted demand for faculty increases, students do appear to respond readily. But when demand falls off (or does not materialize as predicted), the long production cycle means that many young scientists are stranded for extended periods in postdoctoral research/training posts designed to be temporary, with little pay, security or autonomy. This pattern, with the postdoctoral pool building up over a number of years and now extending the total time in PhD plus postdoctoral training for many to 10-12 years, may well be what is discouraging the most able students from S/E studies now.

Following from this analysis, two types of policy suggestions were made. First, efforts to interest more high potential U.S. students in S/E should be broadly focused, not too strictly limited to women and students of color, for the decline in interest by top scoring white males seems to be too steep for a limited focus alone to do enough. Second, the main proposal made here is for the creation of a new matching grant program, strongly encouraged by the federal government's leverage over major research institutions by virtue of its R&D grants to them, designed to fund the substantial improvement of the status of a significant subset of postdoctoral appointments. The new awards would be competitive, probably renewable once, and targeted at the best of more senior postdoctoral appointees through a rigorous peer-reviewed proposal process. These senior research fellow positions would be designed to be competitive to the extent possible with junior faculty positions so as to increase the number of attractive, autonomous early career S/E research positions significantly. While this should add to the aggregate academic research product as a side effect, the main purpose would be to impact the demand side of the market enough to affect the decision making of the most able prospective graduate students of U.S. origin.

To make a lasting difference, these new positions should ideally not be subject to the inevitable up and down cycles of aggregate R&D programs or academic posts. Fiscal partnerships involving universities, industry, and foundations as well as the federal government could help with this but can never make any program invulnerable to budgetary pressures. Nor can a program of this type, even with provision for multiyear support, address the problem of the ultimate narrowing of the career pyramid at the point where the fellowship period ends.[38] Still, it should have some value in encouraging those able students with high confidence in their abilities and a serious interest in pursuing S/E research at least through young adulthood who might otherwise never even enter the competition (i.e., enter graduate school), or have their opportunity to contribute to science.

Appendix A:

AAU/AGS Graduate Institutions Analyzed, by S/E Discipline and GRE Scale

University	Biochem	Math	Physics	Chem Engr	Mech Engr
California, Berkeley		A, Q	A, Q	A, Q	A, Q
California, Los Angeles			A, Q	A, Q	
California, San Diego	A, Q	A, Q	A, Q	A, Q	A, Q
Cal Institute of Tech.	A, Q	A, Q	A, Q	A, Q	A, Q
Columbia	A, Q		A, Q		
Cornell	A, Q	A, Q	A, Q	A, Q	A, Q
California, Santa Barbara		A, Q	A, Q	A, Q	
Florida	A, Q	A, Q	A, Q	A, Q	A, Q
Illinois	A, Q	A, Q		A, Q	A, Q
Indiana		A, Q	A, Q		
Iowa	A, Q	A, Q		A, Q	A, Q
Maryland	A, Q	A, Q	A, Q	A, Q	A, Q
Michigan	A, Q	A, Q	A, Q	A, Q	A, Q
Michigan State	A, Q	A, Q	A, Q		
Missouri	A, Q	A, Q	A, Q	A, Q	A, Q
Northwestern		A, Q	A, Q	A, Q	A, Q
Oregon	A, Q	A, Q	A, Q		
Pennsylvania			A, Q		
Penn. State	A, Q	A, Q	A, Q	A, Q	A, Q
Purdue	A, Q	A, Q	A, Q	A, Q	A, Q
Rutgers	A, Q	A, Q	A, Q	A, Q	A, Q
Southern California	A, Q	A, Q	A, Q		
Texas	A, Q	A, Q	A, Q	A, Q	A, Q
Vanderbilt	A, Q	A, Q	A, Q		
Washington	A, Q	A, Q	A, Q	A, Q	A, Q
Wisconsin	A, Q	A, Q	A, Q	A, Q	

Legend: A – included in analysis of GRE analytical test scores

Q – included in analysis of GRE quantitative test scores

Note: Some institutions do not have doctoral programs in the disciplines studied so this accounts for some of the blanks.

Appendix B:

Participant Institutions in the Consortium on Financing Higher Education (COHFE) Senior Surveys

Amherst College
Barnard College
Bryn Mawr
Carleton College
Columbia University
Cornell University
Dartmouth College
Duke University
Georgetown University
Harvard University/Radcliffe College
Johns Hopkins University
Massachusetts Institute of Technology
Mount Holyoke College
Northwestern University
Pomona College
Princeton University
Smith College
Stanford University
Trinity College
University of Chicago
University of Pennsylvania
University of Rochester
Washington University
Wellesley College
Williams College
Yale University

ACKNOWLEDGEMENTS

The authors gratefully acknowledge support for the research underlying this chapter from the Alfred P. Sloan Foundation. The Foundation, however, bears no responsibility for any errors, omissions or assertions made herein. These are the sole responsibility of the authors. The chapter is a preliminary effort in an on-going research program.

REFERENCES

Adelman, C. (1985). *The Standardized Test Scores of College Graduates, 1964-1982.* Prepared for the Study Group on Conditions of Excellence in American Higher Education. U.S. Department of Education, National Institute of Education.

Association of American Universities. Committee on Postdoctoral Education (1998, March 31). *Report and Recommendations.* Washington, DC: Author.

Bok, D. (1993). *The Cost of Talent: How Executives and Professionals Are Paid and How It Affects America.* New York: Free Press.

Bowen, W. G., and Sosa, J. A. (1989). Prospects for Faculty in the Arts and Sciences: A Study of Factors Affecting Demand and Supply. Princeton, NJ: Princeton University Press.

Breneman, D. W. (1975). *Graduate School Adjustments to the 'New Depression' in Higher Education.* National Board on Graduate Education Technical Report No. 3. Washington, DC: National Academy of Sciences.

Commission on Professionals in Science and Technology. (1997). *Postdocs and Career Prospects: A Status Report.* Washington, DC: Author.

Consortium on Financing Higher Education. (1988). *Five Years Out: Revisiting the COFHE Class of 1982.* Cambridge, MA: Author.

Desruisseaux, P. (1998, September 25). "U.S. Colleges Widen Foreign Recruiting to Offset Loss of Students from Asia." *Chronicle of Higher Education,* A55-A57.

Fechter, A. E., and Gaddy, C. D. (1998). "Trends in Doctoral Education and Employment." *Higher Education: Handbook of Theory and Research,* Vol. XIII. New York: Agathon Press, pp. 353-377.

Fechter, A., and Teitelbaum, M. S. (1997, Spring). "A Fresh Approach to Immigration." *Issues in Science and Technology,* 28-32.

Freeman, R. B. (1971). *The Market for College-Trained Manpower.* Cambridge, MA: Harvard University Press.

Goheen, R. F. (1984). "Cultivating Fresh High-Level Talent in the Humanities." Paper presented at the annual meeting of the Association of Graduate Schools. Boston, MA.

Grandy, J. (1990). *Comparison of Expected with Actual Field of Graduate Study: An Analysis of GRE Survey Data.* ETS Research Report 90-17. Princeton, NJ: Educational Testing Service.

Hartnett, R. T. (1987, September/October). "Has There Been a Graduate Student 'Brain Drain' in the Arts and Sciences?" *Journal of Higher Education* 58(5), 562-585.

Hartnett, R. T. (1985). *Trends in Student Quality in Doctoral and Professional Education.* Talent Trends Project Report, Rutgers University.

Kuhn, T. S. (1962). *The Structure of Scientific Revolutions.* Chicago: University of Chicago Press.

Lloyd, M. (1998, July 17). "India's Brightest Technology Graduates Begin to Stanch the Brain Drain." *Chronicle of Higher Education,* A57-A58.

Maslen, G. (1998, May 22). "Australia Plans Campaign to Promote Its Colleges to Students from Other Nations." *Chronicle of Higher Education,* A52.

Massy, W. F., and Goldman, C. A. (1995). *The Production and Utilization of Science and Engineering Doctorates in the United States.* Stanford, CA: Stanford Institute for Higher Education Research.

National Academy of Sciences, National Academy of Engineering, and Institute of Medicine. (1988). *The Recruitment of the Most Talented Students into Graduate Study in the Sciences, Mathematics, and Engineering: Is There a Problem?* Report of a Steering Committee. Washington, DC: Author.

National Research Council. Commission on Life Sciences. Committee on Dimensions, Causes, and Consequences of Recent Trends in the Careers of Life Scientists. (1998). *Trends in the Early Careers of Life Scientists.* Washington, DC: National Academy Press.

National Research Council. (1969). *The Invisible University: Postdoctoral Education in the United States.* Washington, DC: National Academy of Sciences.

National Research Council. (1981). *Postdoctoral Appointments and Disappointments.* Washington, DC: National Academy of Sciences.

National Research Council. (annual publication). *Summary Report 19xx: Doctorate Recipients from United States Universities.* Washington, DC: National Academy Press.

National Science Foundation. (1989, April 25, working draft). *Future Scarcities of Scientists and Engineers: Problems and Solutions.* Washington, DC: Author.

National Science Foundation. (1990). *The State of Academic Science and Engineering.* Arlington, VA: Author.

Regets, M. (1999). "Has the Use of Postdocs Changed?" National Science Foundation, Division of Science Resources Studies *Issue Brief.* NSF 99-310.

Regets, M. (1998, November 27). "What Follows the Postdoctorate Experience? Employment Patterns of 1993 Postdocs in 1995." National Science Foundation, Division of Science Resources Studies *Issue Brief.* NSF 99-307.

Rosovsky, H. (1990). *The University: An Owner's Manual.* New York: W. W. Norton.

Sanderson, A. R., and Dugoni, B. (1999). *Summary Report 1997: Doctorate Recipients from United States Universities.* Chicago: National Opinion Research Center, University of Chicago.

Shapiro, D. (in press). Modeling Supply and Demand for Arts and Sciences Faculty: What Can We Say About the Projections of Bowen and Sosa 10 Years Late? *Journal of Higher Education.*

Smith, B. L. R. (1990). *American Science Policy Since World War II.* Washington, DC: The Brookings Institution.

Stricker, L. J., and Rock, D. A. (1993). *Examinee Background Characteristics and GRE General Test Performance.* GRE Board Report No. 89-07R. Princeton, NJ: Educational Testing Service.

Wilson, R. (1999, May 14). "Ph.D. Programs Face A Paucity of Americans in the Sciences." *Chronicle of Higher Education,* A14-AA15.

Zumeta, W. (1985). *Extending the Educational Ladder: The Changing Quality and Value of Postdoctoral Study.* Lexington, MA: D. C. Heath/Lexington Books.

Zumeta, W. (1998). "State Higher Education Finance and Policy Developments: 1997." *The NEA 1998 Almanac of Higher Education.* Washington, DC: National Education Association, pp. 65-92.

[1] For purposes of this chapter, the *natural sciences* are defined as the biological sciences, computer sciences, mathematical sciences, and physical sciences. All the engineering disciplines are included within the broad field grouping, *engineering*. *Science and engineering*, or *S/E*, will often be used here to refer to these fields. Sometimes, *science* or *scientists* will be used for variety but, unless the context makes clear otherwise, this also refers to the natural sciences and engineering broadly.

[2] The goal here is to focus upon PhD-level students for these are the people who will be the major creative engines in the research enterprise. In engineering and to some extent computer science especially however, doctoral students are not easily distinguished from master's students in spite of the best efforts of the data collection agencies, so precision in analysis is hampered by this limitation.

[3] The term "supply/demand imbalances" will be defined with more precision later.

[4] We hasten to remind the reader here that we do not claim at this point that the case that graduate programs in S/E are losing ground in attracting top talent is fully proven. At this point, we can simply present some suggestive evidence, describe our research program on the question, and assume the conclusion for purposes of further policy discussion now.

[5] See Smith (1990), Fechter and Gaddy (1998). This very brief history necessarily glosses over many fine points and field differences.

[6] See National Research Council (1969). It should be noted here that postdoctoral study/research appointments have always been much more common in the biomedical disciplines, chemistry, and physics than in other S/E fields. Thus, the following discussion applies most specifically to those disciplines, although the incidence of these appointments has been growing in the other science and engineering fields too.

[7] Both NRC's (1981) and Zumeta's (1985) analyses showed that, at least in the early years of their careers, many former postdoctoral appointees had experienced disappointing labor market rewards. Yet, postdoctoral training did show clear signs of adding substantially to appointees' subsequent research productivity, net of other factors, so it is a plausible investment strategy from a societal point of view. (See Zumeta 1985: chapter 6.)

[8] Measures included stature of graduate institution, registered time-to-the doctorate, receipt of a competitive national fellowship in graduate school, and publication prior to the PhD.

[9] Regets (1999) reports that, across all S/E fields, the median annual salary for a postdoctoral appointee in 1995 was just $28,000, half the median salary of recent PhDs in industry and about one-third less than for those in tenure-track academic positions. Thus, these positions are not attractive for a lengthy stay.

[10] See Hartnett (1987) for various methodological caveats.

[11] This is based on the National Science Foundation's annual fall *Survey of Graduate Students and Postdoctorates*. The latest official data are from the fall 1998 survey.

[12] Since 1993 this category in the NSF data includes persons with permanent residency visas as well as citizens *per se*.

[13] Nor should the U.S. necessarily do so. See Fechter and Teitelbaum (1997) and the discussion of reliance on international students as a policy option, below.

[14] The GRE General Test is the basic set of tests taken by most prospective graduate students in the arts and sciences, consisting of verbal, quantitative, and analytical scales. We are grateful to Robin Durso and Pankaja Narayanan of ETS for their cooperation and assistance with these analyses, and to Jerilee Grandy, consultant to ETS for helpful advice. The years of GRE data available for analysis were 1989, 1992, 1995, and 1998. Each year actually represents a 12-month testing period running from October to October, e.g., the 1989 test year ran from October 1988 through September 1989. For most purposes here,

the changes described span either 1988-89 to 1997-98 or 1991-92 to 1997-98 depending upon which span accurately and efficiently captures the changes over time. Tables and graphs covering all of these years are available from the authors.

[15] According to ETS, only one thorough follow-up study has been done of a large cohort of GRE examinees to see how many enrolled in graduate school the following year (Grandy, 1990). This study tracked a sample of more than 2,100 individuals who took the GRE General Test in the 1987 testing year through graduate school registration in the fall of 1987. Fifty-six percent of the sample enrolled in the fall after taking the test. (Others no doubt enrolled later.) Of those enrolled in fall 1987, 82 percent enrolled in the same field they had indicated on the registration questionnaire.

[16] These criteria do not hold true of undergraduate grades, for example, which vary widely in meaning across institutions and even over time. Significantly, GRE scores correlate with other plausible indicators of student ability including undergraduate grade point average, college selectivity, and college major, net of examinee background characteristics. See Stricker and Rock (1993).

[17] The proportions of all examinees scoring above 700 are shown in the bottom row of the table. This proportion is roughly one-eighth on the analytical and quantitative scales, but less than five percent in recent years on the verbal scale.

[18] Note from the bottom row of Table 3 that, by 1998, only about five percent of U.S. citizen examinees scored at this level on the quantitative and analytical scales and just one percent did so on the verbal scale.

[19] Note that the generalization about the decline applies overall for the S/E fields, but not to each individual field.

[20] The numbers of top scorers (whichever test score cutoff is used) headed for each of the S/E field groupings other than biological sciences were also lower in 1998 than they were nine years earlier (1989).

[21] For example, they may choose directly after, or even before, college to take employment in the burgeoning information technology sector.

[22] These tests are the Medical College Admission Test (MCAT) for medicine, the Law School Admission Test (LSAT) for law, and the Graduate Management Admission Test (GMAT) for business studies.

[23] These data were obtained from the Law School Admission Council.

[24] The data reported in this paragraph are from the Association of American Medical Schools.

[25] GMAT data were provided by the Educational Testing Service.

[26] Graduation data were provided by the American Association of Collegiate Schools of Business.

[27] These include individual GRE scores, the potential to add self-reported undergraduate grade point average, and an index of quality of undergraduate institution. At present, we have been able to analyze only the GRE score data.

[28] Data collection was extended to 1997 but a much lower rate of institutional responses yielded insufficient data for analysis.

[29] We focus on the GRE quantitative and analytical scores because we deem these the most relevant to assessment of S/E talent. It is our understanding that the GRE quantitative and analytical scores are the most utilized by admissions committees in graduate S/E departments.

[30] Permanent residents comprise two percent to six percent of the total in each S/E discipline each year. Analyses of yearly mean GRE quantitative and analytical test scores of permanent residents compared to U.S. citizens revealed differences in means of 3 points or less. Hence our analyses are of U.S. citizens and permanent residents combined.

[31] By agreement, the individual institutions are not to be identified. Whether six or seven institutions are included depends upon the institution-level response rate criterion applied for each survey year (a 40 percent or 50 percent response rate minimum for each survey).

[32] For example, 90 percent of the 1982 respondents who said they planned to pursue an advanced degree immediately after college were so enrolled in February 1983 (COFHE 1988: 73).

[33] Regets (1998, 1999) provides recent evidence that postdoctoral appointment stays are generally getting longer and that many postdocs of recent vintage cite market-related reasons for their appointment.

[34] For a thoughtful discussion of the possibilities and pitfalls here, see Fechter and Teitelbaum (1997).

[35] In light of the premium on research space and equipment in some disciplines, the institutional match might conceivably be in such in-kind resources. Also, universities would be encouraged to seek private or state funds explicitly for purposes of providing their matching share.

[36] Some modest teaching role should be permitted however as this might help the candidate build a record (thus making the fellow positions more attractive) and would also make the arrangement more appealing to universities.

[37] Needless to say, this does not imply that initiatives that have proven effective in attracting more women and minority groups to S/E should be discontinued.

[38] The narrowing may of course be offset for a given cohort by a sudden jump in cyclical R&D support or industrial or academic demand.

INNOVATION POLICY AND ACADEMIC RESEARCH

PART TWO

Chapter 7

Observations on the Post-Bayh-Dole Rise in University Patenting

RICHARD R. NELSON
Columbia University

This chapter is an interim report on a large, and expanding, study of what lies behind the rise in U.S. university patenting and license revenues that has occurred since the late 1970s, on what have been the consequences of those developments, and the policy issues they raise. The early work on this project was focused on Columbia University. Michael Crow, Annetine Gelijns, Holly Raider, Bhaven Sampat, and Richard Nelson were the principal researchers on this early work. Then the project extended to include the University of California and Stanford, with David Mowery and Arvids Ziedonis joining the research group. Recently the project has expanded further, to include scholars at Johns Hopkins University, Penn State, and Duke University. Other scholars at Case Western Reserve University, Purdue and perhaps others may join us.

Before getting into a discussion of the findings, it is necessary to explain briefly the research methodology and the data being explored. The belief is that one cannot understand what is going on without disaggregating, and getting into the details. It turns out that (without exception that can be determined) American research universities have been collecting, at least since the early 1980s, a data set that permits detailed investigation; an "invention report" record. At all the universities studied, university employees are required to file an invention report when their research creates something they think might be commercially valuable. The research report records are collected by the university technology patenting and licensing office (since the mid-1980s almost all universities have one) and can be linked to the record of university patent applications, granted patents, and licensing. Together these records provide a very detailed window into what has been happening. Thus far, the investigation of these records has been largely statistical. The kind of understanding to be achieved requires both statistical analysis of the population of invention reports, and selective detailed study of a number of selected particular cases. The latter part of the inquiry has begun.

The number of patents issued to U.S. universities more than doubled between 1979 and 1984, more than doubled again between 1984 and 1989, and doubled yet again between 1989 and 1997. The number of universities with technology licensing and transfer offices increased from 25 in 1980 to 200 in 1990. Over this same period, university licensing revenues have increased greatly, from $221 million in 1991 to $698 million in 1997 alone. What lies behind these developments?[1]

The widespread impression is that these developments occurred as the direct consequence of the Bayh-Dole Act, which established the presumption that universities would take out patents on inventions resulting from the publicly financed research that they did, and virtually eliminated the need for universities to gain permission from the research funding agency to do so. However, after studying in detail the time series and structure of patents and licensing at Columbia, Stanford, and the University of California, we have come to a somewhat different conclusion.

The sharp increases in university patenting and licensing would seem to be the result, first, of the development and maturation of certain new fields of university research. In particular is the rise of biotechnology, where the research results often seem to promise significant commercial value down the road. Over this period biomedical research rose significantly as a fraction of overall university research, and a large share of that research involved biotechnology in one manner or another. There also was increasing use of computers and specialized software in research across a broad front, and the techniques employed, the results, or both looked commercially promising in a number of cases.

Second, legal and patent office decisions allowed many of the research results in these fields to be patentable. The lion's share of patenting in all three of the universities we studied was concentrated here. The increasing ability to patent in these fields was part of a broader movement in the United States toward strengthening intellectual property rights. The passage of Bayh-Dole itself can be regarded as one aspect of this broader movement.

Stanford and the University of California experienced a significant increase in patenting, largely in biomedical fields, before the passage of Bayh-Dole. In addition, Columbia University's most lucrative patent was applied for before Bayh-Dole. Given the broad developments discussed above, a significant increase in university patenting and licensing was going to happen in any case. The passage of Bayh-Dole legitimated, reinforced, and institutionalized these trends and almost surely speeded them up and magnified them. Nevertheless, in our view they were inevitable. To date no one has had the reason or motivation to do this, although there is concern that some controls may be needed: more on this later.

What have been the consequences of these developments, with respect to the climate of research at American universities, regarding technology transfer, and the progress of science?

There is little evidence that the new climate at universities, where patenting is welcomed and encouraged, has in itself significantly changed the allocation of university research efforts. Federal funding of academic research has increased very rapidly in the biomedical research area, and that research increasingly involves biotechnology, and the use of computers and specialized software. But, given the national changes in patent law and practice, these changes in the menu of research would seem more a source of the change in university attitudes towards patenting and licensing than a consequence. In the three universities examined, there is no discernible evidence that research has become any less fundamental than it used to be. What has happened is that the results of fundamental research in these fields, and using these techniques, have become patentable, and are being patented by universities.

The three universities studied in depth all place a very high premium on the scientific reputation of their faculty. The research that is done there, and the faculty that are selected and tenured, reflect these criteria, and it is unlikely that this will change to any great degree. However, while there is not yet any detailed empirical work on this, there is good reason to believe that the incomes of university researchers and the funding of their labs have become more sensitive to royalty income and research funding by business firms than used to be the case, and some faculty are getting quite wealthy on the basis of their holding of stock in companies that draw on their inventions or knowledge. It would appear that what a university offers a faculty member it wants to attract or hold in terms of salary and research support is becoming quite sensitive to the funds that researcher can be expected to bring in. What this does further down the road to the climate of collegiality at a university is quite uncertain.

What has been the effect of all this on "technology transfer"? The theory behind Bayh-Dole, of course, was that technology transfer from universities to industry would be facilitated if universities got patents on their research results, and licensed these patents to industry, generally on an exclusive basis. Both implicitly, and sometimes explicitly, it was argued that, when universities published their research results and placed them in the public domain, as contrasted with patenting them, companies had little incentive to use them.

It is noteworthy, however, that the two most important university "inventions" studied, Cohen-Boyer, and Axel, were picked up by companies almost immediately after they became known. Nobody was given an exclusive license, and while the patents served as a vehicle to enable the universities to obtain royalty income, it is highly doubtful that they facilitated technology transfer.

More generally, as we get into a wider collection of case studies, it is clear that in fields where companies are technologically sophisticated and aware, when an important breakthrough is made in university research, and published, companies that can use it generally pick it up. For the most part, they do not need an exclusive license in order to induce them to work with it. In at least some cases, it is quite possible that the holding of a patent by the university on a broadly applicable research result or technique, and the threat of a lawsuit for unlicensed use, may have deterred some companies from using the results at least in a way that could be detected, and caused an increase in transaction and real financial costs to those that did take out a license. There is no evidence that the result was overall a significant hindrance to technology transfer in cases where it mattered, but that possibility warrants investigation.

On the other hand, the first look at the cases also seems to reveal a number where simple publication would not have attracted much commercial attention, and where the efforts of the university technology transfer office helped to get attention. Some of these cases resulted in a number of firms taking out a license, some in an exclusive license.

Significant fractions of the licenses given out at the three universities were exclusive. This is only the beginning of digging into the reasons for this. In some cases, the reason clearly was that the university principal researcher already had strong connections with a particular company, or wanted to establish a new company to commercialize the invention. In other cases, not many companies seemed interested and the one that the university preferred as the vehicle insisted on an exclusive license; in some of these instances it looks as if there were other companies who were interested who would not have insisted on an exclusive license. In some cases, it appears that the university thought it could reap more income if it licensed exclusively than if it licensed several firms. It is interesting that in some cases the company originally given the exclusive license did not perform adequately in the eyes of the researcher or the university, or decided to abandon the invention, and another company then obtained the license. In any case, there is little evidence that in the standard run of cases exclusive licensing facilitates technology transfer.

Almost surely, there are occasions where the granting of an exclusive license is necessary for effective technology transfer, or at least speeds up the process. For others, an active role of the university technology transfer office would seem to be important in gaining industry attention and interest, with the kind of licensing policy that bests facilitates technology transfer mostly a matter of judgment. However, for many university inventions of the sort observed, it seems highly likely that technology transfer would occur simply as a result of making the results known. The broadest and most rapid technology transfer calls for widespread licensing by the university of any patents at low rates and without cumbersome bargaining.

On the other hand, it is clear that the institutionalization of university patenting and licensing offices, in the wake of Bayh-Dole, has been associated with a growing belief on the part of universities that their intellectual property rights portfolio should be managed to garner as much revenue as possible. In many cases, managing a patent to facilitate technology transfer, and managing it to reap the highest possible revenues, may be somewhat at odds. The philosophy behind Bayh-Dole, if not the particular theory articulated then, would call for universities to concentrate on doing the former, even if in doing so they sacrifice income. At the universities studied, the officers with the responsibility of setting broad policy are well aware of the potential trade off, and committed to the principle that societal benefit rather than university income ought to be the principal goal. However, this principle may be fragile, and easy to forget.

It is highly important that the impression not get around that universities are managing their intellectual property rights to maximize their own income. Companies that have not been granted a license to work from research results created through projects funded by taxpayer dollars, or which have had to pay a lot to be able to draw on that research, have begun to complain. If the impression gets around that universities are reaping high financial returns from their research results, and are making American companies pay for research results that were achieved with taxpayers' money; the case for public support of university science may begin to fray around the edges. This has not happened yet, but universities should be wary of the possibility.

As earlier noted, a number of the university inventions identified are quite fundamental, and have their principal use in further research, at least over the short run. The potential problems here are not of the universities' making, but stem from the recent proclivity of the patent office and the courts to grant and uphold patents, particularly in biotechnology, on research results that are quite far from commercial applications, although they have promise, and whose principal use is in further research. There is concern that patenting these results, and requiring licenses of those who want to use them as inputs to further research, may seriously increase the financial and transaction cost of doing science. That would not be a good development, and if it occurs, the universities themselves would bear a nontrivial fraction of the costs.   The National Institutes of Health are worried about this possibility.

It has been observed that universities are trying to avoid tying each other up in a tangle of intellectual property rights. But if they do not carefully watch what they are doing, that could happen.

---

[1] This reports on the judgments reached, along with David Mowery, Bhaven Sampat, and Arvids Ziedonis, in the paper forthcoming in *Research Policy*, "The Growth of Patenting and Licensing by U.S. Universities: An Assessment of the Effects of the Bayh-Dole Act of 1980."

Chapter 8

Understanding Evolving University-Industry Relationships

MARYANN P. FELDMAN
Johns Hopkins University

IRWIN FELLER
The Pennsylvania State University

JANET E. L. BERCOVITZ
Duke University

RICHARD M. BURTON
Duke University

1.   INTRODUCTION

Manifest changes in the means by which universities seek to transfer scientific and technical knowledge are apparent after two decades of experience with new legal, economic and policy environments aimed at accelerating the translation of academic research into commercial products. These changes have affected the internal specifications of institutional missions and altered behavioral norms for faculty. U.S. universities have become the *de facto* worldwide template for what Clark (1998) has termed "entrepreneurial universities."

Aspects of these changes are described in a copious literature, written from many different analytical perspectives.[1] Recent studies of university-industry R&D relationships by economists have contributed a more empirical and evaluative dimension, supplementing earlier emphasis on single case studies with broader empirical findings.[2] This chapter proposes to add to this research stream by providing an even broader analytical empirical treatment that considers the relationship between the university and industry in a larger context and incorporates the learning that has occurred on the part of both universities and firms as they search for effective and efficient means of achieving their respective objectives. This approach extends recent work on university-industry technology flows to consider the spectrum of research, technology transfer, educational, and philanthropic relationships between universities and firms and also takes into account the heterogeneous mix of structural influences (e.g., firm size, institution quality, field of knowledge, location) that have been found to be significant in these relationships. Our objective is to build a more general understanding of the interactions that form these relationships, their evolution over time, and ultimately, to inform the current debate in research universities, individually and collectively, concerning missions, priorities, and the allocation of resources.

The integrative component in the relationships between universities and industry is an ongoing search process by both parties (Nelson and Winter 1982, Feller 1990b). University science is conceptualized as an input to industrial innovation. Individual transactions, such as licenses or sponsored research agreements, are one means to initiate the relationship. University characteristics such as university norms, promotion incentives and financial need influence the structure and strategy of the university's technology transfer operations. In addition, technological parameters and firm characteristics are expected to influence the choice of the transaction mechanism and outcome. Examining the behaviors of the participants over time and their evolving relationship, we will be better able to assess the effectiveness and productivity of university-industry interaction, and thus move to firmer footing in determining if these new relationships are a socially efficient way to organize university science and the transfer of academic research findings.

2.   BACKGROUND AND JUSTIFICATION

The Bayh-Dole Act of 1980 marked the advent of a new era in the transfer of university intellectual property to industrial firms (Eisenberg 1996) and altered the working environments of academic scientists (Crow 1998). While universities have long served as a source of technical advance for industry, university-industry collaboration has intensified in recent years due to four interrelated factors: the development of new, high opportunity, technology platforms such as computer science, molecular biology and material science; the more general growing scientific and technical content of all types of industrial production; the need for new sources of funding created by public budgetary stringency; and the prominence of government policies such as Bayh-Dole which aimed to raise the economic returns of publicly-funded research by stimulating university technology transfer (Geuna 1999). Taken together, these changes heralded a new era in university-industry relationships for which the Bayh-Dole Act is arguably the single, most identifiable event.

Initial analysis suggests that the post-Bayh-Dole era is producing significant effects on the number of university patents, as well as the scope of the types of interactions and relationships between universities and industry. For example, before 1980, fewer than 250 patents were issued to universities annually, whereas in 1996, 2,095 patents were issued (AUTM 1996). The number of licenses and revenues from these licenses has likewise increased. In 1996, universities executed for example, 2,741 licenses and options. Cumulative revenue income from licensing agreements was over $2 billion from 1991 to 1996 (AUTM 1996). In addition, 248 new "spin-off" or start-up companies based on university research were formed in 1996, with academic institutions taking equity positions in seventy percent of these new companies (AUTM 1996).

While all U.S. universities acquired broader property rights under Bayh-Dole, considerable diversity exists in policies and contractual mechanisms developed in response to legislation and market opportunities. This diversity may be viewed as a natural experiment as the various actors search for efficient means to organize their activities. For example, institutional policies regarding faculty commercialization incentives, acceptable publication delays and the charters of technology transfer offices vary greatly across research institutions and have evolved over time.

Table 1 demonstrates the substantial variation across major research universities in terms of licensing activity, patenting and new firm start-ups. As a point of reference, total research expenditures for 1997 are included and the universities are ranked by total research expenditures. Data are reported for the University of California System (UC System), (which includes the nine campuses at Berkeley, Davis, Irvine, Los Angeles, Riverside, San Diego, San Francisco, Santa Barbara and Santa Cruz and labs associated with the universities such as the Lawrence Berkeley Labs, Lawrence Livermore Labs and Los Alamos Labs, Scripps Institution of Oceanography, San Diego Supercomputer Center, and the University of California Institute on Global Conflict and Cooperation). By sheer size, the UC System clearly dominates in terms of research expenditures as well as royalties received. In 1997, the UC System received $61,280,000 in royalties for 528 royalty-generating licenses. Columbia University ranks second in terms of royalties while Stanford ranks third. The University of Washington's Research Foundation (WRF), a private not-for-profit organization, is credited by AUTM with starting 25 companies in 1997. WRF manages the intellectual property activity for the University of Washington, Pacific Northwest Laboratories, Washington Technology Center, Fred Hutchinson Cancer Research Center, Washington State University and Spokane Intercollegiate Research & Technology Institute. To facilitate start-ups, WRF manages the Evergreen fund, a seed venture fund, of more than $30 million. The numbers in Table 1 reflect a variety of university strategies, policies and investments.

To facilitate comparisons between the research universities, we calculate two ratios. First, in order to assess the number of new ideas that emerge from the research base, we calculate an invention rate defined as

(1)   Invention rate = Invention Disclosures Received/ Total Research Expenditures

This is a crude measure of how much innovative output the university is able to generate from its R&D base. If we believe that invention disclosures reflect the discovery of economically useful knowledge then this ratio provides a snapshot of the amount of commercially valuable activity generated by the university's research.

Table 2 provides the invention rate for the same research universities listed earlier. The invention rates are normalized to reflect the number of invention disclosures per $10 million in research expenditures. The invention rates range from a high of 6.34 invention disclosures per $10 million at Stanford to a low of 2.43 at Johns Hopkins University.

Second, we calculate the royalties per license. Recognizing that many licenses do not generate revenue, we include only those licenses that actually generate royalties. Thus,

(2)   Royalty Per License = Royalties/ Number of Licenses Generating Royalties

In truth, we expect that university licenses may have a skewed distribution with a few large revenue-generating home runs and many modest projects. The data that we have at hand only allows us to calculate the average revenue.

Table 1. Differences in University Technology Transfer Activities: 1997

University	Total Research Expenditures	Royalties Received	Number of Royalty Generating Licenses	Startup Firms Formed
UC System	$1,586,533,000	$61,280,000	528	13
Johns Hopkins	$942,439,696	$4,686,519	103	3
MIT	$713,600,000	$19,860,549	255	17
Washington Research Foundation	$528,602,441	$11,478,605	142	25
Michigan	$458,500,000	$1,708,939	83	6
Stanford	$391,141,224	$34,014,090	272	15
Wisconsin Alumni Research Foundation	$379,600,000	$17,172,808	133	2
Harvard	$366,710,262	$13,402,273	232	1
Duke	$360,977,000	$1,520,000	N.A.	0
Penn State	$535,373,000	$1,277,775	58	9
UNC-Chapel Hill	$263,517,405	$1,665,909	61	2
Columbia	$244,100,000	$46,105,192	201	4
USC	$238,399,312	$687,004	20	4

Source: 1997 AUTM annual report and Chronicle of Higher Education articles

Table 2: Differences in the Ratios of University Technology Transfer Activities: 1997

University	Invention Rate	Royalty per License
UC System	4.51	$116,061
Johns Hopkins	2.43	$ 45,500
MIT	5.04	$ 77,885
Washington Research Foundation	5.30	$ 80,835
Michigan	3.66	$ 20,590
Stanford	6.34	$125,052
Wisconsin Alumni Research Foundation	5.24	$129,119
Harvard	3.25	$ 57,768
Duke	4.04	N.A.
Penn State	3.44	$ 22,031
UNC-Chapel Hill	3.57	$ 27,310
Columbia	6.02	$229,379
USC	4.74	$ 34,350

Source: 1997 AUTM annual report and Chronicle of Higher Education articles.

Table 2 demonstrates great variation in the royalties per license. The highest average is for Columbia University at over $229,000 per license. The lowest is just over $22,000 for Penn State University. Of course, these simple averages do not take into account the types of technologies that the universities are licensing, the terms of the license, in terms of exclusivity and scope and the other types of contractual agreements such as licensing fee equity swaps. All of these factors are part of university technology transfer activities.

While the aggregate results are intriguing, they fail to resolve competing interpretations or to answer many interesting and controversial questions about the nature and dynamics of university-industry relationships. Some argue, for example, that tapping the expertise and knowledge of American universities will generate a new era of economic growth and international competitiveness (Bowen 1998). Other authors contend, however, that the search for additional revenue streams from industry relationships may detract from the university's basic mission of creating new broad-based knowledge, thus leading to socially undesirable restrictions on the flow of academic R&D, and ultimately to diminished economic growth (Slaughter and Leslie 1997).

University-industry relationships also have proven difficult to manage (Cohen, et al. 1998); yet their numbers and persistence indicate some perceived mutual benefit. Indeed, universities continue to be viewed by many as engines of local economic growth, and continue to be cited as an important factor in regional technology development and revitalization (Raymond 1996). A substantial body of evidence suggests that knowledge spillovers from universities are geographically localized, although the specific factors that condition geographic localization are not well understood (Feldman 2000).

Recent research has expanded understanding of the characteristics of university-industry interaction and provides a platform upon which to build. Mowery, et al. (1999) and Crow, et al. (1998) have focused on intellectual property, studied licensing agreements, and documented increased university-industry interactions, while the work of Cohen, Florida, and Goe (1992) presents findings and highlights issues associated with industry funding of university-industry R&D centers. Preliminary research by Mowery, et al. (1999) indicates substantial variation in licensing agreements across institutions, firms, and technologies. For example, licensing agreements vary significantly in terms of the scope of the license granted— non-exclusive/exclusive scope (by sector or geography), the level of royalty rates, publication delay allowances, duration, and future option rights (Raider 1998, Barnes, Mowery and Ziedonis 1997). Other critical factors such as the attributes of the technology, the characteristics of the corporate partner, the policies of the university holding the patent, the history of relationships between the two players, the role of spatial proximities, or other idiosyncratic factors, have not been studied in detail. In addition, many of the key transaction categories in university-industry relationships, such as sponsored research agreements, university spin-offs, charitable gifts, or the hiring of involved students, as either substitutes or complements for patents and licenses, remain largely unexplored.

Often described in terms of a single variable, such as a licensing agreement, closer inspection reveals that university-industry relationships are multi-faceted, complex, and diverse. Commercializing technology encompasses many transactions between a university and a company. For example, commercialization can involve multiple licenses and require that a company fund a sponsored research project for developmental work to usefully apply the license. In addition, the company subsequently may hire students who worked on the sponsored project. The relationship may be so fruitful that the company ultimately may endow a university chair or make another type of philanthropic gift. Only by considering the complexity of these relationships can we obtain a fuller understanding of their nature. And, only by understanding the nature of university-industry relationships can their impact be estimated.

3.   THEORETICAL FRAMEWORK

Patents and licenses may be used for two important yet different purposes. First, they serve as a measure of the outcomes of recent public policies, university organizational and policy changes, and shifts in corporate strategies as well as a means of linking our work to that of others in pursuit of replicability and increased generalizability.   Second, they provide snapshots of the university and industry participants in what is an evolutionary process of search, transactions, evaluation, reformulation of partners, objectives and policies, and subsequent search for partners.[3] R&D transactions are part of a larger system that incorporates a complex process of technological accumulation whereby knowledge is generated through exchanges that involve social convention and legal rights as well as economic interests. These transactions also involve trust, loyalty, and other motivations that are difficult to measure but appear to be key to innovation.

The elements in these transactions are sponsored research support, patent funding, center participation, licensing agreements, grant sponsorship, student recruitment and hiring, charitable gifts, option agreements, and equity for license. However, as depicted in Figure 1, transactions do not occur in isolation. The institutional environment and the characteristics of companies influence the efficiency, and thus evolution, of these university-industry relationships. Thus, we will examine the series of transactions over time between the dyad of a university and a company.

This theoretical model offers a novel, comparative framework. We will be able to examine not only similarities and differences in the performance of research universities, but also the behavior of firms relative to these universities. For example, we hypothesize that the size of the firm's in-house R&D budget will influence the terms of the relationship, the balance of power between the participants, and the ultimate outcome. Larger firms are expected to have more bargaining power with universities and to negotiate more favorable contractual terms, *ceteris paribus*. Conversely, small firms may be more focused on a university license and may be able to advance the technology in a timelier manner as witnessed by subsequent patents or other outcome measures. This may also vary by sector as different products have different commercialization lags and require different levels of support.

Institutional policies, for example, regarding faculty commercialization incentives vary greatly. To the extent that university policies influence the comparative cost of technology transfer, we expected to see variation in the composition of university-industry relationships across institutions. For example, a private university that emphasizes "service to mankind" is expected to hold fewer exclusive licenses, or to have policies that allow for discrimination on licensing fees by giving breaks to non-profit organizations. Other universities, either public or private, that perform large amounts of industrial R&D are expected to generate higher rates of patents/licenses per R&D expenditure.   In general, we expect that examining the series of transactions over time between a university and a company in institutional environments will dictate differences in the type of transactions that universities undertake with firms.

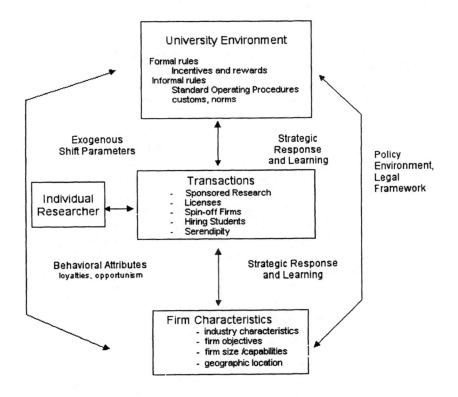

Figure 1: University-Industry Relationship Evolutionary Schema

The characteristics of individual companies also affect the choice and specification of the transaction.   For example, Cohen, Florida, and Goe (1992) found that center participation was higher for engineering technologies, while we expect that biomedical companies are more likely to support sponsored research projects.   New entrepreneurial start-ups are expected to have different transaction profiles with respect to universities when compared to larger companies. There is evidence that small firms are more reliant on university research because they lack in-house resources (Acs, Audretsch, and Feldman 1994). For this reason, we expect that small firms may be more focused on university licenses.

Finally, we expect that the geographic location of the company may also dictate the type of transaction. We expect that geographic distance between the company and the university will result in more formal transactions, less total transactions and will be less productive overall in terms of relationship output such as joint-patenting, joint-publishing and student hiring. Ultimately, we will construct a formal model that links the choice of governance mechanism and outcomes to the characteristics of the firm.

We also expect to see a progression from single transactions to long-term commitments as trust and commitment are built. For example, a firm's licensing experience with a particular university is expected to increase the likelihood of the adoption of a sponsored research agreement. Firm involvement with sponsored research or licensing may increase the likelihood of corporate gifts. Alternatively, firms may engage in opportunistic behavior by contracting directly with faculty members, thus bypassing the university intellectual property apparatus. These elements may be best understood by framing patent and licensing transactions within the larger relationship.

Our framework also incorporates organizational learning effects that dictate evolution in the form of the university-industry relationship (Figure 1). Feedback effects, for example, may include an improvement in contract specification, brought about because the existing specification was found poorly suited to support the integrity of contract. We expect to see that small firms that are able to form productive research relationships with a university may relocate to the same region as that university.

The commercialization of university intellectual property rights involves more than a simple, single transaction. More frequently, it includes actions that spread across the range of university-industry interactions. Relationships with industrial partners encompass inputs such as sponsored research, gifts, contracts, and grants with faculty members, and involve outputs such as invention disclosures, patents, and licenses. These relationships can contain cross-boundary arrangements such as university-industry partnerships, joint ventures, and university-entrepreneur equity swaps.

4. THE MECHANISMS OF UNIVERSITY TECHNOLOGY TRANSFER

Universities form *quid pro quo* relationships with industry through a series of transaction mechanisms. These transactions are primarily motivated to provide funding to universities while transferring knowledge to firms; however, the interactive nature of knowledge generation argues that learning that will also flow from companies to universities. The transaction mechanisms may be formal or informal. Formal mechanisms include sponsored research agreements, or licenses or equity swaps. Informal mechanisms may involve personal networks or the hiring of students. The form of these transactions is influenced by firm strategy and industry characteristics. Recent economic studies of university-industry R&D relationships have contributed an empirical and evaluative dimension, supplementing earlier emphasis on single case studies with broader empirical findings.[4] However, these transactions further reflect economic and legal parameters defined by university policy. In addition, universities are social as well as economic entities and social and behavioral norms as well as economic considerations that vary significantly between types of universities influence relationships with industry.

The elements in university-industry relationships are transactions that occur through the mechanisms of sponsored research support, including center participation, agreements to license university intellectual property, the hiring of research students, and new firm spin-offs. To be inclusive, serendipity is also included as an informal mechanism that might be used to initiate relationships that subsequently develop through more mechanisms. Each of these mechanisms is described briefly in Table 3.

Table 3: Major Mechanisms of University Technology Transfer

Mechanism	Definition
Sponsored Research	An agreement by which the university receives funding for conducting a research project.
Licenses	Access to university intellectual property.
Hiring of Students	Recruitment of students from the university, especially those working on sponsored projects.
Spin-off Firms	A new entity that is formed around the research of faculty or a university license.
Serendipity	Luck or chance.

Sponsored Research entails a contract between the academic entity and the firm. The sponsored research project may be commissioned through the university or may be made directly with a university researcher with the form of the contract determined by the options available to the individual researcher. Sponsored research may take the form of a grant, which is more open ended in terms of outcomes, or a contract in which a set of specific deliverable products and end results are made explicit. Contracts typically entail closer working relationships. Sponsored research may also involve company participation in an industry-funded research center. The university reserves the right to review these agreements, even in the case of faculty research not done through the university. The sponsored research agreement may specify the ownership of any resulting intellectual property and may provide details for licensing of potential patents, divisions of royalties and future sponsored projects. The characteristics of individual companies also affect the choice and specification of the sponsored research transaction. For example, Cohen, Florida, and Goe (1992) found that university-industry research center participation was higher for engineering technologies, while we expect that biomedical companies are more likely to support sponsored research projects.

Another technology transfer mechanism is university licenses that provide the right to use university intellectual property in the form of either patents or trademarks. Transformation of new principles, materials, instruments, and other technological possibilities into products and processes that are competitive with existing or other new alternatives involves both technical and economic risk. Lacking, for example, are detailed treatment of the R&D, manufacturing, or marketing strategies of the firms that licensed academic research and introduced new products and processes to market. Preliminary research indicates that the use and transformation of licenses from universities is complex, diverse, and diffuse. Licenses to academic patents may serve as the critical component of a new product or process; the license may act to enhance selected qualities of a new product but not in any way be essential; the product upon which license income is paid may be profitable only because of extensive in-house R&D, manufacturing competitiveness, or the marketing strength of the licensor.

Numerous scenarios also are reported on the ownership and disposition of licenses among firms. Licenses may be a critical part of the start-up or growth of a small firm; they may revert back to the university if a firm fails to meet contractual markers, and subsequently be assigned to other firms; they may become buried with the failure of a firm even though the technical importance of the license has surfaced. In all, these scenarios point to a largely unexplored area of the contribution of academic research to technological innovation—namely, the uses made by firms of licenses to academic patents.

The second two mechanisms, hiring of students and spin-off companies, are somewhat different in that they involve a more direct technology transfer that takes place through people. The typical model of the advanced research student is the "German model," essentially a scientific apprenticeship. The opportunities to implement this model depend on the workload of professors: more teaching implies less time for research. For example, in Korea from 1966 to 1985 the student-professor ratio increased from 22.6 to 35.8, effectively changing the orientation from research to undergraduate, thereby decreasing the supply of students who could be hired by industry (Kim 1993). From the perspective of companies who fund sponsored research projects, the project provides a mechanism to train students to work on their applications while also screening the students for future employment.

University spin-offs are becoming an increasingly important means to commercialize science. Life-cycle models of scientists suggest heavy investment in human capital early in their careers in order to build reputation and establish a position in a field of expertise (Stephan and Levin 1992). In the latter stages of their career, scientists typically seek an economic return for their human capital. For scientists, starting a company serves the purpose of appropriating the value of their intellectual property as well as providing access to additional funding mechanisms to further the scientist's research agenda. Most critically, academic researchers, especially government-funded researchers, must have the ability to retain rights over their intellectual property (Eisenberg 1987). The potential financial rewards of starting a company coupled with tightening university budgets and competition for the relatively fixed pool of public funding create incentives for scientists to engage in entrepreneurial activity (Powell and Owen-Smith 1998). In this regard, the ability of individual scientists to appropriate the value of intellectual property will be affected by national policies. Consequently, variation in intellectual property procedures among universities is one factor that may influence the academic scientist's decision to commercialize.

From this, we can say that individual scientists who received grants and awards for basic research have the intellectual capital required to start a company. However, there are other barriers to consider. Feldman (1999) has demonstrated that the decision to start a company is very much a socially conditioned action, and if the external conditions are right, a process of social contagion will cause others in the same departments and institutions to follow and to engage in entrepreneurship. In contrast, McFetridge (1993) finds that Canadian academics are immobile and have no incentives to engage in entrepreneurial activity while Keck (1993) concludes that the intellectual orientation of German university professors made them adverse to exploiting new ideas for commercial purposes even after encouragement to do so by university and government policy.

5. REFLECTIVE CONCLUSIONS

Attention to increases in academic patents and licenses has not been matched by commensurate systematic analysis on how patents and licenses are used or their impact on the strategy of the firm and the rate and direction of technological innovation. Academic research findings, whether basic and largely unmodified or "applied" and codified in the form of patents, typically only represent the "raw" material from which commercially competitive technological innovations are constructed (Dasgupta and David 1994, David, Mowery, and Steinmueller 1992, SRI International 1985, von Hippel 1988). Much work remains to be done to fill in and provide depth to the university-industry relationship schema that this chapter has laid out.

ACKNOWLEDGEMENTS

The Andrew W. Mellon Foundation supports this research. This chapter has benefited from discussions with Harriet Zuckerman, Richard Nelson and David Mowery.

REFERENCES

Acs, Z. J., D. B. Audretsch and M. P. Feldman. (1994). "The Recipients of R&D Spillovers: Firm Size and Innovation." *Review of Economics and Statistics.* 76: 336-340.

Association of University Technology Managers, Inc. (AUTM) (1995). *AUTM Licensing Survey Fiscal Year 1991-Fiscal Year 1994.* Norwalk, CT.

Association of University Technology Managers, Inc. (AUTM) (1996). *AUTM Licensing Survey Fiscal Year 1996 Survey Summary.* Norwalk, CT.

Baldwin, D. and J. Green. (1984-1985). "University-Industry Relations: A Review of the Literature." *SRA Journal,* pp. 57-77.

Barnes, M., D. C. Mowery, and A. A. Ziedonis. (1997). "The Geographic Reach of Market and Nonmarket Channels of Technology Transfer: Comparing Citations and Licenses of University Patents," presented at the Academy of Management.

Bowen, R. (1998). *Universities and Their Leadership.* Princeton, NJ: Princeton University Press.

Brooks, H. and L. Randazzese. (1998). "University-Industry Relations: The New Four Years and Beyond" in L. Branscomb and J. Keller, eds., *Investing in Innovation,* Cambridge, MA: The MIT Press, pp. 361-399.

Clark, B. (1998). *Creating Entrepreneurial Universities,* Great Britain: International Association of Universities and Elsevier Science Ltd.

Cohen, W., R. Florida, L. Randazzese, and J. Walsh. (1998). "Industry and the Academy, Uneasy Partners in the Cause of Technical Advance" in R. Noll, ed., *Challenge to the Research University.* Washington, DC: Brookings Institution, pp. 171-199.

Cohen, W., R. Florida, and R. Goe. (1992). *University-Industry Research Centers in the United States.* Pittsburgh, PA: Carnegie Mellon University.

Crow, M. M. (1998). "Universities and the New Manifest Destiny" presented at the AAAS R&D Conference: The Future of Science and Technology in Arizona. March 27, 1998.

Crow, M. M., A. C. Gelijns, R. R. Nelson, H. J. Raider, and B. N. Sampat. (1998). "Recent Changes in University-Industry Research Interactions: A Preliminary Analysis of Causes and Effects," unpublished MS, Columbia University.

Dasgupta, P. and P. A. David. (1994). "Towards a New Economics of Science." *Research Policy* 23: 487-522.

David, P. A., D. Mowery, and E. Steinmueller. (1992). "Analyzing the Economic Payoffs from Basic Research." *Economics of Innovation and New Technology* 2: 73-90.

Davis, L. and D. North. (1971). *Institutional Change and American Economic Growth.* Cambridge: Cambridge University Press.

Eisenberg, R. S. (1987). "Proprietary Rights and the Norms of Science in Biotechnology Research." *The Yale Law Journal* 97 (2): 177-231.

Eisenberg, R. S. (1996). "Public Research and Private Development: Patents and Technology Transfer in Government-Sponsored Research." *Virginia Law Review* 82: 1663-1727.

Etzkowitz, H. (1989). "Entrepreneurial Science in the Academy: A Case of the Transformation of Norms." *Social Problems* 36(1): 14-29, 36-50.

Etzkowitz, H. and L. Peters. (1991). "Profit from Knowledge: Organizational Innovations and Normative Change in American Universities." *Minerva* 29: 133-166.

Etzkowitz, H. and L. Leydesdorff, eds. (1997). *Universities and the Global Knowledge Economy,* London, England: Pinter.

Feldman, M. P. (1994). "The University and High-Technology Start-ups: The Case of Johns Hopkins University and Baltimore." *The Economic Development Quarterly.* 8: 67-77.

Feldman, M. P. (1999). "The New Economics of Innovation, Spillovers and Agglomeration: A Review of Empirical Studies." *Economics of Innovation and New Technology.* 8: 5-25.

Feldman, M. P. (2000). "Location and Innovation: The New Economic Geography of Innovation, Spillovers, and Agglomeration " in G. Clark, M. Feldman and M. Gertler, eds., *Oxford Handbook of Economic Geography,* Oxford: Oxford University Press.

Feldman, M. P. and O. Pfirrmann. (1998). *The Diffusion of Knowledge in Biotechnology*. Paper presented to the 1998 APPAM research conference.

Feller, I. (1990a). "Universities as Engines of R&D-based Economic Growth: They Think They Can." *Research Policy* 19: 335-348.

Feller, I. (1990b). "University-Industry R&D Relationships" in J. Schmandt and R. Wilson, eds., *Growth Policy in the Age of High Technology*, Boston, MA: Unwin Hyman, pp. 313-343.

Feller, I. (1997). "Technology Transfer from Universities." in J. Smart, ed., *Higher Education: Handbook of Theory and Practice*, Volume 12, New York: Agathon Press, pp. 1-42.

Geiger, R. (1993). *Research and Relevant Knowledge*, New York: Oxford University Press.

Geuna, A. (1999) *The Economics of Knowledge Production: Funding and the Structure of University Research*. Cheltenham, UK; Northampton, MA: Edgar Elgar Publishers

Government-University-Industry Research Roundtable. (1986). *New Alliances and Partnerships in American Science and Engineering*. Washington, DC: National Academy of Sciences.

Graubard, S. R. (1994). "The Research University: Notes Toward a New History." in J. R. Cole, E. G. Barber, and S. R. Graubard, eds., *The Research University in A Time of Discontent*. Baltimore, MD: The Johns Hopkins University Press.

Henderson, R., A. Jaffe, and M. Trajtenberg. (1998). "Universities as a Source of Commercial Technology: A Detailed Analysis of University Patenting, 1965-1988." *The Review of Economics and Statistics* 80: 119-127.

Keck, O. (1993) "The National System for Technical Innovation in Germany." in R.R. Nelson, ed., *National Innovation Systems: A Comparative Analysis*. Oxford: Oxford University Press. pp. 115-157.

Kim, L. (1993). "National System of Industrial Innovation: Dynamics of Capacity Building in Korea. " in R.R. Nelson, ed., *National Innovation Systems: A Comparative Analysis*. Oxford: Oxford University Press. pp. 357-383.

Lee, Y. S. (1998). "University-Industry Collaboration on Technology Transfer." *Research Policy* 26: 69-84.

Luger, M. and H. Goldstein. (1991). *Technology in the Garden*, Chapel Hill, NC: University of North Carolina Press.

Mansfield, E. and J.Y. Lee. (1996). "The Modern University, Contributor to Industrial Innovation and Recipient of Industrial R&D Support." *Research Policy* 25: 1047-1058.

McFetridge, D. (1993). "The Canadian System of Industrial Innovation. " in R. Nelson, ed., *National Innovation Systems: A Comparative Analysis*. Oxford: Oxford University Press. pp. 299-323.

Mowery, D., R. R. Nelson, B. N. Sampat, and A. A. Ziedonis. (1999). "The Effects of the Bayh-Dole Act on U.S. University Research and Technology Transfer" in L. Branscomb, F. Kodama, and R. Florida, eds., *Industrializing Knowledge*. Cambridge, MA: MIT Press, pp. 269-306.

Mowery, D. and N. Rosenberg. (1989). *Technology and the Pursuit of Economic Growth*. Cambridge: Cambridge University Press.

Mowery, D. and A. Ziedonis. (1998). "Market Failure or Market Magic? National Innovation Systems and the Transfer of Technology." *Science Technology Industry Review*, 22: 101-136.

Narin, F., K. S. Hamilton, and D. Olivastro. (1997). "The Increasing Linkage Between U.S. Technology and Public Science." *Research Policy* 26: 317-330.

Nelson, R. R. and S. G. Winter. (1982). *An Evolutionary Theory of Economic Change*. Cambridge, MA: Harvard University Press.

North, D. (1981). *Structure and Change in Economic History*. New York: W. W. Norton.

North, D. (1991). "Institutions." *Journal of Economic Perspectives*, Winter, 5: 97-112.

Peters, L. and H. Fusfeld. (1983). "Current U.S. University/Industry Research Connections." in National Science Foundation, *University-Industry Research Relationships: Selected Studies*. Washington, DC: National Science Board.

Powell, W. W. and J. Owen-Smith. (1998). "Universities and the Market for Intellectual Property in the Life Sciences." *Journal of Policy Analysis and Management* 17 (2): 253-277.

Praeger, D. and G. Omenn. (1980). "Research, Innovation and University-Industry Linkages." *Science* 207(2980): 379-384.

Rahm, D. (1994). "Academic Perceptions of University-Firm Technology Transfer" *Policy Studies Journal* 22: 267-278.

Raider, H. (1998). "Repeated Exchange and Evidence of Trust in the Substance Contract," Working paper Columbia University.

Raymond, S., ed. (1996). *The Technology Link to Economic Development, Annals of the New York Academy of Sciences*, Vol. 787. New York: New York Academy of Sciences.

Rosenberg, N. and R. R. Nelson. (1994). "American Universities and Technical Advance in Industry." *Research Policy* 23: 325-348.

Slaughter, S. (1990). *The Higher Learning & High Technology.* Albany, NY: State University of New York Press.

Slaughter, S. and L. L. Leslie. (1997). *Academic Capitalism: Politics, Policies and the Entrepreneurial University.* Baltimore, MD: The Johns Hopkins University Press.

SRI International. (1985). *NSF Engineering Program Patent Study.* Report prepared for the National Science Foundation, Final Report, NSF Contract No. EVL-8319583.

Stephan, P. E. and S. G. Levin (1992). *Striking the Mother Lode in Science,* New York: Oxford University Press.

Vest, C. M. (1997). "Research Universities: Overextended, Underfocused, Overstressed, Underfunded." in R. G. Ehrenberg, ed., *The American University.* Ithaca, NY: Cornell University Press.

von Hippel, E. (1988). *The Sources of Innovation.* New York: Oxford University Press.

Williamson, O. E. (1975). *Markets and Hierarchies: Analysis and Antitrust Implications.* New York: Free Press.

Williamson, O. E. (1985). *The Economic Institutions of Capitalism.* New York: Free Press.

Williamson, O. E. (1991). "Comparative Economic Organization: The Analysis of Discrete Structural Alternatives." *Administrative Science Quarterly* 36 (June): 269-96.

Williamson, O. E. (1993). "Transaction Cost Economics and Organization Theory." *Industrial and Corporate Change.* 2: 107-56.

Williamson, O. E. (1996). *The Mechanisms of Governance,* Oxford: Oxford University Press.

---

[1] See, for example, Baldwin and Green (1984, 1985), Brooks and Randazzese (1998), Etzkowitz and Peters (1991), Etzkowitz and Leydesdorff (1997), Feller (1990a), Geiger (1993), Government-University-Industry Research Roundtable (1986), Lee (1998), Luger and Goldstein (1991), Peters and Fusfeld (1983), Praeger and Omenn (1980), Rahm (1994), Slaughter (1990).

[2] See, for example, Cohen, Florida, and Goe (1992), Feller (1997), Henderson, Jaffe, and Trajtenberg (1998), Mansfield and Lee (1996), Mowery and Rosenberg (1989), Rosenberg and Nelson (1994).

[3] This framework builds upon and extends the work of Williamson (1975, 1985, 1993, 1996), Davis and North (1971), North (1981).

[4] See, for example, Cohen, Florida, and Goe (1992), Feller (1997), Henderson, Jaffe, and Trajtenberg (1998), Mansfield and Lee (1996), Mowery and Rosenberg (1989), Rosenberg and Nelson (1994).

Chapter 9

Elite and/or Distributed Science:

An Analytical and Empirical Guide to Public Policy on the Distribution of Federal Academic R&D Funds

IRWIN FELLER
The Pennsylvania State University

1. INTRODUCTION

The polity requires greater equality, the economy greater merit. The two, which are not absolute opposites, are, however, to a degree, in conflict. The task is to make them as compatible and as reinforcing as possible (Kerr 1994: 28).

The conflicts and compatibilities in the federal funding of elite and distributed academic science highlighted by Kerr's observations are addressed in this chapter. Section 2 provides a brief policy background on the continuing debates about the distribution of federal academic R&D funds, the typical context for discussion of these choices. Section 3 probes conventional definitions of the concepts of elite science and distributed science, and relates these definitions to criteria employed by federal agencies to allocate funds for academic research, especially basic research. Section 4 builds on these definitions and presents data on patterns and trends in elite and distributed science. Section 5 contains the chapter's conclusions.

Allocative efficiency, as represented by competition among individuals and institutions, peer review processes and award criteria centered about scientific merit, and equity, as measured by the shares received by institutions and states, have long contended for influence as the basis for distributing federal funds to support academic research.[1] The standard starting point for treatments of this issue is the concentration of federal academic awards, by institution and by state.[2] In 1998, the top ten university performers accounted for 19.6 percent, the top 20 performers for 33.4 percent, the top 50 for 59.6 percent, and the top 100 for 81.9 percent of federally funded R&D. By state, in 1998, California accounted for 13.4 percent of federal academic R&D expenditures; the top five states accounted for 40.8 percent and the top ten states accounted for 60.0 percent of these expenditures. In contrast, the aggregate share of the ten states with the smallest share of federally funded academic R&D was 1.4 percent, while that of the lowest 20 states was 5.5 percent.

The political implications of these numbers are obvious. If all politics is truly local, at least 40 percent of the U.S. Senate has little stake in the budgetary fate of the National Science Foundation (NSF) or in those programs in other federal agencies that support university-based research. From a related vantage point, the current key leadership roles of senators from traditional "have-not" states, such as Mississippi, Montana, and South Dakota, readily convert NSF statistical series on academic R&D expenditures into a hot button policy issue.

Starting from a political perspective provides limited understanding of the processes that have produced current patterns of concentration, however. Also, to the extent that politics is not always local, with federal support of academic R&D provided to achieve national objectives--such as health, national defense, space exploration, environmental quality, and the pushing outward and filling in of the frontiers of science--data on relative shares by institution or state have little relevance if these patterns are consistent with an effective and efficient allocation of resources.

Moreover, the absolute level of federally-funded academic R&D has increased along with the absolute level of funds received by most universities and all states. Thus, to a degree, the issue of distributed funding represents what Chubin (1994) has termed "relative deprivation," that is, a "disjuncture between federal funding trends on the one hand, and institutional and personal angst on the other" (Chubin 1994: 122).

Finally, and most importantly, even if the political perspective is given its full due measure, it obscures policy options. To set distributed science as a goal in itself fails to comply adequately with Kerr's admonition to make this goal as compatible and reinforcing as possible with scientific merit.

2.   POLICY BACKGROUND

Congressional expressions of the desirability of a distributed system of funding of academic research are longstanding. In the early 1960s, for example, influential members of Congress threatened intervention into what was seen as a bicoastal domination of federal awards, lest the interests of other universities and states, especially at that time those in the Midwest, were not attended to (Greenburg 1967).[3] Hearings on the geographic concentration of federal R&D funds, including academic R&D awards, occurred as early as 1964 (U.S. House of Representatives 1964). These hearings raised claims of unfairness in peer-review mechanisms, harmful economic effects for have-not regions, and calls for equity that anticipate current briefs on behalf of increased dispersion.

Distributive objectives also appear repeatedly in rationalizations of earmarking or pork-barreling episodes. To their proponents, these practices are justified as a needed antidote to the malady of undue concentration of research awards caused by an "old boys network" of representatives from established institutions that are biased against less-prestigious universities (Martino 1992). The Office of Technology Assessment report (1991), *Federally Funded Research: Decisions for a Decade,* also questions in places the dominance of peer review procedures in allocating federal R&D funds. The report suggests that geographically based criteria might be justified to accomplish some of the national goals that are complementary to academic research such as broad-based opportunities for education.

Formative debates about NSF's structure also contained several sub themes related to distributive objectives. These included questions about the access of private universities to publicly provided research funds and whether support was to be supplied on a matching basis to qualified universities or based on awards and grants for specific research projects (Kelves 1977). In 1947, amendments to the bill to establish NSF were offered by Senator Russell (GA) and Senator William Fulbright (AR) that would have required use of a geographic distributional formula in the allocation of the Foundation's grants (Sapolsky 1994: 168). Reflecting these concerns about distribution, NSF's original mandate states that the Foundation is "to avoid undue concentration" as it pursues its objective of strengthening research and education in the sciences and engineering throughout the United States. This mandate is absent in the enabling legislation of most other federal agencies. In recent years, it has placed NSF in the forefront of federal efforts to stimulate the competitive research capabilities of universities in historically have-not states.

Concern about the distribution of federal academic R&D funds appeared most recently in the U.S. Senate, Veterans Affairs/HUD Committee Report, FY1999. The report directed NSF to develop a program for the establishment of three multi-investigator centers in the area of applied molecular biology, and to target development in such centers towards "universities and colleges that do not normally fall within the top 100 of NSF's survey of universities and colleges receiving Federal research support to overcome bias toward more established institutions" (Malakoff 1998: 1438). (The provision was not included in NSF's final appropriations bill.)

Pressures for greater dispersion on behalf of "have-nots"-both institutions and states—find counter-pressures in the interests of those institutions and states that have fared well under the current system of peer-reviewed allocation. Not surprisingly, Congress appears to wish to have it both ways. The recent U.S. House of Representatives Committee on Science (Ehler's) report (1998), *Unlocking Our Future: Towards a New National Science Policy,* for example, expresses an interesting blend of concern about concentration while offering a solution that not only re-emphasizes peer review and competitive processes, but also implies what Wildavsky (1979) has termed a "strategic retreat on objectives" for many states and institutions. After noting the concentrations of federal support of basic research in a small number of states, the report sets forth the normative objective that "all regions of the country ought to be able to share in the benefits of economic prosperity that flow from the fundamental research performed in universities," followed by the prescription, "That to accomplish this goal, it is important that colleges and universities in those regions of the country that have traditionally received little federal research funding be able to compete effectively for peer-reviewed federal grants" (pp. 32-33).

Its solutions, however, would appear to offer little comfort to those advocating major changes in the procedures or criteria for allocating funds. It proposes to have major research universities cultivate working relationships with less well-established research universities in areas of "mutual interest and expertise," and recommends, perhaps more pungently, that "Less research-intensive colleges and universities should consider developing scientific or technological expertise in niche areas that complement local expertise and contribute to local economic development strategies" (p. 33).

This last strategy has been and is in fact the core element in the strategies of many less research-intensive universities (and states). It is, however, a strategy almost fated to perpetuate the concentration of federal academic R&D funds as it implies a retreat from basic research and the new funding opportunities offered by recent increases in the NIH and NSF budgets.

3.   ANALYTICAL AND DEFINITIONAL ISSUES

Science is the classic "winner take all" contest, in which those at or near the top receives a disproportionate share of the rewards, in whatever form they come (Frank and Cook 1995). To the scientists who establish priority claims to breakthrough discoveries and inventions comes most of the laurels;

to those who come after to refine, adapt, extend, correct or apply these discoveries come reputations for "solid" work.

Elite science and distributed science as frequently set against one another in national policy debates confound the two concepts that Steven Stigler has termed intellectual competition and competition for financial resources (Stigler 1994). Elite science relates to the first mode of competition.[4] It is the outcome of competitions in the primacy of ideas as embodied in proposals and publications. Elite is an adjective used to describe the upper end of a quality scale. Elite status is both a prize sought and a prize won.

Elite science (and engineering) is simply another way of identifying those researchers who have been responsible for the major scientific and technological advances of the current generation, or those who are believed to have the potential to generate further such advances. Elite science flows from the disjointed nature of scientific advance and the laurels given to those who are first to perceive or prove these breaks.[5]

Distributed science, by way of contrast, focuses primarily on the competition for resources. It essentially constitutes a claim that funds should be allocated to researchers on criteria other than scientific merit (as gauged at a point in time).

The case for distributed science rests on two major claims. First, a more "equitable" distribution of resources, by geography or institution, is necessary for full intellectual competition to occur. Second, that national (and regional) objectives related to economic development, education, and diversity complement or transcend those associated with scientific excellence or leadership in international comparisons-objectives (and claimed outcomes) typically associated with an emphasis on intellectual competition alone.

Underlying both concepts, albeit with differing interpretations, is the competitive character of American higher education, and its claims on federal and state governments for support of academic research (Rosovsky 1990). This competitive structure is repeatedly highlighted as one of the distinguishing institutional features that have led to U.S. world leadership in science, scholarship, and graduate education (Clark 1995,Kerr 1994).

Competition also is a fundamental force in the conduct of science. As Sacks has observed:

> The history of science and medicine, in a sort of Darwinian way, has taken much of its shape from intellectual and personal competitions that force people to confront both anomalies and deeply held ideologies; and competition, in the form of open debate and trial, is therefore essential to its progress. When these debates are open and straightforward, a rapid resolution and advance can sometimes be achieved (Sacks 1995: 161).

The two concepts of elite (or distinguished) science and distribution are related, of course, but generally under the peer review/scientific merit system, quality comes first, followed by funding. Quality (of proposals, investigators, or institutions) is the single most important factor in the award of the grants, which are the basic elements around which R&D expenditure series are formed.[6] Federal (and other external) funding, though, is often the indispensable input into the performance of the research that leads to or reinforces assessments of individual, program, or institutional quality. Implied in calls for (more) distributed science, is that use of mechanisms other than peer review or competitive processes are needed to cause researchers to shift location (by institution or state).

Smith (1990) aptly stated the *de facto*, pragmatic compromise that has emerged from the tensions between the objectives of elite and distributed science. Citing data which reveal that about 80 percent of all citations are accounted for by 15 percent of the publishing scientists, Smith writes: "Science is, in this sense, an elitist activity. Ways must be found, therefore, to see that those who can use resources most productively get them. But this cannot be done in a fashion that incorporates a privileged status for any institution or principal investigator" (Smith 1990: 179). The solution, according to Smith, has been a system largely based upon review of individual proposals by relevant peers. It "is the only practicable way to reconcile the elite character of science with the norms of American democracy. The system is, furthermore, a self-correcting and evolving procedure, not a static and rigid formality" (Smith 1990). The U.S. system in fact stands in contrast to funding policies in other countries (e.g., France, Germany, Great Britain, and Japan) that target block grants to institutions or chairs (Clark 1995). In these settings, there is truly an "established" elite.

Two further issues require elaboration. The first issue is the unit of analysis in this case, between institutions and states. The two units of analysis are not the same. Increases in the number of research-intensive universities, by definition, serve to make the distribution of federal academic R&D (or indeed of total academic R&D) funds less concentrated (although not equally at all points in the distribution). Increases in the number of research-intensive universities, however, may or may not make the distribution of federal academic R&D funds among states less concentrated.

The second is the distinction between have and have-not institutions (and states) on the one hand, and between elite or distinguished, strong, good, and adequate academic programs, and marginal and weaker academic programs on the other. As documented below, National Research Council (NRC) ratings point to the presence of a substantial percentage of marginal academic programs. Current policy debates about choices between elite and distributed science often fail to set a quality floor in the specification of distributed science.

4.   EMPIRICAL FINDINGS

Different measures exist to assess the distribution of research intensity, research quality, and level of R&D performance among U.S. universities and states. The concepts underlying each measure are different. These differences in findings multiply if further distinctions are made between absolute and relative levels of funding, between levels and trends, between federal and non-federal sources of institutional and state funding of academic R&D, and between total and per-capita measures.

Four "core" measures are reviewed here: (1) number of research-intensive universities; (2) distribution of academic R&D expenditures by institutions; (3) distribution of academic R&D expenditures by state; and (4) NRC ratings of academic program quality. Each measure is subject to technical limitations; some of these limitations are noted in passing but not fully detailed.

4.1   Research-Intensive Universities

The number of American universities defined as "research-intensive" has increased continuously since the end of World War II. While informed observers spoke of some 30 institutions that "really mattered" in the immediate post-war years (Kaysen 1969), the number is currently put at about 175-200, allowing for "indistinct" boundaries among types of higher education universities and colleges (Noll 1998, President's Council of Advisors on Science and Technology 1992).

Employing the Carnegie Classification system, which arrays institutions by the level of federal research funding and the number and breadth of their Ph.D. programs, the number of doctorate-granting institutions increased from 173 in 1970 to 236 in 1994 (Table 1).[7] Within this group, the number of institutions in the Research University I category increased by 52 to 88, or by 69 percent. The number of Research University II institutions first increased, from 40 in 1970 to 47 in 1976, then fell in 1987 to 34, and then increased to 37 in 1994. This pattern reflects the advance of former Research University II institutions into Research University I and the slower rate with which institutions in the Doctorate-granting categories I and II moved into more research-intensive categories.

While the upward movement through the Carnegie ranks was nationwide, major differences exist in the number of research-intensive universities among states and in the size of these institutions. Table 2 lists the number of Research University I and Research University II universities by state according to the 1994 Carnegie survey. Seven states had neither a Research University I nor Research University II university in that year, while California had 12 such universities. New York had 11 and Massachusetts had seven. Graham and Diamond's (1997) analysis also indicates that the "have" states, notably California and New York, were those in which newly established universities were most likely to achieve Research University I status.

RUI status is based on minimum cutoff points; the maximum is unbounded. Thus, the size of research activities ranges greatly among Research University I institutions. For example, West Virginia and Wisconsin each have one Research University I, but in 1998, federal academic R&D expenditures at the University of Wisconsin were $241M, while at West Virginia University, the total was $25M.

4.2   Distribution of Federal Academic R&D

The degree of concentration in federal academic R&D expenditures (as with the total academic R&D expenditures) declined between 1980-1998 (Geiger and Feller 1995; Feller 1999). The share of federal academic R&D received by the 10 top performing institutions fell from 23.2 percent in 1980 to 19.6 percent in 1998; the share of the top 50 fell from 64.3 percent to 59.6 percent; and the share of the top 100 fell from 84.9 percent to 81.9 percent (Table 3).

Significantly, almost all of the loss in share occurs among the top 10 institutions, with some additional loss also experienced by the universities ranked 11-30.[8] Outside of the top 30 institutions, however, each successive group of 10 received approximately the same share in1998 as it did in 1980. Thus, the data point either to a leveling of the peaks or, more accurately, to a rise in the relative elevation of the neighboring institutions, narrowing the distance between them.[9]

A portion of the loss in share of the top 100 institutions is captured by the next set of 100 institutions, as their aggregate share increased from 12.5 Percent in 1980 to 14.2 percent in 1998. Institutions outside the top 200 have made the residual gain. This last increase also reflects the increasing number of institutions receiving federal R&D funding from 555 in 1975 to 648 in 1985, and then to 882 in 1995 (Jankowski 1998). Indeed, one of the most striking features of the U.S. higher education system has been the spread of research (and graduate degree) ethos across institutions.

Table 1. Number of Institutions, by Carnegie Classification

	1970			1976			1987			1994		
	Total	Public	Private	Total	Public	Private	Total	Public	Private	Total	Public	Private
Doctorate-granting institutions	173	109	64	184	119	65	213	134	79	236	151	85
Research University I	52	30	22	51	29	22	70	45	25	88	59	29
Research University II	40	27	13	47	33	14	34	26	8	37	26	11
Doctorate-granting University I	53	34	19	56	38	18	51	30	21	51	28	23
Doctorate-granting University II	28	18	10	30	19	11	58	33	25	60	38	22
Comprehensive universities and colleges*	456	309	147	594	354	240	595	331	264	529	275	254

Source: *A Classification of Institutions of Higher Education, 1994 Edition* (New York: The Carnegie Foundation for the Advancement of Teaching), Tables XIBXIV.

* Category redefined as master's colleges and universities in 1994.

Table 2: Distribution of Research University I and II, by State, 1994

	Research University I	Research University II	Total
Alabama	1	1	2
Alaska			0
Arkansas		1	1
Arizona	2		2
California	10	2	12
Colorado	2		2
Connecticut	2		2
Delaware		1	1
District of Columbia	2	1	3
Florida	3	1	4
Georgia	3		3
Hawaii	1		1
Idaho		1	1
Illinois	4	1	5
Indiana	2	1	3
Iowa	2		2
Kansas	1	1	2
Kentucky	1		1
Louisiana	1	1	2
Maine			0
Maryland	2		2
Massachusetts	5	2	7
Michigan	3		3
Minnesota	1		1
Mississippi		2	2
Missouri	2	1	3
Montana			0

Table 2. Distribution of Research University I and II, by State, 1994 (continued)

	Research University I	Research University II	Total
Nebraska	1		1
Nevada			0
New Hampshire			0
New Jersey	2		2
New Mexico	2		2
New York	8	3	11
North Carolina	3		3
North Dakota			0
Ohio	3	2	5
Oklahoma		2	2
Oregon	1	1	2
Pennsylvania	5	1	6
Puerto Rico			0
Rhode Island	1	1	2
South Carolina		2	2
South Dakota			0
Tennessee	2		2
Texas	2	3	5
Utah	2	1	3
Vermont		1	1
Virginia	3		3
Washington	1	1	2
West Virginia	1		1
Wisconsin	1	1	2
Wyoming		1	1

Compiled from *A Classification of Institutions of Higher Education, 1994 Edition* (New York: The Carnegie Foundation for the Advancement of Teaching).

Table 3: Cumulative Percentage Shares, Federal Academic Research and Development Expenditures, Top 200 Institutions*

Institutions		1980	1990	1998
First	10	23.2	21.0	19.6
	20	38.5	35.7	33.4
	30	49.1	46.4	44.5
	40	57.4	54.7	52.8
	50	64.3	61.6	59.6
	60	69.9	67.7	65.5
	70	74.6	73.0	70.5
	80	78.7	77.4	74.9
	90	82.1	80.8	78.7
	100	84.9	83.9	81.9
	110	87.2	86.4	84.8
	120	89.2	88.6	87.0
	130	90.9	90.3	88.9
	140	92.3	91.9	90.4
	150	93.6	93.1	91.8
	160	94.6	94.1	92.9
	170	95.5	95.0	93.8
	180	96.3	95.7	94.7
	190	96.9	96.3	95.4
	200	97.4	96.8	96.1

Sources: Data for 1980 and 1990 are from the National Science Foundation, Division of Science Resources Studies, Federally Financed R&D Expenditures at Universities and Colleges, Fiscal Years 1980 and 1990. Available at <www.nsf.gov/sbe/srs/srsdata.htm>(webCASPAR categories by multiple sources.)
Data for 1998 are from the National Science Foundation, Academic Research and Development Expenditures: Fiscal Year 1998, Early Release Tables, Table B-33.
*Expenditures are excluded for The Johns Hopkins Applied Physics Laboratory.

Data in Tables 1 and 3 thus point to an increase in the number of research-intensive universities and to wider distribution of federal academic R&D funds. If this was all, the temptation would exist, as once sagely advised by Senator Aiken, to declare victory and move on to more pressing issues.

4.3   Distribution of Federal Academic R&D by State

Federally funded academic R&D increased from $4.1B in 1980 to $15.1B in 1998, or by 277 percent. This increase, coupled with the above noted spreading institutional base of this support, provided the basis for an increase in the absolute level of federally funded academic R&D in all states. Relative rates of growth vary considerably among the states, however. In the period 1980 through 1998, they range from a low of 18.5 percent in Alaska to a high of 583.7 percent in Nevada.

Clearly, if "have-not" states are to increase their relative share of federally funded academic R&D, their rates of increase must exceed the national average. Depending on the period chosen, approximately one-half of the states with the lowest share of federally funded academic R&D have achieved this condition, while one-half have not.

Table 4 presents data on growth rates in federally funded academic R&D for the 12 states (Alaska, Arkansas, Delaware, Idaho, Maine, Montana, Nevada, North Dakota, South Dakota, Vermont, West Virginia, and Wyoming) that ranked at the bottom of the state distribution in 1998. Each state had a share of 0.3 percent or less.

The data are presented for two periods: 1980 through 1998 and 1990 through 1998. Of the 12 states, three (Arkansas, Delaware, Montana) achieved growth rates higher than the national average in both time periods; three (Idaho, Nevada, and South Dakota) had growth rates above the national average in one of the two time periods; and six (Alaska, Maine, North Dakota, Vermont, West Virginia, and Wyoming) had growth rates below the national average in both time periods.

Several factors are acknowledged as common contributors to the low shares for these states: the most notable is a low population, and thus comparatively small higher education system. However, with the exceptions of Nevada, which has had burgeoning growth in its university system, and Alaska, which experienced a singular decline in federally-funded R&D funds between 1990-1998, it is difficult at present to specify aggregate socioeconomic variables that account for the differential growth rate patterns for the remaining 10 states.

For present purposes, the relevant empirical finding is the disconnect between the growth in the number of research-intensive universities and the dispersion of federally- funded academic R&D funds among institutions, on the one hand, and the continued skewed distribution of these funds among states, on the other. While concentration remains less pronounced at the upper end of the state distribution, there is little "trickle down" to states at the lower end of the distribution.

Table 4: Growth Rates in Federally funded Academic R&D

State	Percent Share Federally-funded Academic R&D, 1998	Percent Rate of Growth of Federally-funded Academic R&D	
		1980-1998	1990-1998
Arkansas	0.3	429.7	117.4
Nevada	0.3	583.7	34.0
Alaska	0.2	18.5	-1.2
Montana	0.2	344.2	185.4
Delaware	0.2	267.0	91.5
Idaho	0.2	239.3	64.0
West Virginia	0.2	168.7	9.2
Vermont	0.2	170.3	3.0
North Dakota	0.2	236.6	11.4
Wyoming	0.1	185.7	45.9
Maine	0.1	123.7	44.0
South Dakota	0.1	145.4	70.2
National Average		266.6	56.0

Source: Compiled from National Science Foundation/SRS, Survey of Research and Development Expenditures at Universities and Colleges, Fiscal Year 1998.

4.4   Quality Ratings

Evidence on the distribution of "quality" science among U.S. universities can be inferred from the NRC ratings for 1993. These ratings cover 3,634 research-doctorate programs at 274 U.S. universities. Of these programs, about 62 percent were rated as distinguished, strong, or good; 19 percent as adequate; and 19 percent as marginal or below, based on the scholarly quality of program faculty. By field, 65 percent of the programs in biological sciences, 63 percent in engineering, and 59 percent in physical sciences and mechanical were rated on these categories. These figures point to a considerable distribution of faculty quality across institutions, although again not necessarily across states.

Changes in quality ratings also occur, but in both downward and upward directions. Table 5 presents data on the relative distribution of research-doctorate programs by quartile of such programs appearing in both the 1982 and 1993 studies. Of the 468 programs in the top quartile in 1982, 399 remained in that quartile, 66 moved downward to the second quality grouping, and three fell to the third quartile. Of the 487 programs in the bottom quality quartile in 1982, 363 remained in that quartile in 1993, 113 moved up into the third quartile, and 11 moved up into the second quartile.

This pattern of movement reinforces data contained in Geiger and Feller's (1992) study of the movement of specific institutions among declines and quartiles of academic R&D funding. These up and down patterns of movement in quality ratings and R&D expenditure classes reinforce the earlier description of the U.S. research university system as a highly competitive market system. As in competitive markets, firms can grow in both absolute and relative size, but they also can contract in both absolute and relative size.

Table 5: Relative Distribution of Research-Doctorate Programs Appearing in Both the 1982 and 1993 Studies by Mean Rating of "Scholarly Quality of Program Faculty" in Quality Grouping[*]

Quality Grouping in 1982	Quality Grouping in 1993				
	Top	**2nd**	**3rd**	**4th**	**Total**
Top	*399*	66	3	0	468
2nd	81	*287*	103	12	483
3rd	8	112	*248*	110	478
4th	0	11	113	*363*	487
					1,916

Source: National Research Council (1995), Table 3-8: 42.
[*]Based on average ratings for "Scholarly Quality of Program Faculty"

NRC ratings are useful, too, in highlighting the difference between relative and absolute levels of quality, or alternatively, the relationship between distributed science and quality science. The relationship may be thought of in terms of the shape and position of a frequency distribution. It matters less whether the distribution is normal or skewed, and more whether the lowest ranking segments fall into categories ranked either as adequate or less than adequate.

The latter situation more closely represents the findings of the NRC survey. Data on the frequency and quality scores of those programs falling into the bottom quartile of NRC rankings were compiled for Chemistry, Mathematics, Physics, Electrical Engineering, Mechanical Engineering, and Biochemistry and Molecular Biology-the five largest programs in the survey's broader categories of Physical Sciences, Engineering, and Life Sciences. The relevant data are presented in Table 6. The mean scores for these quartiles were, respectively, Chemistry, 1.38; Mathematics, 1.30; Physics, 1.73; Electrical Engineering, 1.47; Mechanical Engineering, 1.74; and Biochemistry and Molecular Biology, 1.38. These scores correspond to marginal, or less than adequate, points on the NRC scale.[10]

Table 6: Quality Ratings of Universities in the Bottom Quartile, Selected Fields

	Number of Institutions in NRC Study[a]	Number in Bottom Quartile of Quality Ratings	Mean Quality Value for Fourth Quartile	Mean Value for All Programs
Chemistry	168	49	1.38	1.26
Physics	146	37	1.73	2.82
Mathematics	135	40	1.54	2.77
Biochemistry and Molecular Biology	187	49	1.30	2.60
˙Electrical Engineering	126	32	1.47	2.63
˙Mechanical Engineering	110	28	1.74	2.75

Source: Compiled from National Research Council (1995), *Research Doctorate Programs in the United States* (Washington, DC: National Academy Press), Table 2-2: 20, and Appendix Tables K-5, K-8, L-2, L-5, L-7, and N-1.

These low quality ratings raise the question of the desirability of increased attention to distributed science when its academic peers rate the underlying performance capabilities of an institution and its departments so low. Put differently, even if national interests justify explicit attention to a more distributed pattern of academic R&D funds, recipients need greater specification of the quality criteria, whether institutions or states, are to partake of federal R&D funding.

5.   CONCLUSIONS

Empirical findings point to considerable increases in the number of research-intensive universities; a less concentrated distribution of academic research funds among the top 20, 50, and 100 institutions; and an increase in the number of academic programs receiving good and above quality ratings between 1982 and 1993.

These increase trends reflect several key factors in the U.S. higher education system: its competitive underpinnings, the recurrent rise (nanoscience, information technology) and fall (mining engineering) of fields of scientific and technological knowledge shifts in demographic and economic activity that have provided state governments with incentives and resources to strengthen traditional flagship universities and to convert regional universities into research-oriented institutions, the increase in the number of Ph.D. trained faculty, and the dominance of research-intensive, Ph.D.-granting institutions as the standard for institutional and individual excellence among university administrators and faculty. The system for individual and institutional advancement remains highly flexible and open to newcomers. Sufficient examples of notable advances by particular institutions in research funding and quality of program, as well as losses in funding and quality of former leaders, exist to suggest that competitive processes are at work. Moreover, the threat from competitive forces as much as the actual changes produced by these forces keeps universities in a constant effort to be among the best and brightest.

Whether the system will become more or less concentrated, given trends in all forms of external funding of academic R&D and the specific policies of institutions and states, is an open question. Interviews with university leaders and presidents point to highly divergent perspectives on the future structure of the American university system (Feller 1998). The scenarios offered encompass Darwinian shakeouts of the large number of existing institutions, leading to the establishment of a small (er) number of mega-research universities, to statements from upwardly mobile institutions that they are here to stay as major performers of R&D, and to yet more expansively rhetorical statements from representatives of aspiring institutions of "why not '400' (research) universities."

The overarching policy issue questions, then, may not be stylized choices between elite and distributed science, and rather the following:[11]
1. Will increased concentration or dispersion occur in the absence of explicit changes in federal academic R&D funding policies?
1. If a more distributed system of academic R&D than that which currently exists or is projected in the absence of changes in federal policy is desirable, what is the most efficient method for achieving this objective?
2. Is an increase in the number of research-intensive universities either needed or efficient?

ACKNOWLEDGEMENTS

I am indebted to Rolf Lehming for his comments on an earlier version of this chapter and to Darryl Farber and Robert Poulton for their assistance in compiling the data for this chapter. Responsibility for the chapter is mine alone.

An earlier version of this chapter was presented at the American Association for the Advancement of Science's 1999 Annual Meeting, Anaheim, California.

REFERENCES

Chubin, D. (1994). "How Large an R&D Enterprise?" in D. Guston and K. Keniston, eds., *The Fragile Contract*, Cambridge, MA: The MIT Press, pp. 118-144.

Chubin, D., and E. Hackett (1990). *Peerless Science: Peer Review in U.S. Science Policy*, Albany, NY: State University of New York Press.

Clark, B. (1995). *Places of Inquiry*, Berkeley, CA: University of California Press.

Feller, I. (1996). "The Determinants of Research Competitiveness Among Universities." in A. Teich, ed., *Competitiveness in Academic Research*. Washington, DC: American Association for the Advancement of Science. pp. 35-72.

Feller, I. (1998). "A Preliminary Assessment of the Strategies Used by Research Universities to Maintain and Enhance Their Research and Graduate Degree Competitiveness in a Period of Challenged Priorities and Austere Funding: II." Discussion paper prepared for the Social Science Research Council Workshop, "Boundaries of U.S. Higher Education Institutions and the U.S. Higher Education System."

Frank, R., and P. Cook (1995). *The Winner-Take-All Society*, New York: The Free Press.

Geiger, R., and I. Feller (1992). *The Dynamics of the Academic Research System: Institutional Change During the 1980s*. University Park, PA: Institute for Policy Research and Evaluation, The Pennsylvania State University.

Geiger, R., and I. Feller (1995). "The Dispersion of Academic Research in the 1980s." *Journal of Higher Education* 66: 336-360.

Graham, H., and N. Diamond (1997). *The Rise of American Research Universities*. Baltimore, MD: The Johns Hopkins University Press.

Greenburg, D. (1967). *The Politics of Pure Science*. New York: World Publishing Company.

Jankowski, J. (1998). "Statistical Data and Their Impact on University Research Efforts: Trends and Patterns of Academic R&D Expenditures." Presentation to the International Quality & Productivity Center's Conference of Performance Measurements for Research and Development in Universities and Colleges (Washington, DC), May 18-19.

Kaysen, C. (1969). *Higher Learning: The Universities, and the Public*, Princeton, NJ: Princeton University Press.

Kelves, D. (1977). "The National Science Foundation and the Debate over Postwar Research Policy, 1942-1945." *ISIS* 6 (68): 5-26.

Kerr, C. (1994). *Troubled Times in American Higher Education*, Albany, NY: State University of New York Press.

Malakoff, D. (1998). "Legislators Get Creative with New Crop of Earmarks." *Science* 4 (281): 1436-1438.

Martino, J. (1992). *Science Funding,* New Brunswick, NJ: Transactions Publishers.

National Research Council. (1995). *Research-Doctorate Programs in the United States,* Washington, DC: National Academy Press.

National Research Council. (1996). *Trends in the Early Careers of Life Scientists,* Washington, DC: National Academy Press.

National Science Foundation. (1991). *The State of Academic Science and Engineering,* Washington, DC: National Science Foundation, Division of Policy Research and Analysis.

National Science Foundation. (1998). *Science & Engineering Indicators-1998,* Washington, DC: National Science Board.

National Science Foundation. (1998). *National Patterns of Research and Development Resources,* Washington, D.C.: National Science Board.

Noll, R. (1998). "The American Research University: An Introduction." in R. Noll, ed., *Challenges to Research Universities,* Washington, DC: The Brookings Institutions.

Olson, K. (1998). "Total Science and Engineering Graduate Enrollment Falls for Fourth Consecutive Year." National Science Foundation Data Brief, December 17. Washington, DC: National Science Foundation.

President's Council of Advisors on Science and Technology. (1992). *Renewing the Promise: Research-intensive Universities and the Nation.* Washington, DC: Author.

Rosovsky, H. (1990). *The University: An Owner's Manual,* New York: W. W. Norton.

Sacks, O. (1995). "Scotoma: Forgetting and Neglect in Science." in R. Silvers, ed., *Hidden Histories of Science.* New York: New York Review Book. pp. 141-187.

Sapolsky, H. (1994). "Financing Science After the Cold War." in D. Guston and K. Keniston, eds., *The Fragile Contract.* Cambridge, MA: The MIT Press. pp. 159-176.

Smith, B. (1990). *American Science Policy Since World War II,* Washington, DC: Brookings Institution.

Stigler, G. (1994). "Competition." in D. Greenwald, ed., *The McGraw-Hill Encyclopedia of Economics,* New York: McGraw-Hill, second edition. pp. 531-536.

Stigler, S. (1994). "Competition and the Research Universities." in J. Cole, E. Barber, and S. Graubard, eds., *The Research University in a Time of Discontent,* Baltimore, MD: The Johns Hopkins University Press. pp. 131-152.

U.S. Congress, Office of Technology Assessment. (1991). *Federally Funded Research: Decisions for a Decade,* OTA-SET-490, Washington, DC: U.S. Government Printing Office.

U.S. House of Representatives, Committee on Science and Astronautics. (1964). *Geographic Distribution of Federal Research and Development Funds.* Report of the Subcommittee on Science, Research, and Development, 88th Congress, Second Session, Serial J. Washington, DC.

U.S. House of Representatives, Committee on Science. (1998). *Unlocking Our Future: Towards a New National Science Policy.* Report to Congress. Washington, DC.

Wildavsky, A. (1979). "Strategic Retreat on Objectives: Learning from Failure in American Public Policy." in *Speaking Truth to Power*, Boston, MA: Little, Brown. pp. 41-61.

---

[1] To highlight the character of these choices in their most direct form, this paper omits treatment of the appropriateness of criteria other than scientific merit in awarding federal academic R&D, or a detailed examination of the actual mix of competitive, formula, and earmarked allocations which in fact shapes distribution of academic R&D expenditures (U.S. Congress, Office of Technology Assessment 1991).

[2] Throughout this chapter, attention is focused on the distribution of federal academic R&D funds.

[3] "The failure to approve an accelerator for the Midwest would seriously compromise the prospects for approving a $250-million accelerator on the east or west coasts . . . . I say this not with any notion that there might be some kind of political retaliation. I say this from the standpoint of realism" (Senator William Proxmire [D-WI] to Jerome B. Wiesner, White House Science Advisor, 1963, as quoted in Greenburg 1967: 246).

[4] Elite is defined as a measure of achievement and standing in *The Random House Dictionary of the English Language*: "the choice or best of anything considered collectively, as of a group or class of persons." Elite may have pejorative connotations; elite segues into "elitist", which connotes anti-democratic behavior or status. The National Research Council (NRC) ratings of departments avoids the word elite and instead employs the term "distinguished" as the upper end of its 5-point rating scale. The implied opposite of elite is democratic or populist; the implied opposite of distinguished is undistinguished.

[5] As Sacks has observed, "Sudden bursts of discovery change the face of science, and these are often followed by long periods of consolidation, and, in a sense, stasis" (Sacks 1995: 170).

[6] As noted in an NSF overview of patterns of distribution: ". . . the Federal academic R&D funds allocation process results in a higher concentration of funding in some states than in others . . . . When R&D funding distribution is examined in the basis of various demographic and human and institutional resource factors, however, it can be said to be "fairly" distributed in spite of the geographic concentration . . ." (National Science Foundation 1991: 113).

[7] Table 1 abstracts from changes in definitions used to classify universities across Carnegie surveys.

[8] This is a substantial shift in dollar terms. The federal government funded $14.7B of the $25.2B in academic R&D conducted in FY1998. One percent of federally-funded R&D amounts to $147 million; the 5 percentage point drop in shares of the top 10 institutions, amounts to $735 million.

[9] Analysis of the mobility of institutions in and out of deciles for the period 1980–1990 is presented in Geiger and Feller (1992).

[10] Conceptually, each institution in the bottom quartile could have had scores of 2.0 or above, which could reflect a quality floor of adequate. This is not the case. The far larger number of institutions in the bottom quartile for the above five fields had quality scores below 2.

[11] According to some observers, the 175 to 200 current research institutions already represent too large a number, and could be reduced with little if any net loss to the nation's scientific and scholarly enterprise, and possibly a gain to its educational and public service missions. Recent national studies also have raised questions about career prospects, at least in academia, for Ph.D. trained scientists, suggesting, that the national need for distributed opportunities for advanced education in scientific and engineering may be less than implicitly assumed (National Research Council 1998). Students seem to be heeding these cautionary predictions. Graduate enrollments in science and engineering have declined for four consecutive years, from 435,886 in 1993 to 407,644 in 1997 (Olson 1998).

INNOVATION POLICY AND ELECTRONIC COMMERCE

PART THREE

Chapter 10

The Commercialization of Internet Access
Lessons from Recent Experience

SHANE GREENSTEIN
Northwestern University

1. INTRODUCTION

When the National Science Foundation (NSF) commercialized the Internet between 1992 and 1994, it took what might be called a minimalist approach, allowing market forces to develop the technology. It was a grand experiment with markets, and, by some perspectives, an unusual way to develop infrastructure. This experience informs enduring questions about how commercial markets develop new services, a topic that is arising again today as policy makers try to forecast development in broadband markets.

Sufficient time has passed to begin to evaluate the initial record and its lessons. This chapter considers the development of one part of that infrastructure: the commercial access market. I provide an interpretative framework for understanding its development in the United States. I argue that understanding this market requires insights and frameworks from the economics of diffusion, adaptation, and industry evolution.

In brief, this framework helps explain why markets can develop new industries quickly and pervasively. It also explains why this one was especially exceptional in the speed of development. Such an analysis highlights several factors that were quite propitious for the historical diffusion of commercial Internet access. To be brief and overly simple, the NSF got it right, but they also got quite lucky.

Why was the NSF lucky? The economic thresholds for commercial dial-up service turned out to be low. So too were the economic thresholds for expanding service to new geographic territories. In such conditions, it is generally good policy to let decentralized markets do their work, developing infrastructure rapidly in this case, without much guidance from any central authority. Under such conditions commercial markets tend to provide near universal availability, which is precisely what resulted. There is, however, an open question whether this experience provides any or only limited guidance about the future.

On the surface the record of achievement is quite remarkable. Most recent surveys show that no more than ten percent of U.S. households get their Internet access from university-sponsored Internet access providers, the predominant provider of such access just five years ago. Today almost all users go to commercial providers (Clemente 1998), known as Internet Service Providers, or ISPs. As of 1997, this ISP industry was somewhere between a three and five billion dollar industry (Maloff 1997), and it is projected to be much larger in a few years.

What are commercial ISPs in practice? For the most part, they are firms that provide Internet access for a fee. Depending on the user facilities, whether it is a business or personal residence, access can take one of several different forms. It can involve dial-up to a local number or 1-800 number at different speeds, or direct access to the user's server using one of several high-speed access technologies.

Right after commercialization in 1994, only a few commercial enterprises offered national dial-up networks with Internet access, mostly targeting the major urban areas. At that time, it was possible to run a small ISP on a shoestring in either an urban or rural area. These firms were devoted primarily to dial-up. Within a few years, however, there were dozens of well-known national networks and scores of less-known national providers covering a wide variety of dial-up and direct access. There were also many local providers of Internet access serving as links between end-users and the Internet backbone.

What factors shaped these developments? This chapter emphasizes eight factors:
1. There was an uneven maturity to applications which had commercial value;
2. There was a loosely coordinated diffusion process;
3. A significant set of activities involved intermediary functions;
4. Access approached geographic ubiquity due to low economies of scale;
5. National, regional and local ISPs specialized in different markets niches;
6. There were several fleeting business opportunities;
7. Adaptive activity is not yet a fleeting business opportunity;
8. Different firms pursued different strategies for offering new services.
These are discussed below in turn.

2. INTERPRETING DEVELOPMENTS IN THE MARKET FOR ACCESS

2.1 Uneven Maturity in Applications Which Had Value to Commercial Users

Internet access technology is not a single invention, diffusing across time and space without changing form. Instead, access technology is embedded in equipment that uses a suite of communication technologies, protocols and standards for networking between computers. This technology obtains economic value in combination with complementary invention, investment, and equipment.

When the electronic commerce first developed based on TCP/IP standards, it was relatively mature in some applications, such as e-mail and file transfers, and weak in others, such as commercial infrastructure and software applications for business use. This was because complementary Internet technology markets developed among technically sophisticated users before migrating to a broad commercial user base, a typical pattern for new information technology (Bresnahan and Greenstein 1999). The invention of the World Wide Web in the early 1990s further stretched the possibilities for potential applications, exacerbating the gap between the technical frontier and the potential needs of the less technically sophisticated user. As it turned out, commercial markets focused attention on that less sophisticated user, a market opportunity for large scale, simple and potentially profitable access services.

2.2 A Loosely Coordinated Diffusion Process

Unlike the building of every other major communications network in the United States, Internet access was built in an extremely decentralized market environment. Aside from the loosely coordinated use of a few *de facto* standards, (e.g., World Wide Web), government mandates after commercialization were minimal. ISPs had little guidance or restrictions. They had the option to tailor their offerings to local market conditions and to follow entrepreneurial hunches about growing demand.

As a technical matter, there was little barrier to entry into the provision of dial-up access. This was the first obvious adaptation of Internet technologies to commercial use. As a result, commercial factors, and not the distribution of technical knowledge among providers, largely determined the patterns of development of the basic dial-up access market immediately after commercialization.

By historical standards, this situation was relatively uncommon. It is much more typical for decentralization not to matter so much in the early years of a technology. Typically, a primitive technology cannot find uses in more than a few commercial applications, with the technical developments acting as a bottleneck on commercial experiments. Hence, only a few firms bother to experiment.

In Internet access markets, however, because so much technical development took place before commercialization of the Internet, the technical limitations were less binding for most firms. Commercialization coincided, therefore, with thousands of new entrants, each making decisions with a plethora of goals in mind, each using similar technical capabilities.

2.3   A Significant Set of Activities Involve Intermediary Functions

The commercial transaction for Internet access between user and vendor could be brief but most often it was repetitious and on going. A singular transaction arose when the vendor performed one activity, setting up Internet access or attaching Internet access to an existing computing network. If the ISP also operated the access for the user, then this on-going operation provided frequent contact between the user and vendor, and it provided frequent opportunity for the vendor to change the delivery of services in response to changes in technology and changes in user needs.

In many cases, an ISP was better educated about the technological capabilities than the user. In effect, the ISP sold that general knowledge to the user in some form that customized it to the particular needs and requirements of the user. At its simplest level, this provided users with their first exposure to a new technological possibility while educating them about its potential.

More often, access went beyond exposure to electronic commerce, and included the installation of equipment, provision of maintenance and training, as well as undertaking application development. These types of transfers of knowledge typically involved a great deal of nuance, often escaped attention, and yet, were essential to developing electronic commerce as an on-going and valuable economic activity.

2.4 Access Approached Geographic Ubiquity Due to Low Economies of Scale

The U.S. telephone system has one pervasive feature, distance-sensitive pricing at the local level. In virtually every part of the country, phone calls over significant distances (i.e., more than thirty miles) engender per-minute expenses. Hence, Internet access providers had a strong interest in reducing expenses to users by providing local coverage of Internet access for a local population. Unmet local demand represents a gap between what is technically possible and what many users desire. This is a commercial opportunity for an entrepreneurial ISP, a situation where building appropriate facilities could meet local user needs.

We have constructed a series of maps that illustrate the density of ISP locations across the continental U.S. at the county level for the fall of 1996 and the fall of 1998.[1] As the maps show, ISPs tend to locate in all the major population centers, but there is also plenty of entry into rural areas. The maps also illustrate the importance of changes over time. A commercial provider covered many of the areas, which had no coverage in the fall of 1996, in the fall of 1998. Many of the areas that had competitive access markets in the early period were extraordinarily competitive by the end of the period.

Indeed, Downes and Greenstein (1999) show that more than 92 percent of the U.S. population had access by a short local phone call to seven or more ISPs. No more than five percent lacked such access. Almost certainly the true percentage of the population without access to a competitive dial-up market is much lower than five percent.

This near ubiquitous supply of competitive access had two consequences for policy discussions. It raised the issue that some areas of the country characterized by low population densities would be left behind. However, the initial success of commercial markets in rural areas limited the crisis atmosphere; this was not anything like rural electrification in the 1930s. That is, the supply of the Internet access diffused to all but a small percentage of the U.S. population and to all but the lowest density areas; there was no obvious need for a huge or pervasive government subsidy for the industry. Rather, targeted intervention, if it became an issue at all for local governments, quickly turned to discussions about a specific town or a specific county.

Second, in most parts of the country, access to the commercial Internet was determined by demand factors—whether users thought the benefits exceeded the expenses, whether users could learn how to use the Internet quickly, and so on. This also directed policy discussion away from its traditional emphasis on subsidizing the building of infrastructure everywhere and towards the development of access in areas where demand was low, such as low-income areas (see Weinberg 1999; Werbach 1997). In other words, it does not end the debate about the development of universal access, but emphasis shifted from examinations of supply to examinations of demand.

2.5   National, Regional and Local ISPs Specialized in Different Markets Niches

An unexpected pattern accompanied this rapid growth in geographic coverage. First, the number of firms maintaining national and regional networks increased over the two years. In 1996, most of the national firms were recognizable; as they were such firms as IBM, AT&T, Netcom, America Online (AOL), and other established firms who entered the ISP business as a secondary part of their existing services, providing data services to large corporate clients, often with global sub-divisions. By 1998, many entrepreneurial firms maintained national networks and few of these new firms were recognizable to anyone other than a consultant for users of this service.

There was also a dichotomy in growth paths of entrepreneurial firms who became national and regional firms. National firms grow geographically by moving to major cities across the country and then progressively to cities of smaller population. Firms with a regional focus grow into geographically contiguous areas, seemingly irrespective of its urban or rural features.[2]

As it turned out, most of the coverage of rural areas comes from local firms. In 1996, the providers in rural counties with under 50,000 population were overwhelmingly local or regional. Only for populations of 50,000 or above, does the average number of national firms exceed one. In fall of 1998 the equivalent figures was 30,000, indicating that some national firms had moved into slightly smaller areas. In other words, a local or regional provider largely does Internet access in small rural towns.

What should one conclude? It does not pay many large national providers to provide dial-up service for the rural home whereas many small local firms in other lines of business (e.g., local PC retailing) can afford to add Internet access to their existing business. It may also be the case that the local firm may have an easier time customizing the Internet access business to the unique needs of a set of users in a rural setting.

2.6   There Were Several Fleeting Business Opportunities

The geographic patterns illustrated in these maps indicate that the commercialization of the Internet created an economic and business opportunity for providing access. However, this opportunity was fleeting at best. The costs of entry into low quality dial-up access were low, and commercially oriented firms filled voids in specific places. For any firm with national ambitions, coverage of the top 50 to 100 cities in the U.S. was a fleeting advantage and quickly became a necessity for doing business. For any local or regional firm in an urban market, many competitors arose.

It seems unlikely that any future ISP will get much strategic advantage from the scope of its geographic coverage of its dial-up network in the U.S. For any firm with a local or regional focus, there are countless others within every urban area providing similar services, so geographic scope does not provide unique position relative to competitors. There was much debate among ISPs about the value of providing geographically dispersed service. Some ISPs deliberately chose to focus on small geographic region and develop a reputation at that local level. Other ISPs attempted to create national brand names, focusing their attention on expanding their franchises or geographic reach.

2.7   Adaptive Activity Is Not Yet A Non-Fleeting Opportunity

A significant set of activities of many providers in the commercial Internet market involves adaptation. What activity comprises adaptation?[3] Adaptation services involve one of several activities: monitoring technical developments, distilling new information into components which are meaningful to unfamiliar users, and matching unique user needs to one of many new possible solutions enabled by advancing technical frontiers. Sometimes adaptation involves heavy use of the technological frontier and sometimes not. In general, it depends on the users, their circumstances, their background, their capital investments, the costs of adjusting to new services, and other factors which influence the match between user needs and technological possibilities.

Adaptation does not simply happen. In information technology, the agents of change typically come from one of several groups: end-users within an organization, professional staff (such as the MIS group) within an organization, or third party vendors outside the organization (Bresnahan and Greenstein 1999). If the end-users or their staffs do much of the adaptation activity, it becomes an extension of other operations and investments. In contrast, if third parties sell related services to users, adaptation may take several different forms: equipment, consulting about business processes, or both. In the case of diffusion of Internet access, third parties, ISPs, took on a central role.

ISPs commercialized their adaptive role through offering new services. Services at ISPs can be grouped into five broad categories: basic access, frontier access, networking, hosting, and web page design (see Appendix of Greenstein 1999, for precise definitions).

- *Basic access* constitutes any service slower than and including a T-1 line. Many of the technologies inherited from the pre-commercial days were classified as complimentary to basic access, not as a new service.

- *Networking* involves activities associated with enabling Internet technology at a user location. All ISPs do a minimal amount of this as part of their basic service in establishing connectivity. However, an extensive array of these services, such as regular maintenance, assessment of facilities, emergency repair, and so on, are often essential to keeping and retaining business customers. Note, as well, that some of these experimental services could have been in existence prior to the diffusion of Internet access; it is their offering by an Internet access firms that makes them a source of differentiation from other ISPs.

- *Hosting* is typically geared toward a business customer, especially those establishing virtual retailing sites. This requires the ISP to store and maintain information for its access customers on the ISP's servers. Again, all ISPs do a minimal amount of hosting as part of basic service, even for residential customers (e.g., for email). However, some ISPs differentiate themselves by making a large business of providing an extensive array of hosting services, including credit-card processing, site-analysis tools, and so on.

- *Web Design* may be geared toward either the home or the business user. Again, many ISPs offer some passive assistance or help pages on web page design and access. However, some offer additional extensive consulting services, design custom sites for their users, provide services associated with design tools and web development programs. Most charge fees for this additional service.

- *Frontier access* includes any access faster than a T-1 line, which is becoming the norm for high-speed access to a business user. It also includes ISPs that offer direct access for resale to other ISPs or data carriers; it also includes ISP who offers parts of their own "backbone" as a resale to others.[4]

2.8   The Rise of Different Strategies for Offering New Services

By 1998, different ISPs had chosen distinct approaches to developing access markets, offering different combinations of services and different geographic scopes. Table 1 shows the results of surveys of the business lines

Table 1: Services of ISPs

Category definition	Most common phrases in category	Weighted by service territory	Original Sample	Analysis Sample
Providing and servicing access though different channels	28.8, 56k, isdn, web TV, wireless access, T1, T3, DSL, frame relay, e-mail, domain registration, new groups, real audio, ftp, quake server, IRC, chat, video conferencing, cybersitter TM.	28967 (100%)	3816 (100%)	2089 (100%) *Rural ISPs 325 (100%)*
Networking Service and Maintenance	Networking, intranet development, WAN, co-location server, network design, LAN equipment, network support, network service, disaster recovery, backup, database services, novell netware, SQL server	8334 (28.8%)	789 (20.6%)	440 (21.1%) *Rural ISPs (11.0%)*
Web Site Hosting	Web hosting, secure hosting, commercial site hosting, virtual ftp server, personal web space, web statistics, BBS access, catalog hosting	8188 (28.2%)	792 (20.7%)	460 (22.0%) *Rural ISPs (13.8%)*
Web Page Development and Servicing	Web consulting, active server, web design, java, perl, vrml, front page, secure server, firewalls, web business solutions, cybercash, shopping cart, Internet marketing, online marketing, electronic billing, database integration	13809 (47.7%)	1385 (36.3%)	757 (36.2%) *Rural ISPs (23.3%)*
High Speed Access	T3, DSL, xDSL, OC3, OC12, Access rate>1056K	15846 (54.7%)	1059 (27.8%)	514 (24.6%) Rural ISPs (12.0%)

Unit of observation is ISP-Area codes, as found in *the list*. For example, if an ISP offers local dial-up service in 29 area codes, it will be 29 observations. If that same ISP offers high-speed access then it will count as 29 cases of high-speed access. Unit of observation is an ISP in small number of territories. See text for precise definition. Top number is for all 2089 ISPs in analysis sample. *Italicized* percentage is for the 325 ISPs found primarily in rural areas.

of 3816 Internet service providers in the United States that advertise on *the list* in the summer of 1998 (see Appendix of Greenstein 1999). Virtually every firm in the samples provides some amount of dial-up or direct access and basic functionality, such as e-mail accounts, shell accounts, IP addresses, new links, FTP and Telnet capabilities, but these 3816 seem to under-represent both very small and quasi-public ISPs (e.g., rural telephone companies).

Of the 3816 ISPs, 2295 (60.1 percent) have at least one line of business other than basic dial-up or direct Internet access. Table 1 shows that 1059 provide high-speed access, 789 networking, 792 web hosting, and 1385 web page design. There is some overlap (shown in Figure 1): 1869 do at least one of either networking, hosting or web design; 984 do only one of these three; 105 do all three and frontier access. The analysis sample has similar percentages. For such a cautious method, this reveals many different ways to combine non-access services with the access business.[5]

These activities contain much more complexity and nuance than Table 1 can display. ISPs in urban areas have a greater propensity to offer new services. The largest firms also offer services at slightly higher rates, which is also consistent with the hypothesis that urban areas (where large firms are disproportionately located) tend to receive higher rates of new services.

3.   A SUMMARY OF EARLY DEVELOPMENTS IN THE ISP MARKET

3.1 Why Did the Internet Access Business Grow Quickly?

Stated simply, exclusive use did not lead to isolated technical and operational developments. Hence, commercializing Internet access did not give rise to any difficult or insolvable technical and operational challenges. This technology grew among researchers and academics without being isolated from commercial suppliers. That is, the technology grew without generating a set of suppliers whose sole business activity involved the supply of uniquely designed goods for military or government users. Related to this was the fact that the basic needs of researchers and academics were not so different from early commercial users. Hence, simple applications of the Internet invented for academic users—such as e-mail and file transfer using phone lines—migrated to commercial uses without much technical modification.

3.2   Why Did Geographic Ubiquity Arise?

To summarize, the Internet access business was commercially feasible at a small scale and, thus, at low levels of demand. This meant that the technology was commercially viable at low densities of population, whether or not it was part of a national branded service or a local geographically concentrated service. Internet access was feasible in a wide variety of organizational forms, either large or small. Small-scale business opportunities thrive with the help of entrepreneurial initiative, which tend to be widespread throughout the U.S.—including many low density and isolated cities in otherwise rural areas, which were largely not being served by national firms. Small-scale implementation also depended on the presence of high quality complementary local infrastructure, such as digital telephony, and interconnection to existing communications infrastructure. These too were available throughout most of the U.S. due to national and local initiatives to keep the communications infrastructure modern.

3.3   Why Did the Internet Access Business Not Settle into a Common Pattern?

Adaptation activity thrived. Part of this was due to the absence of technical and commercial challenges, which allowed low cost experimentation of the technology in new uses, new locations, new market settings, new applications and in conjunction with other lines of business. More generally, the technology was quite malleable as an economic unit. It could stand-alone or become part of a wider and integrated set of functions under one organizational umbrella. Such malleability motivated experiments with new organizational forms for the delivery of access services, experiments that continue today. Finally, the invention of the World Wide Web brought new promise to the technology. Not only did new business models arise to explore and develop its primitive capabilities and expand them into new uses, but also it motivated firms to experiment with Internet access along side new business lines.

3.4   Why Did Market Forces Lead to Such Extensive Growth?

Adaptive activities have immense social value when there is uncertainty about technical opportunities and complex issues associated with implementation. In addition, as the literature on general-purpose technology would put it, co-invention problems are best situated with those who face them. In this case, those actors were ISPs who knew about the unique features of the user, the location or the application. More generally, commercialization transferred development into an arena where decentralized and unregulated decision-making took over. This was precisely what was needed to customize Internet access technology to a wide variety of locations, circumstances and users. Removing the Internet from the exclusive domain of NSF administrators and employees at research computing centers brought in a large number of potential users and suppliers, all pursuing their own vision and apply it to unique circumstances. In addition, it allowed private firms to try new business models, restructuring in ways that nobody at the NSF could have imagined.

3.5   In What Sense Did the NSF Get Lucky?

As it turned out, the NSF commercialized the Internet access industry at a propitious moment, during the growth of an enormous new technological opportunity, the World Wide Web. Competitive forces sorted through new uses of this opportunity in particular places, enabling some businesses to grow and unsentimentally allowing unsuccessful implementations to fade. To be sure, non-profit institutions, such as the World Wide Web Consortium or the Engineering Internet Task Force shaped some of these developments but profit motives still played a prominent role. Said another way, had NSF stewardship over the Internet continued there would have been some experimentation at computing centers found at universities and government laboratories, but it would not have been possible to replicate all the exploratory activity that did arise in commercial markets.

4.   CHALLENGES FOR THE NEAR FUTURE

The diffusion of broadband access, the widely forecast future for this industry, seems to be taking on a more typical pattern for new technology, where technical and commercial constraints shape the pattern of diffusion. It is unclear what the lowest cost method for the delivery of broadband services will be. It is also unclear what type of services will motivate mass adoption of costly high-speed access to the home. There are technical limitations to retrofitting old cable systems and with developing DSL technology over long distances. It is unclear how many people will be willing to pay for such high-speed services. These uncertainties cloud all forecasts. However, unlike the past, there will not be two decades of incubation of broadband technology by only government-sponsored researchers. Hence, there is no reason to anticipate anything like the speed of diffusion found in the dial-up market, nor take for granted that ubiquity will arise as easily (for more, see Weinberg 1999 or Werbach 1997).

This observation would seem, at first blush, to suggest that this history sheds little light on the future—that past and future challenges are too unique to their time for comparison. However, that conclusion is a bit hasty. Looking forward in the ISP industry, it is possible to identify some technical, commercial and structural challenges which resemble those of the past and which will alter the contours of behavior and outcomes. I will discuss some of these, cognizant that restructuring is still taking place and changing sufficiently fast, so that any discussion runs the risk of becoming obsolete as soon as it is written.

4.1   Lesson 1: The Past Does Offer Guidance for Understanding Patterns of Restructuring

The names of the firms may change and so too may the specifics of the strategies, but the absence of uniformity in the development of Internet access business models should persist into the future. New applications for Web technology are still under development because the technology has potential beyond its present implementations. Not all local markets will experience the same type of competitive choices in access, nor should they. Not all vendors will see the same opportunities and these differences arise for sound economic reasons. Users with more experience still adopt applications closer to the frontier, while users with less experience still demand applications that are more refined. Web technology enables these differences to manifest in new directions and it is not obvious which implementation will succeed with either type of user. In other words, most of the economic fundamentals leading to structure challenges have not disappeared; hence, experimentation with new business models will probably continue.

4.2   Lesson 2: The Subscription Model of Internet Access Will Continue to Change.

Commercial markets inherited an organizational form from their academic ancestors, modifying it slightly for initial use. There is no reason to presume that it will maintain the same operational structure under competitive pressure. Indeed, it is presently under competition from a variety of alternate business models that use dial-up access to subsidize another activity. There are already hints of these potential changes as some ISPs charge very little for access and make up for the lost revenue with other services, such as networking, hosting or web design. AOL has successfully combined access with its "walled garden" of content and AT&T appears intent on pursuing a unique approach to combining content and access. Other recent innovative firms include Netzero.com, which is the most successful to date of many firms who have tried to provide access for free and garner revenue through sales of advertising. There are also many other such experiments altering the explicit definition of basic service, embedding it with more than e-mail, but also with games, streaming, linking and so on, which has the effect of changing the pricing structure too. It is not crazy to predict that access, by itself, could become absorbed into a bundle of many other complementary commercial services, slowly fading as a stand-alone service, as it existed in the academic domain.

4.3   Lesson 3: The Economics of Internet Diffusion Lie Behind Much of the Digital Divide.

Internet access diffused more easily to some users and in some locations. The margin between adoption and non-adoption has become popularly known as the "digital divide." If some of these outcomes are understood as temporary results of a young diffusion process, then many of the differences between those with virtual experience and those without can be framed as the by-product of the economic factors shaping this diffusion episode. Within business the important factors influencing adoption are the density of the location of the business, the availability of basic computer support services nearby, and a firm's previous investment in IT. At the home the important determinants are availability (which is influenced by density) as well as the same factors behind the diffusion of PCs: age, education and income especially, and race for some income levels. It follows, therefore, that policies aimed at digital divide issues, such as the E-rate program, should not address those factors that are only temporary and will resolve themselves through market forces without government intervention. Instead, government programs should target factors which are likely to be more durable over time and which lead to division in adoption behavior; such as density of location, income, education and race.

4.4   Lesson 4: Geographic Pervasiveness Introduces New Economic Considerations.

There is one additional reason to expect the typical business model to remain unsettled. Geographic pervasiveness has entered into calculations today and it was not a relevant consideration at the outset of commercialization. The pervasiveness of the Internet across the country (and the developed world) changes the economic incentives to build applications on top of the backbone, and alters the learning process associated with its commercial development. All ISPs now depend on each other on a daily level in terms of their network security, reliability and some dimensions of performance. Many new applications—virtual private networking, voice telephony over long distances, multi-user conferencing, some forms of instant messaging, and gaming—require coordinating quality of services across providers. It is still unclear whether new business models are needed to take advantage of applications that presume geographic pervasiveness. If so, it will provide a commercial advantage to the firms with national backbones and assets. Pervasiveness also changes the activities below the backbone in the vertical chain. It has altered the scale of the market for supplying goods and services to the access industry, altering the incentives of upstream suppliers, equipment manufacturers or middle-ware software providers, to bring out new services and inventive designs for the entire network. This factor was also not present in the academic network and it is unclear how it will influence the structure of the industry moving forward.

4.5 Lesson 5: Is There a Need for New Communications Policy for the New Millennium?

Until recently, the pace of technical change in most communications services was presumed to be slow and easily monitored from centralized administrative agencies at the state and federal level. It is well known that such a presumption is dated, but it is unclear what conceptual paradigm should replace it. This chapter illustrated how vexing the scope of the problem will be. In this instance, ISPs addressed a variety of commercial and structural challenges with little government interference, but under considerable technical and commercial uncertainty. This occurred because many legacy regulatory decisions had previously specified how commercial firms transact with the regulated public switch network. These legacy institutions acted in society's interest in this instance, fostering experimentation in technically intensive activities, enabling decentralized decision-making to shape commercial restructuring in specific place and times. To put it simply, it was in society's interest to enhance the variety of approaches to new commercial opportunities and existing set of regulations did just that. However, going forward it is unclear whether these legacy institutions are still appropriate for other basic staples of communications policies, such as whether a merger is in the public interest, whether incumbent cable firms should be mandated to provide open access, whether communications infrastructure should be subsidized in under-served areas, and whether Internet services should be classified as a special exemption, immune from taxation and other fiscal expenses. Hence, this industry is entering an era where market events and unceasing restructuring will place considerable tension on long-standing legal foundations and slow regulatory rule making procedures.

REFERENCES

Bresnahan, T. and S. Greenstein. (1999). "Technological Competition and the Structure of the Computing Industry." *Journal of Industrial Economics*, Winter.

Bresnahan, T. and M. Trajtenberg. (1995). "General Purpose Technologies: Engines of Growth?" *Journal of Econometrics* 65: 83-108.

Clemente, P.C. (1998). *The State of the Net: the New Frontier*, New York: McGraw-Hill.

Downes, T. and S. Greenstein. (1998). "Do Commercial ISPs Provide Universal Access?" in Sharon Gillett and Ingo Vogelsang, eds., *Competition, Regulation and Convergence: Selected Papers from the 1998 Telecommunications Policy Research Conference*, Lawrence Erlbaum Associates.

Greenstein, S. (1999). "Building and Developing the Virtual World: The Commercial Internet Access Market." http://skew2.kellogg.nwu.edu/~greenste/research.html

Griliches, Z. (1957). "Hybrid Corn: An Exploration in the Economics of Technological Change." *Econometrica* 25: 501-522.

Hargadon, A.B. (1998). "Firms as Knowledge Brokers: Lessons in Pursuing Continuous Innovation." *California Management Review*, Spring, 40: 3.

Maloff Group International, Inc. (1997). "1996-1997 Internet Access Providers Marketplace Analysis." Dexter, MO, October.

Rosenberg, N. (1977). *Perspectives on Technology*, Cambridge, U.K: Cambridge University Press.

Weinberg, J. (1999). "The Internet and Telecommunications Services, Access Charges, Universal Service Mechanisms, and Other Flotsam of the Regulatory System." *Yale Journal of Regulation*, Spring.

Werbach, K. (1997). "Digital Tornado: The Internet and Telecommunications Policy." FCC, Office of Planning and Policy Working Paper 29, March.

---

[1] See www.kellog.nwu.edu/faculty/greenstein/images/htm/Research/Maps/mapsep1.pdf and www.kellogg.nwu.edu/faculty/greenstein/images/htm/Research/Maps/apoct98.pdf, respectively. Colored areas are counties with providers. White areas have none. For further documentation of these methods, see Downes and Greenstein (1999) or Greenstein (1999). The fall 1996 data cover over 14,000 phone numbers for over 3200 ISPs. The fall 1998 data cover over 65,000 phone numbers for just under 6000 IPS.

[2] Some ISPs, in interviews, reveal that this growth was in response to customer requests for accessing networks (e-mail mostly at first) when these customers traveled outside their primary area. More recently, it is also common to have ISPs discuss the possibility of developing a large customer base for purposes of "selling the base" to a high bidder in some future industry consolidation.

[3] Adaptation has long been a topic of discussion in the economics of technology and economic growth (Bresnahan and Trajtenberg 1995), as well as in the management of technology (Hagedoorn 1998). Studies of this behavior have antecedents in classic studies about diffusion and learning by Griliches (1957), Rosenberg (1977) and many others.

[4] Speed is the sole dimension for differentiating between frontier and basic access. This is a practical choice. There are a number of other access technologies just now becoming viable, such as wireless access, which are slow but technically difficult. Only a small number of firms in this data are offering these services and these are coincident with offering high-speed access.

[5] One of the most difficult phrases to classify was general "consulting." The vast majority of consulting activity is accounted for by the present classification methods as one of these three complementary activities, networking, hosting and web-design.

Chapter 11

Economic Geography and Policy in the Network Age
A Survey of Data, Analysis, and Policy

DANILO PELLETIERE
George Mason University

G. CHRIS RODRIGO
George Mason University

1. INTRODUCTION

The Internet is undoubtedly changing the world in some remarkable ways. Governments that have wielded regulatory and fiscal power within national and sub-national borders are compelled to deal increasingly with global and "spaceless" transactions. The Internet is fast becoming the first and most important medium of information access. This is also true of research in science, technology, social science, and the generation and diffusion of all systematic codified human knowledge.

With this transformation have come all manner of predictions about the Internet's impact on economic geography. Advocates of a "New Economy" suggest that reducing the costs of information will increase economic efficiency at unprecedented rates. Since there is little difference in the costs of distributing digital information to anyone connected to the Internet, whether they are next door or across the globe, these observers have further predicted the death of distance, (Cairncross 1997, Economist 2000c) and that advantages from location will largely disappear. Furthermore, they argue that the benefits of having people connected to the network far outweigh the costs of connection, so that Internet access will be extended almost universally (Krugman 1999, Kling 1999). On the other side, there are those who warn of a growing digital divide. To these observers, the Internet is more likely to exacerbate economic and geographic inequalities than help to overcome them (Benton Foundation 1998). The objective of this chapter is to survey the empirical evidence on how the Internet is re-shaping the spatial patterns of our economies and the resulting policy implications. We provide a brief review of the burgeoning literature in this area and attempt to separate the substantive economic and policy issues from hyperbole.

The clear indication from the evidence presented here is that the Internet will significantly influence spatial patterns of economic development. There is little evidence, however, to suggest that the impact of the Internet on economic geography will be as profound as many might have us believe. More than any previous communications technologies, the Internet has the potential to distribute more information, more quickly to a vast international network of users. This is creating new economic opportunities and income streams. However, both new and familiar problems of location-based inequality are also emerging. This is true of the dispersion and distributions of Internet access itself, the so-called digital divide, but also in the spatial distribution of costs and benefits among those who are connected.

A principal concern of this review is to highlight the important policy issues that emerge in relation to the heterogeneous social and geographic distribution of the Internet and its benefits. We argue that if potential social welfare from this revolutionary new technology is to be maximized, then tough policy options have to be faced and significant public investments made in pursuance of policy objectives.

The next section identifies the features of the Internet, which make it qualitatively different from previous information and communications technologies. Section three provides a review of the quantitative measure of the Internet's impact. Section four follows with a review of the growing empirical literature on the economic geography of the Internet. Section five concludes with an examination of the regional policy implications of the Internet.

2.   WHAT IS THE INTERNET?

The Internet may be best analyzed as a trinity of internationally extensive network of networks. The first of these is the physical network of communication links, computers and other hardware, controlled by Internet-specific software. These determine the capabilities and geographic reach of the network. The second is the information content that resides at the various nodes and the flow of this information between Internet users. The third is the network of users themselves. Users connect with one another from their offices, homes, or other venues to obtain and distribute information. Based on these connections, they make decisions that affect their economic and social behavior in the real world outside.

The embryonic elements of the Internet appeared in the ARPANET, originally designed in the late 1960s to serve as a communication network for defense-related organizations in case of a nuclear attack. Other researchers and academics soon realized the potential of this network. In the mid-1980s, the National Science Foundation (NSF) created a similar, parallel network called the NSFNET to connect its supercomputer centers. The NSFNET adopted the TCP/IP protocol of the ARPANET, to bring into being the primary U.S. backbone. This was soon joined by many other high-speed, TCP/IP fiber-optic backbones maintained by private, for-profit enterprises. In the 1990s, particularly with the development of the World Wide Web and the Mosaic Web browser in 1993, the Internet evolved rapidly from its mainly academic origins to become a major medium for international commercial activity and popular culture (MacKie-Mason and Varian 1997, Lange 1999, Comerford 2000).

2.1   The Internet as a Physical Network

In one respect, therefore, the Internet is a complex but hierarchical network of heterogeneous local, regional, national, and international communications networks, linking together a wide variety of computers located at its nodes.[1] These communication networks are made up of copper cables, fiber-optic lines and wireless communications linkages, connected through routers and other devices that process, store and re-direct standardized packets of digital data. The hardware of the Internet is controlled by means of software packages designed specifically for it, which facilitate the transfer of the digital data between the various computer nodes. The hardware and software are of primary concern to technical specialists who design and maintain the network (Lange 1999, Comerford 2000).

The throughput of the network is determined not only by the capacity of the hardware, but also by the efficiency of the software that controls and regulates the hardware.

2.2   The Internet as an Information Network

The second component of the trinity of networks that constitute the Internet is the set of digitally encoded information sources located at the nodes of the physical network. For most users, the Internet is not the physical network of components. It is instead defined by the information content that they can access, manipulate and distribute on-line. It is the accessibility of information and the links they find or are able to create from one source of information to the next that make up their view of the Internet. Since the information received on-line often appears nearly instantaneously, whether sent from an adjacent site or one halfway across the globe, the information network of the Internet appears to be both spaceless and seamless. Most users are not aware of the geographic extent of the physical infrastructure or of the existence of the various communication protocols and other software and hardware, which provide their seamless and spaceless connections.

2.3   The Internet as a Network of People

The third, and perhaps most important, element of the Internet trinity is the network of people located beyond the hardware and information networks' myriad nodes. The information that is transmitted over the Internet's physical infrastructure influences the behavior of individuals, firms and organizations and changes the nature of the interactions between them.

The Internet is changing the way old relationships are conducted and new relationships are made. The critical advance of functionality brought about by the Internet for the individual user is the expansion of *effective workspace*. The user gains the potential to access up-to-date[2] product, price or other information that was previously distant or even unattainable. The point is pithily stated by Vincent Cerf (2000), a co-inventor of the Internet: "When I have a question, I find myself turning first to the Net - I don't go to the library, to my bookshelf, to the telephone. Only if I can't find it on the Net do I start poking around in some of the older resources." As an increasing array of goods are advertised and ordered on-line without spatial lags in consumer awareness, the *effective local market area* for users has also been increased.

2.4   The Economics of the Internet

Before the genesis of the commercial Internet in the early 1990s, telephones, facsimile machines and overnight express delivery, not to mention telegraph, radio and television were already mitigating the impact of physical distance on information flow in the economy. The question arises why the Internet is widely considered such a revolutionary advance.

The importance of the Internet derives from its greatly increased data transfer efficiency. It is capable of providing previously existing and separate services as a single, coherent bundle with significantly lower hardware requirements. Since these services and many information goods are available through a single relatively affordable device such as a home computer, and information can be sent through a single pipe such as a telephone line or TV cable, they are provided at greatly reduced cost.[3].

The Internet's ability to host a large number of simultaneous information transfers derives from its use of packet switching technology. Packet switching is distinct from the circuit switching technology used in telephone links. A telephone call nails up a dedicated connection that lasts until the end of the call. This is highly inefficient since a normal conversation, with many lulls and breaks, does not use up the full capacity of the dedicated connection. The data stream in an Internet transmission is instead broken up into many small packets, and sent along any available path by the system of routers. Since line capacity is not dedicated to any single connection, this system, introduced in earlier data communication technology, makes much more efficient use of available communication capacity.[4] In practical terms, this has meant that the Internet allows users to receive and send complex video, text, and voice communications to anywhere the telephone network reaches. It has not only reduced the cost of sending information previously sent over other channels, it has also created new and broader opportunities to combine media and information from various locations and sources for personal, public and commercial consumption.

In simple economic terms, lowering the cost of information should increase the demand for it. This in turn generates additional costs (and new types of costs) as available network capacity is absorbed, new information is demanded, and people change behavior based on the new technology.

For example, providing access to the network itself creates substantial costs for service providers. Laying cables, installing routers, erecting the wireless infrastructure and other means of providing and increasing Internet capacity, all require heavy investment. Given the unitary fee structures of most Internet Service Providers (ISPs), only agencies that provide infrastructure services or regulate the constituent hardware/software networks worry about underlying technologies and the costs of providing them at specific locations. During the Internet's early development period, capacity and processing speeds kept well ahead of rising demand. Now, however, as Internet commerce grows, delays may involve significant extra costs and communication that is more reliable has to be assured.

In some ways, then, the hardware and software network of the Internet operates like a system of roads or other network infrastructure: no matter how sophisticated the software and hardware, the capacity to handle traffic will always be limited. Transmission throughput will always be limited by the lowest-capacity link along any route. In the current system, the bottleneck is often the local phone system and especially the last mile of copper cabling. Though rapid advances in technology will continue to expand capacity and reduce transmission costs,[5] demand on the Internet is also expanding apace. In recent years the number of users has expanded at over 50 percent per annum (Adamic and Huberman 1999, Lange 1999, Comerford 2000). As capacity is reached, free riding on public networks will have to be confronted (Huberman and Lukose 1997). More immediately, recent denial of service attacks and viruses such as the ILOVEYOU worm, that send undesired communication from unwitting hosts, have revealed that issues of malicious consumption must be addressed. Therefore, congestion and local bottlenecks will be a continuing irritant requiring ever-increasing investment in the hardware and software components of the Internet.

The costs associated with creating and updating on-line information is not trivial. While the costs of distributing updated information are reduced, the demand for such information is also increased. As numerous governments and non-profit organizations are discovering, on-line public information requires subsidization. Furthermore, as more information and interaction are provided to the public, even more is being demanded. Hence, some new funds for staff positions and Internet related tasks have to be allocated even as the Internet replaces old technology jobs.

Privately operated public information sites face the same dilemma. Though the Internet enables firms to reach a wide market with up-to-date information, they also must compete more than ever on the quality and the timeliness of the information they provide consumers. One option is cross-subsidies from other aspects of the business. Otherwise, on-line information itself must generate revenue. While a large amount of privately provided advertising currently supports information, an increasing number of services are subscription or membership based.[6] Thus, access to the Internet no longer provides access to all its information. There is now a sharper distinction between providing access to the hardware/software network and access to specific information networks.

Finally, one needs to consider how information received over the Internet influences human behavior. The popular vision is of people substituting interaction over the Internet for more costly personal travel or substituting digitally delivered goods for hard copies that would otherwise have to be produced and physically picked up or delivered. It is equally likely, however, that new information will create new demands and indeed complement rather than substitute for existing demand for travel or physical goods (Gaspar and Glaeser 1998). In simple terms, while we are coming to understand the technical capabilities of the Internet, we do not yet fully understand how human beings will fashion its use.

It is also important to remember that the Internet is built up as a network of networks, not as a network of individual connections. Any profit-oriented company will make its most lucrative connection first,[7] i.e. where the highest number of paying users can be reached for the lowest capital outlay. These are likely to be the centers of highest population density, given that human populations are unevenly distributed across the globe. Once the first tier of largest and most easily reached centers is connected, a firm will move to second tier sites, and so on. As the population size of each successive metropolitan region declines, the expected returns from investment will also likely stagnate and then decline.[8] However the fixed costs of incorporating each new region may not significantly decline. In fact, since metropolitan areas themselves tend to be clustered, and the population density within clusters tends to decline with population levels (i.e. from urban to rural settlement patterns) the fixed costs of connecting smaller user networks may even rise as marginal returns from the addition of new users decline

A final issue is that people need information that they cannot only see, but that they can understand and respond to (Kling 1999). Not only are population densities unevenly distributed across space; so also are levels of income and education as well as languages and other socio-demographic characteristics. These may constitute further sources of decreasing returns as networks grow. The original members in a network are likely to be quite similar; with the ARPANET this was government researchers, the U.S. Military, and government contractors. As the network grows, however, new members are increasingly different from the original set and the costs of communicating with and benefiting from each additional member (or network) rise. In other words, simply being able to provide or receive information from new members is not enough: the information must be used in a way that provides value to the network. This is referred to as the costs of overcoming the last inch.[9]

A more specific source of diminishing returns is that as membership of the commercial Internet grows, the levels of affluence of its new members are likely to decline. Though less affluent members may have a larger impact on some markets than the affluent ones, their aggregate impact on Internet-linked economic transactions will likely be progressively smaller.

Thus, along with new opportunities come new costs to be considered. The question that arises is whether the benefits of the Internet outweigh the costs. There are new costs from *expanding* the physical and information networks' capacities to meet rising demand, but there are also additional costs deriving from *extending* the network, that have to be considered. Do the marginal private benefits of expanding and extending the network outweigh the marginal private costs and therefore, is the growth of the physical Internet self-sustaining? Do the marginal benefits to society exceed the marginal social cost, thereby justifying continued public involvement and regulation?

The purpose of considering the Internet, as a trinity of networks is to better understand and differentiate between the various benefits and costs associated with the growth of the Internet. On the one hand the combination and integration of heterogeneous information sources and users into a single network makes the Internet a revolutionary technology that is changing the way people interact with each other by providing unprecedented access to information for its users at relatively low costs. On the other hand, as the demand for such interaction increases, both access and capacity appear to be constrained by familiar factors such as the cost of physical investments and the costs of reducing irresponsible behavior. The next section considers the indicators that can be used to assess the extent of the software and hardware network, the information network, and the network of users separately. Section 4 considers how some of these indicators are being used in analysis.

3.   INDICATORS OF INTERNET ACTIVITY

This section focuses particularly on indicators that track the geographic distribution of the Internet and its effects. Using the Internet trinity, we look at ways of estimating the supply and demand of various types of information on the Net. Finally, we examine options for estimating the Internet's impact on the distribution of people and their consumption and production patterns. As is to be expected, it is relatively easy to develop indicators of characteristics and size for the hardware network. It is considerably more difficult to form estimates of the second two networks of the trinity.

3.1   The Hardware and Software Network

Obtaining indicators of the distribution of hardware components of the Internet is often quite straightforward. It is a matter of counting pieces of equipment, miles of cable, capacity and connectivity levels. These standard infrastructure indicators might be used for any telecommunications or infrastructure network. Immediately below, we examine some standard indicators of the physical distribution of the Internet that have emerged. However, within each class of hardware, there is a great deal of variability in size or capacity not captured by mere numerical aggregates. Further, the Internet is continually and rapidly evolving, with new higher capacity and quality components being added along with superior communication protocols and software. Invariably, some of this unevenness and dynamism are not well captured by simple snapshots of the physical infrastructure.

3.1.1 Number of Hosts

A number of providers such as Matrix Information and Demography Services (MIDS), the Internet Software Consortium (ISC) and others, provide a count of hosts. A host is a computer with an IP (Internet Protocol) address, which can be anything from a single home PC to a large server with multiple users, that is in relatively constant contact with the Internet. [10] While it is relatively straightforward to count the number of hosts, it is difficult to fix a particular host in a geographic location. Though these data are readily available, they must be used with caution or as part of a broader analysis (Moss and Townsend 1996, Kellerman 2000). Since there is much variation in the size and use of hosts, host counts are best considered a very rough indicator of Internet size (Zook 2000b).

3.1.2 Network Capacity and Performance

A more important indicator may be the level and location of Internet transmission capacity. Unlike a host count, this indicator says something about the potential of a particular node to transmit information. On the one hand, high information carrying capacity says little about whether this capacity is well used and for what purpose. On the other hand, low transmission capacity or complete lack of access, is a clear indication of poor accessibility. Moss and Townsend (2000a) point out, that given the nature of competition in the market for commercial Internet traffic, knowledge of the capacity installed and the nodes connected, reveal considerable information about the expected returns from linking particular geographic locations.

The most common indicators of Internet capacity are those that relate to the Internet backbone, the network of high-speed communication links that constitute the arteries of the Internet system in the United States and abroad. For example, we might simply count the number of backbone connections. Node-to-node transmission capacity is measured in megabits per second (Mb/s). Gorman (1998) and Moss and Townsend (2000a) use Mb/s capacity of existing backbones between U.S. cities as an indicator of regional connectivity. Moss and Townsend (2000a) found that in the spring of 1999 there were 39 such inter-metropolitan connections, whereas in the previous year there had been 29.

3.1.3 Price and Other Indicators

A number of recent studies have focused on price differentials relating to Internet access across regions and countries (OECD 2000, Booz Allen and Hamilton. 2000). As suggested earlier, one of the most attractive features of the Internet is its relatively low price. Since price can be a barrier to access even where ample capacity exists, the spatial distribution of prices constitutes important data for policy research. Prices can also be seen as an indicator of the capacity that is being effectively made available for consumption. Price data is most often collected by surveys; for example, Booz, Allen, and Hamilton surveyed people over 12 years old who said they used the Internet more than once a month (Booz Allen and Hamilton 2000)

Other useful indicators include computer usage and telephones penetration rates since Internet access is mostly over existing telephone lines with personal computers (Department of Commerce 1999). Surveys of related communication infrastructure, such as miles of fiber-optic cables, could also estimate the potential penetration of the Internet. A similar indicator is the number and type of firms that provide Internet access in a region (Greenstein 1998). This gives an indication of the market structure for Internet service as well as an indication of the types of services provided.

3.2   The Information Network

The physical infrastructure data says little about the information available on the Internet. Data on information production, consumption and distribution, however, are hard to come by. Network congestion and aggregate quality of service can be estimated easily. For example, a common Internet weather report provided daily by MIDS, uses average round-trip times (latencies) to about 4000 nodes, hosts, servers and routers throughout the world, to indicate aggregate congestion levels (Lange 1999). It is difficult, however, to pin down the flow of information more specifically, and such reports may be misleading (Lukose and Huberman 1999). Even when we know something about the flow of information between two nodes, there is no expedient or direct way to ascertain what was transferred, its value to the recipient, or if it was paid for. This makes the taxing of information products and services provided over the Internet somewhat challenging.

3.2.1   User Consumption Surveys

The primary way to collect information on how consumers use Internet-hosted information is user surveys that focus on tracking the nature of web-based information consumption. This means finding out who uses the Internet, what they do on-line and what motivates their Web-surfing. Many market research firms and research institutions such as NUA and Forrester Research,[11] carry out these surveys on a regularly basis, mostly for the largest metropolitan regions or entire countries.

One available public source of survey data on the Internet is the Computer Supplement to the Current Population Survey (CPS) conducted by the U.S. Census Bureau and the Department of Commerce.[12] The CPS supplement has asked Americans about computer and Internet related behavior on a nationwide basis periodically since 1989. Though this CPS data can be used for estimates of spatial patterns of use (Pelletiere and Rodrigo 1999), small sample sizes limit its usefulness for smaller metropolitan regions. A variation has used the CPS computer supplement to estimate the level of Internet use for a specific profession or other grouping. (Kolko 1999a) These data are then combined with local demographic information to develop estimates of Internet use in a local economy. This method, however, may obscure interesting interregional variations in Internet use.

3.2.2   Other Indicators of Information Access

It is possible to generate and collect hit rates for a site, the average length of stay, and other usage statistics for individual web pages. Such statistics tell us a great deal about the web surfing behavior of individuals, various aggregates, or even the average user (Huberman, et al. 1998, Adamic and Huberman 1999). Site-specific information along these lines can be valuable for commercial and policy decision-making. Many firms base their advertising decisions on hit-rates and related information gathered from such site-visit statistics. As with host counts, however, such data say little about the geographic locations from where these hits originated or what the value or utility of those hits were to the user. Obvious exceptions are sites that record an on-line sale and a delivery address for a good or service in a database. Another possible approach is the user-logs of ISPs. Adamic and Huberman (1999) use AOL user logs to study on-line behavior. This data might be linked up to subscription information to create a geographic database. The problem here is that such data is proprietary, and its use may raise privacy concerns.

3.2.3   Site Surveys

User surveys can also be used to infer information production patterns. Users can be asked whether they transmit e-mail, maintain their own websites, transact e-business and so on. In a process similar to the host count, it is possible to survey the content of Internet sites and web pages. These surveys can simply count the sites that contain a particular key word or words. Sites can also be classified further according to the variables of interest.[13] For example, a recent survey of over 850 million pages found that

42.6 million pages (or 5.0 percent) were related to sex. 36.8 million sites (4.5 percent) were related to education, and 34.7 million (4.2 percent) to music (Kellerman 2000). Obviously, this gives us only an aggregate glimpse of the information being produced for consumption on the web. It gives little insight into the actual usage of the sites.

It is possible to use this information to differentiate between geographic locations in a limited sense. One example is ZDnet's list of most wired cities and towns using the number of websites devoted to information about a particular city.[14]

3.2.4 Domain Names

One of the more interesting and robust indicators of Internet activity is the count of domain name registrations (Moss and Townsend 1997, Zook 2000a). A domain name is what most Web-users employ to track down particular site. Examples of domain names are netscape.com, gmu.edu, sierraclub.org or bild.de. Zook (2000a) argues that registering a domain name suggests a commitment to use the Internet "in a more sophisticated manner," and provides a rough indicator of sites where information is being produced for consumption on-line.

An interesting characteristic of domain names is that they can be used to aggregate sites according to their top-level domain name (TLD) classification such as .com, .org, .net, or .edu.[15] This provides a rough way of categorizing Internet sites. Zook (2000a, 2000b), for example, separates .com sites from non-commercial sites. A problem with this is that the above TLD format is used almost exclusively in the United States. In other countries, the country code such as .de or .jp. is most often used as the TLD. This dual standard complicates international domain name research (Zook forthcoming).

A further characteristic of domain names is that registrants are required to give a mailing address. Therefore, a domain name is nominally associated with a geographic location. There are two important caveats.

First, due to domain name speculation[16] many domain names may be registered but never used. Zook (2000b) controlled for observable signs of speculation, such as the words for sale in the registration address, or addresses where more than 25 domains are registered. This procedure removed 35,000 domain names, or 2 percent of the total number of names in his dataset.) Second, the mailing address given may not be the location where the Internet site is created, maintained or stored. Zook (forthcoming) compared the registration address of .com websites with entries in the CorpTech database of up-to-date firm office addresses and found that 84 percent matched at the city (three digit zip code) level. Hence, domain name registrations do appear to give a strong indication of the geographic location where information is being produced for the Internet and the physical location of firms active on the Internet.

3.3 The Network of Users

The Internet's influence on spatial patterns of production and consumption derives from the information made available to people in their roles as consumers, producers, and citizens. Its impact on firms and other organizations is similarly mediated. One approach has been to simply track changes in the location of various production and consumption activities over the period in which information and communications technologies have become more prevalent.[17] The problem as far as this survey is concerned, is that this addresses the impact of the information age on firms and other economic variables rather the Internet-specific impact.

An alternative approach might focus expressly on businesses or people known to be actively using the Internet.[18] More recently, there have also been some attempts at correlation and regression analysis that include on-line information consumption and use variables (Kolko 1999a and 1999b, Pelletiere and Rodrigo 1999).

Most studies confine analysis to information technology industries or industries that use information intensively.[19] Emerging evidence suggests that the impact of the Internet may be greatest in traditional sectors such as retailing, wholesaling, and business-to-business procurement (OECD 1998). Therefore, it may well be necessary to examine changes in employment, distribution systems, firm location, market extent and other factors across a broad range of industries.

4. EMPIRICAL STUDIES

Given the recent vintage of the Internet and lags in published population and economic data, this literature is in its infancy. Still a number of interesting and consistent findings emerge.

4.1 Studies of the Internet Physical Infrastructure

The empirical literature suggests that the penetration and reach of the Internet is widely differentiated over space. Though Internet access continues to expand rapidly, there is no clear evidence that network capacity or network access is becoming more evenly dispersed across regions. Rather, network connections, capacity, and density seem to be rapidly increasing in population centers and among specific population groups that are already central to the network and the economy. The gap between these locations and other regions would continue to grow.

In a study of Internet backbones Gorman (1998) found clear evidence of spatial differentiation in access and capacity. Simple binary connectivity, i.e. whether there is or is not a connection between two nodes, yields a simple four tier hierarchy with Washington, D.C., Chicago, and San Francisco in the first tier, Atlanta, New York and Dallas in the second tier and so on. The first tier cities appear to owe their position to their geographic location in the national network. Chicago, located in the middle of the country is a central hub and D.C. and San Francisco are coastal hubs for the network. D.C. also owes its position to the Federal origins of the network.

When network density, (i.e., the number of links between nodes), is considered, the gap between the top and bottom tiers widens. Seven cities are found to dominate the entire system. Another important finding is that, while LA is not important as a location in the national network (i.e., it is located at the periphery and therefore not a hub) its economic weight alone evokes strong demand to which the market has responded by providing numerous connections. By factoring bandwidth into his calculations to account for capacity of links between nodes, Gorman finds that the hierarchy based on network capacity becomes even more accentuated. He pushes the analysis further by separating out direct and indirect connections available in each city, affirming the dominance of the hub cities.

Gorman concludes that the factors shaping the geographic pattern of Internet infrastructure and the prominence of core cities are network centrality (based on geographic location), the role of the federal government (the original developer of the Internet), and the demand for Internet and information services in the local economy. Malecki and Gorman (2000) compared the rank order of population centers to the rank order of access to Internet capacity. While population is the best determinant of connectivity, economic, geographic, and historical factors are also important. Some cities such as Miami or Philadelphia are less connected than their populations would suggest due to these factors, while others such as Washington are more connected.

Gorman concludes (1998) that there is a potential for greater government involvement to provide universal service. Implicitly, Gorman is advancing the notion that as capacity is raised to match rising demand in a few large cities, market-driven investment would further accelerate demand in these self-same urban locations through positive feedback linkages, to the detriment of other, less-favored locations.

Moss and Townsend (2000) found that even as investment in backbone capacity rose, the same seven highly interconnected cities found by Gorman

(1998) continued to dominate national data networks. While the average capacity of inter-metropolitan backbone links increased 500 percent, the number of cities connected directly to the backbone increased by 45 percent from 72 to 105. The hierarchy of cities, however, did change slightly within tight bands. Among the top seven, for example, Dallas and Atlanta moved up, while Chicago and New York declined in relative terms. Washington, DC remained number one. Moss and Townsend found that economically distressed cities failed to keep pace. Overall, the gap between what Moss and Townsend (1996) call the leaders and the losers has been growing.

Greenstein (1998) looked at the geographic distribution of ISPs and came to a similar conclusion. Looking at location, the quality of service and the price of Internet access, characterizing over 14,000 local phone numbers that provided residents with local access through ISPs, he finds distinct economies of scale in the provision of Internet service. These economies occur in both the scale and quality of connections and the provision of value-added services. Obviously, these economies can only be achieved where there is sufficient traffic.

Similarly, the current costs incurred by ISPs derive from the provision of value added services such as websites, information updates and enhanced user interfaces. As digital information goods, once these services are developed and produced, they can be replicated an infinite number of times at negligible marginal cost. Therefore, concentrations of population and demand within the population are a distinct determinant of the ISP market structure, the number of firms, firm capacities, and the services they provide. This limits the spread of ISPs and access to Internet services in less populated areas. Even so-called national firms were providing access to less than 30 percent of the population in 1997, but most were represented in major metropolitan areas. Greenstein does not address the extent to which observed patterns are the result of existing telephone tariff structures, or the economics of capacity expansion or other localized costs.

The recent Department of Commerce report (1999: 81-88), *Falling Through the Net* finds that though telephone penetration was nearly the same (94 percent) in rural and urban areas in 1997, between 1989 and 1997 rural areas fell further behind in modem penetration and computer ownership, particularly for lower income and disadvantaged groups. Central cities lagged behind their suburban counterparts to a lesser degree.

In summary, the empirical evidence thus far seems to support the hypothesis that the economics of developing the physical network lead to decreasing (rather than increasing) returns over space given the lumpy and heterogeneous nature of the current population distribution and the operation of normal market mechanisms. Recognition of these rather disquieting patterns and trends, has led to the Federal Communication Commission

(FCC)'s rural broadband initiative and other recent efforts in Congress, private foundations, and elsewhere, to actively promote rural Internet access.

4.2   Studies of the Information Network

Having access to the Internet is not the same thing as using it. Accessing information available on the Internet is distinct from producing information for other peoples' consumption. A number of recent studies have tried to trace geographic patterns relating to information production and use; they suggest that Internet use is diffusing outward geographically.

According to the Department of Commerce (1999), the percent of non-Hispanic whites using the Internet in 1998 was 40.6 percent in urban areas and 31.3 percent in rural areas with even greater disparities among other races. Though overall the gap between rural and urban areas has grown between 1989 and 1997 (p. 85-86), Internet penetration (as proxied by modem ownership and e-mail use) is growing at a faster rate in some rural areas. This is occurring most notably in the Northeast where the percentage of rural households with e-mail is higher than that for urban ones (p. 105).[20]

The same cannot be said about information produced on-line. Zook (2000a, 2000b & 2000c) uses domain names as a proxy for information production. Comparing the concentration of addresses associated with .com domain name registrations across, states, metropolitan areas and cities, he finds them highly clustered around information content producing centers, related industries and areas in which associated employees actually live.

In making these comparisons, Zook employs a domain names to number of firms ratio that compares local to national concentrations. He calls it a firm specialization ratio, and it is similar to the location quotient of regional economics.[21] If a region has the same number of .com domains per firm as the nation as a whole, the ratio equals 1. A ratio greater than 1 indicates the region has a higher concentration of domain names than the nation. For example, San Francisco had a firm specialization ratio of 3.07 in 1998 -- three times more domains per firm than the nation as a whole. Similar concentration ratios can be developed from jobs, income or other data to yield further economic insights (Zook 2000a, 2000b, 2000c, Pelletiere and Rodrigo 1999).

Zook concludes that the Internet is not bringing about the elimination of place-based networks in favor of cyberspace. He too finds that New York, Los Angeles and San Francisco are centers for domain name activity, with a higher concentration of domains per firm than the national average. He also finds that some new second tier centers may be emerging in high technology regions such as Provo-Orem, Utah; Denver-Boulder-Greeley, Colorado; and Austin-San Marcos, Texas. When he reduces the scale of observation from metropolitan areas to cities, however, many smaller suburban cities, within the large first tier metropolitan regions mentioned above emerge as hot spots for domain name registrations. This suggests an even greater geographic concentration of Internet information production activity. Zook (forthcoming) concludes that this pattern is broadly replicated internationally with the existing international urban hierarchy of cities with New York, London and Tokyo dominating.

In these analyses, Zook expressly avoids raising the issue of causality. His analysis of domain names tell us where the decisions are being made to use the Internet as a more sophisticated tool to distribute information, but it may reflect the enduring underlying structure of these economies rather than changes brought about by the Internet itself.

4.3   Studies of the People Network

The capacity and use of the Internet is not evenly distributed nationally but primarily concentrated in a few large metropolitan areas. Internet content *production* appears to be even more highly concentrated in a few cities and even neighborhoods. Even though the Internet does not appear to be as space-transcending as we might have been led to believe, we need to ask whether it is a significant enough technology to change the places where people work, live and shop. The answer here appears to be yes.

Hamermesh and Oster (1998) test the impact of telecommunications on scholarly publications in Economics by tracing the location of the authors during the period before the paper was written (checked by interviews) and the impact of distance on the numbers of papers produced. They also check the impact of distance on the productivity of papers by tracing the number of subsequent citations realized by different types of papers. They find a sharp increase in the number of papers co-authored by authors who were not in the same metropolitan area during the four years before publication. They also found, however, that papers co-authored across a distance, received fewer subsequent citations and there has been no decline in their relative disadvantage between the 1970s and the 1990s. Papers co-authored in proximity are more successful in this sense; they have also been increasing in number over this period.

Gaspar and Glaeser's work (1996, 1998), a theoretical consideration of the substitution of electronic interaction for face-to-face interaction, asks whether the external benefits of proximity can be substituted for by on-line interaction at a distance. Though they conclude that the benefits of proximity are likely to be complemented by on-line interaction, they also find that the question is one that must be established empirically. They provide what they term suggestive evidence from historical data. Using Japanese data, they found that the use of telephones is highly correlated with proximity. They also find that since 1980, and the rise of facsimile machines and e-mail, business travel has increased significantly, suggesting that increased electronic communications leads to increased face-to-face interaction. There is also a high correlation between telephones and urbanization. They test this last relationship using Japanese, US, and international cross-sectional data as well as U.S. time series data. They conclude that as telecommunications capacity improves the demand for all types of interactions rises, indicating continued dramatic advantages from communicating and interacting in person.

Other research has also focused on the substitutability or complementarity of on-line interaction for geographically proximate interaction.

Based on earlier work by Glaeser, et al. (1992, 1997) on the growth of cities, Kolko (1999a, 1999b) sets out to empirically test whether proximity in cyberspace can substitute for physical proximity to customers, suppliers and employees. Kolko (1999a) considers whether the Internet has affected the location of information intensive industries in the service sector that have previously relied on face-to-face interaction. This is a sector that might be most influenced by the Internet.

In order to test the role of the telecommunications technology explicitly, Kolko (1999a) models changes in employment in the industry from 1977 to 1995 with suppliers and customers as independent variables. He uses the proportion of workers using computers for e-mail at work for that industry from the 1993 CPS survey, as an interaction term. Kolko concludes that firms with high information technology usage have moved farther away from customers and suppliers in the intervening 18 years relative to low information technology-use firms. Notable exceptions, however, are legal and management services firms. This might initially suggest that firms dispersed as information and communication technologies enabled them to become more footloose. However, the coefficient on the interaction term for workers using computers at work went up. According to Kolko, this result indicates that the presence of a qualified labor pool became more important during this period. It is inconsistent with the notion that the Internet allows workers to telecommute from great distances. Kolko concludes on balance that information technology has complemented the economic advantages of cities rather than substituted for them.

Kolko (1999b) considers three hypotheses for why Internet adoption is higher in cities. The first is the Gasper and Glaeser (1998) hypothesis that the Internet and other information and communications technologies are actually complements of face-to-face interaction. Second is that, while the Internet does substitute for face-to-face interaction, cities providing other advantages such as skilled labor and better infrastructure. The third hypothesis is that the Internet substitutes for long but not short distance communication, so that it disproportionately benefits those cities that are in relative isolation.

Kolko uses the number of .com domains per 1000 people as the dependent variable in his model. As the independent variables, he has used industry mix (percent of workforce in programming occupations), education and income, physical telecommunications infrastructure (fiber-optic to copper wire ratio), and the average distance between metropolitan area residents and persons outside the metropolitan area, as well as population, federal procurement, and industry controls. He also tests the relationships in 1998, and then for various years from 1994 to 1998. He finds that the Internet is a complement, not a substitute, for the advantages of cities. He finds that the relationship between population and domain density was positive suggesting that the Internet grows where face-to-face communication is most feasible. He also finds a positive relationship between the Internet and other benefits of cities. The observed relationship strengthened over the time surveyed, so it could not be attributed to any initial advantage the cities might have enjoyed. Similarly, the relationship between isolation (a higher average distance between an MSA resident and those outside the MSA) strengthens over this period. Therefore, he concludes that the Internet complements face-to-face communication; it does not substitute for the advantages of cities, and isolated cities such as Seattle and Denver turn out to be disproportionate winners in the emerging information economy.

In our own work (Pelletiere and Rodrigo 1999), using a database of 67 fast growing MSAs, we find a significant differentiation in the relationship of Internet content produced and Internet use. Internet content production was proxied by a domain/employment specialization index (DESI), and the use variable was the percentage of CPS survey respondents using the Internet at the office. [22] Using change in total personal income as the dependent variable and initial local economic structure and Internet penetration as independent variables, we found that while the DESI is significant as a predictor of metropolitan income growth, use of the Internet at work is not. This suggests an economic difference between information production (supply), which Zook (2000b) has found to be highly clustered, and information consumption (demand), which the literature shows to be subject to wider diffusion propensity.

When we tested the impact on income growth for individual sectors, however, we found that the relationship between Internet use, income growth in manufacturing and wholesale trade was positive. The relationship was reversed for finance, insurance and real-estate (FIRE) services. Both

Internet content production and consumption were highly significant for the service sector. In general terms, our findings supported the hypothesis that information consumption and production are distinct economic activities with distinct economic impacts. While overall an increase in the DESI was the best predictor of income growth, there was considerable variation between sectors.

This section has presented some of the emerging empirical evidence on the impact of the Internet on regional economies. This survey has clearly not been exhaustive: a number of the hypotheses are still to be tested. Research on the impact of the Internet continues to be hampered by the relatively recent vintage of the Internet revolution and lack of sufficient time series data or significantly disaggregated cross-sectional data.

Still, the findings thus far are relatively consistent. Empirical studies confirm that location still matters, whether one looks at the Internet as a physical, informational, or people and goods network. However, the importance of some local economic factors is diminishing while that of others is increasing. For example, as Kolko shows for the services industry, the importance of proximity to suppliers and consumers may be decreasing, however the importance of labor supply proximity is increasing. Finally, we see the need to distinguish between Internet access and the uses that local people are making of it, i.e. what information can be accessed, and how it may be used.

5.   EMERGING REGIONAL POLICY QUESTIONS

The Internet, in its present form, offers unprecedented opportunities for information exchange and distribution in various media at an extraordinarily low cost to users. Therefore, a priori, it might appear that the Internet offers the opportunity to overcome existing spatially defined information gaps and asymmetries. But there are significant costs associated with the expansion of the Internet and growing concern about the digital divide: (i.e., the Internet may be compounding rather than diminishing existing economic inequalities based on race, location, education and other variables).

According to the survey, three types of problems that bear on the digital divide issue. The first is whether or not a person in a specific location has access to the physical network itself and how much capacity is available.

The second problem relates to differentiated access to information and information goods of value. Just having a physical connection to the Internet, whether through a public or private ISP, does not guarantee access to high quality, beneficial or necessary information. As the costs of maintaining information sites become better known, the market could become differentiated as follows. At one end there may concentrate less timely, lower-quality, publicly available information. At the other end, high quality information will be available on a willingness-to-pay basis. While this may be interpreted as the most efficient market outcome given the peculiar attributes of information goods, this can no longer be assumed the welfare-maximizing outcome. (DeLong and Froomkin 1999)

Finally, there is the problem of inequalities that exist in the potential population of users, in their current ability to benefit from the Internet, and the ability for those already on-line to derive further benefits. It is often assumed that an Internet connection will overcome many inequalities by giving everyone access to the same information. The prospects of distance learning are poorly understood at present. Are those who are not acculturated to electronic media, and indeed to formal education, capable of being reached in this way, when they have not benefited from existing channels of education?

Concerns expressed in the empirical literature about an emerging digital divide, therefore, appear to be well founded. Extending Internet access beyond a privileged core will involve increasing investments in communication infrastructure. As the affluence and size of the communities connected declines, so will the prospects of adequate private returns, at least in the short term. This suggests that market forces alone may not be able to realize the full potential of the information revolution and posits the need for public investment. Apart from investment in hardware and physical infrastructure, however, staggeringly large investments in human capital would have to be made to enable any significant proportion of humanity to develop the capability to use the Internet and consume information goods. In other words, the Internet does not eliminate the need for on-site education as a prerequisite for development; it actually necessitates such foundation building and complements its beneficial effects. This is borne out by the problems faced in the U.S. in taking computer literacy and Internet access to not just the economic underclass, but even to blue-collar workers and children in remote schools. Bridging the last inch in the U.S. alone is likely to prove a giant leap. To trot out a sobering statistic often quoted in this debate, 80 percent of the world population has yet to make a single phone call.

Therefore, though they have been conceptually separated here for clarity, the networks of the Internet trinity clearly do not exist in isolation. A policy that focuses on extending the hardware and software network to a region, without making complementary investments in the local information network and the cultural capability of local users, is doomed to fail. If spatial as well as other inequalities are to be overcome, this will have to be done through explicit policy initiatives that address all three aspects.

The question arises, however: What opportunities or obstacles to regional economic development policies does the Internet itself creates?

For example, after strong lobbying by the Internet industry, Congress has made the Internet tax-free status official, despite the strong objections of most state and local officials. Recently, however, even some high-tech executives have questioned the wisdom of this.[23] The costs of this to localities may be significant (Goolsbee 1998).

This may be compounded by the fact that since many goods that traditionally have been purchased, shipped and taxed in a physical form can now be distributed digitally (i.e., music, reports, graphics, and magazines), it is difficult to determine exactly where they are produced and their value.

In a clear sense, recent Congressional and state actions to exempt Internet commerce from sales taxes is an indirect subsidy for Internet commerce. While the stated intent is to institute taxes once the industry matures, experience suggest this may not be politically practicable. Much of what are currently construed as the cost benefits of Internet commerce are not due to any technical advantage but to the advantageous tax status. Consumers and citizens have increasingly come to view the Internet as an untaxed good to which they are entitled. Our attitude towards the Interstate highway system has developed in a similar fashion, but it is difficult to imagine tolls for specific stretches or costly projects on the Internet in the future. On this note, it is important to recognize that neither the attributes of information goods nor the technical aspects of the Internet mean that economic activities that use or benefit from the Internet cannot be taxed. If they are to be taxed, however, we must recognize that it may not be in the old established ways.

Many industry experts and reformers are already calling for congestion pricing, tariff structures that are based on usage and other market-based approaches to ensure the efficient use of publicly provided Internet infrastructure. As time goes by, while these demands will be increasingly difficult to ignore, they will also be more difficult to implement.

The example of taxes shows in clear terms, that for policy makers and policy analysts the question is not *whether* policy in any general sense is needed if the digital divide is to be addressed, but exactly what policies are needed. As a physical network and a network that links people and physical goods, our experience with past network architectures may be helpful, but we must also come to terms with unprecedented challenges and opportunities that the information network and the production and distribution of information goods pose (Delong and Froomkin 1999).

Finally, as Section Two illustrates, we need to continue to develop and improve the indicators we have to measure the changes and implications of the Internet. The mapping of the physical infrastructure and the people and goods networks is a problem similar to those we have faced with previous economic infrastructures. Mapping and measuring the information network is a very different proposition (Moss and Townsend 2000b). The functionality and on-line appearance of information nodes can be easily and frequently reconfigured. Information can be moved on line to any other location in the network relatively easily and quickly. Above all, what exists today can cease to exist tomorrow. While some policies such as including better geographic information in the new IPv6 address system (note 10) are relatively straight forward (Moss and Townsend 2000b), the Internet and its economic implications must be better understood and new indicators are still to be developed.

REFERENCES

Adamic, L.A. and B.A. Huberman. (1999). "The Nature of Markets in the World Wide Web." Xerox Palo Alto Research Center; ftp://ftp.parc.xerox.com/pub/dynamics/

Booz, Allen and Hamilton. (2000). The Competitiveness of Europe's ICT Markets: The Crisis Amid the Growth. Presented at the Ministerial Conference, March 9-10, 2000.

Beardsell M. and V. Henderson. (1999). "Spatial Evolution of the Computer Industry." *European Economic Review* 43: 431-56.

Benton Foundation. (1998). "Losing Ground Bit by Bit: Low Income Communities in the Information Age." Washington, D.C.

Cairncross, F. (1997). *The Death Distance*, Boston, MA: Harvard Business School Press.

Cerf, V. (2000). "An Interview with Vincent Cerf." *IEEE Spectrum* 37 (1): 43-44.

Comerford, R. (2000). "The Internet." *IEEE Spectrum* 37 (1): 40-44.

DeLong, J. Bradford and A. M. Froomkin. (1999). "Speculative Microeconomics for Tomorrow's Economy." November 22; http://econ161.berkeley.edu/oped/virtual/technet/spmicro.html

Department of Commerce. (1999). *Falling through the Digital Divide: Defining the Digital Divide*, Washington, D.C.: National Telecommunications and Information Administration. http://www.ntia.doc.gov/ntiahome/digitaldivide/

Economist. (1999). "Survey: Business and the Internet." June 26.

Economist. (2000a). "How to be Perfect." February 12, p. 82.

Economist. (2000b). "Dotty about Dot.commerce? The E-commerce Boom is Changing Business for the Better." February 26, p. 24.

Economist. (2000c). "Survey: E-Commerce." February 26.

Economist. (2000d). "Internet Economics: A Thinkers Guide." April 1, pp. 64-66.

Gaspar, J. and E. L. Glaeser. (1998). "Information Technology and the Future of Cities." *Journal of Urban Economics* 46: 136-156.

Glaeser, E. L, H. Kallal, J. Scheinkman and A. Shleifer. (1992). "Growth in Cities." *Journal of Political Economy* 100 (6): 1126-1152.

Goolsbee, A. (1998). "In a World Without Borders: The Impact of Taxes on Internet Commerce." NBER Working Paper 6863.

Gorman, S. (1998). "The Death of Distance but not the End of Geography: The Internet as a Network." Presented at the Regional Science Association Annual Meeting Santa Fe, October 29, 1998.

Greenstein, S. (1998). "Universal Service in the Digital Age: The Commercialization and the Geography of U.S. Internet Access." NBER Working Paper 6453.

Hammermesh, D. and S. Oster. (1998). "Tools or Toys? The Impact of High Technology on Scholarly Productivity." NBER Working Paper #6761.

Huberman, B. , P. Pirolli, J. Pitkow and R. M. Lukose (1998). "Strong Regularities in World Wide Web Surfing." *Science* 280: 95-97.

Huberman, B. and R. Lukose. (1997). "Social Dilemma's and Internet Congestion." *Science* 277: 535-537.

Kellerman, A. (2000). "Its not only what You Inform - It's Also Where You do it: The Location of Production, Consumption and Contents of Web Information." New York University Unpublished Paper. http://urban.nyu.edu/research/telecom/

Kling, A (1999). "The Last Inch and Metcalfe's Law." Arguing in My Spare Time No. 2.12 http://home.us.net/~arnoldsk/aimst2/aimst212.html.

Kolko, J. (1999a). "Can I get Some Information Here? Information technology, Services Industries, and the Future of Cities." Unpublished Paper: Harvard University. http://www.economics.harvard.edu/~jkolko/papers.html.

Kolko, J. (1999b). "The Death of Cities? The Death of Distance? Evidence from the Geography of Commercial Internet Usage." Selected papers from the Telecommunications Policy Research Conference 1999.
http://www.economics.harvard.edu/~jkolko/papers.html.

Krugman, P. (1991). "Increasing Returns and Economic Geography." *Journal of Political Economy* 99: 483-99.

Krugman, P. (1999). "Networks and Increasing Returns: A Cautionary Tale." http://web.mit.edu/krugman/www/metcalfe.htm.

Lange, L. (1999). "The Internet." *IEEE Spectrum* 36 (1): 35-40.

Lukose, R. and B. Huberman. (1999). "Economic Modeling of the World Wide Web." Internet Ecologies Group, Xerox Palo Alto Research Center. http://www.parc.xerox.com/iea.

MacKie-Mason, J. and H. Varian. (1997). "Economic FAQs about the Internet." in L. McKnight and J. Bailey, eds., *Internet Economics*, Cambridge, MA: MIT Press, pp. 27-62.

Malecki, E. and S. Gorman. (2000). "Maybe the End of Distance is Not the End of Geography: The Internet as a Network" in S.D. Brunn in *The Wild Worlds of Electronic Commerce*, New York: Wiley and Sons.

Moss, M. and A. Townsend. (1996). "Leaders and Losers on the Internet." Research Report. Taub Urban Research Center, New York University.

Moss, M. and A. Townsend. (1997). "Tracking the 'Net: Using domain Names to Measure the Growth on Internet in U.S. Cities." *Journal of Urban Technology* 4(3): 47-61.

Moss, M. and A. Townsend. (1998). "Spatial Analysis of the Internet in U.S. Cities and States." Presented at the Technological Futures-Urban Futures Conference at Durham England April 23-25. http://urban.nyu.edu/research/telecom/

Moss, M. and A. Townsend. (2000a). "The Internet Backbone and the American Metropolis." *The Information Society Journal* 16(1): 35-47.

Moss, M. and A. Townsend. (2000b). "The Role of the Real City in Cyberspace: Measuring and Representing Regional Variations in Internet Accessibility." in Information, Place and Cyberspace, Donald Janelle and David Hodge, eds., Berlin: Springer Verlag: Forthcoming.

OECD. (1998). *The Economic and Social Impacts of Electronic Commerce: Preliminary Findings and Research Agenda*, Paris: OECD.

OECD. (2000). *OECD Information Technology Outlook 2000: ICTs, E-commerce and the Information Economy*, Paris: OECD.

Pelletiere, D. and G. C. Rodrigo. (1999). "Does the Internet Complement or Substitute for Regional External Economies: A proposed Framework for analysis and preliminary results." Paper presented at Association for Public Policy Analysis and Management Annual Research Conference, November 6.

Shapiro, C. and H. Varian. (1999). *Information Rules: A Strategic Guide to the Network Economy*, Boston, MA: Harvard Business School Press.

Taggert, S. (1999). "The 20-ton Packet: Ocean Shipping is the Biggest Real-Time Data Streaming Network in the World." *Wired*, October.

Varian, H. (1999). "Market Structure in the Network Age." Prepared for the Understanding the Digital Economy Conference, Department of Commerce, Washington, D.C., May 25-26. Revised June 17. http://sims.berkeley.edu/resources/infoecon

Zook, M. (2000a). "Internet Metrics: Using Host and Domain Counts to Map the Internet." *Telecommunication Policy Online*: 24 (6/7).

Zook, M. (2000b). "The Web of Production: The Economic Geography of Commercial Internet Content Production in the United States." *Environment and Planning A* 32 (3): 411-426.

Zook, M. (forthcoming). "Old Hierarchies or New Networks of Centrality? - The Global Geography of the Internet Content Market." *American Behavioral Scientist.*

---

[1] The lowest level is made up of numerous local area networks (LANs). Each LAN connects computers accessible to users in a single organization or campus. The LANs are linked one to another through regional, mid-level networks, which in turn are connected to the system of national backbones. A backbone is a high-speed, fiber-optic, data communication network linking together multiple regional networks. The U.S. backbones are then connected to backbone networks in other countries to form an international network.

[2] It is important to note that there is no guarantee the information on-line is up-to-date. However, it can be said that digital information on the Web is more easily distributed once it is up-dated and therefore perhaps more likely to be up-to-date at any given time than hardcopy sources.

[3] An analogy with Henry Ford's Model T automobile is apt. The Model T was not a better car than those produced previously. In many of its functions, it was more basic. The real significance of the Model T was that its relatively low cost, deriving from assembly line production, enabled a far greater number of people to travel faster, more cheaply and independently, than had been the case before with individual and mass modes of transportation or the high-priced luxury automobiles of the time.

[4] The analogy to a road network is again appropriate, as containerized shipping has revolutionized the distribution of physical goods in the last part of the twentieth century in a similar way. Today large shipments are broken up to fit standardized containers with routing instructions printed on the outside. The containers are more easily stored and transferred between trucks, trains, and boats (Taggert 1999).

[5] TeraBeam Networks of Seattle has just unveiled a laser link of very high capacity (2 Gigabit/second) that overcomes the bottleneck introduced by the "last mile" of copper cabling. The communication link is carried on a tiny laser beam emitted from a small transmitter/receiver mounted just outside an office window. On account of its low cost, the system could be extended to form a fiber-less, high speed communication web over an entire city, a web that links to the ultra high-speed fiber optic inter-city networks already in place across the entire nation (*Economist*, March 25, 2000, pp. 66-7).

[6] This is often part of a two-tiered system where older or less valuable information is provided on a public site while more recent or valuable information is presented on a members-only or fee based part of the site.

[7] Which Krugman calls DeLong's law after Berkeley economist Bradford DeLong.

[8] In Krugman's (1999) hypothetical example, the populations of cities are distributed according to the rank-size rule (i.e. the biggest city is twice the size of the second biggest, and the second biggest is 1/3 bigger than the third), so that the first city has 120 people, the next has 60 people, the next 40 and so on. In this hypothetical world, which actually approximates the current distribution of urban populations quite closely, connecting the populations of the first two cities will yield 7200 potential links (120X60). Connecting the next city to the network, however, will also yield an additional 7200 potential links (180x40) and the returns from the next connection decline to 6600 additional connections.

[9] The "last inch" is a play on the "last mile." It refers to the distance that information must travel the inch from the eyes of a user to his brain for analysis and action. Kling (1999)

claims that the last inch is a more substantial obstacle to returns from Internet commerce than the last mile discussed above.

[10] Every computer connected to the Internet has an IP address, which employs a 32 bit numeric code to identify each network node. The 32-bit code is based on the IPv4 (version 4) protocol that is soon to be superseded by the IPv6 protocol based on a 128-bit address space (Comerford 2000).

[11] See www.nua.ie, or www.forrester.com.

[12] www.census.gov/population/www/socdemo/computer.html

[13] For example, the Cyberspace Policy Research Group has been surveying government web sites across many countries and classifying them according to different criteria, including how easy it is to find any particular information. http://www.cyprg.arizona.edu.

[14] This was used in a broader index as an indication of how much information about the city was available on the web, and how savvy its residents and other interested parties were in using the Internet to publicize the strengths and weaknesses of the city. www.zdnet.com/yil/content/mag/9903/cities1.html

[15] These are also referred to as CONE (Com, Org, Net, Edu) domains. Others TLDs include, .gov and .mil for government and military sites.

[16] As with real estate speculation, domain name speculation occurs when a person buys domain names not for own use but to realize a profit on resale. A variation of this is domain name protection. A much-publicized example of domain protection occurred when the George W. Bush campaign bought up domain names involving various permutations of the candidate's name to keep them out of the hands of rivals. Firms do this as well. Wired magazine has over 75 ".com" addresses registered (Zook 2000a). In many cases, diverse domain names lead to the same site, or different divisions of the same firm.

[17] For example, Audretsch & Feldman (1996) looked at changes in the location of innovation (as proxied by patent citations and the Small Business Innovation Database). Audretsch and Stefan (1996) looked at the location of researchers in the biotech sector.

[18] As discussed in the previous section, Zook's work with domain name registrations is one form that such an analysis might take.

[19] This is true in fact for many studies including, Audretsch and Feldman (1996); Audretsch and Stephan (1996), Kolko (1999a).

[20] The fact that this is occurring in the Northeast where population densities are higher may in fact support the density hypothesis.

[21] For example, the employment location quotient for a region would be [Local Employment in Industry/Regional Employment]/[National Employment in Industry/ National Employment].

[22] [Regional CONE Domains/Regional Employment]/[National CONE Domains/National Employment].

[23] Andy Grove, Chairman of Intel Corp as quoted in "Intel Exec Calls for E-commerce Tax" Washington post.com, 6/6/2000.

Chapter 12

Industrial Location in the Information Age
An Analysis of Economic Development for High-Tech Industries

DARRENE HACKLER
George Mason University

1. INTRODUCTION

Information technology (IT) has become a popular means to attain goals for entities such as businesses, governments, communities, and even individuals. While the effects of IT are frequently prophesized, IT is invisible and its hard-to-measure nature stymies most systematic attempts to unravel the causal process. Given the difficulty of studying IT, the central premise of the research is to examine whether IT has the effect on firms that popular literature has noted. Consequently, this chapter investigates how IT affects firms with a theoretical and empirical analysis of industrial location.

Prominent newspapers, trade magazines, and journals currently suggest that firms that depend on IT in production are more flexible.[1] IT enables firms to respond quickly to relative changes in the market economy. Such flexibility is the central characteristic of how popular literature refers to the influence of IT on firm location decisions. A firm can substitute IT for certain essential inputs to become free from traditional location constraints. Firms with great reliance on IT can locate wherever the firm can maximize profit—even if that location is Sioux Falls, South Dakota, home of Gateway Computers.

Footloose is the term coined to explain flexibility in firm location (Audretsch and Feldman 2000, Hackler 2000). Footloose describes the ability and action of firms to locate in areas other than traditional economic centers. Footloose refers to three types of firm location decisions: the start-up of a firm outside of the urban center; the expansion of a firm outside of the urban center; and the relocation of a firm from the urban center to the suburbs or to another central city that is not traditionally considered an economic center. Firms most able to harness IT may be more likely to locate outside of urban centers leading to the decentralization of industry. Examples of this phenomenon are prevalent in newspapers and trade magazines. Citibank's relocation of its credit card processing department from New York City to Sioux Falls, South Dakota is an example from the service sector. In manufacturing, the only manufacturer of DRAMS in the United States. Micron Computers, is not located in the Silicon Valley of California but in Boise, Idaho. The question at hand is to determine if the data support the headlines that claim that the IT industry is footloose.

While popular sentiment indicates that IT is changing how certain types of firms make location decisions, the disciplines of urban and regional economics explain the location of firms with location theory and business location determinants. Firm location, or the demand for a production site, is often posited to be a function of the preferences of employers and employees, price differentials, concentration of industry, labor pool, local fiscal incentives, and other amenities. Speculation that IT enables footloose location decisions suggests that business location determinants have a greater effect on the location decision of a firm that relies on IT in production than a firm that uses little or no IT in production. Popular literature suggests that with the onset of the information age, industrial location patterns are better understood if the industry is considered IT-intensive in the production of goods. Such industry is commonly referred to as high technology, or high-tech, because the level of technology or IT is an essential production input.

To examine whether IT is creating footloose location decisions, this chapter compares the location patterns of high-tech industry to low-tech, or non-IT-intensive, industry in manufacturing. Manufacturing is an appropriate sample population because of earlier studies that note location tendencies of manufacturing employment as a function of business location determinants. In addition, these manufacturing employment studies show that manufacturing has been decentralizing from traditional manufacturing hubs and central cities.[2] Thus, determining the role of IT in these location tendencies and decentralization is noteworthy.

Under the proposition of footlooseness, high-tech manufacturers are expected be more flexible in location decisions than low-tech manufacturers. This flexibility relates to how high-tech firms weight business location determinants in comparison to low-tech firms. Footlooseness suggests that IT enables a high-tech firm to assign greater weights to all determinants since it is freer to select a location that maximizes profit—where the difference between revenues and expenses is greatest (Greenhut 1956). However, a low-tech firm is less able to move freely and may be sticky even if location determinants adversely affect its production. In general, flexibility in location is reflected in how a firm responds to business location determinants such that a quantitative change in a determinant generates a greater response in absolute value from a high-tech firm.

For example, labor wages are an important location determinant, and microeconomic theory details that a decrease in wages can increase the likelihood of firm growth in an area. The combination of footlooseness with location theory and firm profit maximization suggests that a high-tech manufacturer is better positioned to take advantage of this location for start-up, expansion, or relocation. While a decrease in wages can increase all manufacturing growth, it increases the likelihood of high-tech manufacturing growth even more because high-tech firms can use IT to overcome constraints.

Examination of footlooseness requires more than one-dimensional comparisons of location determinants, thus location models for both high- and low-tech industry are developed using location theory to identify business location determinants. Econometric analysis of these high- and low-tech models provides the results necessary to determine whether high-tech industry, in response to business location determinants, is more footloose than low-tech industry. If the popular contention of high-tech footlooseness is supported, the benefits that high-tech industry is claimed to amass in locations it selects can be multiplied. Such economic development issues are the heart of the fascination with high-tech industry.

2.   WHY HIGH-TECH?

High-tech industry is claimed to be an economic driver. A study by the Milken Institute has shown that economic growth in the United States is highly reliant on high-tech growth (DeVol 1999). The proposed research is highly relevant in today's information-driven economy, especially for cities seeking to attract high-tech industry in order to stimulate the local economy. Cities can gain or lose jobs and revenues depending on where firms choose to locate. Thus, cities have an incentive to influence firm location decisions. This is most often accomplished through economic development policies such as tax incentives, land subsidies, and job training programs. From the firm's perspective, the decision of where to locate is not only affected by what cities do but also by specific constraints, such as proximity to an adequate labor pool, transportation, and price differentials. Historically, this is why industry clustered in urban centers, such as Chicago, Illinois; Los Angeles, California; and, New York City, New York.

If high-tech industry is footloose, traditional constraints are weakened, and economic development policies may be more successful in attracting high-tech industry. Cities seek to increase economic growth with high-tech manufacturing for various reasons. Most important is that high-tech manufacturing wages are, on average, fifty percent more than wages for low-tech manufacturing (Hadlock, Hecker, and Gannon 1991). In addition, manufacturing firms are sticky because of the amount of capital investment made to locate in a city. The opportunity cost of relocating is greater for manufacturing than for service and retail firms, thus manufacturing will most likely remain in the city longer. Economic development policies seek such sustained business and employment growth since it can enhance the region and make it more economically viable.

The implications for economic development policy are a direct outgrowth of the research underlying this chapter. If high-tech manufacturing is footloose, a high-tech location model will indicate what location determinants drive high-tech location decisions. With knowledge of these factors, policymakers may be able to more effectively target high-tech firms with economic development policies and successfully take advantage of high-tech manufacturing location tendencies. The information age brings a completely new set of decision criteria not only to the locating firm, but also to the geographic areas in which a firm may locate. Footlooseness suggests that politically entrepreneurial regions and cities will have more success in attracting high-tech industry since it has more available location options. Local economic development policy structured to attract footloose high-tech manufacturing will be more successful in attracting these industries if the policy is flexible and concentrates on the factors driving high-tech industrial location.

With IT permeating many processes from assembly line to decision-making, an understanding of high-tech industry is most appropriate both from theoretical and practical perspectives. High-tech location patterns are examined using a detailed data set of manufacturing establishments and employment with labor market, demographic, and economic characteristics for the 1987 to 1994 period. The following section introduces procedural issues such as the definition and identification of high-tech industry and identifies the appropriate data to provide focus to the research. Location theory provides the necessary background and business location determinants for the development of the high- and low-tech industrial location models. From this, the models of high- and low-tech industrial location are introduced with the central hypotheses, variable descriptions, and expectations. The next section provides an overview of what business location determinants are driving high-tech manufacturing location in comparison to low-tech manufacturing and the policy implications of the results at the state, metropolitan, and city level. Finally, general economic development policy conclusions round out the chapter.

3. DATA, MODELS, AND HYPOTHESES OF INDUSTRIAL LOCATION

In order to analyze whether high-tech's industrial location pattern is more footloose than low-tech's, IT-intensity is defined on an industry basis *ex ante* and is based on the proportion of technical occupations in the total industry labor force. The definition is applied to all manufacturing industries at the four-digit standard industrial classification (SIC) level in order to select high-tech and low-tech industry populations. According to this definition, high-tech manufacturing industries employ a proportion of the following technical occupations in excess of the national manufacturing average: engineers, engineering technicians, computer scientists, mathematicians, and life scientists (geologists, physicians, and chemists) (Glasmeier 1985, 1991).

In much of the previous research on industrial location of high-tech manufacturing, employment is used as an indicator of location. However, establishment data, or the number of firms/production sites, are more advantageous for a number of reasons. Establishment data provide exact location down to the zip code level and do not suffer from data suppression due to privacy like employment data. Concern for location decisions restricts the appropriateness of data. Establishment data also better capture not only the entity at which the location decision occurs but also the target of most economic development policies. Given that business growth is often greatest among small- and medium-sized firms, inferences about high-tech growth based on establishment data are more appropriate. Employment data cannot distinguish whether growth is due to an increase in the number of firms or one existing firm that hires more employees. Thus, the research utilizes establishment data for analyzing industrial location.

Data on the number of firms at a smaller geographical area than the county were not available until 1987. Since the Economic Census of 1987, nationwide zip code data exist on firm location, reported for establishments, at the four-digit standard industrial classification (SIC) level for 1987, 1992, 1994. Such data will better inform regional and local policy.[3] The U.S. Postal Services designates each zip code a Post Office name that is matched to the appropriate city.[4] Thus, the number of establishments in an industry for each zip code is associated with a city and aggregated with all other zip code data for that city. The aggregation allows for location pattern analysis at the city level.

Table 1: Variable Information and Expectations

Variable	Measure	Expectation High	Low	Qualitative Expected Differential[5]
State				
Corporate Tax Rate (CT)	Corporate tax rate	-	-	More high-tech
State Labor Skills (CG)	College graduates as % of state population	+	+	More high-tech
Higher Education Expenditures (HE)	Higher education expenditures per capita	+	-	More high-tech
Metropolitan				
Wages (MW)	Average manufacturing wage	-	-	More high-tech
Union Membership (UM)	% Union membership	-	-	More high-tech
Civilian Labor Force Density (CL)	Civilian labor force per square mile	-	-	More high-tech
Employment Density (IE, LE, ED)	High-tech/Low-tech/total employees per square mile	+	+	More high-tech
Housing Affordability (HA)	Median value of owner-occupied housing units/median household income	-	-	More high-tech
County Labor Skills (CC)	College graduates as % of county population	+	+	More high-tech
Quality of Schools (QS)	% High school graduates of 12th grade enrollment	+	+	More high-tech
Restaurants (R)	Restaurants per 100,000 population	+	+	More high-tech
Core (CORE)	Dummy variable equals one for core, zero for non-core	-	-	More high-tech
City				
Federal Contracts (D)	Department of Defense procurement $ per 100,000 population	+	+	More high-tech
Property Crime (PC)	Property crime per 100,000 population	-	-	More high-tech
Establishments (TH, TL, TE)	Number of high-tech/low-tech/total establishments	+	+	More high-tech
Property Tax Rate (PT)	Property tax collected/assessed value (nominal property tax rate)	-	-	†
Public Expenditures (TC)	% of Total Current Operations on Police, Fire, Parks and Recreation, Solid Waste/Sanitation	+	+	†

Dependent Variables

High-Tech Establishments Growth ($HIT_{i, t} - HIT_{i, t-1}$)	Absolute growth of high-tech establishments from 1987 to 1994
Low-Tech Establishments Growth ($LIT_{i, t} - LIT_{i, t-1}$)	Absolute growth of low-tech establishments from 1987 to 1994
Total Establishment Growth ($TES_{i, t} - TES_{i, t-1}$)	Absolute growth of total establishments from 1987 to 1994

Interactive Variable

High-Tech Dummy (HD)	Dummy variable equals one for high-tech, zero for low-tech

3.1   Central Hypotheses

If high-tech manufacturing is footloose due to IT, variables in a model of industrial location may have a stronger or larger relative effect on location of high-tech firms.   IT, therefore, serves as an intervening variable in an industrial location equation.   The behavioral model of industrial location below is posited to be a function of various labor market, demographic, and economic characteristics for cities, metropolitan regions, and states.   The proposed theory of IT impact asserts the following hypotheses:

Hypothesis I: Variation in industrial location is greater for high-tech manufacturing   industry   than   for   low-tech manufacturing industry.

Hypothesis II: Coefficients on business location determinants are significantly   greater   for   high-tech   manufacturing industry.

Econometric analyses of the high- and low-tech models of industrial location will provide evidence to test each hypothesis and help determine if IT has increased a firm's ability to locate in areas that are more favorable to its production process.

3.2   Business Location Determinants and Variable Hypotheses

The structural models below include a series of business location determinants found to be instrumental in predicting location. This chapter is not an in-depth analysis of how one type of determinant, like fiscal institutions or amenities, affects high-tech growth. Instead, a combination of determinants allows for detailed testing of the existence of high-tech footlooseness. The independent variables exemplify four categories of business location determinants: agglomeration economies, labor market conditions, business climate, and quality of life. These categories represent three geographical classifications, state, metropolitan, and city. The analytical focus is on the industrial location patterns of high- and low-tech industry in cities, one city is not independent of surrounding cities in a metropolitan area nor is it able to separate itself from state policy. To investigate what determinants are important to both high- and low-tech firms and how the high- and low-tech preferences differ, the models pose a full representation of various geographical considerations in a location decision.

Such a statistical approach is unique to the urban economic literature. The models explain both inter-metropolitan and intra-metropolitan location with the inclusion of state, metropolitan, and city location determinants. With the utilization of establishments, the models represent a varied approach to industrial location and growth (Bartik 1991b, Carlton 1979, Charney 1983, Gyourko 1987, Harris 1986, Howland 1985). The variables in the model are listed according to geographic reference in Table 1. The table details hypothesized sign for each variable in the high- and low-tech models as well as the expected qualitative differential. While location theory suggests the relationship between such variables and industrial growth, footlooseness suggests that a qualitative differential is expected between high- and low-tech industries for each variable. Given that footlooseness imparts that high-tech industry is more able to react to changes in location determinants, the response of high-tech industry to each determinant should be greater in absolute value than the response for low-tech industry. Thus, the qualitative differential does not differ for each variable but is essential to later reporting of the results.

3.2.1   State Determinants

While the state level variables are not numerous, the theoretical contribution of a select number depicts inter-regional location decisions of firms. Site location options are often not in the same state. Such observations indicate that states must offer different location packages based on state fiscal priorities, labor pool attractiveness, policy mechanisms, and overall growth and fiscal health. State corporate tax rates are an indicator of state business climates while state labor skills (college educational attainment) and higher education expenditures in the state explain state labor market conditions. The corporate income tax rate is a cost to the firm of doing business in a particular state. Consequently, a negative relationship with respect to industrial location is expected for both high- and low-tech industry (Fox 1981, Wasylenko 1991, Bartik 1985, Newman 1983, Plaut and Pluta 1983, Schmenner 1982).

In the same vein, higher education expenditures per capita should be a public expenditure in which high-tech firms are greatly interested. Relating to the development of a potential labor pool with a higher technical-skill level, the cost of taxes on the firm may be somewhat offset with such an expenditure (Fisher 1997, Ó hUallacháin 1990, Partridge 1993, Plaut and Pluta 1983, Wasylenko and McGuire 1985). Thus, a positive relationship is hypothesized for high-tech industry. As for low-tech industry, this expenditure, while beneficial to the further growth and success of the state, does not directly influence low-tech's desired labor pool qualities and is viewed as an opportunity cost vis-à-vis other possible public expenditures. A negative relationship with low-tech location is expected.

The final state variable is state labor skills, measured as the percentage of the state's adult population that is college educated. As with higher education expenditures, a population with more college-educated individuals is more likely to have a suitable labor pool for high-tech firms. A positive relationship is hypothesized for high-tech industry because firms are concerned with finding a technically skilled labor force. While high rates of college educational attainment may be indirectly influenced by what a state spends on higher education, a low-tech firm would benefit from a higher-skilled workforce regardless. Thus, the hypothesized relationship for low-tech manufacturing would also be positive (Ó hUallacháin 1990).

3.2.2 Metropolitan Determinants

The metropolitan variables capture determinants that are not confined to the city in which a firm decides to locate thereby allowing intraregional analysis. The models decipher what location determinants are important to locating within a metropolitan area from the categories of agglomeration economies, labor market conditions, and quality of life indicators at either the county or MSA level. Theoretically guided by agglomeration economies and the externalities, metropolitan areas are the bases from which urbanization economies are derived. Firms accrue benefits from being located in an urban area. The urbanization effect is tested with the county's employment density (high-tech employment in the high-tech model and low-tech employment in the low-tech model).[6]

Some of the variables included in the metropolitan classification also furnish additional theoretical background for location decisions relative to the labor market. High-tech manufacturing, by the definition utilized, requires higher-skilled labor. Therefore, both the wage and the measurement of skills are essential to the model. The average manufacturing wage in the county for all manufacturing industries captures another cost to the firm, thus the wages variable is expected to be negatively related to both high- and low-tech industry (Carlton 1979, Digby 1983, Helms 1985). For labor skills, both the high- and low-tech model use college educational attainment as a proxy. Given that a labor pool is accessible in the entire metropolitan area, the variable measures the percentage of the adult population that has graduated from college in the county. In a similar manner to the state variable, county labor skills is hypothesized to be positively related to both high- and low-tech location.

A final labor market condition at the metropolitan level is union membership, measured as the percentage of the workers who are union members in the MSA. Unionization of the labor force is often transferred into higher labor costs for the firm and is expected to negatively affect firm location (Bartik 1985, Newman 1983, Plaut and Pluta 1983).

The metropolitan area is also viewed from the perspective of future employees who desire areas with a moderate cost of living, quality schools for their children, and other cultural amenities. A firm's location decision is somewhat affected by such quality of life factors for employees and managers (Krall 1998). In these models, when housing affordability—a ratio of the median value of occupied housing in the county to the median household income in the county—increases, housing is actually less affordable. Housing affordability is hypothesized to have a negative relationship with both high- and low-tech location (Glasmeier 1991, Luce 1994).

The quality of schools in an area is also important to employees with children and thus locating firms (Fox 1981, Wasylenko 1980). Quality of schools is measured as the percentage of publicly enrolled twelfth grade students who graduated from high school.[7] The quality of public schools should be important to a locating low-tech firm not only in terms of employees' preferences but also because of the possible labor pool that is developing—attracting students who finish and have no plans for continuing their education. A positive relationship is also expected in high-tech location. The final quality of life variable is an amenity, number of restaurants. A sizeable number of restaurants often indicate that an area is well developed and able to provide for an expanding population desiring the conveniences and environment that restaurants indicate. As an amenity to an area, restaurants per 100,000 population in the county are hypothesized to have a positive relationship with both high- and low-tech location (Carlino and Mills 1987).[8]

Business climate is also addressed at the metropolitan level with a vacant land proxy. While data on actual vacant land are difficult to obtain for geographical areas other than states, availability of land or parcels that can be redeveloped for industrial use is a strong factor in industrial location models (Bartik 1991a, Fox 1981, Luce 1994, Wasylenko 1980). In order to capture this dynamic, a measure of county density is created. Civilian labor force per square mile in the county serves as a proxy for vacant land. With manufacturing often demanding larger parcels of land than services and some retail, lower labor force density may convey larger portions of land available for industry. Therefore, a negative relationship between civilian labor force density and industrial location is hypothesized.

The final metropolitan variable is unique to the study's testing of footlooseness in high-tech industry. It attempts to measure whether high-tech manufacturing is dispersing from central cities and if this is occurring at a greater rate for high-tech industry because of IT. To analyze this hypothesized negative relationship for high-tech manufacturing, a dummy variable, CORE, is constructed such that it is equal to one if a city is in the core of the metropolitan area and zero otherwise.[9] The dummy variable CORE is expected to be negative for both high- and low-tech manufacturing because of the general decentralization of industry over the past few decades.[10] However, high-tech manufacturing is expected to be footloose and decentralizing from the core at a greater rate than low-tech manufacturing.

3.2.3   City Determinants

The final classification of geographical variables is at the city level. Determinants that can influence such a decision are related to local agglomeration economies, quality of life characteristics, and business climate. Agglomeration is not only important to the metropolitan area but also to a distinct local area. Localization economies are the benefits a firm gains from similar firms doing business in the same locality. Business activity of similar firms illustrates this dynamic. Therefore, the total number of high-tech manufacturing firms in a city for the high-tech model and the total number of low-tech manufacturing firms in a city for the low-tech model are expected to positively affect further growth of each industry (Ó hUallacháin 1990).

A city variable that emphasizes quality of life in a location is property crime. Property crime is measured as the difference between total and violent crimes per 100,000 population. Firms making a location decision factor the level and type of crime activity as a cost of doing business in a city (Kasarda and Irwin 1991). As any other cost, property crime incidence is hypothesized to negatively affect both high- and low-tech industrial location decisions.

The final set of variables focusing on location determinants is related to business climate. Federal support of industry indicates a favorable local business climate. For high-tech growth, past levels of federal funding is an important determinant of future growth (Glasmeier 1991, Markusen, Hall, and Glasmeier 1986). Federal support, measured as contract dollars per 100,000-city population, is expected to be positively related to both high- and low-tech growth (Chinitz 1991, Glasmeier 1985, 1991, Ó hUallacháin 1990).

Location literature advances the role of local government policy on the local business climate and industry growth.[11] While initially tested, local policy variables, property tax rate, and public services are not in the final model based on evidence from a series of statistical tests. This result has been noted before. Wasylenko found in his survey of fiscal incentives that studies using "firm level data generally did not find that taxes or business climate were determinants in business location decisions" (Wasylenko 1991: 26). The establishment data for the dependent variable may be a partial reason. In addition, the significance of local policy variables varies with the geographical area studies. Insignificance of local variables often results from samples of larger geographical areas like states and MSAs (Carroll and Wasylenko 1994, Glickman and Woodward 1989, Howland 1985, Luce 1994, Mills 1983, White 1986, Woodward 1990). Most intra-metropolitan analyses of industrial location find that location decisions are sensitive to intrametropolitan variation in business cost and property taxes (Charney 1983, Gyourko 1987, Herzog and Schlottmann 1993, Luce 1994).

The research at hand is somewhere in the middle with a sample of much smaller areas, cities, in which both inter-metropolitan and intra-metropolitan location determinants are included. The sample accounts for local, metropolitan, and state factors, yet local policy still does not matter. Since the ratio of suburban to central cities is high, the few large central cities seem to distort estimation, increasing standard errors. Finally, the insignificance and resulting removal of the local policy variables from the final models could be reflective of their actual impact. Ziegler (1990) states that the theoretical price a firm is facing with local policy variables is not relatively large enough to affect the estimation, and businesses associate lower taxes with relatively lower levels of public good provisions (services). Findings in the location literature are somewhat mixed on local policy variables and vary according to the variable being explained (establishments data) and the geographical areas in the sample. While reducing some local emphasis in the model, the three local variables, federal contracts, property crime, and total establishments, still allows for some local differentiation in high- and low-tech manufacturing.

3.3 Analytical Framework

The model specifications are non-linear levels models seeking to explain changes in local business activity of high- and low-tech manufacturing by the level of local characteristics (Bartik 1991a). Since the location decisions of firms in this study are assumed profit maximizing, growth of industry in a city occurs when firms select a site because that is where the differences between revenues and expenses are greatest. The location determinants are inputs into the site demand function and production of city industry growth. Thus, the non-linear specification is multiplicative, like a Cobb Douglas production function. The assumed multiplicative relationship indicates that all variables (location determinants) have an effect on industrial location, but that effect is dependent on the values of the other variables in the model (Gujarati 1995). Thus, the research uses the exponential regression models (log linear) below to estimate high-tech and low-tech industrial location:

(1) $\ln(HIT_{i,t} - HIT_{i,t-1}) = \ln \beta_1 - \beta_2 CT_{i,t-1} + \beta_3 CG_{i,t-1} + \beta_4 HE_{i,t-1} - \beta_5 \ln MW_{i,t-1} - \beta_6 UM_{i,t-1} - \beta_7 \ln CL_{i,t-1} + \beta_8 \ln IE_{i,t-1} - \beta_9 \ln HA_{i,t-1} + \beta_{10} CC_{i,t-1} + \beta_{11} QS_{i,t-1} + \beta_{12} \ln R_{i,t-1} + \beta_{13} \ln D_{i,t-1} - \beta_{14} \ln PC_{i,t-1} + \beta_{15} \ln TH_{i,t-1} - \beta_{16} CORE_i + \mu_{i,t-1},$

(2) $\ln(LIT_{i,t} - LIT_{i,t-1}) = \ln \beta_1 - \beta_2 CT_{i,t-1} + \beta_3 CG_{i,t-1} - \beta_4 HE_{i,t-1} - \beta_5 \ln MW_{i,t-1} - \beta_6 UM_{i,t-1} - \beta_7 \ln CL_{i,t-1} + \beta_8 \ln LE_{i,t-1} - \beta_9 \ln HA_{i,t-1} + \beta_{10} CC_{i,t-1} + \beta_{11} QS_{i,t-1} + \beta_{12} \ln R_{i,t-1} + \beta_{13} \ln D_{i,t-1} - \beta_{14} \ln PC_{i,t-1} + \beta_{15} \ln TL_{i,t-1} - \beta_{16} CORE_i + \mu_{i,t-1}$

(3) $\ln(TES_{i,t} - TES_{i,t-1}) = \ln \beta_1 - \beta_2 CT_{i,t-1} + \beta_3 CG_{i,t-1} + \beta_4 HE_{i,t-1} - \beta_5 \ln MW_{i,t-1} - \beta_6 UM_{i,t-1} - \beta_7 \ln CL_{i,t-1} + \beta_8 \ln ED_{i,t-1} - \beta_9 \ln HA_{i,t-1} + \beta_{10} CC_{i,t-1} + \beta_{11} QS_{i,t-1} + \beta_{12} \ln R_{i,t-1} + \beta_{13} \ln D_{i,t-1} - \beta_{14} \ln PC_{i,t-1} + \beta_{15} \ln TE_{i,t-1} - \beta_{16} CORE_i + \beta_{17} HD - \beta_{18}(HD)CT_{i,t-1} + \beta_{19}(HD)CG_{i,t-1} + \beta_{20}(HD)HE_{i,t-1} - \beta_{21}(HD)\ln MW_{i,t-1} - \beta_{22}(HD)UM_{i,t-1} - \beta_{23}(HD)\ln CL_{i,t-1} + \beta_{24}(HD)\ln ED_{i,t-1} - \beta_{25}(HD)\ln HA_{i,t-1} + \beta_{26}(HD)CC_{i,t-1} + \beta_{28}(HD)QS_{i,t-1} + \beta_{29}(HD)\ln R_{i,t-1} + \beta_{30}(HD)\ln D_{i,t-1} - \beta_{31}(HD)\ln PC_{i,t-1} + \beta_{32}(HD)\ln TE_{i,t-1} - \beta_{32}(HD)CORE_i + \mu_{i,t-1}$

Table 1 provides variable abbreviations and associated measurement.[12] The first equation describes the absolute growth of high-tech manufacturing firms in a city while the second equation is the same for low-tech manufacturing growth. Although the two models provide results of what is driving high- and low-tech location, the two models are unable to determine the differences between the two. The third equation is a high-tech interactive dummy model that tests whether the responses of high- and low-tech manufacturing to location determinants are statistically different and that high-tech's response is greater in absolute terms.

The combination of these three models is essential for the following reasons. First, the high-tech interactive dummy model produces the same coefficients and standard errors as the separate high- and low-tech estimations. As a result, F-tests show significant evidence against pooling the models.[13] Second, either relying on the combination of the high- and low-tech models or only on the high-tech interactive dummy model provides evidence on only two of three queries. It is essential to the analysis to determine significance of both high- and low-tech coefficients for variables as well as whether the interactive term indicates significantly different responses of high- and low-tech manufacturing to changes in the variables.

3.4   Sample

Five geographical regions were purposively selected. Industrial location for high- and low-tech manufacturing is analyzed during the period of 1987 to 1994 in the following metropolitan regions: Los Angeles, California; New York City, New York; Phoenix, Arizona; Minneapolis-St. Paul, Minnesota; and El Paso, Texas. The metropolitan sample represents geographical diversity and a mix of traditional manufacturing centers and second-tier cities, cities that are not considered traditional manufacturing centers.[14] The traditional large cities in the sample are Los Angeles and New York City. The second-tier cities are Phoenix and Minneapolis-St. Paul. While the second-tier cities are mainly reputed as high-tech centers, the traditional centers also have a solid share of high-tech industry. The final city, El Paso, adds a level of diversity to the selected sample. While each of the other cities, at some point in their history, attracted high-tech industry, El Paso has a reputation of being a low-tech haven. Its location on the border of western Texas and proximity to the *maquiladora* region in Mexico has been a driver of this bias. The addition of El Paso to this purposive sample provides a control for the other second-tier cities that are often touted for their high-tech allure.

Table 2: Expectations and Findings

Variable	Expectation High	Low	Actual High	Low	Qualitative Differential
State					
Corporate Tax Rate	-	-	+**	+**	Less high-tech***
State Labor Skills	+	+	+**	+**	Less high-tech
Higher Education Expenditures	+	-	-	-**	Less high-tech**
Metropolitan					
Wages	-	-	-***	-**	Less high-tech***
Union Membership	-	-	-	-**	Less high-tech***
Civilian Labor Force Density	-	-	-**	-**	Less high-tech***
Employment Density	+	+	+***	+**	Less high-tech***
Housing Affordability	-	-	-**	-*	More high-tech
County Labor Skills	+	+	+	+**	Less high-tech***
Quality of Schools	+	+	-*	-**	Less high-tech
Restaurants	+	+	-*	-**	Less high-tech**
Core	-	-	+***	+	More-high-tech[a]
City					
Federal Contracts	+	+	+	+	N/A
Property Crime	-	-	+	+	N/A
Establishments	+	+	-***	-	More high-tech**
Property Tax Rate	-	-	N/A	N/A	
Public Expenditures	+	+	N/A	N/A	

Note: $*p < .10$; $**p < .05$; $***p < .01$.

Qualitative Differential: Explains the actual difference between high- and low-tech coefficients in absolute value.

N/A: Not applicable because variables were dropped from both high- or low-tech models.

[a]While high-tech industry's response is greater than low-tech's response, the relationship is not in the direction expected.

4. OVERVIEW OF FINDINGS

The models produce interesting evidence that is contrary to popular belief. Table 2 compares the expectations and actual findings for each variable while Table 3 reports the OLS estimation results for the high-tech, low-tech, and the high-tech interactive dummy location models.

High-tech manufacturing does not differ greatly from low-tech manufacturing. For the high-tech model, six of fifteen variables exhibit significance in the direction hypothesized. Cities with growth in high-tech establishments are in states with higher corporate tax rates and higher state labor skills; in metropolitan areas with larger high-tech employment densities, lower manufacturing wages, lower housing costs, lower quality of schools, fewer restaurants, lower civilian labor force density (more vacant land), and in the core of a metropolitan area; and in cities with fewer high-tech establishments.

Table 3: High-Tech, Low-Tech, and High-Tech Interactive Dummy Model Results

Variable	High-Tech Coefficient[a]	Low-Tech Coefficient[b]	High-Tech Dummy Coefficient[c]
State			
Corporate Tax Rate	.0659**	.3126**	-0.2477***
State Labor Skills	.4440**	.6359**	-0.1920
Higher Education Expenditures	-.9204	-3.1250**	2.2046**
Metropolitan			
Wages	-3.0176***	-7.6727**	4.6551***
Union Membership	-.0044	-.0896**	0.0852***
Civilian Labor Force Density	-.3166**	-1.4510**	1.1344***
High-Tech/Low-Tech Employment Density	.3062***	1.4147**	-1.1085***
Housing Affordability	-1.983**	-1.478*	-0.5056
County Labor Skills	.0057	.1187**	-0.1129***
Quality of Schools	-.0470*	-.0694**	0.0224
Restaurants	-1.0260*	-2.8345**	1.8085**
CORE	.2722***	.3120	-0.0397
City			
Federal Contracts	.0117	.0040	0.0077
Property Crime	.0228	.0050	0.0177
High-Tech/Low-Tech Establishments	-.0271***	-.0038	0.0233**
(Constant)	43.99***	109.4902***	-65.5004***
R^2	.9587	.9898	.9963
Adjusted R^2	.9510	.9879	.9956
Standard Error of Regression	.1128	.0857	.1001
Sum of Squared Residuals	1.0306	.5957	1.6264
Sample Size	97	97	194
F-statistic	125.2214***	524.4444***	1410.114***

Note: *$p < .10$; **$p < .05$; ***$p < .01$
[a] Dependent variable for the high-tech model is the absolute growth of high-tech establishments.
[b] Dependent variable for the low-tech model is the absolute growth of low-tech establishments.
[c] Dependent variable for the high-tech interactive dummy model is the absolute growth of all establishments.

For the low-tech model, eight variables are significant and in the hypothesized direction. Low-tech manufacturing growth is greatest in states with higher corporate tax rates, higher state labor skills, and lower higher education expenditures; in metropolitan areas with larger low-tech employment densities, lower manufacturing wages, lower rates of unionization, lower housing costs, higher county labor skills, lower quality of schools, fewer restaurants, and lower civilian labor force density (more vacant land).

The majority of the variables have the same qualitative effect on industry growth. In highlighting the differences of each model, three variables that are insignificant in the high-tech model enter in the low-tech model with greater explanatory power: higher education expenditures, county labor skills, and union membership. Two variables are significant in the high-tech model but are not in low-tech model: total number of establishments and core. In the low-tech model, the unionization effect is somewhat expected because while the rate of unionization in the U.S. has been declining over the past few decades, some states, metropolitan areas, and industries still have high unionization rates, especially in low-tech manufacturing. The significantly negative coefficient on higher education expenditures is also expected given that the expenditure does not directly influence low-tech's desired labor pool qualities and is viewed as an opportunity cost vis-à-vis other possible public expenditures. Most interestingly, higher education expenditures are thought to positively affect high-tech growth, and the results show that it is not statistically significant from zero, reflecting that it remains a cost of doing business.

The significantly positive effect of county labor skills for low-tech growth but not for high-tech growth is peculiar. While low-tech firms benefit from a higher-skilled labor pool, proximity to an educated labor pool should also be more important to high-tech firms. With both models showing the importance of labor skills at the state level, high-tech growth may not be as dependent on intrametropolitan differences in labor skills as it is with interstate. There is indication that labor pool quality is more important to the high-tech firm when comparing states—a first stage business location decision.

Noting that a group of variables influencing high- and low-tech growth in manufacturing is similar, further differentiation of the high-tech model from the low-tech model is most important to the study's central purpose. The relative significance of the total number of high-tech establishments in the city presents evidence contrary to the theory of localization economies. While insignificant in the low-tech model, high-tech growth is actually enhanced with a decrease in the number of similar firms. High-tech firms may find that if the competition from similar firms becomes to great, the benefits of localization are actually curtailed. Chinitz (1991) believes that the effect of IT on high-tech industry diminishes the importance of localization economies. In combination with the positive relationship for the urbanization economies variable (high-tech employment density), there is evidence that IT promotes location decisions based on an urban area's benefits rather than a singular location that has firms producing similar goods.

The high-tech model also differs in significance of the core dummy variable. The direction of the significant relationship is positive and thus highly contrary to the popular belief that drives this research. The first central hypothesis tests the general assumption of whether IT enables high-tech firms to be less restricted by traditional location constraints such as transportation, price differentials, or concentration of industry. Consequently:

Hypothesis I: Variation in industrial location is greater for high-tech manufacturing industry than for low-tech manufacturing industry.

Given the assumption of high-tech industry footlooseness, the coefficient on CORE in the high-tech model is expected to be negative; yet, the estimated coefficient of CORE in the high-tech model is 0.272 (see Table 3). This signifies that high-tech growth is actually greater in the central cities. The estimated coefficient for CORE in the low-tech model is not significantly different from zero. In fact, the smaller coefficient for CORE in the low-tech model indicates a weaker relationship and larger variation in low-tech location. Consequently, the results of the high- and low-tech models do not confirm Hypothesis I. Evidence suggests that high-tech manufacturing is not dispersing from the urban core. Moreover, the results show support for the idea that low-tech manufacturing is actually dispersing more quickly than high-tech manufacturing. The first tenet of footlooseness in high-tech industry is unfounded.

With evidence disputing the reality of high-tech footlooseness, the high-tech interactive dummy model incorporates the ability to further test the final hypothesis of the research. The interaction term provides results for the hypothesized qualitative differential, shown in Table 2, to determine whether high- and low-tech manufacturing responds significantly different from each other. The second central hypothesis of the study, while not contingent on the first, is related to the assumption that reliance on IT in high-tech industries generates consequential differences in how high-and low-tech firms evaluate location factors. As inputs into the demand for a production site, a firm selects a location that enables it to maximize profit. The second hypothesis that the models test is:

Hypothesis II: Coefficients on business location determinants are significantly greater for high-tech manufacturing industry.

Footlooseness insinuates that high-tech manufacturing will respond more greatly to changes in location determinants. The expectation is that the significant interaction terms indicate that high- and low-tech manufacturing do respond differently to location determinants in the model. In addition, the interaction term should indicate that the high-tech coefficient is greater in absolute percentages. While nine variables are significantly different in the high- and low-tech models, total number of establishments is the only variable that induces a significantly greater response from high-tech manufacturing. High-tech growth is significantly greater than low-tech growth for every one percent decrease in the number of establishments in a city, but the differential is minor at only 0.02 percent (see Table 3 for estimated coefficients). Thus, there is little evidence to support Hypothesis II.

In general, the findings suggest that high-tech manufacturing location does not differ greatly from low-tech in terms of the business location determinants driving location. The resulting patterns are the opposite of what the popular literature suggests. High-tech industry is less variable in location decisions. Lower variation from traditional core locations is a result of smaller response to changes in location determinants. Jointly, the findings serve important notice to not only the body of popular literature emphasizing footlooseness in high-tech industry, but the findings also suggest that cities with economic development packages seeking high-tech industry are at a great disadvantage. High-tech industry is less likely to be footloose in response to those incentives.

4.1   State Policy Implications

Cities that are experiencing growth of high-tech establishments are in states with a high corporate tax rate and higher state labor skills. Cities with low-tech growth are similar except low-tech growth also entails lower expenditures per capita on higher education. However, the results do not indicate a clear policy direction. The analysis overall indicates that the ability to attract high-tech industry is severely limited, and the state level results confirm this problem.

This contradictory finding does not particularly benefit policymakers attempting to attract high-tech industry. Localities still desire high-tech industry and thus want to influence their location choices. While policymakers can influence corporate tax rates and possibly enhance the state labor pool through an appeal to increasing state economic competitiveness, there is a long time horizon before the effects of such policies are felt. However, the real predicament is that low-tech industry is more responsive to changes in the corporate tax rate and labor skills, so the effort may have the exact opposite effect. Given high-tech manufacturing is not footloose, policymakers should focus on the few variables that do favor high-tech location, leaving corporate tax rates and state labor skills to float at the margin.

The significantly positive relationship of corporate tax rates is the most perplexing from a policy standpoint since it deviates from location theory—even though Carroll and Wasylenko (1994) found a similar result in a study of state manufacturing employment growth. The result many indicate that the aggregation of all other taxes are low.[15] If the other state taxes and conditions are beneficial to a firm, the state may be selected even if the corporate tax rate is relatively high in comparison to other states. The contrary result doubles in magnitude when it is taken into consideration that low-tech manufacturing adjusts more to changes in the tax rate.

Also of policy importance is that higher education expenditures are significant in the low-tech model but not in the high-tech model. This is interesting for two particular reasons. First, high-tech growth appears to be influenced by higher education given its need for higher-skilled labor. In combination with the positive coefficient for state labor skills, the insignificance of higher education expenditures may imply that the growth of high-tech establishments is more responsive to the composition of the labor pool than how much is spent on higher education. Higher education expenditures are still a fundamental cost to firms that may not be as focused on the needs of high-tech industry.[16] Second, the insignificance amassed with the other two state results indicates that high-tech manufacturing is less responsive, in general, to state location determinants. Thus, again, policymakers would be better served in not concentrating on the business location determinants.

4.2   Metropolitan Policy Implications

For the metropolitan factors, cities experiencing growth of high-tech establishments are in metropolitan areas with larger high-tech employment densities, lower manufacturing wages, lower housing costs, lower quality of schools, fewer restaurants, lower civilian labor force density (more vacant land), and in the core of a metropolitan area. Cities with low-tech growth are similar to those with high-tech growth except on two variables. Low-tech growth is influenced by unionization rates but not dependent on being located in the core. Of greatest consequence to policy is that the CORE dummy variable deviates from the expectation with a positive and very significant coefficient in the high-tech model. The core, central cities have a greater number of high-tech firms and either grew more than suburbs or declined less than suburbs over the period examined. Either way, the implication refutes the popular conception that high-tech industry is footloose. This, in addition to the results for most metropolitan variables, suggests that high-tech industry is definitely not more footloose than low-tech industry. High-tech growth was less responsive on all but one other location determinant, housing affordability. Policy seeking to attract high-tech industry should note the relative stickiness of high-tech manufacturing relative to low-tech manufacturing.

Of the labor market conditions, high-tech employment density and wages, while important to high-tech location, are not suitable policy handles because they are difficult if not impossible to manipulate. Wages are determined in the market for labor while employment density is a product of other city successes in gaining high-tech industry. Finally, given the importance of interstate labor skills and that local labor pool must be appropriately trained, not just educated, county labor skills are not really the exact labor market in which high-tech industry is interested.

Only in the quality of life determinants does high-tech growth react attractively. Housing affordability has a strong relationship with high-tech growth. However, the reality is that policymakers do not have great control over housing affordability without creating perverse incentives, as rent control does. Low-income housing efforts are also not feasible, if the preferences of high-tech employees are heeded. Consequently, affordable housing quickly becomes out of the range of policy control.

While not a major driver of high-tech growth, land use and zoning issues, the availability of vacant and/or industrially zoned land, does have some probability of policy control. If the area is already too populated, nothing can be done retroactively, and future growth policy is the only tool. In cities without such preconditions, land use and zoning may have success in ensuring land is available to locating high-tech firms. However, even zoning policy is limited given local conflicts over excessive growth and the ability of the policy to have positive outcomes in the short term. Again, while land use and zoning seem to be manipulative factors, high-tech growth is less likely than low-tech growth because of high-tech's relative stickiness. High-tech manufacturing is not footloose, and the primary determinant (housing affordability) influencing its growth is not very controllable with policy. It would heed policymakers not to concentrate on the metropolitan business location determinants in hopes of attracting high-tech industry.

4.3   City Policy Implications

While theoretically important, none of the city factors post significant results in the low-tech model, and only one is significant in the high-tech model—growth in high-tech establishments is occurring in cities that have few high-tech establishments. The city factors in the models of high- and low-tech location are fewer than in the metropolitan section. This is partly due to the lack of city level data that is appropriate to serve as location determinants, and early analysis determined that local fiscal policy variables should not be included in the models. Such evidence suggests that the nature of the sample data declines the importance of local variables.

Of greater consequence to the research as a whole is that with limited local policy handles on high-tech growth, local policy to attract high-tech industry is rendered powerless. The importance of fewer high-tech firms in a site location demonstrates the basic problem. Current policymakers lack control over the pre-existing number of firms, but they now possess the knowledge that a threshold exists at which further industrial attraction is ineffective. In the end, policymakers who recognize such barriers will not only appreciate what few determinants can be manipulated but also where not to allocate additional resources.

5.   CONCLUSIONS

Overall the econometric results suggest that contrary to popular belief, high-tech manufacturing is not footloose. Not only is high-tech manufacturing not dispersing from central cities but also it is definitely not dispersing at a greater rate than low-tech manufacturing. Additionally, the models present no evidence to support the popular idea that IT enables high-tech firms to locate more freely. In fact, high-tech growth responds less than low-tech growth to changes in most business location determinants. The research is in direct contradiction of studies claiming that high-tech manufacturing is more likely to be decentralizing from central cities than high-tech services (DeVol 1999, Glaeser 1998). The results suggest that traditional central cities are not losing the competition for high-tech industry. In fact, high-tech manufacturing shows agglomerative tendencies, more of the urbanization than localization type, where central cities possess an edge over suburban cities.

Understanding that high-tech manufacturing is not as footloose as previously suggested increases the importance of knowing what creates high-tech growth so that policy can be more targeted and effective. While high-tech growth is less responsive than low-tech growth, several location determinants are statistically significant in explaining high-tech manufacturing location decisions. Thus, cities still seeking to attract high-tech industry will have an improved knowledge of high-tech location decisions. Though not always in the direction expected, state taxes and workforce skills, county wages, housing affordability, quality of schools, land use and zoning, high-technology employment, and city high-tech establishments base affect high-tech growth. Policymakers who take heed of what few determinants can be manipulated will allocate scarce economic development resources more efficiently.

Given that footlooseness is an inappropriate depiction of high-tech industrial location, the sphere of policy influence that entrepreneurial state and local policymakers have is somewhat limited. First and foremost, the coefficients in the high-tech growth model indicate a small impact and often in a direction contrary to theory. Thus, the results indicate where the return on development investment is low. This knowledge is useful since it shows local policymakers where it is not salient to offer incentives or spend money. Such a finding challenges the way local government perceives economic development. Since most cities seek to attract small operations, getting the economic incentives right will not waste scarce local resources.

Policymakers have only a small number of the business location determinants that are maneuverable and that influence high-tech growth. Policies attracting high-tech industry cannot be predetermined for all states and cities since some have endowments that set them either ahead or behind the competition. Thus, the research indicates that policy actions to affect business location determinants fall into two categories, preconditions and manipulative factors. Preconditions are macro elements that are out of the sphere of influence for policymakers. Wages and high-tech employment density and establishments base are such preconditions. Manipulative factors are state taxes, workforce skills, housing affordability, quality of schools, and land use and zoning. While local policymakers may have the means to manipulate these determinants, the policies would not always be free of perverse incentives, rest at a steady state that is capable of being manipulated, or actually attract high-tech over low-tech industry.

For example, high-tech growth shows great response to zoning issues, vacant and industrially zoned land being an indicator of growth. Yet, even availability of vacant land, while zoning can have some effect, could be a precondition if the area is already too populated. In addition, low-tech growth has a statistically greater response to such policy. Consequently, while the categories of preconditions and manipulative factors give some structure to possible policy actions, location determinants can belong to either category, depending on local endowments.

Within the category of manipulative factors, policy actions do not have a similar temporal horizon. Local policymakers are most concerned with having a quick turnaround so that resources spent this year will show growth soon after. However, policies seeking to affect state taxes and workforce labor skills are long-term policy options. Only land use and zoning, barring any standard local conflict, could make the jurisdiction available to locating high-tech firms in the short term. Moreover, as cited above, zoning carries a number of other external problems. Regardless of whether policymakers have control over land use and zoning, high-tech growth is less likely than low-tech growth because of high-tech's relative stickiness. Policymakers need to get the incentive right, but first they must pay attention to whether it is a policy that will achieve its intended outcome. In the case of high-tech industry growth, local economic development dollars would be better spent elsewhere.

In summary, high-tech industry is not footloose. Changes in business location determinants do not stimulate much growth nor are significant determinants necessarily maneuverable. Thus, policy has little effect on high-tech growth, especially at the local level. The research suggests that economic development policy targeting the attraction of high-tech firms is a misallocation of resources. This is a notion that has been commonly forwarded in the economic development literature, particularly regarding tax incentives.[17] While the results do not offer a quick fix for struggling cities, the research provides some direction where cities should not be allocating resources. Policymakers must not only acknowledge the differences between high- and low-tech industries but also be willing to accept that the attraction of high-tech industry does not come at minimal cost to the city, nor does it ensure it comes at all.

REFERENCES

Armington, C., C. Harris, and M. Odle. (1983). *Formation and Growth in High-Technology Businesses: A Regional Assessment*, Washington D.C.: Brookings Institution, Business Micro Data Project.

Audretsch, D. and M. P. Feldman. (2000). "The Telecommunications Revolution and the Geography of Innovation." in J. O. Wheeler, Y. Aoyama and B. Warf, eds., *Cities in the Telecommunications Age: The Fracturing of Geographies*, New York, Routledge, pp. 181-199.

Barkley, D. (1988). "The Decentralization of High-Technology Manufacturing to Nonmetropolitan Areas." *Growth and Change*, Winter, pp. 13-30.

Barkley, D. and S. Hinschberger. (1992). "Industrial Restructuring: Implications for the Decentralization of Manufacturing to Nonmetropolitan Areas." *Economic Development Quarterly* 6(1): 64-79.

Bartik, T. J. (1985). "Business Location Decisions in the United States: Estimates of the Effects of Unionization, Taxes, and Other Characteristics of States." *Journal of Business and Economic Statistics*, January, pp. 14-22.

Bartik, T. J. (1991). "The Effects of Property Taxes and Other Local Public Policies on Intrametropolitan Pattern of Business Location." in H. W. Herzog, Jr. and A. M. Schlottmann, eds., *Industry Location and Public Policy*, Knoxville: University of Tennessee Press, pp. 57-80.

Bartik, T. J. (1991). *Who Benefits from State and Local Economic Development Policies?*, Kalamazoo, MI: W.E. Upjohn Institute for Employment Research.

Bergsman, S. (1994). "Silicon Valley's Real Estate Gamble." *Financial World* 163(4): 50-51.

Bradbury, K. L., Y. K. Kodrzycki, and R. Tannenwald. (1997). "The Effects of State and Local Public Policies on Economic Development: An Overview." *New England Economic Review*, March/April, pp. 1-12.

Cairncross, F. (1995). "The Death of Distance." *Economist* 336 (7934).

Carlino, G. and E. Mills (1987). "The Determinants of County Growth." *Journal of Regional Science* 27: 39-54.

Carlton, D. W. (1979). "Why Do New Firms Locate Where They Do: An Econometric Model." in W. C. Wheaton, ed., *Interregional Movements and Regional Growth*, Washington, D.C.: The Urban Institute.

Carroll, R. and M. Wasylenko. (1994). "Do State Business Climates Still Matter? Evidence of a Structural Change." *National Tax Journal*, March, 67: 19-37.

Charney, A. H. (1983). "Intraurban Manufacturing Location Decisions and Local Tax Differentials." *Journal of Urban Economics* 14: 184-205.

Cheshire, P. C. and A. W. Evans, eds. (1991). *Urban and Regional Economics*. Cambridge, University Press.

Chinitz, Benjamin. (1991). "A Framework for Speculating about Future Urban Growth Patterns in the US." *Urban Studies* 28(6): 939-959.

DeVol, R. C. (1999). "America's High-Tech Economy: Growth, Development, and Risks for Metropolitan Areas." Santa Monica: Milken Institute, p. 127.

Digby, M. (1983). "Evaluating State Industrial Development Programs." *Public Administration Quarterly*, Winter, 6: 434-449.

Elstrom, P., P. M. Eng, P. Judge, and G. McWilliams. (1997). "It Must Be Something in the Water." *Business Week* 3541: 138-144.

Fisher, R. C. (1997). "The Effects of State and Local Public Services on Economic Development." *New England Economic Review*, March-April, pp. 53-82.

Forkenbrock, D. and N. Foster. (1996). "Highways and Business Location Decisions." *Economic Development Quarterly* 10(3): 239-249.

Fox, W. F. (1981). "Fiscal Differentials and Industrial Location: Some Empirical Evidence." *Urban Studies* 18(1): 105-111.

Glaeser, E. (1998). "Are Cities Dying." *Journal of Economic Perspectives* 12(2): 139-160.

Glasmeier, A. K. (1985). "Innovative Manufacturing Industries: Spatial Incidence in the United States." in M. Castells, ed., *High Technology, Space, and Society*, Beverly Hills, CA: Sage Publications.

Glasmeier, A. K. (1991). *The High-Tech Potential: Economic Development in Rural America.* New Brunswick, NJ: Center for Urban Policy Research.

Glickman, N. and D. Woodward. (1989). *The New Competitors*, New York: Basic Books.

Gordon, P., H. W. Richardson, and G. Yu. (1997). "Settlement Patterns in the U.S.: Recent Evidence and Implications." 36th Annual WRSA Meeting, Royal Waikolan Resort, Hawaii.

Greenhut, M. L. (1956). *Plant Location Theory and Practice: The Economics of Space.* Chapel Hill: The University of North Carolina Press.

Gujarati, D. N. (1995). *Basic Econometrics*, New York: McGraw-Hill, Inc.

Gyourko, J. (1987). "New Firm Activity and Employment Changes Among the Localities in the Philadelphia Area, 1980-1983." in A. Summers and T. Luce, eds., *Economic Development within the Philadelphia Metropolitan Area*, Philadelphia: University of Pennsylvania Press.

Hackler, D. (2000). "Industrial Location in the Information Age: An Analysis of Information-Technology-Intensive Industry." in J. O. Wheeler, Y. Aoyama, and B. Warf, eds., *Cities in the Telecommunications Age: The Fracturing of Geographies*, New York: Routledge, pp. 200-218.

Hadlock, P., D. Hecker, and J. Gannon. (1991). "High Technology Employment: Another View." *Monthly Labor Review*, July, pp. 26-30.

Hansell, S. (1991). "R. Michael McCullough of Booz, Allen & Hamilton: Where Do We Go from Here?" *Institutional Investor* 25(7): 33-34.

Hanson, G. (1996). "Agglomeration, Dispersion, and the Pioneer Firm." *Journal of Urban Economics* 39: 255-281.

Harris, C. S. (1986). "Establishing High-Technology Enterprises in Metropolitan Areas." in E. M. Bergman, ed., *Local Economies in Transition*, Durham, NC: Duke University Press.

Helms, L. J. (1985). "The Effect of State and Local Taxes on Economic Growth: A Time Series-Cross Section Approach." *The Review of Economics and Statistics*, February, 67: 574-582.

Henderson, J. V. (1994). "Where Does an Industry Locate." *Journal of Urban Economics* 35: 83-104.

Henry, M. S., D. Barkley, and S. Bao. (1997). "The Hinterland's Stake in Metropolitan Growth: Evidence from Selected Southern Regions." *Journal of Regional Science* 37(3): 479-501.

Herzog, H. W., Jr. and A. M. Schlottmann. (1993). "Industrial Location in the United States: Some New Evidence of Public Policy Efficacy." *Survey of Business*, Summer/Fall, pp. 9-16.

Howland, M. (1985). "Property Taxes and the Birth and Intraregional Location of New Firms." *Journal of Planning, Education and Research*, April, 4: 148-156.

Kasarda, J. and M. Irwin. (1991). "National Business Cycles and Community Competition for Jobs." *Social Forces* 69(3): 733-761.

Krall, M. (1998). "In Search of the Good Life." *Business Facilities Online*, pp. 1-7.

Krider, C. and P. Oslund. (1995). "Analysis of Tax Policy Impact on Business." Lawrence, Institute for Public Policy and Business Research, The University of Kansas, p. 37.

Kieschnick, M. (1981). "Taxes and Growth: Business Incentives and Economic Development." Washington, D.C.: Council of State Planning Agencies.

Luce, J. (1994). "Local Taxes, Public Services, and the Intrametropolitan Location of Firms and Households." *Public Finance Quarterly* 22(2): 139-168.

Luker, W., Jr. and D. Lyons. (1997). "Employment Shifts in High-Technology Industries, 1988-96." *Monthly Labor Review*, June, pp. 12-25.

Lyons, D. (1995). "Agglomeration Economies among High Technology Firms in Advanced Production Areas: The Case of Denver/Boulder." *Regional Studies* 29(3): 265-278.

Markusen, A., P. Hall, A. Glasmeier. (1986). *High Tech America: The What, How, Where, and Why of the Sunrise Industries*, Boston: Allen and Unwin.

Mills, E. S. (1983). "Metropolitan Central City Population and Employment Growth during the 1970's." Philadelphia: Federal Reserve Bank of Philadelphia.

Moriarty, B. M. (1980). *Industrial Location and Community Development*. Chapel Hill: University of North Carolina Press.

Newman, R. J. (1983). "Industry Migration and Growth in the South." *Review of Economics and Statistics* 3: 14-22.

Ó hUalláchain, B. (1990). "The Location of U.S. Manufacturing: Some Empirical Evidence on Recent Geographical Shifts." *Environment and Planning A* 22: 1206-1222.

Oslund, P. and A. Fetisova (1998). "Business Taxes and Costs: A Cross-State Comparison." Lawrence, Institute for Public Policy and Business Research, The University of Kansas.

Papke, L. E. (1987). "Subnational Taxation and Capital Mobility: Estimates of Tax-Price Elasticities." *National Tax Journal* 40(2): 191-204.

Partridge, M. (1993). "High-Tech Employment and State Economic Development Policies." *Review of Regional Studies* 23(3): 287-305.

Plaut, T. and J. E. Pluta (1983). "Business Climate, Taxes and Expenditures, and State Industrial Growth in the U.S." *Southern Economic Journal*, Summer, 50: 99-119.

Rycroft, R. and D. Kash (1992). "Technology Policy Requires Picking Winners." *Economic Development Quarterly* 6(3): 227-240.

Schmenner, R. W. (1982). *Making Business Location Decisions.* Englewood Cliffs, NJ: Prentice Hall Publishers.

Steinacker, A. (1998). "Economic Restructuring of Cities, Suburbs, and Non-metropolitan Areas: 1977-1992." *Urban Affairs Review* 34(2).

Summers, A. A. and P. D. Linneman (1990). "Patterns and Processes of Urban Employment Decentralization in the U.S. 1976-1986." Comparisons of Urban Economic Development in the U.S. and Western Europe, Bellagio, Italy.

Tonn, B. (1990). "Recommendations for Decentralized Information Technology Innovation and Management." *Information Society* 7(2): 139-154.

Wasylenko, M. (1991). "The Role of Fiscal Incentives." in H. W. Herzog, Jr. and A. M. Schlottmann, eds., *Industry Location and Public Policy*, Knoxville, TN: University of Tennessee Press, pp. 13-30.

Wasylenko, M. and T. J. McGuire. (1985). "Jobs and Taxes: The Effect of Business Climate on States' Employment Growth Rates." *National Tax Journal* 38: 497-511.

Wasylenko, M. (1980). "Evidence of Fiscal Differentials and Intrametropolitan Firm Relocation." *Land Economics* 56(3): 339-349.

Wheat, L. F. (1986). "The Determinants of 1963-77 Regional Manufacturing Growth: Why the South and West Grow." *Journal of Regional Science* 26: 635-659.

White, M. J. (1986). "Property Taxes and Firm Location: Evidence from Proposition 13." in H. S. Rosen, ed., *Studies in State and Local Public Finance*, Chicago: University of Chicago Press.

Wilson, R. (1989). "State Business Incentives and Economic Growth: Are They Effective? A Review of the Literature." Lexington, KY: Council of State Governments.

Wolkoff, M. J. (1985). "Chasing a Dream: The Use of Tax Abatements to Spur Urban Economic Development." *Urban Studies* 22: 305-315.

Wollman, H. (1988). "Local Economic Development Policy: What Explains the Divergence between Policy Analysis and Political Behavior." *Journal of Urban Affairs* 10: 10-28.

Woodward, D. P. (1990). "Locational Determinants of Japanese Manufacturing Start-ups in the United States", University of South Carolina.

Wyly, E. K., N. J. Glickman, and M. Lahr. (1998). "A Top 10 List of Things to Know about American Cities." *Cityscape: A Journal of Policy Development and Research* 3(3): 7-32.

Ziegler, J. (1990). "Industrial Location and State and Local Tax and Other Financial Incentives." *Arkansas Business and Economic Review*, Spring, pp. 25-30.

---

[1] See Audretsch and Feldman (2000), Bergsman (1994), Elstrom (1997), Cairncross (1995), Hackler (2000), Hansell (1991), Tonn (1990).

[2] Several studies note the decentralization of industry and employment: Barkley (1988), Barkley and Hinschberger (1992), Gordon, Richardson, and Yu (1997), Hanson (1996), Henderson (1994), Henry, Barkley, and Bao (1997), Lyons (1995), Ó hUallacháin (1990), Steinacker (1998), Summers and Linneman (1990), Luker and Lyons (1997), Wyly, Glickman, and Lahr (1998).

[3] While zip code level data is available for firm location, many of the independent variables essential to the industrial location model are disaggregated to no further than the city level. However, at the city level, no firm location data are collected.

[4] Each metropolitan area had zip codes with assigned Post Office names different from the actual city that contained it. For example, zip codes in Van Nuys, California have Post Office names for Van Nuys, but Van Nuys is really part of the City of Los Angeles. Data was aggregated for the City of Los Angeles. Using ArcView Geographical Information Systems, each zip code is assigned to the city in which contains a majority of its geographical boundaries. Some zip codes were associated with more than one city. If a zip code was located in both city A and B and the majority of the zip code's geographical boundaries were in city A's boundaries, the zip code data were aggregated for city A.

[5] Qualitative Expected Differential: Explains the difference expected between high- and low-tech coefficients in absolute value. For example, the state corporate tax rate, while negatively related to high-and low-tech growth, is expected to affect high-tech growth less than low-tech growth. Local property tax rate and public expenditures were dropped from both high- and low-tech model with a series statistical tests.

[6] This variable also controls for cyclical variations.

[7] Unfortunately, school districts do not share coterminous geographical boundaries with counties or cities that hinders the construction of variables that appropriately represent quality of schools in an area. The county is the chosen level of analysis because of the number of counties in the sample that are geographically small. California and Arizona counties are the exception, yet, fifteen of the twenty-four in the study are geographically smaller counties and assumed to have fewer school districts.

[8] Restaurants are establishments for each county in SIC code 5812, Eating Places, from the County Business Patterns series for 1987.

[9] Each geographical region is divided into two areas, the core CBD and the area outside of the CBD. Gordon, Richardson, and Yu (1997) utilize a similar approach to understand business location decisions.

[10] To allow the core to absorb a larger area than the CBD proper, a three-mile circle (measured by freeway distance) with the core at the center creates a geographical divider. Freeway distance data will be used from the U.S. Bureau of the Census' Tiger Database.

[11] See: Herzog and Schlottmann (1993), Armington, Harris, and Odle (1983), Bartik (1985), Newman (1983), Papke (1987), Plaut and Pluta (1983), Wasylenko and McGuire (1985), Bartik (1991b), Carroll and Wasylenko (1994), Forkenbrock and Foster (1996).

[12] All dollars are constant and converted to the 1982-84 base using the consumer price index.

[13] The interactive model estimation, in addition to the high- and low-tech location models, allows high- and low-tech variables to have different coefficients such that 79 percent of the remaining variation from a basic pooled model of the high- and low-tech data is explained.

[14] Second-tier cities are those attracting industry and jobs over the past ten to fifteen years.

[15] For example, sales and property taxes are also a cost to doing business in a state. Also, the variations in each state's corporate tax rate include allowable deductions, income allocation methods, and even economic development incentives. For more discussion of these items, see Krider and Oslund (1995), and, Oslund and Fetisova (1998).

[16] Glasmeier (1985) reports similar findings with respect to education.

[17] See: Bradbury, Kodrzycki, and Tannenwald (1997), Partridge (1993), Rycroft and Kash (1992), Wasylenko and McGuire (1985), Wilson (1989), Wolkoff (1985), Wasylenko (1991), Wheat (1986), Wollman (1988), Kieschnick (1981), Moriarty (1980).

Chapter 13

Brokering Trust in Online Privacy:
Analysis of Issues and Options

PRISCILLA M. REGAN
George Mason University

Public opinion surveys and anecdotal reports indicate that the public is both excited about the potential opportunities offered by the Internet and at the same time wary about loss of privacy online. A recent survey (Harris and Westin 1998) revealed that 81 percent of Internet users who buy products and services over the Internet are concerned about threats to their personal privacy while online and 72 percent are concerned about someone tracking what Websites people visit and using this information improperly. Press reports of "identity theft" are increasing as individuals find that their alter-egos are applying for credit with information that likely was obtained by "data-mining" for Social Security numbers and demographic information on the Internet.

The issue of online privacy has been a key component of policy deliberations about the National Information Infrastructure (NII) and has been on the government's agenda since the early 1990s. Deliberations have taken place in congressional committees and subcommittees, advisory committees, agency task forces, regulatory commissions, and international bodies. Policy makers have not ignored concerns about online privacy protection but to this point the policy response has been one of caution. Policy makers have been more receptive to the concerns of industry advocates who argue that government regulation will stifle innovation and that self-regulation will generate a robust electronic marketplace that protects both privacy and profits.

It appears that the critical component in the public's comfort level with conducting personal, social, and/or business affairs online is a sense of trust in understanding how personally identifiable information flows in the online world and a sense of trust in believing what Web sites say they are doing with that information. The capacity to trust that individuals and organizations will do what they say they will do is a key component of a social system. Trust is one of the ingredients that fosters the level of "social capital" that makes systems operate smoothly and without undue interference and overt regulation (Putnam 1995, Fukuyama 1995). But trust has to develop or evolve; it cannot be forced.

People appear to be transferring their skepticism and cautions, if not outright distrust, about organizations in the physical world to the online world. The physical world biases create a predisposition to mistrust, which may be exaggerated by the faceless nature of the online world. Moreover, the ways in which trust could be developed in the online world are still somewhat unclear. Repetition of contacts, reputation and brand names, for example, are all components that foster trust in the physical world and are likely to be critical in the development of trust online.

In the faceless, ephemeral world of the Internet how does one actually determine what is happening and if one is told by a Web site that certain things are happening why would one believe that Web site? The issue of online privacy is intrinsically related to the concept of trust. Individuals want to know two things when they visit a Web site: what is that Web site doing with my personally identifiable information; and, how do I know I can believe that the Web site is doing what it says it is doing? Developing mechanisms to provide answers to these questions has proven difficult. If the individual is inherently unlikely to place trust in what a Web site says, then some mechanism is necessary to broker the trust relationship between the individual and the Web site. Privacy notices, privacy icons or seals, privacy-enhancing technologies, privacy laws, and privacy agencies are all possible options.

This chapter analyzes both the privacy issues that have been presented in the online world and the policy options that have been offered in response. The chapter proceeds in three parts: first, the policy problems are explored; second, the policy deliberations are briefly summarized; and third, the policy options are presented and analyzed.

1.   ONLINE PRIVACY ISSUES

In cyberspace there are not clear visual cues about the level of privacy available. In fact, many newcomers initially assume that all of their activities in cyberspace are basically private if no one in physical space is observing them as they use their computers. Unless they have been made aware of the fact that "clickstream data" or "mouse droppings" leave "electronic footprints" that become a detailed digital record, they would not intuitively realize that they could be observed. The automatic capturing of this data is not obvious to the user.

There are a number of ways in which information may be captured as one surfs the Internet. First, each site that a user visits obtains the user's Internet Protocol (IP) address. The IP address is the unique address that a user has when connected to the Internet. It locates that computer on the Internet. Although the IP address may not yield personally identifiable information, it does allow tracking of Internet movements from a particular computer. Second, "cookies" can be placed on the user's hard drive so that a Web site can determine a user's prior activities at that Web site when the user returns. This transactional information reveals not only what pages the user viewed but also how the user arrived at the Web site and where the user went on departure. A user can set up her browser to warn her every time a cookie is about to be stored in her computer. This enables a user to see the contents of a cookie before the computer accepts it. Doing this slows down surfing on the Web; the costs of monitoring cookies are borne by the user. A user also can read the cookie file on the hard drive and can delete the cookies that are stored there. Some sites require users to accept cookies; if a user has deleted a cookie file, a new file will be created on the next visit to the site.

The more or less automatic capture of information through IP addresses and cookies are new techniques for collecting transaction information online. The policy problems posed by these techniques though are similar to the secondary uses of personally identifiable information in the physical world. In both instances, questions about notice of information practices and consent to those practices are key. Moreover, the quality of the information in terms of its accuracy, relevance, and timeliness may present policy issues. For example, a particular computer's accessing of a Web site does not mean that a particular person has accessed that site. Similarly browsing for particular information on the Web does not reveal the intent behind that browsing.

In addition to this more or less automatic capturing of transactional information, Web sites often request, and sometimes require, a visitor to reveal certain personally identifiable information or demographic information. The 1999 Georgetown Internet Privacy Policy (GIPP) Survey found that, from a sample of 361 commercial Web sites, 335 sites (92.8 percent) collected personal identifiable information and 205 sites (56.8 percent) collected demographic information (see Table 1).

Table 1. 1999 GIPP Survey
Personal Information Collected (Base=361)

Type of Information	Number of Sites Collecting	Percent Collecting
Personal Identifying Information		
Name	293	81.2%
E-mail	328	90.9%
Postal Address	227	62.9%
Phone Number	189	52.4%
Fax Number	59	16.3%
Credit Card Number	141	39.1%
Social Security Number	17	4.7%
Demographic Information		
Age/Date of Birth	111	30.7%
Family Information	23	6.4%
Gender	91	25.2%
Education	37	10.2%
Zip Code/City/State	108	29.9%
Income	37	10.2%
Preferences/Interests	76	21.1%
Occupation	58	16.1%
Other	57	15.8%

Source: Culnan (1999: 6).

Public opinion surveys indicate that almost 90 percent of respondents are concerned about threats to their privacy online. An AT&T survey asked Internet users about how comfortable they generally feel providing specific types of information to Web sites: 82 percent were comfortable revealing their favorite TV show; 76 percent were comfortable revealing their email addresses; 54 percent were comfortable revealing their name; 44 percent their postal address; 17 percent their income; 11 percent their phone number; and 3 percent their credit card number (Cranor, et al. 1999). The survey also found that 96 percent of respondents believed the most important factor affecting the release of information was whether or not the information would be shared with other companies and organizations. The 1998 Georgia Institute of Technology survey confirmed this concern that over 66 percent of survey respondents said the lack of information about how personal information would be used was a reason for not filling out online registration forms (GIT 1998).

Organizations maintaining Web sites are tracking public attitudes about online privacy for three reasons. First, Web site operators believe that there is more potential online traffic than is currently occurring. Some people are not going online. In a 1998 Harris/Westin/PWC survey respondents who defined themselves as "not likely to access the Internet in the next year" gave privacy protection as the factor most likely to influence their decision to go online and security of financial transactions as a close second (Harris 1998). Moreover, some people leave Web sites when personally identifiable information is requested. A 1997 survey found that 41 percent of respondents exited Web sites as soon as they saw a registration request (Boston Consulting Group 1997).

Second, public opinion surveys indicate that although more people are going online, they are not fully using the opportunities of the online world. For example, many people are browsing for information but not making purchases online. A 1999 National Consumers League survey found that 42 percent of those online use the Internet to gather information about products and services while 24 percent use the Internet to purchase goods or services. The 1998 Harris/Westin survey similarly reported that 23 percent had made online purchases. The responses to the 1998 AT&T survey reveal a somewhat different picture with 77 percent of online users reporting that they have made online purchases. It is important to note that this surveyed online users and although they may have made purchases online, they still were worried about privacy: 87 percent of respondents were concerned about threats to privacy online and 87 percent believed that tracking the Web sites that people visit and using that information improperly is very serious. The April 1998 10th Georgia Institute of Technology survey showed an over 10 percent increase in personal shopping online over a six month period.

Third, the information that people divulge online may not be accurate. The 1998 Georgia Institute of Technology survey reported that individuals have provided false information when registration is required. Similarly, a 1997 survey conducted by TRUSTe found that 27 percent of respondents furnished false information in response to a registration request (Boston Consulting Group 1997).

2.   POLICYMAKING FOR ONLINE PRIVACY

During the decades of discussions about information privacy, various codes of "fair information practice" have been developed to give meaning to the notion of privacy defined as individual control over personally identifiable information (Rule et al. 1980; Regan 1995; Schwartz and Reidenberg 1996; Cate 1997; Gellman 1997). In the early 1970s, the HEW Secretary's Committee (Department of Health, Education and Welfare 1973) developed the first of such codes and the British Younger Committee (1972) developed a very similar code. Both provided that: (1) there be no secret record systems; (2) an individual be able to find out what personally identifiable information is in a record and how it is used; (3) an individual be able to consent to uses of information for a purpose other than that for which it was collected (secondary use); (4) an individual be able to correct or amend an incorrect or incomplete record; and (5) organizations ensure the reliability of their information and prevent misuse of that information. This code of fair information practice became the core of the Privacy Act of 1974, which legislated policy for systems of records held by federal agencies.

In 1977, the Privacy Protection Study Commission (PPSC) reviewed the issue of information privacy policy and concluded that the core of an effective policy would be one that meet three objectives: to *minimize intrusiveness* (to create a proper balance between what an individual is expected to divulge to a record-keeping organization and what he seeks in return) to *maximize fairness* (to open up record-keeping operations in ways that will minimize the extent to which recorded information about an individual is itself a source of unfairness in any decision about her made on the basis of it) and, to *create legitimate, enforceable expectations of confidentiality* (to create and define obligations with respect to the uses and disclosures that will be made of recorded information about an individual (PPSC 1977)).

Efforts to articulate more clearly the essence of information privacy continued as computerization enabled collection and exchanges of more and more personally identifiable information. These efforts were by no means limited to the United States (Flaherty 1989; Bennett 1992). Indeed, the most comprehensive of these codes of fair information practices is the one crafted by the Organization for Economic Cooperation and Development (OECD 1980). The OECD code emphasized eight principles: collection limitation; data quality; purpose specification; use limitation; security safeguards; openness; individual participation; and accountability.

Recognizing the importance of privacy protection in fostering trust and confidence in the National Information Infrastructure (NII), two study commissions developed information privacy principles for the NII in the early 1990s. The Information Policy Committee of the White House's Information Infrastructure Task Force (IITF) issued several principles for providing and using personal information beginning with three general principles of information privacy, information integrity, and information quality (Information Infrastructure Task Force 1995). The National Information Infrastructure Advisory Council (NIIAC) approved thirteen privacy and security principles (National Information Infrastructure Advisory Council 1995). In both cases, these study commissions echoed many of the traditional principles developed earlier, often modifying, if not weakening, some of the core principles such as consent and redress. But both commissions also struggled with questions about fair information practice that are new in the online environment. The IITF and the NIIAC recognized emergent principles including the need to provide some opportunity for individuals to use technical controls, such as encryption, to protect the confidentiality and integrity of personally identifiable information. Both acknowledged that individuals should be able to remain anonymous as they conducted some online activities. The importance of educating the public about the privacy implications of online activities was highlighted in the codes developed by the IITF and the NIIAC.

In 1998 the National Telecommunications and Information Administration (NTIA) of the Department of Commerce and the OMB issued for public comment a discussion paper, "Elements of Effective Self Regulation for Protection of Privacy" (NTIA 1998). In this document a set of principles of fair information use for the online world, especially with respect to electronic commerce. Included among these were notice; choice; data security; data integrity; access; correction and amendment; and accountability. Additionally three possible enforcement mechanisms were discussed: consumer recourse (way that complaints and disputes can be resolved); verification (attestation that policy assertions are true); and consequences (sanctions).

In addition to policy formulation by executive agencies and task forces, the Federal Trade Commission (FTC) has also provided a forum for policy discussions. In April 1995 the FTC held its first public workshop on privacy, followed by a series of hearings in October and November 1995, and public workshops in June of 1996, 1997 and 1999. Under Section 5 of the FTC Act, the Commission may enforce actions against "deceptive trade practices." It has brought two major enforcement actions against deceptive online information practices. Both cases, one in 1998 against GeoCities and one in 1999 against Liberty Financial Companies, had to do with Web sites misrepresenting the purposes for which they were collecting personal information and their practices for uses of such information. Based on its public hearings, surveys of Web sites, and investigations the FTC has cautiously endorsed the principle of industry self-regulation and concluded that legislation is not necessary (FTC 1999).

Despite the general political climate endorsing self-regulation, the threat or possibility of legislation keeps pressure on organizations to craft effective self-regulatory mechanisms. In this sense, Congress can play an important role by providing incentives, signaling concerns and suggesting appropriate measures. The number of bills introduced regarding online privacy indicates that there is legislative concern and that legislative proposals are being formulated. In the 106th Congress, there are over a dozen bills that explicitly address online privacy including, for example, the Electronic Rights for the

21st Century Act (S.854), Online Privacy Protection Act (S.809), Internet Consumer Information Protection Act (HR 2882), and Social Security On-line Privacy Protection Act (HR 367). In addition to concerns about online privacy, there are a number of bills addressing medical information privacy, privacy of wireless communications, financial privacy, encryption and telemarketing. Most of these bills have been referred to committee and in many cases hearings have been held.

The only privacy bill that has successfully passed Congress and been signed by the President is the Children's Online Privacy Protection Act of 1998 (COPPA). The area of children's online privacy was the one area where the FTC in its 1998 report to Congress recommended that Congress develop legislation that would give parents controls over the online collection and use of personal information from children (FTC 1998). The FTC is currently drafting proposed rules to implement this law. It has been especially difficult to develop methods to obtain "verifiable parental consent" given the difficulties of authenticating identity on the Internet and the absence of intermediaries that might serve to negotiate such consent.

3. POLICY OPTIONS FOR ONLINE PRIVACY

3.1 Self-Regulation

As mentioned previously, the current political climate favors self-regulation as a method to protect online privacy. The theory is that if privacy is important to consumers, then online organizations will respond to the perceived consumer demand and will provide privacy protection. In essence the market will respond and outside regulation will not be necessary. The counter-argument, in part, is that the online world does not represent a perfect market and that market failures, in particular information asymmetries, need to be corrected. Advocates of self-regulation recognize the legitimacy of some of these concerns but respond that the online marketplace is still evolving and that the threat of government regulation, largely provided through media and public interest oversight, will provide additional incentives for effective self-regulation. Concerns about stifling market and technological innovations have trumped concerns about the commodification and misuse of personal information.

To this point, three types of self-regulatory mechanisms have received the most attention. Each will be described and analyzed below.

3.1.1   Privacy Notices

Because of the non-obvious nature of cyber-tracking, some visual cues about when and how such tracking occurs may be necessary in order to make cyberspace somewhat more comparable to what people have become accustomed to in physical space. This is most commonly being done through the posting of "privacy notices" or "information practice statements" on Web sites. In order to be effective as a visual cue, these statements need to be prominently displayed preferably on the home page and any other page where information is gathered. Although more Web sites are posting such notices (FTC 1998; Culnan 1999), the quality of these notices in terms of the completeness of information revealed varies enormously.

In order to demonstrate how these notices work, it may be instructive to examine the "privacy information" that the *New York Times* posted on its Web site in August of 1999. It should be pointed out that this notice is generally regarded as one of the best as compared to other notices. The notice is found on the bottom of the homepage under the copyright notice, with the printing for the privacy notice in a slightly smaller font and lighter color type than the copyright notice. If one clicks on "privacy information," one goes to a four-page disclosure of privacy practices http://www.nytimes.com/subscribe/help/privacy.html). The response to the question "What information does *The New York Times* on the Web gather/track about you?" reveals four types of information:

- Registration information including e-mail address and demographic information (country, zip code, age and gender with household income being optional);
- Premium services require credit card information;
- "Cookies" are collected to recognize the user and her privileges, as well as to track site usage, and ads displayed by a third-party advertising server may also contain cookies; and,
- IP Addresses are logged for systems administration and troubleshooting purposes but not to track behavior on the site.

The "privacy information" notice also discusses what *The Times* does with the information it gathers (statistical analysis and banner advertising, optional promotional e-mail, and data security) and with whom *The Times* shares information (shares aggregate information with advertisers and other partners, does not release personal information to third parties, and does provide you with copy of your registration information upon request but does not provide copy of tracking information). The "privacy notice" states that the Forums or message boards that *The Times* offers are public and could result in unsolicited e-mail. From the "privacy notice," one can click to a FAQ About Cookies (www.nytimes.com/subscribe/help/cookies.html).

The Federal Trade Commission, acting under its authority to identify "unfair and deceptive trade practices," has been following the development of self-regulatory mechanisms particularly the posting of privacy or information practice notices on commercial Web sites. In 1998, the FTC surveyed a sample of 1400 commercial Web sites and found that more than 85 percent collected personal information from consumers, 14 percent provided some notice with respect to their personal information practices, and 2 percent provided a comprehensive privacy policy notice (FTC 1998). Largely in response to these results and the perceived likelihood of federal legislation, several large private sector companies formed the Online Privacy Alliance, drafted privacy guidelines, and encouraged online posting of such policies. A year later the FTC concluded that sufficient increase in the number, if not necessarily the quality, of Web site notices had occurred to indicate that self-regulation was working and that legislation was not needed (FTC 1999). The FTC based its conclusion on a 1999 survey that was commissioned by several large corporations and conducted through the Georgetown Business School. This survey sampled 361 commercial Web sites drawn from 7500 of the most-often visited Web sites, and found that more than 92 percent of the sites collected personal information, 66 percent posted a privacy notice or information practice statement, and over 43 percent posted a privacy policy notice (Culnan 1999). Several groups criticized the FTC's interpretation of the survey results because few Web sites actually posted the full set of fair information practices that the FTC and the Clinton administration had advocated (Center for Democracy and Technology 1999).

Although such notices have the potential of providing visual cues in cyberspace, they are less effective than visual cues in the physical world. First, people do need to go through extra steps to find and read the notices. Reading privacy notices slows down the online experience. Rather than just reading the article on *The Times Online* or purchasing the book from Amazon.com, people have to go through additional steps to figure out the privacy environment. They then have to make a judgment about whether that environment is compatible with their privacy preferences. If it is not, then they have to go through steps to change that environment to better suit their preferences or leave that Website and go elsewhere. In response to scenarios presented in the 1998 AT&T survey, less than a third of respondents said they would be more likely to provide information if a site had a privacy policy (AT&T 1998).

Second, notices may not completely address fair information practices. The Georgetown survey of Web sites found that of 236 Web sites that collected personal information and had a privacy disclosure 89.8 percent addressed notice, 61.9 percent addressed choice, 40.3 percent addressed access, and 45.8 percent addressed security. In general the Web sites surveyed fell short of the full complement of fair information practices.

Moreover, on Web site notices, the defaults may be set in ways that are not obvious. For example, on the registration page for *The New York Times on the Web*, the e-mail preference options ("Yes, send me e-mail for new features, events, special coverage, and special offers from advertisers.") are already clicked on; people who do not want those e-mails have to click them off. In effect, the default here is set at a low level of privacy preferences.

Finally, and perhaps most importantly, it is not intuitively obvious that the Web sites are doing what they say they are doing. Since much of the action online takes place behind the computer screen, users cannot easily tell what a company is doing with the information it has collected. Enforcing standards or auditing practices are beyond the normal ability of an individual user. Some Web sites, including *The Times,* have registered with third parties, such as TRUSTe and BBB *OnLine*, which verify the practices of the Web site.

3.1.2   Privacy Seals

To remedy the lack of verifiability and enforceability of Web site notices, a few third party intermediaries have been formed. To date, the most popular are TRUSTe, formed from a partnership between EFF and CommerceNet, and BBB *OnLine*, a subsidiary of the Better Business Bureau. Both provide a system of "seals" and "trustmarks" displayed on Web sites that have contracted with TRUSTe or BBB *OnLine*. The terms of the contract may vary somewhat but in general the seal indicates that the Web site complies with certain fair information practices and that TRUSTe or BBB *OnLine* will receive complaints about the Web site's information practices and will audit the Web site's practices. If it is found that Web sites are not complying with the terms of the seal program, then the seal will be revoked and the Web site may be referred to legal authorities for further action.

TRUSTe's clients are primarily large companies, such as AOL, IBM, Netscape and eBay. It has been reported that there are more than 500 licensees represent over 90 percent of all Internet traffic (Electronic Frontier Foundation 1999). BBB *OnLine* was formed in March 1999 and is targeted to more mid-size and small firms, which make up BBB's traditional base.

The Center for Democracy and Technology (CDT) examined the practices and policies of three seal programs: BBB *OnLine*, TRUSTe, and WebTrust (CDT 1999). In general, CDT found that the fair information standards of all the programs did not fully address fair information practice principles. In particular seal programs fell short on the principles of access and correction, collection limitation, and disclosure limitation. Moreover, CDT pointed out that consumers have to read the fine print to determine the meaning of the seal. Sites with the same seals may have quite different policies; however, such discrepancies are to be eliminated in the near future.

The use of privacy seals redirects the costs or privacy protection to some extent. Web sites are now subject to some outside control and have to pay a license fee to receive that control. The Web sites are assuming more of the cost of privacy protection than they do under the option of privacy notices. Consumers do bear some time costs in that they need to look for the seal and click it on to determine what level of protection is ensured. If seals become ubiquitous on the Web, consumers may be able to easily discern their meanings.

Responses to the 1998 AT&T survey indicate that almost 60 percent of respondents would be more likely to provide information if the site had both a privacy policy and a seal of approval from "a well-known organization such as the Better Business Bureau or AAA" (AT&T 1998). Key to support for the seal component appears to be whether the organization backing the seal is one which consumers already trust. This is not surprising but may have implications for the development of seal programs. In initial discussions about seals, one of their advantages as a policy option was that there would be competition among seal programs, which would provoke the offering of stronger privacy protections. If successful entry into the privacy seal market is dependent upon existing reputation as a trusted organization, this will narrow the range of organizations likely to risk entrance.

3.1.3 Technical Privacy Interfaces/Filters

In order to avoid interruptions in Web surfing to check for privacy notices or for privacy seals, the World Wide Web Consortium has advocated use of the Platform for Privacy Preferences (P3P). P3P provides a technical means for consumers to specify their privacy preferences, to communicate those preferences to every Web site they visit, and to compare those preferences to the practices of the Web site as they are specified in a machine-readable proposal (EFF 1999; Reagle and Cranor 1998). In this way P3P acts as a "social protocol" in that it mediates the human components of the interaction between the individual and the Web site (Cranor and Reagle 1998). The consumers' Web browsers, browsers' plug-ins or proxy servers read the Web site proposals and determine whether they match the preferences of the consumer. If there is a match, the user accesses the Web site; if there is not a match, the user is automatically denied access or is asked if she wishes to enter the Web site despite its information practices. Consumers can also tailor preferences with specific sites or types of sites.

The primary advantages of this technical option are that consumers do not need to repeatedly make decisions about their privacy preferences and that their Web surfing is not interrupted. The costs of privacy protection to the individual are concentrated primarily at the time at which initial privacy preferences are set. If the consumer finds that her preferences are set too high, then she can reset them. If the Web site finds that it is losing traffic, then the Web site might consider resetting its practices to restrict the collection and/or reuse of personally identifiable information. There is some feedback to the individual directly and to the Web site somewhat indirectly that can approximate the supply/demand communication that a market needs in order to function.

The major disadvantage with this option is that individuals do not know for certain that the Web site is following the agreement or if the Web site, for example, is actually collecting cookies. The essence of this approach is a contract that is negotiated through technical interfaces. Enforcement or auditing of practices is not built into this solution. In order to be effective, it may be necessary to employ this option in conjunction with a seal program or audit mechanism.

Another technical option is an Open Profiling Standard (OPS) proposed by Netscape and Microsoft and supported by some forty private sector firms. OPS is a software standard that would enable computer users to control the release of personal information by enabling them to enter profile and preference information one time in a standard format and to establish specific rules about the use and disclosure of this information. An advantage of this approach is that it saves users time. There appear to be some problems, however. First, the OPS requires a form of digital signatures to ensure that the identity and authenticity of both user and Web site. Second, OPS may result in release and exchange of more information than consumers intend as OPS is designed for release, not suppression, of information (OECD 1998). Finally, people may not be interested in using such a system. In the 1998 AT&T survey, 86 percent of respondents said that they had no interest in feature that would automatically transfer data "to sites with acceptable privacy policies accompanied by notice to users" and 94 percent said they had no interest without an accompanying notice (Cranor, Reagle and Ackerman 1999).

3.2   Regulation

Although the current political climate favors self-regulation, the issue of the appropriate role of government in the online world has not been settled and the possibility of government regulation of several areas of Internet activity, including privacy, is a real one. Before discussing particular forms of regulation, it is important to note that the global, open network architecture of the Internet appears to be an inherent limitation on the effectiveness of government regulation. The continuous technological evolution of the Internet and its applications may also be a limitation on the effectiveness of regulatory options.

Despite these political, global and technological barriers, the thirty-year discussion in the United States and other countries about the need for government action to protect information privacy validates the consideration of regulation to protect online privacy. There is public opinion data that also support the possibility of this option. In a 1998 Harris/Westin survey 80 percent of Internet users agreed with the Clinton administration's self-regulatory stance with the consideration of legislation only if the private sector fails to implement effective policy. But, only 34 percent of male users and 19 percent of female users were in total agreement that business incentives would be sufficient to address the problem. In the October 1998 Georgia Tech Survey, over 40 percent of respondents agreed strongly, and over 30 percent agreed somewhat, that there should be new laws to protect privacy on the Internet. Less than 10 percent disagreed strongly with the statement. There would appear to be some public skepticism, even among Internet users, that self-regulation will be effective and over two-thirds of the public expressing support for new laws.

3.2.1   Legislating Information Practices

One often-discussed option is to legislate some variant of "fair information practices" and give them the force of law on the Internet generally or as protection of certain categories of personally identifiable information. Traditionally, the United States has adopted a sectoral approach to information protection, legislating some protections for certain areas such as federal agencies, credit, banking, cable, education and video and leaving other areas without protection, for example medical. Many other countries, the Europeans in particular, have adopted an omnibus approach requiring by law that all organizations comply with certain fair information standards.

In addition to the debate about whether legislation might be appropriate for all or particular sectors, a second issue in considering legislation is what fair information principles should be legislated. Although, as discussed above, there is a basic rubric of fair information practices, there is also variation within that rubric.

There are two major problems with a legislative option. First, it is responsive or reactive rather than proactive. Legislative standards are unlikely to pass unless there is a record of information abuses. People must somehow learn about abuses of their personal information and be willing to go public with their stories. More importantly, this approach is always addressing the problem that "was" rather than addressing the problem that is in the planning stages. Rather than providing guidelines for what is legally appropriate, this approach allows organizations to experiment with uses of information until those uses exceed expectations in a dramatic manner. Second, this approach tends to give individuals rights of redress to correct information misuses. The burden of enforcement falls to the individual and necessitates expenditures of interest, time, and money.

3.2.2   Establishing an Agency

Most countries have created a national-level institution with some degree of responsibility for monitoring the collection and use of personal information. In some countries, such as Germany, this is referred to as a "Data Protection Agency" and in others, such as Canada, it is referred to as a "Privacy Commissioner." The powers of such agencies also vary from licensing to regulation to advice (Bennett 1992; Flaherty 1989). Although the United States considered the establishment of such a federal entity as early as 1974, there has not been sufficient support for its creation and its opposition has been adamant and has maintained good political connections.

The question of the creation of a privacy entity as a policy option surfaced in the discussions of the National Information Infrastructure Task Force (IITF). The IITF evaluated three institutional possibilities. The creation of a federal agency with regulatory authority was considered but the IITF recognized that it would be inconsistent with the existing sectoral and fragmented approach, it would be expensive, and it would appear as antithetical to a "smaller government" philosophy. A second option was the creation of a federal entity without regulatory authority, but with other authority such as coordination, representation, advocacy, ombudsman, advice and/or education. Although the IITF recognized some shortcomings in each of these, it also saw some value to many of these functions. Third was the creation of a non-governmental or advisory entity. The value of this approach was seen as its low cost and easy implementation, but the IITF noted that it might not have the stature or breadth that seems necessary for online privacy issues.

With the recent focus on self-regulation, privacy notices, and the possibility of technical solutions, the option of establishing a new agency has receded from public discussions. However, as the limitations of other approaches highlight the need to find ways of brokering trust, the value of an agency may be recognized. One of the primary, and shared, shortcomings of the self-regulatory mechanisms discussed above is that there is no assurance that they ensure that an organization is actually doing what it indicates. The fundamental flaw is that there is no real accountability and hence no way to broker or negotiate individual or public trust.

4.   DISCUSSION

In addressing online privacy protection, the fundamental policy issue is how best to convey to individuals and the public that Web sites are doing what they say with personally identifiable information. The critical question in evaluating different options is how effective that option is in conveying trust about information practices. Fundamentally the question of trust is one of enforcement or compliance. From the perspective of conveying trust, there is less concern with the specific content of the information practices of a Web site and more concern with whether the Web site is doing what it says regardless of that may specifically be. The focus of analysis is not on whether, for example, the Web site discloses, or does not disclose, personally identifiable information to its affiliates but how individuals and the public can know whether the stated policy is followed. The focus of concern is on mechanisms that ensure accountability of the Web site. Some means of verifying that the practices are followed is pivotal.

In developing a verification and accountability scheme, individuals themselves need to be able to learn the details of the personal information practices of Web sites. Part of trusting an organization is that the organization is accountable to its current and potential customers and clients. Openness about how that organization is ensuring compliance appears essential. Secret practices, whether they issue from self-regulation, regulation, or technical advancements, are not going to foster trust. The terms of the information practices that a Web site is following must be accessible to all users and potential users. A seal program that did not post the practices represented by that seal does not assist the individual user in beginning to develop trust about that Web site.

Although providing knowledge and the possibility for individual involvement is necessary, a policy option that relies upon individual oversight to ensure whether the Web site complies with its own stated privacy notices, statutory requirements, or technical safeguards is unlikely to convey trust. Common to all three approaches is that the responsibility of overseeing privacy practices falls to the individual, regardless of whether the terms of the practice result from self-regulation, legislation, or technical standards. The difficulties inherent in individual oversight are enormous. Given the complexity of information practices and the number of Web sites an individual might visit, it is simply beyond the capacity of an individual to provide any time of meaningful oversight. If an individual were to assume this burden, she would realize its enormity and realize that the most rational response would be to be wary all of the time. The skepticism necessary to monitor this situation is not likely to lead to trust.

A more fundamental dilemma with focusing on individual empowerment is that the larger social or public consequences of online privacy protection are not addressed. Relying on individual decisions to protect privacy in a context where organizational and market forces push aggressively in the opposite direction is likely to result in less privacy than would be optimal from a collective standpoint (Regan 1999). When individuals mistrust the personal information practices of an organization and when the organization responds by increasing its information collection and surveillance practices, a "spiral of mistrust" (Samarajiva 1997) occurs. This spiral does not only affect the individual and organization in question, but becomes part of the larger social context. The effect is that, both from the individual perspective and from the social perspective, not only is there less privacy, there is also less trust.

To address the weaknesses inherent in individual enforcement, one response has been to propose the placement of a number of organizations between the individual and the Web site. But this proposal will not itself be sufficient to convey trust. Instead, there appears to be a temptation in crafting policy solutions to begin an infinite regress. The Web site adopts a policy which meets with the requirements of a seal program; the Web site posts both its policy and the seal; the seal program audits the Web site to ensure Web site compliance; and, the seal program hires an outside auditor to ensure that it conducted the initial audit properly. But is the outside auditor trustworthy? At each point, someone has protected itself by providing a form of outside control, but none of those forms of outside control necessarily ensures trust. If the reputation of any one of the organizations is impeccable, for example, the *New York Times*, or Better Business Bureau, or Ernst and Young then that organization may be able to convey trust regardless of the number of other organizations involved. But this is trust conveyed by prior reputation. Online trust is then dependent in trust conveyed from the physical world. Success in the online world then becomes dependent on success in the physical world. But this does not foster the innovation that the private sector espouses.

Simplicity in enforcement mechanisms may be a key virtue. Constructing a house of cards with many points of vulnerability appears not to hold the answer. A Rube Goldberg construct will not convey trust. It might be better to strive for simple, understandable, and transparent. If these become the criteria, then logically a few premises seem to follow. The involvement of fewer organizations is better than many. More obvious information practices are to be preferred over less obvious. More responsibility to parties with direct involvement is preferred to either less responsibility to such parties or more responsibility to parties with indirect involvement.

An enduring issue in debates about online policy, privacy and otherwise, involves the appropriate role of government and law. The truth is that in most areas of social and economic life, government and law do play basic roles. As social and economic activities move online, does it follow that government and law should remain behind. In large part what is being searched for in mechanisms that convey or broker trust is a mechanism that has the force of law behind it. Law is one of our primary methods of ensuring accountability and in conveying trust. If a legal agreement is not kept, there are ways of holding the parties to that agreement accountable. Consequences follow. A system that is backed by law will convey more trust than one backed by a service agreement or the threat of legislation.

Using traditional contract law, however, is unlikely to be sufficient. Harms resulting from online collections and uses of personal information are not obvious, either to the individual or to a third party. Additionally, a contract law approach is remedial addressing harms after they have occurred. For these reasons legal requirements need to be accompanied by a system of oversight. Monitoring or auditing by a disinterested third-party seems necessary to convey trust. But, as pointed out above, this third-party has to be trusted or has to be held accountable. Government organizations, although they may not be trusted in and of themselves, can be held accountable and for that reason may have a better chance at brokering trust than any other organization.

REFERENCES

Agre, P. E. and M. Rotenberg. (1997). *Technology and Privacy: The New Landscape*, Cambridge, MA: The MIT Press.

Bennett, C. J. (1992). *Regulating Privacy: Data Protection and Public Policy in Europe and the United States*, Ithaca, NY: Cornell University Press.

Boston Consulting Group. (1997). *Internet Privacy Study*. http://www.truste.org/news/article003.html.

Cate, F. H. (1997). *Privacy in the Information Age*, Washington, D.C.: Brookings.

Center for Democracy and Technology. (1999). *Behind the Numbers: Privacy Practices on the Web*. http://www.cdt.org/privacy/990727privacy.pdf.

Cranor, L. F., J. Reagle, and M. S. Ackerman. (1999). *Beyond Concern: Understanding Net Users' Attitudes About Online Privacy*. AT&T Labs-Research Technical Report TR 99.4.3. http://www.research.att.com/library/trs/TRs/99/99.4/99.4/report.htm.

Cranor, L. F. and J. Reagle Jr. (1998). *Designing a Social Protocol: Lessons Learned from the Platform for Privacy Preferences Project*. http://www.w3.org/People/Reagle/papers/tprc97/tprc-f2m3.html.

Culnan, M. (1999). *Georgetown Internet Privacy Policy Survey: Report to the Federal Trade Commission*, Washington, DC: Georgetown University. Available at: http://www.msb.edu/faculty/culnanm/gippshome.html.

Department of Health, Education and Welfare (HEW). (1973). *Records, Computers, and the Rights of Citizens*, Washington, DC: Government Printing Office.

Electronic Frontier Foundation (EFF). (1999). *Architecture is Policy–Case Study: Cooperative development as standards-based Implementation for Privacy on the Internet.* http://www.eff.org/privacypaper.html.

Federal Trade Commission (FTC). (1999). *Self-Regulation and Privacy Online: A Report to Congress.* Washington, DC: Federal Trade Commission. http://www.ftc.gov/os/1999/9907/privacy99.pdf

Federal Trade Commission (FTC). (1998). *Privacy Online: A Report to Congress*, Washington, DC: Federal Trade Commission. http://www.ftc.gov/reports/privacy3/toc.htm.

Flaherty, D. H. (1989). *Protecting Privacy in Surveillance Societies: The Federal Republic of Germany, Sweden, France, Canada, and the United States*, Chapel Hill, NC: University of North Carolina Press.

Fukuyama, F. (1995). *Trust: The Social Virtues and The Creation of Prosperity*, New York: The Free Press.

Gellman, R. (1997). "Does Privacy Law Work?" In P. E. Agre and M. Rotenberg, *Technology and Privacy: The New Landscape*, Cambridge, MA: MIT Press.

Georgia Institute of Technology (GIT). (1998). *GVU's Tenth WWW User Survey.* http://www.gatech.edu/gvu/user_surveys/survey-1998-10.html.

Harris, L. and A.F. Westin. (1998). *E-Commerce and Privacy: What Net Users Want*, Sponsored by Price Waterhouse and Privacy and American Business, Hackensack, NJ: P&AB).

Information Infrastructure Task Force (IITF). (1995). *Privacy and the National Information Infrastructure: Principles for Providing and Using Personal Information.* http://www.iitf.nist.gov/documents/committee/infopol/niiprivprin_final.html.

National Information Infrastructure Advisory Council (NIIAC). (1995). *Common Ground: Fundamental Principles for the National Information Infrastructure.* Washington, DC: National Information Infrastructure Advisory Council.

National Telecommunications and Information Administration (NTIA). (1998). *Elements of Effective Self-Regulation for the Protection of Privacy and Questions Related to Online Privacy.* http://www.ntia.doc.gov/ntiahome/privacy/6_5_98fedreg.htm.

OMB Watch. (1997). *A Delicate Balance: The Privacy and Access Practices of Federal Government World Wide Web Sites.* http://ombwatch.org/ombw/info/balance.html.

Organization for Economic Cooperation and Development (OECD). (1980). *Guidelines on the Protection of Privacy and Transborder Flows of Personal Data.* http://www.oecd.org//dsti/sti/it/secur/prod/PRIV-EN.HTM.

Organization for Economic Cooperation and Development, Directorate for Science, Technology and Industry, Committee for Information, Computer and Communications Policy (OECD). (1998). *Implementing the OECD "Privacy Guidelines" in the Electronic Environment: Focus on the Internet.* http://www.oecd.org/dsti/sti/it/secur/prod/reg97-6e.htm.

Privacy Protection Study Commission (PPSC). (1977). *Personal Privacy in an Information Society.* Washington, DC: Government Printing Office.

Putnam, R. D. (1995). "Bowling Alone: America's Declining Social Capital," *Journal of Democracy* 6(1):65-78.

Reagle, J. and L. F. Cranor. (1998). *The Platform for Privacy Preferences.* Note-P3P-CACM-19981106. http://www.w3.org/TR/1998/NOTE-P3P-CACM/

Regan, P. M. (1995). *Legislating Privacy: Technology, Social Values, and Public Policy,* Chapel Hill, NC: University of North Carolina Press.

Regan, P. M. (1999). *Privacy as a Common Good in a Digital World.* Presented at the Annual Meetings of the American Political Science Association, Atlanta Marriott Marquis and Atlanta Hilton Towers.

Rule, J. B., D. MacAdam, L. Stearns and D. Uglow (1980). *The Politics of Privacy: Planning for Personal Data Systems as Powerful Technologies,* New York: Elsevier.

Samarajiva, R. (1997). "Interactivity as Though Privacy Mattered." In P.E. Agre and M. Rotenberg, *Technology and Privacy: The New Landscape,* Cambridge, MA: MIT Press, pp. 277-309.

Schwartz, P. M. and J. R. Reidenberg. (1996). *Data Privacy Law: A Study of United States Data Protection,* Charlottesville, VA: Michie.

Westin, A. F. (1967). *Privacy and Freedom,* New York: Atheneum.

World Wide Web Consortium (W3C). (1999). *Platform for Privacy Preferences: P3P Project.* http://www.w3.org/P3P/#overview.

INNOVATION POLICY AND GLOBALIZATION ISSUES

PART FOUR

Chapter 14

National Technology Policy in Global Markets
Developing Next-Generation Lithography in the Semiconductor Industry

GREG LINDEN
University of California, Berkeley

DAVID C. MOWERY
University of California, Berkeley

ROSEMARIE HAM ZIEDONIS
University of Pennsylvania

1.   INTRODUCTION

During the late 1980s and early 1990s, U.S. policymakers confronted an unusual combination of political success and economic challenge in the international landscape. As the Cold War waned, competition from firms in industrial and industrializing allies, such as Japan and South Korea, placed severe pressure on U.S. firms in many industries, including the high-technology industries whose early growth had benefited from Cold War-related defense spending. One result of this juxtaposition of events was a series of federal initiatives designed to link the activities of the vast network of federal laboratories, many of which were established as part of the Cold War defense build-up, to the technological needs of industry.   The Cooperative Research and Development Agreement (CRADA) was one of the most widely employed vehicles in these initiatives, particularly in the Department of Energy (DoE) laboratory system.

At the end of the decade, both the political success and the economic challenge are more muted.   In particular, U.S. firms in many high-technology industries, notably the semiconductor and computer industries, appear to have improved their competitive performance.   The causes of this improved performance remain poorly understood, and may well have had as much to do with the greater stability of U.S. macroeconomic policy during the 1990s as with the sectoral federal programs that were initiated during the late 1980s and early 1990s (Mowery 1999).   Political support for these programs has declined, and federal funding for CRADAs and for the Energy Department's role in industrial competitiveness has diminished.   Federal funding for CRADAs in the DOE has shrunk from more than $346 million in fiscal 1995 to an estimated level of less than $95 million in fiscal 1999.   The total number of active CRADAs with DOE laboratories has declined from nearly 1700 in fiscal 1996 to fewer than 700 in fiscal 1999 (U.S. Department of Energy July 1999).

Nevertheless, CRADAs continue to be widely employed by federal agencies to support industrial collaboration and U.S. firms continue to confront significant competitive challenges.   This chapter examines the structure and goals of one of the largest of these recent CRADAs, involving the Department of Energy and the "Extreme Ultraviolet Limited Liability Company" (EUV LLC).   Founded in 1997, the EUV LLC is a consortium owned by three U.S. semiconductor manufacturers, Intel Corporation, Motorola, and AMD.   The EUV LLC has established a CRADA with three of the largest DOE laboratories—Sandia, Lawrence Livermore, and Lawrence Berkeley National Laboratories—to develop technologies for "next-generation lithography" (NGL) in the semiconductor manufacturing industry.

The EUV initiative relies on both government-industry and intra-industry collaboration to develop a technically effective and commercially feasible next-generation lithography technology.   The role of U.S. semiconductor equipment firms is especially important to the successful development of new manufacturing technologies, and equipment producers face severe uncertainties about the timing and characteristics of the transition from current optical lithography technologies to their (still uncertain) replacement. The collaborative development by semiconductor firms of technological "roadmaps," consensus forecasts of the timing and characteristics of previous major technological transitions in the industry, has not eliminated the presence or the economic costs of uncertainty over the timing of technological transitions.

The EUV CRADA also has interesting lessons for the design of effective government-industry partnerships.   How does this CRADA build on the successes and failures of previous CRADAs with DOE laboratories (Ham and Mowery 1995, 1998)? Although the structure of this CRADA appears to avoid some of the difficulties of previous DOE CRADAs, the transition from pre-commercial R&D to the manufacture and support of high-quality manufacturing tools poses significant challenges to public and private managers. Finally, like other initiatives in public-private collaborative R&D, this CRADA confronts the dilemma of national technology policies in global industries—what role should non-U.S. firms play in R&D collaborations that involve federal funds or federal facilities?

2.   COOPERATIVE RESEARCH AND DEVELOPMENT AGREEMENTS

A CRADA is a contractual arrangement between a federal laboratory and participating firm that enables the laboratories to conduct joint R&D projects with the private sector. Under the terms of a CRADA, the private-firm partner can be assigned the rights to any intellectual property resulting from the joint work, while the federal government retains a nonexclusive license to the intellectual property. The Federal Technology Transfer Act of 1986 created CRADAs, but government-owned, contractor-operated federal laboratories, such as those in the DOE laboratory system, were allowed to conduct CRADAs with private firms only with the passage of amendments to the Act in 1989.[1] Federal agencies and research laboratories have signed hundreds of CRADAs each year since the late 1980s; between 1989 and 1995, DOE signed over 1500 CRADAs to support collaborative technology projects with private firms. Many of the CRADAs signed by DOE included cost-sharing provisions that provided laboratory support (either funding or "in-kind" contributions) for up to 50 percent of total project costs.

A series of case studies of CRADAs between the Lawrence Livermore National Laboratory and individual firms by Ham and Mowery (1995, 1998) found that CRADAs were most effective for projects that drew on the historic missions and capabilities of the DOE laboratories. This finding echoed the arguments of the Energy Department Task Force on Alternative Futures for the Energy Department Laboratories (1995, more commonly known as the Galvin Committee) that the defense laboratories are poorly suited to the task of civilian technology development in areas not directly linked to their historic missions.[2] The case studies suggested that CRADAs experienced a number of operational problems, stemming from insufficient budgetary and managerial flexibility in project operations; insufficient commitment by the collaborating parties to the joint project, frequently reflected in limited interaction between the research teams; limited laboratory researcher familiarity with the needs of the eventual users of the technologies being jointly developed; and insufficient internal R&D resources and technical expertise within the collaborating firm(s) to absorb and apply the results of collaboration. The EUV CRADA has addressed some but not all of these issues in the design and implementation of CRADAs, as we discuss in detail below.

3.   THE EUV CHALLENGE

The technical challenges facing the EUV LLC CRADA are embedded in the larger problem facing the semiconductor industry as a whole—whether and when to shift to a new lithography technology. The semiconductor industry thus faces two types of uncertainty. The first is *timing uncertainty*: When will semiconductor producers be ready to buy the lithography tools of the future in sufficient volume to justify their development and manufacture by suppliers? The second is *technological uncertainty*: Which technology will prove best suited to replace the current dominant design? Similar uncertainties attend the adoption of new technologies in many other industries. These challenges are heightened in the case of semiconductors by two features. First, the scale and duration of the investments necessary to develop and commercialize a complete next-generation lithography (NGL) system are considerable—well in excess of $1 billion and 8-10 years in duration.[3] Second, and perhaps even more important, is the fact that this technology transition, like previous cases in semiconductor manufacturing, requires complementary investments by numerous suppliers of materials, equipment, and optics, as well as semiconductor manufacturers.

3.1   Semiconductor Optical Lithography Technology: An Overview

Optical lithography technology currently is employed in semiconductor manufacturing to create interconnected patterns of electronic circuitry on a silicon wafer by transferring a pattern from a reusable template ("mask") onto the wafer surface. All lithography tools use the same basic arrangement of elements: the light passes through the pattern-bearing mask, then through a reduction lens (typically 4x reduction or greater) to the wafer, where it exposes a light-sensitive coating called "photoresist," which is then processed by other tools to create a circuit layer.

Lithographic tools (referred to as "steppers") play a critical role in semiconductor manufacturing and are very expensive (about $5 million each), typically accounting for 20 percent of the costs of an advanced fabrication facility.[4] These tools have played a pivotal role in technological progress within the semiconductor industry, making possible the shrinkage of semiconductor "linewidths" (the size of the smallest feature on a semiconductor component) from several microns to 0.25-micron (250 nanometers) or less.[5]

3.2 Next-Generation Lithography: Timing Uncertainty

Optical lithography manufacturing technologies have displayed a remarkably robust and unexpectedly lengthy "old age."[6] Like the sailing ships of the late 19th century, optical lithography technology has displayed unexpected possibilities for extension and improvement in the face of (potential) competition from alternatives. This characteristic of optical lithography technology, however, creates uncertainty about the timing of the transition to a "post-optical" alternative.

Industry experts currently expect that a next-generation lithography (NGL) technology will be needed for volume manufacturing by the middle of the next decade; but similar forecasts have been made for almost 20 years. Around 1980, optical lithography was projected to extend only through 0.8-micron linewidths. By the mid-1980s, the expectation had become 0.5-micron, meaning that a successor technology would not be needed until the mid-1990s. Later improvements, such as the introduction of "phase-shift" masks around 1990, raised expectations that optical lithography could be extended to at least 0.35-micron linewidths. It now appears that optical lithography using a 193nm light source will remain feasible for semiconductor devices with linewidths of 0.12 microns and possibly for linewidths of 0.09 microns by 2005.

The cumulative effect of numerous incremental improvements in optical lithography thus has extended the life of this technology by more than 20 years and has advanced its technical capabilities at least nine fold. As a result, the date of expected need for post-optical technologies has remained "five to ten years in the future" for more than a decade. The continuing uncertainty about the timing of the large-scale introduction of NGL has a chilling effect on investments by equipment suppliers in the development of new technologies.

3.3 Next-Generation Lithography: Technological Uncertainty

An additional element of uncertainty is created by the fact that no single technological solution has yet been shown to be unambiguously superior to all others for "post-optical" lithographic applications in the manufacture of semiconductors. Six different technologies are listed in the 1998 "Update" to the *International Technology Roadmap for Semiconductors* (SIA 1998), a consensus industry forecast prepared by SEMATECH, for the 0.065-micron linewidth devices that are expected to enter production in 2006.[7] These six NGL contenders (summarized in Table 1) are:

1) **Electron-Beam Direct Write (EBDW) Lithography:**   Electron beams a few thousandths of a nanometer in wavelength are used to draw patterns directly on the wafer. Because it imprints patterns directly on the wafer instead of using a mask, EBDW is less costly than the other NGL options. The direct-write system, however, suffers from low throughput and is generally considered too slow for mass production. As a result, EBDW has been used primarily for very low-volume products, such as fabrication masks or small-lot custom chips. This is the most mature NGL technology, developed by IBM and Bell Labs during the 1960s. The Japanese semiconductor research consortium ASET, [8] as well as Hitachi and Fujitsu, continue to invest in EBDW development.

2) **Proximity X-Ray Lithography (PXRL):**   This lithography technology uses X-rays of approximately 1 nm wavelength through a 1x mask placed in close proximity to the wafer to expose a circuit layer. The 1:1 mask ratio places a heavy burden on defect prevention in the mask-making process; a minuscule defect will become insignificant on the final chip in a 4x reduction process, but retains its original size in a 1x process, with a correspondingly greater chance of rendering the entire chip defective.   The power source for this technology, a large synchrotron, costs up to $50 million, but operates as many as 20 lithography tools (Smith and Cerrina 1997). ASET, Mitsubishi, NEC, Toshiba, NTT, and IBM all have made major investments in this technology's development, but it has never been used for volume production.[9]

3) **Ion-Beam Projection Lithography (IPL):** A beam of hydrogen or helium ions is projected through a 4x-stencil mask. Ions (electrically charged atoms) scatter less than either electrons or light, which makes more precise imaging possible. Whereas most masks use an absorbing material over a transmissive substrate, a stencil mask uses only the absorbing material and permits the beam to pass through openings. This technique requires two "complementary" masks for most layers in wafer processing, increasing costs and slowing throughput.   Focused ion beams have several industrial uses, such as very fine measurement and machining applications, but have been the focus of little investment for semiconductor lithography. The projection technique currently under consideration was developed in Europe in the late 1980s and has been supported as one of several NGL projects by a European consortium

known as MEDEA with the involvement of Infineon (formerly Siemens Semiconductor).[10]

4) **Electron-beam Projection (EPL) Lithography**: An electron beam is projected onto a 4x mask that uses differential scattering of the electrons to form a high-resolution image on the wafer. The electrons expose a small area of the wafer that must be "stitched" to other exposed areas to create the whole pattern. The system retains the high resolution of electron beams but has higher throughput. One version of this technology, "SCALPEL," was developed by Lucent in 1989, and in 1999, IBM and Nikon revealed the existence of a joint project to develop a closely related system ("PREVAIL").[11] In November 1999, Motorola, Texas Instruments, and Samsung announced that they would cooperate with Lucent in commercial development of the SCALPEL system.

5) **157-nm Lithography**: This technology, based on a fluorine (F2) laser, is an extension of the existing optical architecture, although it appeared in the industry's roadmap only in 1998.[12] Fluorine-based 157-nm lithography was the focus of research at Bell Labs in the 1980s. Until recently industry experts doubted its feasibility for manufacturing applications (Bloomstein et al. 1997). This technology requires new materials for masks and photoresist, which makes it as uncertain as the alternatives. All major lithography suppliers have launched 157nm development programs. The major proponent of this technology in the United States is MIT's Lincoln Lab, whose 157nm research is partially funded by Intel. In April 1999, Infineon announced a three-year, $27 million program on 157nm lithography funded by the German Ministry of Education and Research.

6) **Extreme Ultraviolet (EUV) Lithography**: EUV uses waves of approximately 13 nm ("extreme ultraviolet"). The waves are reflected off a series of mirrors, one of which contains the 4x mask; each mirror must be very precisely shaped (slightly aspherical) and coated with dozens of super-fine alternating layers of molybdenum and silicon. Because of the unique multilayer technology, eliminating mask defects is more technically challenging for EUV than for most of the other technologies. Nevertheless, the system offers high resolution at acceptable levels of throughput and the technology has advanced rapidly. Besides the EUV LLC, proponents of EUV include ASET in Japan and EUCLIDES in Europe.[13]

Table 1: Technological Alternatives for Next-Generation Lithography

Technology	Wavelength	Key Characteristics	Chip Companies Funding Development	Main Challenges
Electron-Beam Direct Writing (EBDW)	0.004 nm	Maskless, low throughput	ASET[‡]	Increasing throughput
Proximity X-Ray Lithography (PXRL)	1 nm	1x mask	IBM, ASET[‡]	Reducing mask defects
Ion Projection Lithography (IPL)	.00005 nm*	Complementary stencil masks	Infineon (Siemens)	Mask improvement
Electron Projection Lithography (EPL)	0.004 nm*	Scattering mask, small exposure field	Lucent, IBM, Motorola, Samsung, Texas Instruments	Mask improvement; stitching small fields
157nm ("Optical extension")	157 nm	Extension of existing architecture	Infineon (Siemens), Intel	New materials for optics and photoresist
Extreme Ultra-Violet Lithography (EUVL)	13 nm	Multilayer coated optics, including mask	EUV LLC, ASET[‡]	Reducing defects in masks; compact source

* - The beam width for IPL and EPL is larger than the wavelength

[‡] - Chip companies in ASET's EUV program are Fujitsu, Hitachi, Matsushita, Mitsubishi, NEC, Oki, Sanyo, Sharp, Sony, and Toshiba.

As the right column of Table 1 makes clear, the main challenge facing most next-generation lithography technologies (with the exception of maskless electron beam direct write) is that of creating very fine masks. This challenge is particularly acute for EUV lithography because the multilayer coatings make it problematic to correct embedded errors that do not occur in the other technologies.

3.4   Managing Uncertainty: Intra-Industry Collaboration

Equipment suppliers and semiconductor manufacturers thus confront great uncertainty about the timing of the exhaustion of the technological possibilities for optical lithography, along with uncertainty about which technology will replace optical lithography. These uncertainties may retard the development and deployment of NGL technology because of the need for coordinated investments over a number of years by many different user and supplier firms. The willingness of these firms to make these substantial and risky investments will be heavily affected by their expectations about timing and technology choice.

The U.S. and global semiconductor manufacturing and equipment industries have instituted a number of efforts to prevent these uncertainties from paralyzing the development of new lithographic technologies. SEMATECH, a U.S.-based consortium of semiconductor manufacturers, has sponsored a series of meetings to develop an industry "roadmap" of future technological evolution that (among other things) includes forecasts of the timing of introduction and a list of the leading technologies for use in next-generation lithography. By promoting and publicizing these consensus forecasts by major potential adopters of these technologies, SEMATECH hoped to provide clearer guidance to the equipment suppliers that must make substantial development investments.[14] Even the most careful efforts to create such a consensus can be foiled by underlying disagreements among firms and technical experts, and any such consensus can be overtaken by events.

Development of consensus on the leading technological successor to optical lithography has been difficult. In November 1997, SEMATECH held a workshop with lithography experts from all over the world that failed to reach agreement on the best next-generation lithography candidate. A second workshop was held in December 1998, where attendees identified EUV and EPL as the two leading candidates. Although the selection of these technologies as the most likely replacements for optical lithography by workshop participants will guide SEMATECH's investments (roughly $40 million per year) in support of lithography development, semiconductor manufacturers have maintained their investments in the other NGL alternatives. Diversified development investment by manufacturers forces suppliers of lithography tools and masks to spread their investments over numerous technologies, slowing the development of the eventual "winner."

The semiconductor industry is no stranger to these timing uncertainties. A recent example is the planned transition to 300mm wafers from the current 200mm-wafer standard (Ham, Linden, and Appleyard 1998). The shift in wafer size, a basic input to the production process, requires changes throughout the production tool set. Indeed, developing new tools for this "systemic" technological transition will cost nearly $10 billion, far more than the NGL development effort.

In 1994, worldwide industry agreement was reached on the new standard wafer size, and buyers and suppliers collaborated on an unprecedented global scale to define standardized infrastructure needs for fabrication plants using the new larger wafer size. As part of this "roadmap," leading semiconductor manufacturers established a clear set of technical and performance specifications for 300mm equipment, reducing technological uncertainty for equipment suppliers about the characteristics of equipment that users would adopt.

Industry consensus on the requirements for 300mm equipment, which reduced technological uncertainty, did not translate into valid forecasts of the timing of the transition. As recently as November 1997, chip makers predicted that seven 300mm pilot lines would be operational in 1998 and that the first high-volume 300mm fabs would appear in 2000. In the event, however, the first 300mm pilot line did not appear until 1999, and 300mm-based volume production will be delayed at least until 2002. Furthermore, this delay means that the first 300mm tool sets will need to be capable of manufacturing devices with linewidths as small as 0.13 microns, rather than the 0.25-micron linewidths originally predicted, a "forecasting error" of two generations. These forecasting errors have increased the costs of developing 300mm tools.

These delays in the deployment of 300mm equipment resulted from a severe three-year industry downturn that began in 1996. The effects on equipment producers of the inaccurate industry forecasts were magnified by technological developments. Many of the productivity enhancements planned for 300mm-based factories were instead introduced in existing 200mm plants, further delaying the need for new production capacity. Chip sizes also have not increased as expected, providing yet another reason for manufacturers to stay with smaller wafers.[15] The consequences of the delay have been most severe for equipment suppliers. Ironically, equipment firms that made the greatest effort to comply with the original timetable, having spent $25 million or more to develop each tool, were left worse off.[16] In other words, the industry "roadmap" for the timing of the transition to 300mm manufacturing equipment left some equipment suppliers worse off than a lack of consensus.

In the case of NGL, the timing uncertainty magnifies the effects of technological uncertainty. Suppliers of lithography, mask, and resist technologies must diversify their investments across most or all of the alternative technologies, although the probability that any one of these will be needed, as well as the timing of the technological transition, remains uncertain.

4.   THE EUV CRADA

Reflecting the political salience of the semiconductor industry as a producer of "dual-use" technologies and as an industry widely viewed as "strategic" for economic competitiveness, the federal government has supported research in NGL technologies for more than two decades. Like their private-sector counterparts, federal decision-makers (largely in DARPA and the Department of Energy) have faced considerable uncertainty about the direction and timing of the transition to post-optical lithography. Until the late 1980s, the bulk of federal funding was allocated to proximity X-ray technology. More recently, however, federal NGL programs have funded a broader portfolio of alternatives to optical lithography, and public funds currently support research on at least four of the six technologies discussed in the previous section. EUV lithography has received considerable public funding from the Department of Energy during the past decade, most of which operated through CRADAs between individual DOE laboratories and U.S. producers of semiconductor equipment and components. The CRADA in which the EUV LLC is participating differs considerably from these previous undertakings, however, not least in its large size and its reliance on private firms for funding.

4.1   DoE Programs in EUV before the EUV LLC: Intra-Government Rivalry

EUV-related CRADAs began during the early 1990s, and involved the three DOE labs currently involved in the EUV LLC CRADA—Lawrence Berkeley (LBL); Lawrence Livermore (LLNL); and Sandia National Laboratories (SNL). The National Institute of Standards and Technology (NIST) provided support services, including precise measurements of mirror surfaces created at LLNL. By 1996, the labs (mainly Sandia and Lawrence Livermore) had contributed about $30 million of DOE funding, matched by a similar contribution (partly in-kind) from eight participating firms.[17]

Although there were obvious potential gains from a coordinated effort by the laboratories, rivalries among the laboratories and their industrial collaborators impeded the development of a more coordinated approach until 1996. Facing Congressional cuts in funding for collaborative technology development programs at its laboratories, DOE refused to renew funding for EUV research beyond September 1996. Intel's suggestion that it might be willing to fund further research led to the release of minimal DOE funding to keep the technological assets in place for six months while a new plan was negotiated. Intel's search for partners to share the project's financial burden led to the formation of the EUV LLC and the CRADA between the LLC and the three DOE laboratories.

4.2   EUV LLC: An Experiment in Intra-Government Collaboration

Intel established the EUV LLC in 1997 to serve as a CRADA partner with the DOE laboratories. Intel is the majority shareholder in the LLC while Motorola and Advanced Micro Devices are also shareholders.[18] With a three-year budget of $250 million, the LLC project is one of the largest CRADAs involving DOE laboratories to date. A large share of the budget is used to pay the salaries and overhead of over 100 scientists and engineers participating in the project at the three DOE laboratories. The remainder is used to fund new equipment for the labs (much of which will remain with the labs at the end of the CRADA) and to provide financial support for U.S. companies involved in collaborative development of system components. Although some research on masks and photoresist is performed at the R&D facilities of LLC members, most of the activity takes place at the DOE laboratories. The exchange of engineers among the laboratories, LLC member firms, and system component manufacturers, plus frequent inter-organizational communication, is at the heart of the collaborative effort (Gwynne 1999).

The primary goal of the CRADA is the creation of an "engineering test stand" (a prototype system) in the three years ending April 2000 (with a possible extension). Following this "proof of concept," the technology will be made available to lithography equipment suppliers for further development into tools that will enter production by 2007. The benefits of participating in the CRADA for LLC members hinge on the successful commercialization of EUV technology. LLC member firms receive exclusive access to the first commercial versions of the EUV system until they have been provided an agreed-upon number of tools to meet their initial requirements. In addition, their access to the LLC R&D means that member-firm engineers will gain experience with EUV technology that may permit them to implement the new system more rapidly than their non-participating competitors. The LLC owns any intellectual property produced by the EUV CRADA that is relevant to EUV lithography systems and, according to CRADA participants; the LLC has filed more than 60 patent applications.

Reflecting the fact that they provide all of the funding for the CRADA, the LLC, rather than the DOE laboratories, receives any royalties (some of which will be shared with an inventing laboratory under separate agreement(s)) on sales of EUV tools.[19] Nonetheless, the benefits of early access to the tools almost certainly outweigh those associated with royalties. According to the late Sander H. Wilson of Intel, formerly director of business programs at EUV LLC, "If this technology doesn't work, we're going to be out on the order of $250 million. On the other hand, if it works, what we want to do is recover our investment. But more importantly, what we want is access to the tools prior to our competitors who didn't take that risk."[20]

5. HOW DOES THE EUV LLC BUILD ON THE EXPERIENCE OF PREVIOUS CRADAS?

As we noted earlier, field research evaluating the performance of individual CRADAs highlighted a number of problems. In some cases, these problems impeded progress within the CRADA and contributed to the failure of the collaboration, while in others, they reduced the value of the collaboration for both laboratory and firm personnel. How if at all do the structure and management of the EUV CRADA address these problems?

Perhaps the most important difference between the EUV CRADA and those examined in Ham and Mowery (1998) is the relationship between the private firms and the participating DOE laboratories. Rather than a jointly funded undertaking, in which both laboratory and firm participants shared management responsibility, the EUV CRADA is one in which the private firms provide all of the operating budget, as well as contributing a number of pieces of costly laboratory equipment. The participating DOE laboratories provide unique facilities and research skills, but they do so in a capacity that resembles that of a research contractor, rather than a collaborator with significant control over the agenda or budget. As such, the EUV LLC exemplifies the "contractor principle" for public laboratories first enunciated in the Rothschild Report (Department of Trade and Industry 1971), which recommended greater reliance by public research facilities on research contracts to ensure their responsiveness to the requirements of their clients in the public or private sectors.

Consistent with the "contractor principle," the EUV CRADA avoids an important pitfall in the previous DOE laboratory CRADAs that relied in part on funding from the DOE headquarters. The availability of matching funding from DOE created strong incentives for laboratory personnel to market the research facilities and capabilities of DOE laboratories. These marketing efforts created some unrealistic expectations among private-firm participants about the size, cost, and likely time horizon of technical and commercial benefits from the CRADA. The availability of public subsidies for these CRADAs encouraged laboratory personnel to pursue activities that occasionally were too distant from the historical strengths and capabilities of laboratories, especially those specializing in nuclear weapons design.

In the case of the EUV CRADA, however, the private firms that are providing the operating budget are unambiguously in charge of the research agenda. Moreover, the LLC's continued financial support depends on the ability of laboratory personnel to address the challenges of the collaborative research agenda, reducing some of the incentive conflicts associated with previous CRADAs that drew in part on DOE funds. Rather than competing among themselves for private-firm partners in order to obtain additional funds from DOE headquarters, these three large DOE laboratories are motivated to collaborate by the structure of the EUV LLC CRADA. Indeed, one participant interviewed for this study characterized the level of cooperation among the labs as unusually high, and argued that this effective collaboration was attributable in part to the unusual nature (and large size) of this CRADA.

Private financing also may allow for greater flexibility in CRADA administration, enabling the project to "ramp down" more gradually as part of a transition from laboratory to prototype development and, eventually, larger-volume production of the equipment under development (see below for additional discussion). At the same time, however, the scope of the technological challenges posed by this CRADA is such that participation yields benefits for the DOE laboratory personnel. The ambitious technological goals of this CRADA contrast with those of some earlier CRADAs studied in Ham and Mowery (1998)—in several cases, the availability of DOE funding led laboratory researchers to pursue short-term "job-shop" projects with limited technical benefits for the laboratories' missions. More technically challenging CRADAs also address another long-standing problem for the DOE laboratories, especially those focusing primarily on national security missions—maintaining and in some instances, enhancing, and the technical expertise of laboratory researchers.

Retaining highly trained researchers at the national laboratories is especially significant in an environment of declining (or flat) defense spending and limited growth in laboratory staff. Solving problems of weapons design and maintenance in a world of smaller defense budgets will require greater use of and familiarity with the capabilities of firms that are focused on the far larger commercial market for related technologies. The EUV CRADA thus provides important benefits for laboratory researchers, even as it increases the risk that especially capable laboratory personnel may choose to leave the DOE laboratories for more lucrative private-sector employment opportunities.

Another important contrast with many other CRADAs is the sheer scale of this undertaking, whose 3-year budget is $250 million. Given the relatively high operating costs of the DOE laboratories when indirect charges are included, private firms in small-budget CRADAs often had problems in gaining or maintaining access to senior laboratory staff researchers. The scale of this CRADA, however, means that even senior laboratory managers and researchers are more likely to become involved. In addition, the size and technical capabilities of the participating firms dwarf those of the private-sector participants in many of the CRADAs examined in Ham and Mowery (1998). As a result, the firms leading the EUV CRADA are better able to sustain the considerable investments in supporting this collaboration. These include frequent face-to-face meetings, temporary assignment of firm personnel to work in the DOE laboratories, and the necessary in-house investments in related R&D that improve these firms' ability to evaluate, absorb and exploit the results of the project.

Although these characteristics of the EUV CRADA appear to represent improvements over the structure of previous DOE CRADAs, significant political and management challenges remain. Perhaps the greatest challenge is that of "handing off" the results of this CRADA to enterprises capable of developing commercial versions of the EUV tool. The LLC members are semiconductor manufacturers who have expressed no interest in entering the production of manufacturing equipment (indeed, any such entrant would face serious competitive challenges in selling equipment to semiconductor manufacturers who are competitors).

The role of leading semiconductor manufacturers in supporting the development of the EUV technology and the initial period of exclusive access by LLC members to commercial versions of the EUV tool could impede commercialization of EUV as the standard for the NGL technology. The EUV LLC partners, rather than their competitors, will have early access to commercial versions of the EUV equipment. Thus, competitors of the EUV LLC partners may elect not to adopt the technology, choosing instead to pursue alternative NGL technologies with no delays in early access to commercial tools. Such reluctance could fragment the market for EUV or other NGL technologies, making it difficult for equipment manufacturers to recover their development investments.[21]

Other difficult issues affecting the commercialization of an EUV prototype are associated with the management of the intellectual property produced by the LLC and with the need to assemble a substantial portfolio of patents to develop the EUV technology. LLC members require access to the intellectual property of non-member firms to develop this technology. LLNL, Lucent, and Ultratech are among the organizations that control EUV-related intellectual property, and commercial development of the technology requires that they license their patents to the EUV LLC. At least one of these owners of EUV-related intellectual property (Lucent) is a manufacturer of semiconductor devices who competes with the LLC member firms. This fact may reduce Lucent's willingness to license a group of competitors that will in turn profit from the application of Lucent's patents to EUV. Moreover, since Lucent is committed to the development of a substitute for EUV (SCALPEL), facilitating the development of EUV could undercut the returns to its SCALPEL-related intellectual property, further reducing its incentives to license.

Still another uncertainty affecting the development of EUV concerns the ability of U.S. equipment firms to support the investments in product development, high-quality manufacture, and product support that are necessary to commercialize this technology. In particular, product-support issues (maintenance, troubleshooting, spare parts) have proven critical to the success and failure of semiconductor equipment producers in the past[22] and remain a serious issue at many U.S. equipment suppliers. The uncertain commercialization capabilities of many equipment producers (particularly U.S.-based equipment firms) argue in favor of widespread dissemination of EUV-related intellectual property, in order that as many equipment firms as possible have an opportunity to undertake the costly investments. The policies of the EUV LLC member firms emphasize profitable (and therefore, restricted) licensing, which may limit entry by prospective producers of the equipment and could impede the commercial development of EUV. Moreover, as we note in the next section, potential licensing of foreign equipment producers has already sparked political controversy and is likely to remain contentious.

6.   FOREIGN PARTICIPATION: A PERENNIAL ISSUE

The "handoff" of technologies from the EUV LLC to private firms has significant political as well as commercial dimensions.   Current and prospective U.S. producers of NGL tools are small by comparison with their foreign rivals and have a small share of the global market for optical lithography tools.   In 1996, non-U.S. companies dominated the global lithography market; the Japanese firm Nikon held a 40 percnet market share, Canon, also based in Japan, had a 30 percent share of the market, and ASML of the Netherlands held a 20 percent market share.[23]

In order to ensure the acceptance of EUVL as a global standard for next-generation lithography, the members of the EUV LLC sought the participation of at least one of these three foreign firms in the CRADA. Although the governing legislation for the CRADA (the 1986 Technology Transfer Act) does not prohibit granting licenses to foreign firms, it requires "substantial U.S. manufacture" of transferred technologies (for products sold in the United States). The DoE, however, can waive this requirement, if such a license creates a "net economic benefit" to the United States.

Discussions among the LLC member firms, DOE and foreign firms over their participation in the EUV CRADA attracted Congressional criticism in October 1997. Although the language of the EUV CRADA was not revised in response to the Congressional criticism, at least one leading foreign lithographic equipment supplier, Nikon, elected not to participate in the CRADA because of the controversy.[24] Senior managers at Intel expressed disappointment over the decision by Nikon not to participate in the EUV CRADA.

The EUV CRADA also was criticized by representatives of Ultratech Stepper, a partner of Intel in a previous EUV CRADA with LLNL. Echoing criticisms of other CRADAs, Ultratech claimed that its exclusion from the EUV LLC was unfair and subsidized potential competitors.[25] Ultratech wished to be a full partner in the EUV LLC, which excludes equipment firms from full membership in order to encourage the maximum number of potential suppliers of these technologies to take licenses. In addition to unsuccessfully lobbying Congress for changes in the structure of the EUV CRADA, Ultratech created a partnership (in which it remains, to date, the only partner) called United States Advanced Lithography (USAL) to develop EUV lithography equipment. USAL has entered into a non-exclusive agreement with the EUV LLC to monitor progress in the CRADA. Another U.S. equipment firm, the Silicon Valley Group (SVGL), which has a small market share in advanced optical lithography tools, also has a non-exclusive agreement with the EUV LLC.

In February 1999, DOE permitted ASML, which also heads an EUV lithography program in Europe ("EUCLIDES"), to negotiate a license with EUV LLC. Descriptions in the press of ASML's agreement with DoE, which is not public, state that it requires ASML to produce any EUVL tools sold in the U.S. at a U.S. factory comparable to its Netherlands facility. The Dutch firm also must use a sufficient quantity of U.S.-produced components to meet local content goals, and is required to establish a U.S. research center.[26] ASML, which is also a partner for Lucent's SCALPEL technology and a participant in a European effort to develop ion-beam projection lithography, signed a contract with EUV LLC in June 1999.

The U.S. semiconductor firms providing the bulk of the financial support for the EUV CRADA currently display little concern over "dependence" on foreign suppliers of equipment. Indeed, the failure of U.S. semiconductor producers during the early 1990s to make more substantial procurement commitments to the optical lithography tools developed under SEMATECH sponsorship by GCA contributed to the failure of this firm. The overriding concern of U.S. semiconductor producers at present is the availability of a reliable EUV tool that is cost-effective and well supported in the field. Historically, non-U.S. equipment firms have been more adept in meeting these needs.

In addition, of course, the costs of developing an EUV tool are so high that commercial success for any U.S. equipment firm that succeeded in this task will require substantial foreign sales. Political criticism of the EUV CRADA also overlooked its importance to U.S. suppliers of components for EUV lithographic systems. More than one-third of the CRADA budget was used to fund the development of specialized system components, such as the light source, optics, and mirror coatings, at U.S. firms who may eventually supply both U.S. and foreign producers of EUV lithography tools.

The debate over foreign participation in the EUV CRADA, like similar debates in other programs, thus seems to pit political perceptions against economic realities. Perhaps because of the different premises of the protagonists in this debate, it seems no closer to resolution in this project than in any prior programs. The issues in the EUV debate have divided the U.S. semiconductor industry, splitting chip manufacturers from equipment suppliers and creating frictions within each of these groups. By creating internal divisions in the semiconductor industry, globalization of its markets and technology sources thus may erode the U.S. industry's historically powerful domestic political influence.

This debate over foreign participation and Nikon's decision not to participate in the EUV CRADA illustrate the limits of the "contractor principle" in the DOE laboratories. Despite the commitment by private firms to cover the costs of the CRADA and the apparent conformity of the provisions of the CRADA with DOE regulations concerning foreign participation, political criticism, along with "domestic manufacture" requirements appear to have led to Nikon's withdrawal. Working with public laboratories introduces additional constraints into the operation of even privately funded collaborative R&D projects.

7.   CONCLUSION

For students of U.S. technology policy, the development of next-generation lithographic technologies for the semiconductor industry is a case study in "post-Cold-War" technology policy and government-industry collaboration. It involves limited public financing for R&D on a technology of considerable importance to both defense-related and civilian applications, and it utilizes a publicly financed R&D infrastructure whose mission has been greatly diminished in the wake of the Cold War. Numerous hurdles must be surmounted before the technical success of the EUV CRADA can be assessed, and we limit our concluding discussion to the general issues of program design and policy that this initiative illustrates.

7.1 Balancing Political and Economic Goals

The NGL technology development programs highlight difficult issues about the rationale (and the political defense of this rationale) for federal support of R&D, especially R&D with commercial applications. After all, the rationale for much of the hundreds of billions devoted to federally supported R&D for most of the past 50 years was the contribution of such programs to national defense. In the aftermath of the Cold War, and in the absence of any compelling alternative rationale, such programs are justified in economic terms. This in turn creates two critical tensions.

First, the economic rationale provides much less restraint on the naturally strong redistributive behavior of elected officials. The demise of the Cold War justification for federal R&D spending has supported significant growth in Congressional earmarking of R&D appropriations for state- or district-specific programs, bypassing the peer review process (Brainard and Cordes 1999). There is little evidence of such "pork-barreling" in federal NGL programs, but another, closely related tension is apparent. Reconciling the political requirement that such policies produce visible economic returns for domestic taxpayers with the economic realities of an industry whose manufacturers and equipment suppliers operate in global markets has proven difficult. Political criticism over precisely this issue nearly jeopardized the EUV program's viability, limited participation by non-U.S. firms, and contributed to internal divisions within the U.S. semiconductor industry.

7.2 Should Federal Technology Programs Focus on Those in Need or Those Best Able to Benefit?

The EUV CRADA illustrates some significant improvements in the design and management of CRADAs. As we noted above, the reliance within this CRADA on private financing appears to have reduced some of the disincentives to inter-laboratory collaboration created by the financial structure of many previous DOE CRADAs that were partially financed with funds from the Department itself. In addition, the reliance of this CRADA on private funds means that the R&D agenda and the management of the CRADA are of considerable salience to these firms. This characteristic of the EUV CRADA enforces closer involvement by the firms in the joint R&D and creates stronger incentives for DOE laboratory staff to meet the expectations of their private-sector partners. These desirable incentives were lacking in many previous DOE CRADAs.

Nevertheless, these sources of strength in this CRADA raise other difficult issues for policy. Should federal R&D policy and the substantial federal laboratory infrastructure be used to help only those industries that can finance such assistance, or should these programs focus on industries or firms that are in severe economic distress? After all, Intel and its partners are underwriting the costs of the EUV LLC and the EUV CRADA with their considerable profits of the 1990s. It is unlikely that these firms would have funded such a costly project with a distant and diffuse payoff during the 1980s, when Intel was nearly bankrupted by losses in the DRAM market.

There are several reasons to argue that this policy of "helping the strong" is desirable from a program design viewpoint, although it may be difficult to defend politically. First, technology programs alone rarely are sufficient to restore the fortunes of declining industries or firms. In the semiconductor equipment industry, this conclusion receives strong support from the GCA case (Grindley, et al. 1994). Even SEMATECH, which assuredly received considerable federal assistance, involved collaborative R&D (managed by the participating firms) for firms that were economically battered but still strong in technological and managerial capabilities. Failing industries and firms much more frequently require assistance across the board, spanning management, finance, marketing, and other functions—technology alone rarely will suffice.

Second, firms that lack internal financial or technological resources often find it difficult to manage the requirements of R&D collaboration, either within an industry or between industry and government. Collaborating firms must have sufficient internal technical resources to "absorb" and apply the results of R&D; moreover, these capabilities are essential to the task of defining and monitoring the progress of collaborative R&D. In addition, the financial requirements of collaboration, including the need to devote considerable management time and resources (e.g., rotating personnel through a collaborative research site or project) are considerable. Indeed, a recurrent problem in many of the DOE CRADAs examined in Ham and Mowery (1995, 1998) was precisely the difficulty faced by small, undercapitalized firms in managing the interface with the joint research project.

However successful the design of the EUV CRADA appears to be thus far, this undertaking will face considerable challenges in moving from laboratory prototype to commercially feasible and successful production technology. Indeed, this phase of the project involves working with firms in the semiconductor equipment industry that often lack the financial and managerial resources to support their considerable technological assets. Moreover, this is a phase of this CRADA in which the incentives of its financial supporters may conflict with the requirements of commercial development—as we noted earlier, these conflicts appear to be particularly salient in the area of intellectual property. In addition, of course, participation in this phase of the EUV project by foreign equipment firms, several of which may be better positioned to commercialize the EUV technology, remains controversial.

7.3 How Should Uncertainty Be Managed?

Finally, our discussion of the EUV project highlights the uncertainties that pervade this undertaking, and the limited ability of intra-industry collaboration to offset the effects of such uncertainties on the costs and incentives of would-be developers of equipment. What is the appropriate role for public R&D investments in this situation? Clearly, these uncertainties argue strongly in favor of avoiding excessive commitments of public funds to any single technological alternative or to any single estimate of the timing of introduction of "next-wave" technology. As such, it seems appropriate for federal agencies to diversify their R&D investments among the various competing alternatives for NGL lithography, as they have done for most of this decade.

This diversification principle also suggests the desirability of limiting investments of public funds to the earlier stages of R&D, which has the added advantage of being less costly. This consideration should favor the reliance by an undertaking such as the EUV CRADA, which involves development activity, on private rather than public funding. However, this design principle also should lead to the relatively liberal dissemination of the results of such research, rather than restrictive patents or licenses. These uncertainties also mean that many projects will "fail," in the sense of not yielding commercial products. Such "failures" are to be expected and valued for their illumination of dead ends, rather than condemned as illustrations of managerial incompetence, mendacity, and the like. Moreover, the likelihood of such "failures" is yet another reason to use public funds for the earlier, and less costly, phases of R&D.

The uncertainties that we have emphasized in this chapter apply with particular force to its content and conclusions. The EUV CRADA is very much a work in progress. Its ultimate success or failure are unknown and at present, unknowable. Our current observations about the superiority in design and finance of this undertaking, along with our attempt to distill lessons for federal technology policy, must therefore be treated with great caution and skepticism. In scholarship as in complex technology development programs, diversity in opinion and experimentation in method are indispensable.

ACKNOWLEDGEMENTS

The Alfred P. Sloan Foundation and the Andrew W. Mellon Foundation provided support for this research. We are grateful to David Attwood, Charles Gwyn, Gib Marguth, and Bill Spencer who provided many valuable insights but who bear no responsibility for errors, omissions, or conclusions in this chapter.

REFERENCES

Barnett, J. (1998). "Intel Powers up Research Labs." *The Oregonian,* March 1.

Bloomstein, T.M., M. W. Horn, M. Rothschild, R. R. Kunz, S. T. Palmacci, and R. B. Goodman. (1997). "Lithography with 157 nm Lasers." *Journal of Vacuum Science and Technology B* 15(6): 2112-2116.

Brainard, J., and C. Cordes. (1999). "Pork-Barrel Spending on Academe Reaches a Record $797-Million." *Chronicle of Higher Education,* July 23, A44.

Cataldo, A. (1999). "IBM Builds Prototypes Using X-ray Lithography." *Electronic Engineering Times,* April 19.

Department of Trade and Industry, United Kingdom. (1971). *A Framework for Government Research and Development, Cmnd 4814,* London: HMSO.

Garcia, M.L., and O.H. Bray. (1997) *Fundamentals of Technology Roadmapping, Report SAND9797-0665,* Albuquerque, NM: Sandia National Laboratories.

Grindley, P., D.C. Mowery, and B. Silverman. (1994). "SEMATECH and Collaborative Research: Lessons in the Design of High-Technology Consortia." *Journal of Policy Analysis and Management* 13(4): 723-758.

Gwynne, P. (1999). "Unusual Energy Dept.-Industry Partnership to Build 21st Century Computer Chip May be Co-Op Model." *Research-Technology Management* 42(2): 2-4.

Ham, R.M., G. Linden, and M. Appleyard. (1998). "The Evolving Role of Semiconductor Consortia in the U.S. and Japan." *California Management Review* 41(1): 137-163.

Ham, R.M., and D.C. Mowery. (1995). "Improving Industry-Government Cooperative R&D." *Issues in Science and Technology,* Summer, pp. 67-73.

Ham, R.M., and D.C. Mowery. (1998). "Improving the Effectiveness of Public-Private R&D Collaboration: Case Studies at a U.S. Weapons Laboratory." *Research Policy* 26: 661-675.

Henderson, R. (1995). "Of Life Cycles Real and Imaginary: The Unexpectedly Long Old Age of Optical Lithography." *Research Policy* 24: 631-643.

Holstein, W.J. (1998). "U.S.-Funded Technology Stays Here, For Now." *U.S. News & World Report*, May 18.

Mowery, D.C. (1999). "America's Industrial Resurgence: An Overview," in D.C. Mowery, ed., *U.S. Industry in 2000*. Washington, DC: National Academy Press.

OTA. (1993). *Contributions of DOE Weapons Labs and NIST to Semiconductor Technology Report #OTA-ITE-585*, Washington, DC: U.S. Government Printing Office.

Randazzese, L.P. (1996). "Semiconductor Subsidies." *Scientific American*, June, pp. 46-49.

Robertson, J. (1999). "Chip Makers Gripe Bitterly, But Litho Costs Keep Soaring." *Semiconductor Business News*, July.

SIA. (1997). *National Technology Roadmap for Semiconductors: Technology Needs, 1997 Edition*, San Jose, CA: Semiconductor Industry Association.

SIA. (1998). *International Technology Roadmap for Semiconductors: 1998 Update*, San Jose, CA: Semiconductor Industry Association.

Smith, H.I., and F. Cerrina. (1997). "X-Ray Lithography for ULSI Manufacturing." *Microlithography World*, Winter, pp. 10-15.

Stix, G. (1995). "Lithography Becomes Political Pork." *Scientific American*, May, p. 30.

Takahashi, D. (1998) "Applied Materials Profit Drops, Forecasting an Industry Slump." *Wall Street Journal Interactive Edition*, July 13.

U.S. Department of Energy Task Force on Alternative Futures for the Department of Energy National Laboratories. (1995). *Alternative Futures for the Department of Energy National Laboratories*, Washington, DC: U.S. Department of Energy.

U.S. Department of Energy. (1999). *"Preliminary A-11 Data,"* July.

---

[1] The Federal Technology Transfer Act of 1986 and its 1989 amendment extended the legislative framework developed in the Stevenson-Wydler and Bayh-Dole Acts of 1980, which authorized recipients of federal research to gain title to the intellectual property created in such projects.

[2] The Committee's report criticized the "idea that the [DOE] laboratories are, or could become, cornucopias of relevant technology for a broad range of industries," and argued that the laboratories should focus their technology collaboration activities on areas that were directly relevant to laboratory missions.

[3] SEMATECH's estimate reported in Chad Fasca and Dylan McGrath, "Advanced Lithography At Critical Juncture," *Electronic News*, October 13, 1997.

[4] See Robertson (1999). Lithography also accounts for one-third of manufacturing costs (Silicon Valley Group Form 10-K for fiscal year ended 9/30/98).

[5] A micron is one millionth of a meter, and a nanometer is one thousandth of a micron (i.e., one billionth of a meter). The dramatic shrinkage in linewidths has required the use of shorter-wavelength lithography exposure sources, because the wavelength is one of the

key factors limiting the size of features that can be drawn on the chip. The wavelength of visible light extends down to roughly 400 nm. For about thirty years, lithography tools used a 435 nm light source to produce circuit lines that gradually became as narrow as 0.6-micron. In the early 1990s, high-end lithography adopted a 365 nm light source, which has been used for feature sizes down to 0.35-micron (350 nm) using enhanced lithography techniques. Laser-based tools, with a wavelength of 248nm, are currently used to make feature sizes as small as 180 nm, and a new generation of 193 nm laser-based tools was introduced commercially in 1999 to fabricate feature sizes down to 0.13-micron.

[6] For a detailed treatment of this topic, see Henderson (1995).

[7] The International (formerly the "National") Technology Roadmap for Semiconductors is coordinated and funded by SEMATECH under the aegis of the Semiconductor Industry Association, an industry trade group. Recent editions of the Roadmap can be accessed at http://www.itrs.net/ntrs/publntrs.nsf.

[8] The Association of Super-advanced Electronics Technologies (ASET) is a multi-year research collaboration funded primarily by Japan's Ministry of International Trade and Industry with projects related to semiconductors, flat panel displays, and hard disk drives. Its average annual budget is about $90 million, of which nearly two-thirds goes to semiconductor research.

[9] See Cataldo (1999).

[10] Micro-Electronics Development for European Applications (MEDEA) is a four-year, $2.5 billion program funded jointly by government and industry. MEDEA's IPL project has a budget of $36 million covering four years.

[11] SCALPEL: Scattering with Angular Limitation Projection Electron Beam Lithography, PREVAIL: Projection-Reduction Exposure with Variable Immersion Layer.

[12] The 1997 National Roadmap was updated in 1998 to reflect the input of newly formed Working Groups with membership from Europe and Asia, and 157nm lithography appears for the first time in the resulting document (SIA 1998).

[13] ASM Lithography of the Netherlands leads the Extreme UV Concept Lithography Development System (EUCLIDES). The collaboration is partially funded by the European Commission, with an EU contribution of $9 million for Year 1, as well as in-kind contributions from participating firms.

[14] A recent report on "Fundamentals of Technology Roadmapping" (Garcia and Bray 1997) argues that

"...at the industry level, technology road mapping involves multiple companies, either as a consortium or an entire industry (industry technology road mapping). By focusing on common needs, companies can more effectively address critical research and collaboratively develop the common technologies.

...This level of technology roadmap allows industry to collaboratively develop the key underlying technologies, rather than redundantly funding the same research and under funding or missing other important technologies. This can result in significant benefits because a certain technology may be too expensive for a single company to support or take too long to develop, given the resources that can be justified. However, combining the resources across companies may make developing the technology possible and consequently the industry more competitive."

[15] The main cause of unexpected reductions in chip sizes is the same unexpected advance in optical lithography that is creating timing uncertainty for the developers of next-generation lithography.

[16] See Takahashi (1998).

[17] The eight firms in EUV CRADAs were AT&T, Intel, AMD, KLA Instruments, and Ultratech Stepper, as well as JMAR Industries Inc. of San Diego, Tropel of Rochester, NY, and Micrion of Peabody, MA (*Electronic Materials Technology News*, August, 1996).

[18] Despite reports that other partners have been solicited, no additional firms have publicly announced their participation in the EUV LLC as of December 1999.

[19] The DOE labs will be free to use the technology in other applications.

[20] *The Oregonian*, November 1, 1998.

[21] The SEMATECH consortium ultimately abandoned a similar policy of exclusive access (involving a two-year period of exclusivity) by member firms to tools incorporating SEMATECH-funded improvements because of opposition by equipment firms participating in the consortium, who argued that the more restrictive policy limited the market for their tools (Grindley, et al. 1994).

[22] See Grindley, et al. (1994) or Randazzese (1996) for a discussion of the case of GCA, formerly a leading U.S. semiconductor equipment supplier. GCA's attempts to commercialize its state-of-the-art optical lithography tool, despite assistance from SEMATECH, ultimately failed, partly because of the firm's poor reputation for product quality and field support.

[23] VLSI Research data reported in *Electronic Business Today*, July 1997.

[24] See Holstein (1998).

[25] See Barnett (1998).

[26] *Electronic Engineering Times*, February 24, 1999, *The Oregonian*, March 3, 1999.

Chapter 15

International Knowledge Transmission and Innovation in High-Technology Industries

SHERYL WINSTON SMITH
Harvard University

1.   INTRODUCTION

Knowledge, which lies at the heart of innovation, comes from a wide range of sources. Nations that fail to understand and utilize knowledge from other nations, neglect a vital aspect of innovation in a globally interdependent world.   At the same time, domestic infrastructure for innovation remains critical to the ability to generate, absorb, and implement knowledge from both domestic and global origins.

Policy debates about the economic impact of free trade are as vigorous and unresolved as they are old.   One aspect that has not been examined sufficiently is the relationship between openness and the creation and use of technological knowledge, on which an innovation based economy so strongly depends. This chapter describes mechanisms of knowledge transmission in an increasingly global economy and asks how international flows of knowledge impact innovation in dynamic, high–technology industries that rely heavily on investment in research and development (R&D).

While globalization certainly has an impact on innovation, the mechanism through which this operates is not well understood. This chapter puts forth a hypothesized relationship between domestic innovation and openness and analyzes the policy implications of such a relationship. The rest of this chapter proceeds as follows. Section 2 provides background. Section 3 presents a conceptual framework and Section 4 presents a short literature overview.   Section 5 outlines the policy issues and Section 6 concludes.

2.   BACKGROUND

Innovation depends on developing and finding knowledge and embodying it in new or better products or processes. The sources of this knowledge include not just the research within a company, but its connections to other research. For example, these connections include university research, and the knowledge gained through the course of business, including insights into innovation by competitors, and interactions with suppliers, contractors, and customers, all of whom can be sources of knowledge that flows into the innovation process. The nature of the innovation process has evolved. Recent trends in innovation reflect the increasing importance of a variety of sources of knowledge and organizational forms. Innovation increasingly has become decentralized, with the importance of central R&D laboratories of large companies decreasing. Firms have become more reliant on outside sources of technology, such as suppliers and contract R&D, which involves relationships with foreign as well as domestic firms (Branscomb and Florida 1998). Networks and collaborative research ventures have become more prominent forms for the organization of innovation (Fountain and Atkinson 1998, Mowery 1998, Rothwell 1994).

Technological innovation is becoming increasingly distributed internationally. In part, this is because the sources of knowledge are more globally distributed than in the past. Convergence of the industrial economies towards more equal states of technological advance means that knowledge is generated around the world. While the United States continues to account for the greatest share of industrial R&D in the OECD, this share has dropped from 55 percent in 1973 to 46 percent in 1994 (National Science Board 1998). Likewise, the U.S. share of outputs from innovation, such as the production in high-tech industries and patenting activity, has also declined. The U.S. share of world production of high-tech products declined from approximately 37 percent in 1980 to under 32 percent in 1995, having dropped even lower in the early 1990s (National Science Board 1998). Of companies granted U.S. patents, U.S. companies accounted for only two of the ten highest patenting companies in 1996, compared to six of the ten in the period 1977–1996 (National Science Board 1998). Just over half of all U.S. patents have been assigned to U.S. inventors in the 1980s and 1990s: 56 percent for 1982–86; 52 percent for 1987–91; and 55 percent for 1992–96 (Office of Technology Policy 1998).

Innovation increasingly involves international collaboration. For example, the share of internationally co-authored papers in scientific and technical publications has more than doubled from six percent of all papers in 1981 to 15 percent in 1995 (National Science Board 1998). Importantly, international relationships have become an increasingly significant factor in industrial innovation. As indicated in Table 1, both the share of overseas R&D relative to domestic R&D funding and the share of industry funding in the U.S. that is performed by foreign affiliates have increased substantially. International strategic technology alliances have also increased in prominence, from 136 in 1980 to 483 in 1996 (National Science Board 1998).

Table 1. U.S. R&D Abroad and R&D of Foreign Affiliates in the United States

	U.S. company financed R&D performed abroad/ U.S. domestic	Foreign affiliate R&D performed in U.S. /U.S. domestic
1980	NA	5.0
1985	6.4	NA
1987	8.5	7.3
1990	9.7	10.4
1995	12.0	13.8

Sources: NSF *Science and Engineering Indicators*, 1998, Chapter 4: Appendix tables 4–3, 4–50, 4–53.

International trade in intellectual property has been increasing steadily. In particular, U.S. receipts of royalties and license fees, or exports of intellectual property, have been increasing strongly, and more rapidly than the increase in payments, or imports of intellectual property, resulting in a growing surplus for the U.S. As shown in Table 2, the growth in receipts by U.S. parents from affiliated foreigners shows the greatest rate of increase, perhaps suggesting the increasing importance of intra-firm technology transfer.

Table 2. Trade in Intellectual Property in Millions of U.S. Dollars

	U.S. receipts of royalties and license fees	U.S. payments of royalties and license fees	U.S. receipts of royalties and license fees from affiliated foreigners
1986	8,113	1,401	6,174
1990	16,634	3,135	13,250
1993	21,695	5,032	15,688
1996	32,823	7,854	24,710

Sources: U.S. Bureau of Economic Analysis, "U.S. International Private Services, 1986–1997." Receipts and payments are between U.S. companies and affiliated or unaffiliated foreigners. Data on royalties and license fees are aggregated and includes all industries (not only manufacturing).

Innovation occurs in the context of increasing globalization in the world economy. International trade and investment have increased substantially over the last several decades. The indicators in Table 3 illustrate the trend towards globalization. U.S. exports, imports, and direct investment abroad have all increased in recent years, indicating a greater participation in global markets through trade and investment. In both popular and policy literature, the importance of this increasing interdependence of economies has been the subject of much attention.[1]   A growing policy literature links structural changes in the economy, technological innovation, and globalization as the several forces underlying the knowledge driven economy (Atkinson and Court 1998, OECD 1998, Vickery 1998).

Table 3. Exports, Imports, and Foreign Direct Investment as a Percent of U.S. GDP

	U.S. exports of goods and services/GDP	U.S. imports of goods and services/GDP	U.S. direct investment abroad/GDP
1985	9.2	11.6	5.7
1989	11.8	13.2	7.0
1993	11.7	12.5	8.6
1997	14.6	16.0	10.7

Sources: *Statistical Abstract of the United States*: 1998 (GDP, export, and import data); USDIA, 1982–1997, BEA (investment data).

Communications and computing equipment are particularly compelling sectors to consider.   Innovation in information technology is integral to the knowledge economy. By some measures, information technology is one of the most innovative sectors.   The number of U.S. patents granted in these areas has been increasing much faster than the number of U.S. patents overall.   From 1982–96, the number of U.S. patents in information technology increased dramatically, from seven percent of all U.S. patents in 1982 to 14.5 percent in 1996 (U.S. Department of Commerce, Office of Technology Policy 1998).

Information technology has become increasingly global in scope. Largely, the numerous international mergers and alliances in telecommunications are driven by the combined pressure of the drive for expanding international markets through the development of new technologies. In part, this is by necessity: in order to have global communications as easy as domestic communications, companies need to have international reach, including standards that work together, as well as access to networks and equipment. The drive for global scope and integrated wireless communications features prominently in these deals, which highlights the importance of better understanding the relationship between globalization and innovation.

Communications and computing are increasingly international by a number of measures. Exports and imports have become increasingly prominent in computing and communications production. Table 4 shows that the volume of both exports and imports relative to production has increased substantially, which highlights the importance of flows in both directions. Over the time period from 1980–1994, exports relative to U.S. production increased from 27 percent to 42 percent in computing and from.

Table 4. Export and Import Share of Production, 1980 and 1994

	Exports/prod. (U.S.)	Exports/prod. (G-7)	Exports/prod. (ANBERD 14)	Imports/prod. (U.S.)
Computing equipment				
1980	27.0	33.3	34.4	8.2
1994	42.3	44.0	48.5	69.3
Change	15.3	10.8	14.1	61.1
Communication machinery				
1980	14.5	21.7	23.0	23.7
1994	27.9	28.3	30.4	42.4
Change	13.5	6.7	7.4	18.6
Total manufacturing				
1980	9.4	16.1	17.3	8.9
1994	13.0	19.9	21.6	18.1
Change	3.6	3.8	4.3	9.2

Sources: OECD Main Industrial Indicators database. Note: G-7 includes Canada, France, Germany, Italy, Japan, the United Kingdom and the United States; ANBERD14 includes Australia, Canada, Denmark, Finland, France, Germany, Italy, Japan, the Netherlands, Norway, Spain, Sweden, the United Kingdom and the United States.

14 percent to 28 percent in communications machinery, compared to an increase from nine percent to 13 percent in manufacturing as a whole. During the same time period, imports as a share of U.S. production increased as well. In computing and in communications equipment both inward and outward foreign direct investments have increased. Comparatively, the share of exports in production in the U.S. has been lower than the share of exports in production in other industrial economies. Table 4 shows the export share of production in computing, communications, and total manufacturing for the United States, the G7 countries, and a larger grouping of industrial economies. However, the share of exports in production has increased in the United States. On the other hand, the globalization of innovation in information technology has been mixed. Three-fourths of the top 20 information technology companies are U.S. companies (*Economist*, 4/22/00). As well, overseas R&D spending relative to all company financed R&D in industrial machinery (which includes computing equipment) and in electronics (which includes communications equipment) has varied, as shown in Table 5.

Table 5. Overseas R&D by U.S. Companies as a Percent of Total

	Industrial machinery	Electrical equipment	All industries
1985	6.4	6.4	6.4
1987	11.7	4.1	8.5
1990	10.7	8.3	9.7
1993	4.1	4.5	10.1
1995	5.2	5.1	12.0

Sources: NSF *Science and Engineering Indicators*, 1998, Appendix table 4-50.

By some measures, internationalization is increasingly integral to growth in communications and computing. The dramatic increases in trade in these industries underscores this point. Innovation in these industries is a global phenomenon, as evidenced by half the U.S. patents in these sectors granted to inventors abroad.

3.   CONCEPTUAL FRAMEWORK

Conceptually, it is expected that international connections should increase the flow of knowledge. Openness should promote knowledge transmission through increased communication and transfer of goods and ideas. International trade creates communication channels, enhancing the flow of knowledge in the normal course of business. More directly, international trade allows knowledge to be transmitted through reverse engineering of products or through the incorporation of intermediate inputs that embody innovations from abroad. Knowledge transmission also occurs through the investment of multinational companies (MNC). As a group, MNCs account for a large portion of industrial innovation, through their investments in R&D, patenting, and technology payments (e.g., licensing between parent and affiliate). Moreover, by having a presence in more than one nation, they are conduits for information. This is especially, but not only, the case when R&D is performed directly by the foreign affiliate.

At the same time, innovation depends not only on the availability of knowledge but also on the ability to absorb and implement knowledge in an innovative fashion. Thus, simply increasing the flows of knowledge raises the possibility of innovation but if something is done with this knowledge. This absorptive capacity is a function of the infrastructure that is in place for innovation. A large component of this infrastructure is science and technology resources.

Moreover, increasing channels of information transmission is also a function of whether there is knowledge abroad that is novel and relevant. That is, channels of knowledge transmission are more likely to result in innovation if the potential for useful knowledge being exported from a given country is relatively high. In this regard, an important consideration is the infrastructure for innovation in the nations from which knowledge could be transmitted. Again, science and technology resources are a large component of this infrastructure.

It is helpful to think of two extreme cases. First, in a completely closed economy, with no trade, no FDI, no R&D overseas and, in the limit, no international communication, the likely effect would be that domestic innovation and productivity would slow down dramatically in the long run.

Second, in a completely open economy, with no impediments to trade, investment, and R&D overseas, and unfettered international communication, domestic innovation would still be limited by the domestic capacity to generate new knowledge and receive, absorb, and implement domestic and international knowledge. As well, with free and rapid flow of knowledge there might be disincentives to domestic innovation. Such disincentives include firms not being able to appropriate the benefits of innovation and the potential for free riding. The real relationship between trade and protection and domestic innovation probably lies somewhere on this continuum. A hypothetical representation of the relationship between domestic innovation and international connections is depicted in *Figure 1* below. This possible relationship needs to be tested empirically. The expectation is that openness should increase domestic innovation, at least to a given point before dropping off. Investigating the shape of the hypothetical curve given in *Figure* will permit the formulation of appropriately directed policies that will take into account the impact of trade policy on domestic innovation.

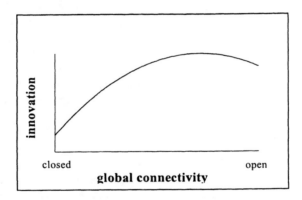

Figure 1. Schematic Curve Suggesting Hypothetical Relationship between Openness and Innovation

4. LITERATURE CONTEXT

The literature points to international trade as an important conduit for knowledge, but it also shows that this is neither automatic nor complete. Likewise, the global reach and innovative resources of MNCs provide avenues for international knowledge transmission. Furthermore, the sourcing of innovation by MNCs draws on the local resources, but can also allow knowledge spillovers. Taken together, the literature strongly suggests that globalization affects innovation in many ways, but the task remains to understand the relative importance and magnitude of these several factors.

In economic theory, knowledge is a public good: it is non–rival, that is it can be shared by more than one user without diminishing the ability of anyone else to use it; as well it is at least partially non–excludable, or difficult to prevent others from using it.[2] In particular, the non-rival nature of consumption of knowledge leads to spillovers.[3] Not surprisingly, R&D is essential to both creating knowledge and absorbing it. Absorptive capacity is an important component of R&D spillover; spillovers are more likely to occur if the "receiver" is advanced enough to find new knowledge, recognize its importance, and otherwise prepared to incorporate this knowledge effectively (Cohen and Levinthal 1989). R&D in a nation thus affects the likelihood and magnitude of R&D spillovers from other nations. At the same time, mechanisms that mitigate the flow of knowledge from the entity that invested resources in innovation include patents and other intellectual property restrictions. The most fundamental barrier may be the capability of the receiving institution to understand and use the knowledge. Geography is a barrier to knowledge diffusion. R&D spillovers occur more easily within nations than between them. Jaffe and Trajtenberg (1998) show that domestic patents are cited both sooner and more frequently than foreign patents. The empirical literature also shows that within a nation knowledge diffuses most quickly within a limited geographic range (Jaffe 1993, Mansfield 1995). Technological similarity also mediates knowledge transmission. Several empirical studies have examined this effect. International knowledge transmission has been related to the closeness between domestic and foreign R&D (Jaffe and Trajtenberg 1998, Park 1995). Branstetter (1996) finds that foreign R&D has a greater impact on firm level innovation the closer the patent portfolios are. The gap between the levels of technological advancement in both nations also conditions knowledge transmission (Keller 1997).

Technical knowledge gained from R&D performed in one nation ultimately diffuses to other nations. International trade enhances this diffusion. International trade theory suggests that dynamic gains from trade result from the impact of international trade on innovation, in part through increased knowledge transmission.[4] One approach to investigating these relationships has involved examining the impact of R&D spending abroad on domestic productivity. The results of several such empirical studies suggest that R&D from other nations contributes to domestic innovation. (Coe and Helpman 1995, Helpman 1997). Another approach to studying the impact of trade on innovation considers trade in inputs. International trade in differentiated inputs allows international knowledge transmission through increasing the variety or quality of inputs (Grossman and Helpman 1991).

Again, several empirical studies identify international R&D spillovers through trade in inputs, other studies find relationships between R&D abroad and dynamic changes in the production structure in another country (Bernstein and Mohnen 1998, Nadiri and Kim 1996).[5] Trade also has been related to international patenting (Eaton and Kortum 1996).

By virtue of their international operations, multinational firms are conduits for knowledge transmission. Economic theory posits that the multinational firm transfers technology more efficiently than separately organized firms do by internalizing arms length transactions. While MNCs face disadvantages competing in a foreign market, R&D gives them a unique exploitable assets, particularly R&D.[6] MNCs are among the most innovation intensive firms, accounting for a large portion of R&D and patenting (National Science Board 1998). The relative competitiveness of U.S. MNCs in share of world export is related to R&D (Kravis and Lipsey 1992). It is reasonable to expect that particularly innovative firms are likely sources of knowledge spillovers, and thus MNCs may lead to knowledge transfer to other domestic firms. Empirical studies of FDI within developed nations support the importance of multinational firms in generating R&D spillovers. Barrell and Pain (1997) find that knowledge-based assets are an important determinant of outward FDI within Europe, and that this FDI leads to productivity improvements. Likewise, Lichtenberg and van Pottelsberghe de la Potterie (1996) find that technology sourcing through outward FDI and import flows result in R&D spillovers.

The correct physical location of R&D abroad by MNC provides even greater opportunity for knowledge transmission. In part, geographical barriers to knowledge transmission are mitigated through integration of R&D abroad with R&D at home. A firm that performs R&D in more than one nation also has a broader window on innovation. An R&D presence abroad gives the MNC an opportunities to interact formally and informally with the local environment and thereby transmit knowledge spillovers. Thus, MNCs are often direct conduits for international knowledge transmission through overseas R&D activity in affiliate R&D laboratories and through contract or sponsored research. Evidence suggests that MNC location decisions are related to innovation in the destination country in order to facilitate knowledge spillover to the firm through access to science and technology resources (Dunning and Narula 1995, Hirschey and Caves 1981). Importantly, these location decisions are likely a function of relative innovation levels between the domestic and foreign resources. For example, Kogut and Chang (1991) found that Japanese direct investment in the U.S. is a function of technological abilities in both markets. As well, Kuemmerle (1997) found that MNCs engage in overseas R&D to complement and augment their ability to innovate.

Finally, globalization affects innovation through several indirect factors. Competition resulting from openness is one of these effects. The outcome, however, is ambiguous. On one hand, competition from imports can spur innovation; an argument that trade policy can be competition policy. On the other hand, competition can impede domestic innovation by inducing companies, or even entire industries, out of the market.[7] Openness also increases market size and potential for economies of scale and scope as well as greater opportunities for learning by doing. Increasing internationalization of high-tech industries also affects innovation. It is impossible to read the business pages without seeing evidence of the extent to which globalization is affecting the international character of high technology industries. Recent international mergers and other transactions in high technology industries are based in part on concerns related to globalization. Clearly, such international combinations have implications for innovation. Notably, the increasing internationalization in high–tech industries also has an ambiguous relationship to innovation. Some factors point to positive effects on innovation. The ability to incorporate and utilize worldwide sources of knowledge could be expected to increase innovation. Increased demand and potentials for economies of scale from the expanded market size might also drive innovation. Conversely, increased industry concentration might act against innovation. Thus, the impact of the increasing international character of high-tech industries depends on the relative balance between these several influences.[8]

5.   POLICY ISSUES

The discussion above illustrates the increasing ways in which innovation and globalization interact. In particular, the occurrence of knowledge transmission through international channels has important consequences for innovation. To the extent that knowledge is exchanged through international transactions of trade and investment and through R&D presence in multiple nations, the extent and level of these actions matter for innovation policy. The increased importance of trade and FDI in the world economy, particularly in high-tech industries, makes this especially true. Likewise, the increasingly international nature of innovation and the evolution of innovation towards relying on outside sources of knowledge also foretell the importance of considering the impacts of globalization for an innovation based economy.

The relationship between globalization and innovation has a wide effect, necessitating consideration within several areas of policy. Foremost, while theory and evidence suggest that increasing international interactions should increase knowledge transmission, much about the process remains mysterious. The mechanisms through which this happens, the extent of knowledge spillovers generated through international channels, and the ultimate effects on the greater economy all need to be much more fully understood and analyzed. Incorporating these considerations into domestic science and technology policy is essential in an interdependent world. Likewise, the reverberations of trade policy are indirectly felt through the economy through the effect on knowledge transmission and innovation. Thus, the relationship between openness and innovation needs to be included in the making of trade policy. In addition, understanding international knowledge transmission also affects other areas of domestic policy. The crucial importance of absorptive capacity in the innovation infrastructure means that potential benefits from globalization depends in part on the education and quality of the workforce, as well as policies which impact industrial R&D. In these many ways, a comprehensive policy that encourages and facilitates innovation in a global context demands that we understand the multiple channels through which knowledge transmission occurs and to address both static and dynamic consequences of international knowledge transmission.

The dynamic consequences of learning through international knowledge transmission are of great importance. Incorporating a new input might enable innovation, but moreover the knowledge embodied in that input contributes to learning. On one level, the embodied knowledge contributes to the cumulative stock of knowledge available to that nation. Beyond the importance of the embodied knowledge however is also the extent to which that knowledge enables future innovation. Moreover, path dependence in innovation can compound the impact of the accumulating knowledge and the increasing learning that occurs, for example through "learning by doing" and "learning to learn".[9]

While globalization of trade and R&D may be international in scope, largely beyond the ability of any one nation to control, policy plays an essential role in determining its consequences. Policy modulates and conditions how domestic innovation responds to globalization. Careful consideration of the interdependencies among multiple aspects of policy will better enable the United States to realize gains from globalization and prepare to adjust to attendant losses. More than anything, adapting to dynamic effects of globalization requires the integration and understanding of the intertwined effects of myriad policy realms: research and technology policy and international trade policy in particular, as well as the interface with education and labor policies.

5.1   Research and Technology Policy

Foremost, research and technology policy must explicitly consider the broader global context. Global innovation demands rethinking a key paradigm of U.S. policy: the United States as unrivalled leader in technological innovation. While much of the U.S. science and technology policy was shaped by circumstances of U.S. dominance in technological innovation, current policy cannot proceed on this assumption. Two options follow from this recognition: to strengthen domestic innovation and to optimize global knowledge gathering by U.S. firms. Moreover, these goals are linked. A solid innovation infrastructure at home is essential to the ability to find and utilize knowledge from abroad.

The appropriation of benefits from knowledge creation is a question of dynamic consequence. Largely the policy debate about the overseas R&D activity of foreign affiliates in the United States has been framed by the fear of "losing" knowledge to other nations rather than a focus on how to best respond to globalization. The significance of R&D activities of multinationals is related to the important question of the extent to which technology transfer is a "contact sport" (Reid and Schriesheim 1996). Affiliates may monitor and capture benefits from abroad, but spillover benefits may also accrue in the host country (Graham 1992, Graham and Krugman 1995). Understanding how the value of U.S. R&D is captured in the U.S. economy involves studying the factors that contribute to learning in interactions such as overseas R&D, international research ventures and alliances, and in the R&D of foreign affiliates in the United States.

The dynamic elements of learning extend beyond the intra-firm transactions of MNC. In particular, the relationships with suppliers as well as customers are important aspects of international knowledge transmission. Learning about organization and management of innovation and other dynamic benefits may be conditioned by the extent to which domestic suppliers are an integral part of the supply chain for foreign affiliates, as being part of supply chain represents real opportunity for learning and innovating. As well, interactions with university researchers are an opportunity for knowledge transmission facilitated by R&D presence.

Enabling the U.S. to appropriate the results of domestic R&D also requires thinking about the relationships between publicly funded knowledge and privately sector investment in R&D. In particular, the symmetry between U.S. university relationships with foreign industry and the ability of U.S. industry to form academic relationships abroad needs to be considered. Asymmetry becomes a political as well as economic issue when academic research is better integrated with industry in the U.S. than it is in other nations, or if university-industry relationships are more transparent and accessible to foreign firms in the U.S. than to U.S. firms abroad.[10] Access to participation in publicly funded programs and research consortia must also be considered.

5.2 Trade Policy

Knowledge transmission and innovation need to be taken into account as an explicit part of the formulation of trade policy. There needs to be a better understanding of how openness affects innovation, particularly given its global character. Only in this manner, can policy incorporate and integrate technology and trade goals in a complementary fashion. Importantly, concomitant consideration helps point out that free trade does not have to be pitted against technology concerns, but rather can be used as a tool to enhance innovation and hence economic growth.

The participation of U.S. firms in international research collaborations presents many issues that need to be better considered from the standpoint of innovation. Especially in the evolving wireless communications sector and other emerging areas, it is not realistic to assume that U.S. standards will be dominant. Thus, U.S. industry needs to be part of determining standards, through international research ventures, participation in consortia, and coordination with international programs such as OECD and WTO guidelines for international investment.

Moreover, while convergence has accelerated in Europe with the increasing integration of the EU, the consequences of this for U.S. innovation have not been studied well. For example, recent international mergers in several high technology sectors, including drugs and communications, are likely to impact domestic innovation.

5.3 Education Policy

Education in science and mathematics is an important aspect of the domestic innovation infrastructure. The science and mathematics skills of U.S. students have been compared unfavorably to other countries (National Science Board 1998). The National Research Council (1999) indicated the inadequacy of current undergraduate science and engineering education for a high-tech world. In a similar vein, the American Electronics Association (1999) pointed out the decline in higher degrees in science and technology and the significance of this to high-tech industry in the United States.

An international comparison of elementary and secondary school science and mathematics achievement found that the performance of U.S. students relative to other nations declined with increasing grade level.[11] Moreover, the top U.S. students compare poorly to top students elsewhere. Likewise, the content of U.S. science and math classes is not as challenging as many nations, particularly Japan and Germany (U.S. Department of Education 1996, 1998).[12]

A skilled, educated workforce increases absorptive capacity and enables the benefits of international knowledge transmission to be utilized. Clearly, poor science and math education does not portend well for an innovative economy. Thus, improving K–12 and undergraduate science and math education is important to promoting innovation. In part, this involves better integration of science and math into the curriculum and requiring greater math skills from all college and even high school graduates. Another component of improving the skill match between technology driven innovation and the workforce is to further encourage masters' education in science and engineering to be better tailored to needs of industry. Recognizing the importance of support for graduate education is also important.

5.4   Labor Policy

The distributional impact on labor and the relative impacts on particular industries is a perennial source of conflict between trade and labor policy. The relationship among globalization, innovation, and technology with regard to employment and wages needs to be better understood. Domestic policy also can mediate this through training workers for appropriate high-skill, high wage sectors, by learning to adapt to evolving patterns of production and innovation, and through policy to encourage broad access and facility with information and communication technologies in the workforce.

5.5   Data Collection and Funding

Understanding the impacts of international trade and investment on knowledge transmission and innovation remains limited by available data. More complete data on R&D and innovation in foreign affiliates of U.S. corporations abroad and of the affiliates of foreign companies in the U.S. at a detailed industry level by individual country is needed. The trend towards increased cooperation between BEA and NSF in such analysis should be continued and accelerated. As well, data collection should be expanded and standardized. One policy option is to fund an international data project to understand globalization of innovation in the world economy. Funding from several nations and coordinated research efforts with ongoing efforts in EU would encourage this.

5.6   Service Sector

It is increasingly necessary to recognize the importance of the service sector in the economy, particularly the information industry and financial sector. Significantly, globalization is increasing dramatically in this area. Service is an important and growing sector which is increasingly technology-driven. Moreover, the service sector is becoming more international in scope. A particularly important component of this is the growing interdependencies between computing and communications in the service sector. While the service sector is not high-tech in the traditional way of thinking about high-tech industries, the integration of the information and communications industry with services makes it increasingly important to consider the service sector in technology policy.

6.   CONCLUSIONS AND POLICY AGENDA

Twin dangers accompany the issue of the impact of globalization on innovation. The first, to overstate the potential for globalization to influence domestic affairs (i.e., to give too much power to "global forces" and not enough to domestic policy). The second, to underestimate the interplay of domestic policy, particularly policy towards innovation and the secondary policies that relate to it, with the greater global context. Only by understanding the impact of globalization can these errors be moderated. Ultimately, research and innovation policy in the United States must encourage domestic innovation, but it must do so with full consideration of the broader global context in which it operates. From this analysis it should be clear that policy towards innovation must be considered in global context. Areas frequently evaluated at best in isolation and often in conflict must be jointly analyzed in order to maximize benefits, minimize actual losses and avoid the opportunity cost of not taking advantage of global sources of knowledge.

Ultimately, globalization has a significant effect on the relationship among international trade, domestic innovation, and productivity. As globalization increases and as innovation becomes increasingly international, it becomes more important to understand the link between them and its consequences. That said it is certainly not the case that international trade policy is the most important effect on domestic innovation and productivity. Indeed, the several other policy areas I mention matter for domestic innovation, especially education and labor, as well as "industrial policy" stated or unstated.

Importantly, several factors suggest that the impact of globalization on innovation is likely increasing in significance. The two factors outlined in Tables 1 and 2, the increasing share of high-tech industries in international trade and the increasing dependence of innovation on a greater variety of sources, point towards the growing relationship between innovation and international connections.

To some extent, the impact of globalization on innovation may have a differentially greater effect on the United States than on most other nations. As innovation is increasingly distributed internationally the predominance of U.S. industries and companies shrinks as a share of innovation related measures (e.g., patents, industrial R&D, overseas R&D). In other words, the United States has relatively more to lose. This is compounded by issues such as whether the United States is better or worse at learning from abroad, a dynamic question, as well as the static question of net knowledge flow, for example through FDI into the United States and FDI in R&D abroad and the flow of people internationally.

Looking at the big picture, international trade and protection relate to the ability of the United States to innovate and compete. Protection will likely hurt long-run innovation. Usually trade barriers end up protecting weaker industries. Protectionism allows neglect of the very domestic issues that can influence the balance: such as science and technology education and training an adequately skilled workforce, or the human capital component of absorptive capacity. Moreover, it is important to keep in mind that knowledge is hard to contain, making protectionist barriers an inefficient solution. While we can erect barriers, a likely effect is to look inward, and not take advantage of knowledge and innovation abroad. The take home message is that globalization cannot be "fought" with protectionist policies. Certainly, the United States would not become more innovative by erecting trade barriers. At best, this might prevent some catching-up or leap-frogging by others, but this is a separate issue from spurring domestic innovation and provides only a temporary advantage. The United States needs to scan the horizon broadly and actively, and to have the ability to absorb and implement knowledge from an ever-wider variety of sources.

REFERENCES

American Electronics Association. (1999*). Cybereducation: U.S. Education and the High-Tech Workforce, A National and State-by-State Perspective*, Washington, DC.

Arrow, K. J. (1962). "The Economic Implications of Learning by Doing." *Review of Economic Studies* 29: 155-173.

Atkinson, R. D. and R. H. Court. (1998). *The New Economy Index: Understanding America's Economic Transformation*, Washington, DC: Progressive Policy Institute.

Barrell, R. and N. Pain. (1997). "Foreign Direct Investment, Technological Change, and Economic Growth Within Europe." *Economic Journal,* November, *107*: 1770-1786.

Bernstein, J. I. and P. Mohnen. (1998). "International R&D Spillovers Between U.S. and Japanese R&D Intensive Sectors." *Journal of International Economics* 44 (2): 315-38.

Branscomb, L. M. and R. Florida. (1998). "Challenges to Technology Policy in a Changing World Economy." in L. M. Branscomb, and J. H. Keller, eds., *Investing in Innovation: Creating a Research and Innovation Policy That Works*, Cambridge, MA: The MIT Press.

Branscomb, L. M. and J. H. Keller. (1998). *Investing in Innovation: Creating a Research and Innovation Policy That Works*, Cambridge, MA: The MIT Press.

Branscomb, L. M. and J. H. Keller (1998). "Towards a Research and Innovation Policy." in L. M. Branscomb, and J. H. Keller, eds., *Investing in Innovation: Creating a Research and Innovation Policy That Works*, Cambridge, MA: The MIT Press.

Branscomb, L. M., F. Kodama, and R. Florida. (1999). *Industrializing Knowledge: University-Industry Linkages in Japan and the United States*, Cambridge: MIT Press.

Branstetter, L. (1996). "Are Knowledge Spillovers International or Intranational in Scope?" NBER Working Paper 5800.

Coe, D. and E. Helpman. (1995). "International R&D Spillovers." *European Economic Review* 39: 859-887.

Cohen, W. and D. Levinthal. (1989). "Innovation and Learning: The Two Faces of R&D." *Economic Journal* 99: 569-596.

Connolly, M. P. (1998). "The Dual Nature of Trade: Measuring Its Impact on Imitation and Growth." *Federal Reserve Bank of New York Staff Reports,* No. 44.

Dunning, J. H. and R. Narula. (1995). "The R&D Activities of Foreign Firms in the United States." *International Studies of Management and Organization,* Spring-Summer, 25: 39-73.

Eaton, J. and S. Kortum. (1996). "Trade in Ideas: Patenting and Productivity in the OECD." *Journal of International Economics 40*: 251-278.

The Economist (1997). "One World?" October 18, 345: 79-80.

The Economist (2000)."Financial Indicators, Technology Shares." April 22, 355: 96.

Fountain, J. E. and R. D. Atkinson. (1998). "Innovation, Social Capital, and the New Economy: New Federal Policies to Support Collaborative Research." Progressive Policy Institute Policy Briefing: Washington, DC.

Graham, E. M. (1992). "Japanese Control of R&D Activities in the United States: Is This Cause for Concern?" in T. S. Arrison, C. F. Bergsten, E. M. Graham, and M. C. H. Harris, eds., *Japan's Growing Technological Capability: Implications for the U.S. Economy*, Washington, DC: National Academy Press.

Graham, E. M. and P. R. Krugman. (1995). *Foreign Direct Investment in the United States*, Washington, DC: Institute for International Economics.

Griliches, Z. (1992). "The Search for R&D Spillovers." *Scandinavian Journal of Economics, Supplement,* 94: 29-47.

Grossman, G. M. and E. Helpman. (1991). "Trade, Knowledge Spillovers, and Growth." *European Economic Review* 35: 517-526.

Grossman, G. M. and E. Helpman. (1995). "Technology and Trade." in G. M. Grossman and K. Rogoff, eds., *Handbook of International Economics, Volume III*, Amsterdam: Elsevier Science B. V.

Helpman, E. (1997). "R&D and Productivity: The International Connection." NBER Working Paper 6101.

Hirschey, R. and R. Caves. (1981). "Research and Transfer of Technology by Multinational Enterprises." *Oxford Bulletin of Economics and Statistics,* May, 43: 115-130.

International Monetary Fund. (1997). *World Economic Outlook*, Washington, DC: International Monetary Fund.

Jaffe, A. (1993). "Geographic Localization of Knowledge Spillovers As Evidenced by Patent Citations." *Quarterly Journal of Economics* 108 (3): 577-598.

Jaffe, A. (1996). *Economic Analysis of Research Spillovers: Implications for the Advanced Technology Program.* Washington, DC: National Institute of Standards and Technology, U.S. Department of Commerce.

Jaffe, A. B. and M. Trajtenberg. (1998). "International Knowledge Flows: Evidence From Patent Citations." NBER Working Paper 6507.

Keller, W. (1997). "Trade and the Transmission of Technology." NBER Working Paper 6113.

Kogut, B. and S. J. Chang. (1991). "Technological Capabilities and Japanese Foreign Direct Investment in the United States." *Review of Economics and Statistics,* August, 73: 401-413.

Kuemmerle, W. (1999). "Foreign Direct Investment in Industrial Research in the Pharmaceutical and Electronics Industries-Results from a Survey of Multinational Firms" *Research Policy,* March, 28: 179-93.

Lawrence, R. (2000). "Does a Kick in the Pants Get You Going or Does It Just Hurt? The Impact of International Competition on Technological Change in U.S. Manufacturing." in

R.F. Feenstra, ed., *The Impact of International Trade on Wages*. Chicago: University of Chicago Press.

Lawrence, R. and D. Weinstein. (2000). "The Role of Trade in East Asian Productivity Growth: the Case of Japan." in J. Stiglitz and S. Yusuf, eds., *Rethinking the East Asian Miracle*, New York and Oxford: Oxford University Press for the World Bank.

Lichtenberg, F. and B. van Pottelsberghe de la Potterie. (1996). "International R&D Spillovers: A Re-Examination." NBER Working Paper 5668.

Mansfield, E. (1995). "Academic Research Underlying Industrial Innovations: Sources, Characteristics, and Financing." *Review of Economics and Statistics 77* (1): 55-65.

Mokyr, J. (1990). *The Lever of Riches*, New York and Oxford: Oxford University Press.

Mowery, D. C. (1998). "Collaborative R&D: How Effective Is It?" *Issues in Science and Technology (Online)*, Fall.

Nadiri, M. I. and S. Kim. (1996). "International R&D Spillovers, Trade and Productivity in Major OECD Countries." NBER Working Paper 5801.

National Research Council. (1999). *Transforming Undergraduate Education in Science, Mathematics, Engineering, and Technology*, Washington, DC: National Academy Press.

National Science Board. (1998). *Science and Engineering Indicators—1998*, Arlington, VA: National Science Foundation.

Nelson, R. R. (1998). "The Agenda for Growth Theory: A Different Point of View." *Cambridge Journal of Economics* 22 (4): 497-520.

Nelson, R. R. and P. M. Romer. (1996). "Science, Economic Growth, and Public Policy." in B. L. R. Smith and C. E. Barfield, eds., *Technology, R&D, and the Economy*, Washington, DC: Brookings Institution and American Enterprise Institute for Public Policy Research.

Organization for Economic Cooperation and Development. (OECD). (1997). *Science, Technology and Industry-Scoreboard of Indicators 1997*, Paris: OECD.

Organization for Economic Cooperation and Development. (OECD). (1998). "Open Markets Matter." *OECD Policy Brief*, No. 6.

Park, W. (1995). "International R&D Spillovers and Economic Growth." *Economic Inquiry* 33 (4): 571-91.

Reid, P. P. and A. Schriesheim. (1996). *Foreign Participation in U.S. Research and Development: Asset or Liability*, Washington, DC: National Academy Press.

Rodrik, D. (1998). "Symposium on Globalization in Perspective: An Introduction." *Journal of Economic Perspectives* 12 (4): 3-8.

Rothwell, R. (1994). "Industrial Innovation: Success, Strategy, Trends." in M. Dodgson and R. Rothwell, eds., *Handbook of Industrial Innovation*, Brookfield, VT: Edward Elgar.

Scherer, F. M. (1992). *International High-Technology Competition*, Cambridge, MA: Harvard University Press.

Scherer, F. M. (1994). *Competition Policies for an Integrated World Economy*, Washington, DC: Brookings Institution.

Smith, S. W. (1999). "The Industrial Perspective on University-Industry Relationships in Japan and the United States." in L. M. Branscomb, F. Kodama, and R. L. Florida, eds., *Industrializing Knowledge University-Industry Linkages in Japan and the United States*, Cambridge, Mass: MIT Press.

Stiglitz, J. E. (1987). "Learning to Learn, Localized Learning, and Technological Progress ." in P. Dasgupta and P. Stoneman, eds., *Economic Policy and Technological Performance*, Cambridge: Cambridge University Press.

U.S. Bureau of Economic Analysis. (1998). *U.S. International Private Services, 1986–1997 (IDN-0215)*. Washington, DC: U.S. Bureau of Economic Analysis.

U.S. Bureau of Economic Analysis. (1998). *U.S. Direct Investment Abroad, 1982-97 (IDN-0217)* Washington, DC: U.S. Bureau of Economic Analysis.

U.S. Department of Commerce, Office of Technology Policy. (1998). *The New Innovators: Global Patenting Trends in Five Sectors*, Washington, DC.

U.S. Department of Commerce, Office of Technology Policy. (1999). *The Digital Workforce: Building Infotech Skills at the Speed of Innovation*, Washington, DC.

U.S. Department of Education, National Center for Education Statistics. (1996). *Pursuing Excellence: A Study of U.S. Eighth-Grade Mathematics and Science Teaching, Learning, Curriculum, and Achievement in International Context*, Washington, DC: U.S. Government Printing Office.

U.S. Department of Education, National Center for Education Statistics. (1998). *Pursuing Excellence: A Study of U.S. Twelfth-Grade Mathematics and Science Achievement in International Context*, Washington, DC: U.S. Government Printing Office.

U.S. International Trade Commission. (1997). *The Dynamic Effects of Trade Liberalization: An Empirical Analysis*, Washington, DC.

Varian, H. R. (1992). *Microeconomic Analysis*, New York and London: W. W. Norton.

Vickery, G. (1998). "Industrial Performance and Competitiveness in an Era of Globalization and Technological Change." *OECD DSTI/IND 97*: 23/Final.

World Bank. (1998). *World Development Report 1998/1999: Knowledge for Development*, New York, NY: Oxford University Press.

[1] See for example Rodrik (1998).

[2] See, for example, Nelson and Romer (1996) for a detailed argument on the properties of knowledge; see, for example, Varian (1992) for a textbook exposition of public goods.

[3] When knowledge spillovers occur, the innovator is unable to fully appropriate the gains from innovation, as the benefits of innovation are realized partly by others. Pure knowledge spillovers result from the embodied and disembodied knowledge from innovation in one realm spilling over into the creation of new products or new processes in another realm. This can be distinguished from market spillovers, which result from the improved quality of products or lower cost processes in the original field. However, market spillovers may look like productivity improvements in another field due to the inability to adequately account for improved quality inputs in the original field, which is different from a pure knowledge spillover. See discussion in Griliches (1979, 1992) and Jaffe (1996).

[4] See Grossman and Helpman (1991), Grossman and Helpman (1995), Lawrence and Weinstein (1999).

[5] See, for example, Keller (1997) and Connolly (1998).

[6] See Caves (1996) and Dunning (1995).

[7] See for example Lawrence (2000), Lawrence and Weinstein (1999), Scherer (1992), and Scherer (1994).

[8] See for example Scherer (1994).

[9] For discussion of path dependence in technological innovation, see for example Mokyr (1990). Learning by doing is put forward in Arrow (1962), and incorporated in many analyses of innovation and growth. See, for example, Grossman and Helpman (1991) and Romer (1996). Learning to learn, see Stiglitz (1987) among others.

[10] See Branscomb, Kodama, and Florida (1999) for comparison to Japan, See OECD (1997) and Nelson (1998) for discussions of differences in the nature of university-industry relationships under different national innovation systems.

[11] The Third International Mathematics and Science Study (TIMSS) project compares science and mathematics education in 4th, 8th, and 12th graders. Overall, United States students score above the international average in both science and math in 4th grade, somewhat below the international average in math and somewhat above in science in 8th grade, and below the international average in both math and science by the 12th grade.

[12] United States 8th grade math corresponded more closely to 7th grade math in Germany and Japan. The nature of the material taught to advanced students also diverges; in the United States advanced students tend to cover different material (e.g., algebra and geometry are done earlier) whereas in Germany advanced students (in Gymnasium) cover the same material but with greater depth and attention to developing understanding of how to think mathematically and theory.

Chapter 16

Globalization and Environmental Regulation

GRAHAM K. WILSON
University of Wisconsin-Madison

1. GLOBALIZATION AND REGULATION

A wide range of authoritative indicators establishes what we sense in our daily lives: the effects of international influences and factors are increasing. This trend is most easily observed in economic activity. Goods and money move around the globe at levels that until recently seemed unimaginable. Even nations, such as the United States, whose economies were only marginally dependent on trade, are drawn into world trade. While total trade, the sum of exports and imports, was 6.5 percent of U.S. Gross National Product (GNP) in the period 1946-59, it was 15.3 percent in the period 1980-1992 (*Economic Report of the President* 1994). U.S. trade dependence continued to increase, growing 44 percent between 1992 and 1996. By 1996, trade was equivalent to 30 percent of U.S. Gross Domestic Product (GDP) (U.S. Trade Representative 1997). Cross border investment stock (assets in the United States owned by foreigners plus assets owned by Americans overseas) grew from 15.45 of GNP in 1960 to 41 percent in 1992 and has continued at a faster rate than the growth in GNP overall (*Economic Report of the President* 1995). The United States, although it remains less trade dependent than other countries such as the United Kingdom, is now fully part of international markets.

Globalization creates a number of potential problems for national regulatory agencies and their political masters. The basic issue is what is the role of national regulatory policy in a global economy. This chapter focuses on the regulation of environment and consumer protection. This type of social regulation has been at the heart of the debate about globalization because it is the type of regulation that appears to set states against markets in pursuit of public policy goals. Social regulation attempts to change the outcome of market forces in pursuit of policy outcomes that frequently involve public goods such as clean air and water. Social regulations impose costs on industries and so are naturally opposed. Particularly in the United States, fierce struggles between business and environmental interest groups have been waged over regulation to promote a cleaner environment with business threatening to move to less regulated environments.

Many proponents of social regulations fear that globalization has shifted the advantage in this struggle in favor of business. For example, the protesters against the World Trade Organization (WTO) in Seattle in 1999 and against the World Bank and International Monetary Fund (IMF) in Washington, DC in 2000 contended that globalization empowered the business opponents of stricter regulation. International organizations, the protesters asserted, were biased in favor of business, while the increased mobility of capital and labor facilitated corporations switching investment and production to plants in countries with the weakest, and therefore least costly, regulations.

Distinguishing between globalization and internationalization helps to clarify some of the issues involved. The term globalization is used to refer to forces promoting integration on a worldwide scale that are not amenable to government controls (Berger and Dore 1996, Garrett 1995, Garrett and Lange 1995, Keohane and Milner 1996, Schwartz 1994). The most obvious examples are the economic forces unleashed by global economic integration. Products such as apparel and clothing may be designed on one continent (perhaps Europe), manufactured in another (probably Asia) and sold in a third (such as North America.) Globalization is itself something that results, in part, from the past decisions of governments such as lifting capital controls and reducing tariffs. Once those economic forces were unleashed, they produce strong downward pressure on national regulation.

Globalization need not be a purely economic phenomenon. The popularity of American styles and movies with young Japanese and Europeans, for example, or the spread of a rights discourse that once seemed particularly American are reminders that globalization can be a cultural as well as an economic phenomenon. As is the case with the forces of economic globalization, cultural globalization may well result from decisions of governments (for example, to end or reduce restrictions on the proportion of television programming that consists of imported, usually American material). However, again once unleashed, the forces of cultural globalization have a life of their own. Governments can probably do little to prevent their teenagers from embracing American styles.

Internationalization, by contrast, consists of governments making policy in negotiations with each other or by handing over the authority to formulate policy to an international organization. It is therefore easier to monitor the institutional basis of internationalization than globalization; we can see actual people in governmental and international institutions making the relevant decisions. Those decisions can be made in government-to-government negotiations. Increasingly, however, important decisions are made within international organizations, even if member governments subsequently ratify them. The clearest examples of internationalization arise within the European Union (EU) whose member states have given it authority to make binding decisions in a number of policy areas, including two of particular importance to this chapter, namely environmental and trade policy. On a more global scale, members have granted the WTO significant authority to settle trade disputes.

In sum, globalization is an economic and cultural process while internationalization is a political process. The consequences of globalization are the results of the workings of global economic and social forces, not of identifiable current political decisions. Several different types of problems for regulators stem from the distinction of globalization and internationalization that may be distinguished.

First, regulators may be pushed into a "race to the bottom." The almost total elimination of capital controls in the developed world and the drastic reduction of tariffs on manufactured goods has created fierce competition between nations for investment. This is similar to the fierce rivalry noted between states within the USA. This competition is likely to be particularly intense within economic zones such as the European Union or the North American Free Trade Agreement (NAFTA) that have attempted to eliminate all trade barriers. One means by which nations can compete for business investment is by lowering taxes; another is by reducing the cost and impact of regulations. Nations may become involved therefore in a competition for investment based on reducing their fiscal resources and the force with which they protect consumers and the environment.

Second, regulators increasingly encounter international organizations that diminish their ability to regulate. Some of these international organizations may themselves be regulatory bodies that pre-empt national regulatory authority, the regulatory agencies of the EU being perhaps the best example. A more difficult situation arises, however, when domestic regulators in one policy area find that their freedom to regulate is limited by the actions and policies of an international organization that has an entirely different policy focus. The best known examples are of collisions between trade and environmental policy. In the final days of the General Agreement on Tariffs and Trade (GATT), before it was re-organized into the World Trade

Organization (WTO), the United States' use of its Marine Mammal Protection Act to ban the import of tuna that were caught in ways that endangered dolphins conflicted with GATT obligations. As a campaigner for freer trade, the United States was placed in an embarrassing situation and revised the Act. In a more recent case brought against the United States within the framework of the WTO, the United States was found to be in breach of international trade law by banning the import of shrimp caught by fishermen in less developed countries such as India, Bangladesh and Malaysia in a manner that protected endangered sea turtles. The United States has attempted to revise its laws and regulations to comply with WTO rulings but has been blocked by domestic legal difficulties (Wilson 1999).

A third problem for national regulators is that they face considerable pressure from international corporations to harmonize regulations. Corporations understandably wish to avoid the problems of being in compliance with a law or regulation in one country only to be out of compliance in another. This is a familiar problem domestically for American corporations that have wished to avoid situations in which regulations differ from one state to another. Business has generally opposed (to the dismay of conservatives) moves to devolve more regulatory power from the federal to the state level. Such complications arise more frequently as international trade increases. European bans on genetically altered food is creating serious problems currently for United States shippers of grain, long used to mixing grain from different farmers and therefore until recently mixing conventional and genetically altered grain in their silos. Differences in regulations between nations have even greater potential to disrupt trade in services (such as insurance) where the very nature of the product being sold is defined by laws and regulations. Corporations, generally inclined in the modern era to favor freer trade, are also well aware of the potential for environmental or consumer regulations to be used as shields against foreign competition by domestic industries. Corporations favoring trade liberalization therefore have an interest in making sure that domestic regulators achieve harmony with foreign counterparts. A similar story can of course be told about American farmers' fears that EU policies against the use of growth hormones in beef cattle or genetically modified cereals are merely new forms of long standing policies aimed at protecting American farmers from foreign competition.

Although internationalization and globalization have been seen as reducing the likelihood of effective regulation there are a number of ways in which they may enhance the prospects for effective regulation.

First, as Vogel (1995) has argued, countries that have adopted stringent regulations that have a significant impact on their production costs have a major interest in using international organizations to raise costs in other countries. The United States and Germany, Vogel argued, forced to adopt stringent and costly regulations by strong environmental movements in their own country will push their competitors to adopt similarly costly measures. The more integrated are markets and the stronger the related international organizations, the more likely it is that there will be a leveling up rather than a leveling down of regulatory standards. Vogel's argument is clearly dependent, however, on the strength of environmental groups. If these groups were weaker, the globalization of trade could be followed by measures to weaken high regulatory standards rather than to export them to competitor countries.

Here the special character of the United States in world hegemony comes into play. Hegemons, according to international relations theory, are supposed to be able to prioritize the maintenance of the international and international economic system over domestic concerns (Keohane 1984, Gowa 1993). Nations that had acted as hegemons in prior eras were less subject to interest group and popular pressure: Great Britain, for example, during its period of hegemony, was not yet a full democracy as a large proportion of the male working class had yet to attain the franchise and government was still dominated by the aristocracy. In contrast, the United States became the hegemon in an era in which its political system was famously, or notoriously, open to pressures from domestic interests and popular opinion. While the international power of its leaders is indeed great, so also is their vulnerability to domestic pressure. Even groups that think of themselves as relatively weak may exert significant ability to influence policy in directions that may be contrary to U.S. foreign policy and global responsibilities. Environmental groups may feel weak and under financed in comparison to business; they clearly have the ability to exert leverage. If President Clinton, or more probably his successor, is to regain fast track authority for negotiating further trade liberalization, the environmental groups will have to be won over. For at present, the environmental groups are a crucial component of a projectionist coalition based on labor, a component that brings not only added lobbying power but intellectual and moral respectability in the United States to that coalition. In this context, the name of the game in Washington is to emphasize the compatibility of environmentalism with trade, not the possibility of weakening environmental commitments to promote competitiveness.

It is important to note, the protestations of American domestic environmental groups not withstanding, that they have enjoyed qualified victories when they have become involved in conflict with international trade organizations. On the two most notable occasions when the United States was required by international bodies to revise its environmental laws to comply with its trade policy commitments (tuna/ dolphin under GATT and shrimp/turtle under WTO) a very substantial resistance developed.

Indeed, the United States came into compliance with the GATT ruling on tuna only after the complaining countries had settled for a compromise that they negotiated with five U.S. domestic environmental groups. The U.S. implementing legislation followed the terms of the agreement negotiated between sovereign nations and U.S. domestic interest groups. Although the agreement has its critics, it resulted in increased protection for dolphins throughout the eastern Pacific. The leverage of public interest groups in American domestic politics was sufficiently great not merely to avoid a reduction in environmental standards but to raise the level of international environmental protection. The U.S. has yet to come into compliance with the WTO ruling on shrimp/turtle but once again we can be confident that the outcome will not be significant defeat for environmental groups. As Vogel's argument requires, the environmental groups have sufficient power in the United States to make it more rational for policy makers there to try to raise standards in other countries than to weaken their own.

It has been interesting, and again consistent with Vogel's arguments, to watch the United States act as sponsor of environmental groups within the WTO. American leaders, including President Clinton himself, have pressed for greater transparency in WTO decision making, meaning greater openness to lobbying by groups such as environmentalists. In the period following the initial ruling against the U.S. on shrimp/turtle, the United States engaged in vigorous lobbying of the WTO that helped contribute to a final ruling by the appeals panel that contained significant procedural gains for environmentalists. Their right to submit briefs to WTO hearings on trade laws was accepted (previously many members of WTO had argued that only governments had this right) and the WTO leadership attempted to open a dialogue with the groups. In the words of the *Economist*, the current head of the WTO, Mike Moore, "is reaching out to the most vocal of all the WTO's critics, environmentalists."

Globalization, like Internationalization, has unexpected consequences that enhance the prospects for effective regulation. There have been unexpected gains from globalization that public interest groups such as environmentalists have enjoyed. Environmentalists have been adept at using the forces of globalization (cheap air travel and phone calls, the Internet) to build international movements and coalitions (Ayres 1999).

One consequence of this internationalization of public interest groups has been that they have been able to mount campaigns at the point of greatest corporate weakness. The British political scientist, Grant Jordan, provides a telling example (Jordan 1998). Shell wished to dispose of a North Sea oil storage facility, the *Brent Spar*, by sinking it in deep waters in the Atlantic. Shell persuaded most scientists and the British government that this was the most environmentally friendly way to dispose of the storage facility.

Environmentalists in Britain and in other European countries condemned the plan. The British government had been so convinced that it not only approved its plan but also defended it vigorously within the EU. The British prime minister, John Major, left his meeting with Kohl only to be informed that Shell itself had retreated and now intended to follow the more expensive option of dismantling, not sinking the Brent Spar. Why had Shell retreated? In brief the explanation was that a campaign which included boycotts of gas stations in Germany and the Netherlands was hurting Shell profits and public image. Shell's character as a transnational corporation allowed environmentalists to pressure Shell wherever they were strongest and Shell was weakest. Shell had sufficient influence with the British government to protect its interests; the British government unquestionably had the legal power to issue the permit to Shell that it needed to sink the *Brent Spar.* Unfortunately for Shell, its own commercial interests were vulnerable to pressure in Germany and the Netherlands where environmentalists were stronger and more militant than in Britain. Shell needed to ask not whether it had the requisite influence where the legal authority to make the decision resided, in Britain; it had. Instead, Shell needed to ask how vulnerable it was where its opponents were strongest (Germany and the Netherlands.) Thus, internationalization can undermine the capacity of global corporations to resist environmentalist pressures by allowing their critics to pressure them where they are weakest.

Globalization may even make business willing to promote certain types of internationalization. Business generally remains anxious, for understandable reasons, to avoid further extensions of traditional regulations. In order to fend off further command and control regulation or restrictions on trade adopted in the name of environmental protection, corporations have themselves become agents for spreading a certain type of regulation. This type of regulation, of course not legally binding and therefore not formally regulation focuses on managerial procedures. Businesses are encouraged, or in a sense required, to adopt specified forms of self-regulation if they wish to remain contractors or suppliers of major corporations. Some of these requirements are issued in forms that appear mandatory rather than voluntary, except in the sense that suppliers can choose to lose important business by not complying. Thus, on September 15, 1999, the Ford Motor Company issued a notice to all suppliers to register a minimum of one facility to international standards by December 31, 2001 and all manufacturing sites by July 1, 2003. Ford offered its suppliers training in order to meet these requirements.

The two most important forms of corporate self-regulation in this area are ISO 14000 and EMAS. The International Standards Organization (ISO) regulations are in fact a series beginning at 14000; EMAS stands for

Environmental Management and Auditing System. They differ significantly in character. ISO 14000 is a voluntary system of self management whose main tenets are that companies adopt procedures for evaluating their current environmental record, adopt plans for improvement, procedures for evaluating progress and for setting new goals. Firms that adopt such procedures receive a certificate. ISO 14000 does not mandate specific targets or levels of performance. Indeed, one U.S. firm holding an ISO 14000 certificate was adjudged by regulators to be in breach of existing environmental laws. EMAS in contrast derives from a European Union directive issued in 1996 and whereas ISO 14000 covers all types of organization, ISO is focused on producing industries. EMAS requires firms to comply with all existing laws but then to adopt plans for additional improvements. Auditors from a panel approved by government audit firms at least once within each three-year period. A list of firms in compliance is maintained by an industry organization such as a Chamber of Commerce.

EMAS is clearly a more stringent procedure involving external evaluation of performance, not just process. Yet though government is more directly involved with EMAS in establishing the scheme and by approving and monitoring auditors, it is similar to ISO 14000 in resting on the idea of improving environmental performance though non governmental means; private sector auditors, not civil servants, carry out inspections and identify underperformance. It is perhaps predictable, therefore, that ISO 14000 has had more appeal than EMAS, even in Europe; EMAS is heavily concentrated in Germany.

Table 1. EMAS versus ISO 14000, 1999

	EMAS	ISO 14000
Germany	2,238	1,450
Sweden	165	645
France	34	365
UK	71	1,009
Netherlands	23	210
Italy	13	166

Source: Wisconsin Department of Natural Resources, Office of the Secretary, November 1999.

It is more surprising that so far ISO 14000 has made only very limited progress in the United States. American business has often claimed that it is willing to accept environmental goals but opposes inflexible government regulations. Yet, its take up rate of ISO 14000 has been slow in spite of its voluntary nature. In Europe, 5,800 ISO certificates have been issued, in Japan around 2,500 and in the whole of North America, around 500.

However, while there is no indigenous enthusiasm for ISO 14000 in the United States, it is now being spread by American transnational corporations. For example, as one executive at Ford put it somewhat melodramatically in an interview with the author in 1999, that if they do nothing one day "the Europeans will slam the door" on them through environmental regulations that have trade consequences.

2. REGULATION AND INTERNATIONALIZATION: HOW MANY GAMES?

It is clearly inadequate to characterize the interaction of international forces and regulation in terms of a simple race to the bottom. The question is how might we best summarize the interaction of globalization, internationalization and regulation for policy.

The most powerful analogy that has been put forward to capture the interaction of international and domestic policy goals of opening foreign markets to U.S. industry through is Putnam's "two level game" (Evans, et al. 1993). National leaders are increasingly involved in interacting with leaders of other nations; they are also involved simultaneously with thinking about how to deal with powerful domestic actors (interest groups, legislators, and other politicians) on the same issue at home. Thus, national leaders play one "game" of thinking about how to win in international negotiations. National leaders also need to think about how to win the usual "game" of domestic politics so that they can secure approval for their policy at home. Their skill lies in combining these two games. Perhaps one of the most celebrated examples of a leader winning an international game and losing the domestic was Woodrow Wilson who suffered the rejection of his prized League of Nations at home having secured its approval internationally.

There are indeed examples of the interaction of foreign and domestic forces and regulation that are well captured by the idea of a two level game. The struggles between environmentalists seeking to protect endangered species such as dolphins and turtles on the one hand and the agency (the U.S. Trade Representative, USTR) pushing an international policy of trade liberalization provided good examples. U.S. Presidents and legislators have had to struggle to reconcile powerful domestic forces pushing for environmental goals around the world with attempts to open foreign markets for U.S. firms through trade liberalization.

Putnam's valuable analogy of national leaders playing two games (the international policy making game and the domestic policy making game) simultaneously does not fully capture the interaction of domestic and international factors in regulation, however. The two level game analogies miss at least two important aspects of the relationship between international factors and regulation.

First, international and domestic levels are not nearly as separated as the two level game analogies suggests. Domestic interests are active at the international level seeking to influence policy makers not only in bodies such as the EU (which after all takes on daily more the character of a state than an international organization) but in truly international organizations such as the WTO. Domestic interests have won the right to submit their arguments direct to WTO hearings without relying on national governments as intermediaries. Social movements have also been adept at acting internationally. German Greens are currently pressuring a paper manufacturer in their country, Handel, to force its pulp suppliers in British Columbia to adopt sustainable forestry practices. Indigenous peoples from British Columbia have been flown to Germany to take part in protests aimed at Handel. Using email, the Internet, air travel and cheap international phone calls, domestic social movements have gone global with their concerns. The boundary between the domestic and the international has been eroded.

The second reason why the two level game analogies is inadequate is that it does not consider the independent impact of international organizations. International organizations like domestic institutions not only have their own power structures but they also generally have a particularly strong sense of their primary mission. The commitments and values of the individuals who work in the organization, even the language and concepts used in analyzing problems and situations make some policy outcomes more likely, others less so. For example, the EU is not a neutral setting in choices between more and less integrative policy options and the WTO is not neutral between more or less trade liberalization. International bodies charged with environmental protection are not neutral about proposals to protect the environment. These organizations are also surrounded by a penumbra, a policy network of generally sympathetic journalists, commentators, and interest groups and agencies of national and sub national governments with which they have contacts all of which can generate domestic support for international regulations. In certain areas of environmental policy, these international networks may be "epistemic communities" united by common beliefs, assumptions and concepts (Haas 1992). Even while Margaret Thatcher inveighed against the growing power of Brussels, some European Union directives (for example on the cleanliness of bathing beaches) attracted great support in Britain due to the mobilization of public opinion.

The significance of the independent influence of international organizations and the policy networks of which they are part is that they are not purely international. Policy advocates who have succeeded at the international level can reach down into the politics and society of individual nations and communities to build support. Thus, there is no simple separation of the international and domestic policy arenas. Rather, policy coalitions and networks increasingly cross borders and the domestic/international divide and may achieve their objectives in multiple ways.

3.   COMBINING NATIONAL AND INTERNATIONAL REGULATION

Nations differ in the degree to which they favor investing resources in policies such as environmental or consumer protection. The causes for this variation are hard to determine and no doubt deeply rooted in political culture and past history. While we might assume that those nations that are the most keen on environmental protection in general will be the keenest on international regulation. However, as Vogel argued, nations with high standards and therefore high costs have important economic incentives in persuading other countries to adopt similarly costly measures. There is also an interaction, however, between nations' preferences on environmental policy and their policy capacities. Countries with a tradition of lax enforcement of regulations such as the Mediterranean members of the EU are often willing to vote for stringent regulations that they have no intention (or capability) of enforcing precisely because they know that their industries will not in practice have to bear the cost of the regulations.

The standard assumption has been that the more liberal economies gain from globalization. As their own economies are less encumbered by restrictive regulations, they have the flexibility to attract capital and compete in export markets. It is less clear, however, that economies that are more liberal will benefit from the internationalization of regulation for reasons that are connected to what is often seen as one of their strengths, the absence of institutionalized influence for interest groups. The recent success of the American economy in achieving higher rates of growth and employment than many European nations is often linked to a capacity for quick adaptability to changing economic conditions unencumbered by major economic interests having a major role in policy making. In Europe, in contrast, important aspects of governance are sometimes shared with major economic interests, as in Germany where economic interests run important programs such as health care and training or policy is made through negotiations between the major economic interests and government, as in the "neocorporatist" states such as the Netherlands. These countries are often said to have a different forms of capitalism from the United States, forms that are labeled "organized capitalism" because economic interest groups rather than market forces play such a conspicuous role in their economies.

States that are more practitioners of "organized capitalism" than of markets that are more liberal have other policy options because of the institutional capacity that they possess. Governments can not only pass laws or adopt regulations but can also entrust the implementation of policies to the organizations representing business and labor, or can negotiate flexible implementation arrangements with the "social partners" (typically business and labor) that share in policy making in neocorporatist systems. While Americans might suppose that inviting interest groups to share in policy implementation is akin to asking the fox to share in running the chicken coup experience in Europe suggests that such arrangements are often very effective in achieving public policy goals without the costs of inflexibility, inefficiency and conflict that reliance on laws and regulations generally entails. Countries that have economies characterized by organized capitalism have the option of pursuing internationally agreed goals through flexible agreements with industries rather than through "command and control" regulations. The Netherlands, for example, has promised to attain Kyoto levels of reduction in green house gases. It will do so through agreements or as they are known, "compacts" with major industries. Industry promises to attain the best environmental standards in the world; government promises to leave them free to do so. Government may also provide tax allowances as an incentive to do so. The growth of EMAS in Germany draws on that country's long traditions of industrial self-governance intended in part to avoid action by the state. Again, this provides a more flexible means for pursuing internationally agreed goals than "command and control regulation. A more organized political economy, precisely the feature of those economies most often criticized by American commentators for promoting rigidities in those economies in fact provides greater flexibility in pursuing regulator goals.

Calls for stricter standards at the international level will generally be experienced by liberal states as a call for more regulation in the command and control format. This is the only policy capacity that they have. The United States does not have a tradition of entrusting major responsibilities to interest groups. Indeed, it would generally be seen as dangerous and improper to allow interest groups to have a major role in policy implementation; the tradition of attacking "iron triangles" an the power of "special interests" illustrates a much greater skepticism about interest groups than exists in many European nations. The structure of the American interest group system also makes it difficult to share governance with them. In Germany, the Netherlands and other countries with economies that can be characterized as organized capitalism, generally a single organization speaks for business, farmers, labor and individual industries such as chemicals. This is not so in the United States where numerous interest groups compete with each other to be voice of business, farmers, environmentalists et cetera. It would be very difficult for an Administration to work with the Chamber of Commerce, for example, in preference to the National Association of Manufacturers, the Business Roundtable, the National Federation of Independent Business or any of the other numerous groups that claim to speak for business. For their part, business organizations like interest groups in other fields know that if a willingness to compromise with government can be portrayed as weakness, they will lose members to competing groups. Achieving the partnership between government and economic interest groups that exists in the Netherlands, for example, is very difficult in the United States. For lack of an alternative, the United States is forced to rely on laws and regulations in spite of their well know disadvantages. The United States is therefore particularly likely to be placed in the dilemma of choosing between the international disgrace or infamy of blocking what are seen as essential measures or advocating the costs of additional command and control regulation. Our regulatory traditions are based on a legalism that usually creates inflexibility The danger for the United States in a competitive, global economy as Nivola (1997) has argued is that the American style of regulation is an important source of competitive disadvantage.

4. CONCLUSION

In the study of the impact of international forces on political systems, it is a truism that not all countries react in the same way or are influenced by a international force in the same way (Gourevitch 1986). Perhaps the time has come to start to assess the different ways in which regulators in advanced democracies will be affected by the common international environment of globalization and internationalization.

Most discussion of internationalization and regulation has focused on the danger of a "race to the bottom" in standards. Though this is one possible influence, the interaction between globalization, internationalization and regulation is in reality much more complicated and unpredictable. Indeed, international influences can as readily raise and lower the prospects for regulation. The ability of the international environment to promote as well as retard regulation will be welcome to some countries that prioritize goals such as environmental protection. However, attitudes towards the capacity of the international environment to promote increased regulation will depend also on the domestic capacity of countries such as the Netherlands with flexible and adaptable partnerships between businesses. Government may feel better able to embrace international initiatives than countries such as the U.S. for whom accepting higher levels of protection may also mean accepting a new wave of costly and inflexible command and control regulation.

ACKNOWLEDGEMENTS

The author would like to acknowledge the assistance of Matthew Zierler with the research for this chapter.

REFERENCES

Ayres, J. M. (1999). "From the Streets to the Internet: The Cyber-Diffusion of Contention." *Annals* AAPSS, November, pp. 132-143.

Berger S. and R. Dore, eds. (1996) *Globalization and Its Limits,* Ithaca, NY: Cornell University Press.

Evans, P., H. Jacobson and R. D. Putnam. (1993). *Double Edged Diplomacy: International Diplomacy and Domestic Politics,* Berkeley, CA: University of California Press.

Economic Report of the President. (1994). Washington, DC: Government Printing Office.

Economic Report of the President. (1995). Washington, DC: Government Printing Office.

Garrett, G. (1995). "Capital Mobility, Trade and the Domestic Politics of Economic Policy." *International Organization* 49: 657-687.

Garrett, G. and P. Lange. (1995). "Internationalization, Institutions and Political Change." *International Organization* 49: 627-635.

Gourevitch, P. (1986). *Politics in Hard Times: Comparative Responses to Economic Crises,* Ithaca, NY: Cornell University Press.

Gowa, J. (1993). "An Epitaph for Hegemonic Stability?" in J. S. Odell and T. D. Willett, eds., *International Trade Policies: Gains from Exchange between Economics and Political Science,* Ann Arbor, MI: University of Michigan Press, pp. 55-74.

Haas, P. (1992). "Introduction: Epistemic Communities and International Policy Co-ordination." *International Organization* Winter, 46: 1-36.

Jordan, G. (1998). "Indirect Causes and Effects in Policy Change: Shell, Greenpeace and the Brent Spar." Paper prepared for delivery at the 1998 Annual Meeting of the APSA, Boston MA.

Keohane, R. O. (1984). *After Hegemony: Co-operation and Discord in the World Political Economy*, Princeton, NJ: Princeton University Press.

Keohane R. O. and Milner H. V. (1996). *Internationalization and Domestic Politics*, Cambridge, UK: Cambridge University Press.

Nivola P., ed. (1997). *Comparative Disadvantage? Social Regulation and the Global Economy*, Washington, DC: Brookings Institution.

Schwartz, H. M. (1994). *States versus Markets: History, Geography and the Development of the International Political Economy*, New York: St Martin's.

U.S. Trade Representative. (1997). *1997 Trade Policy Agenda and 1996 Annual Report of the President of the United States on the Trade Agreements Program*, Washington, DC: GPO.

Vogel, D. (1995). *Trading Up: Consumer and Environmental Regulation in a Global Economy*, Cambridge, MA: Harvard University Press.

Wilson, G. K. (1999). "Dolphins and Tuna, Shrimp and Turtles: An American Tale or Policymaking Goes Global?" Paper presented to the Annual Convention of the American Political Science Association, Atlanta, Georgia.

Chapter 17

Towards The Knowledge-Based Economy
United States and Its APEC Partners

NICHOLAS S. VONORTAS
George Washington University

ADAM TOLNAY
Georgetown University.

1.   INTRODUCTION

In the future, the economies that perform the best will be those whose governments help develop and manage their knowledge assets most effectively for innovation. Technology policy will thus need to revert to innovation policy that will be much more technology-user centered and demand based than technology policy has been until now. As such, innovation policy must also be better integrated with general economic policies that affect incentives to innovate, policies that shape the regulatory and institutional environment in which innovation takes place, and policies that provide appropriate safety nets for the parts of the population that fail to follow the ever increasing pace of change.

Globalization, the revolution in information and communication technologies, and the breakdown of institutional barriers to change internationally have worked to speed up change and have raised the value of tacit skills needed to use codified knowledge effectively (Lundvall and Borras 1996). These two outcomes together, a faster rate of change and a rise in the value of tacit skills needed to make use of increasingly cheap codified knowledge, in turn favor those individuals, firms and nations with the ability to learn. Accordingly, the ability to learn becomes the key asset of the knowledge-based economy.

This approach to the knowledge-based economy has important implications for both firm strategy and policy. On the strategy front, firms must learn to link changes in their intellectual capital and the worth of their business and balance sheets (ITAG 1999). Yet, this is nothing new. A firm's intellectual capital—or intangible assets in more traditional economic parlance that includes both the stock of knowledge and the ability to enhance it—has always been a source of competitive advantage. The dominant conceptualization of multinational corporations is, after all, based on the ability of such organizational structures to exploit their superior intangible assets (Buckley and Casson 1998; Caves 1982, 1996; Dunning 1998). What is new is mounting evidence that for an increasing number of firms in high technology manufacturing and service sectors the intangible component of value far outweighs the value of their tangible assets. As far back as ten years ago, Fumio Kodama (1991, 1995) noticed that several large manufacturing firms in Japan were spending more on building their intangible assets through research and development (R&D) than on building their tangible assets through investment in traditional capital. He argued that these firms were turning into "thinking organizations." This process has, in the meanwhile, intensified in manufacturing and has exploded of late in knowledge-intensive service sectors.

This chapter outlines some of the basic features of the knowledge economy and delineates the relative position of the United States in the emerging global economy through a survey of quantitative indicators. The chapter then briefly discusses the seemingly most fruitful avenues for increasing collaboration between the U.S. and fellow Asia Pacific Economic Cooperation (APEC) countries. APEC is a forum for nations on both sides of the North and South Pacific Ocean dedicated to the pursuit of economic growth and integration through trade and other forms of economic cooperation) member countries to support and strengthen the fledgling global knowledge-based economy.

The rest of the chapter is organized as follows. The next (second) section introduces some basic characteristics of the knowledge-based economy. The third section focuses more on the knowledge economy of the United States and provides a collection of proxy indicators as to its rapid development in recent years. The fourth section discusses some of the policies that have contributed to the development of the U.S. knowledge-based economy during the past few decades. Finally, the fifth section of the chapter turns to the potential of using the United States as a lever for collaboration in the development of knowledge-based economies in the APEC region, a necessary step in the creation of a truly global knowledge economy. It suggests focal points and possible avenues of cooperation that, on one hand, will allow diffusion of some of the strengths of the American system around the Pacific Rim and, on the other hand, will allow the United States to learn from its partners.

Taken as a whole, the policies of the last twenty years have produced undeniable successes for the United States. At the time of this writing, the country is enjoying the longest period of growth in its history based on resurgent industrial competitiveness (manufacturing and services) and the ability of the expansive economy to create huge numbers of new jobs in knowledge-intensive sectors. On the negative side, a failure to focus attention on policies that assist those who have not benefited from the changing economy has led to a situation captured most strikingly by the widening disparity in incomes and general quality of life between skilled, knowledge-based workers and progressively displaced, lower skilled workers.

2. THE U.S. KNOWLEDGE-BASED ECONOMY IN NUMBERS

Quantification of the knowledge-based economy is currently the subject of extensive research and discussion. No consensus has emerged regarding the most appropriate indicators to use nor has sufficient data been compiled to allow the construction of potentially very useful indicators (e.g., various types of knowledge spillovers). The set of indicators shown below is highly selective, limited by space, availability, and the biases of the authors. They are, nevertheless, some of the better and most current indicators.[1]

2.1 General Indicators

With gross domestic product (GDP) approaching $9 trillion, the United States is by far the largest national economy in the world. This product is the effort of a working population of approximately 100 million people. Importantly, the country has managed in the 1990s to reverse the relative decline of GDP growth rates of the previous two decades. Figure 1 shows America surging ahead of the European Union and Japan in the 1990s on both counts.

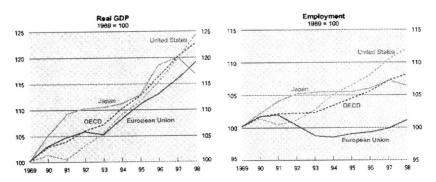

Figure 1 The Macroeconomic Context
Source: OECD 1999a: 15.

Such performance is remarkable considering that the leading economy has traditionally been expected by convergence theorists to grow at lower rates (Baumol, et al. 1994). The growth differential has remained, if not intensified, during the last two to three years of the decade leading the U.S. into the longest stream of continuous growth in its history. Explanations of this performance have varied, but one of them, offered by the chairman of the Federal Reserve Board, has captured everyone's attention. The United States, it is now commonly agreed, is enjoying the returns of its long dedication to information technology.[2]

There is mounting evidence that the United States is leading advanced economies into the era of the knowledge-based economy. This can be captured only imperfectly by existing indicators that still largely reflect the manufacturing era (OECD 1996).

According to the OECD (1999b), the term "knowledge-based industries" refers to industries that use technology and/or human capital intensively. In addition to R&D-intensive manufacturing sectors typically identified with high and medium-high technology (Appendix 1), this definition includes the following service activities: communications, finance, insurance, real estate, business services, community, social and personal services (including, among others, health and education). Knowledge-based industries accounted for more than 50 percent of OECD business value added in the mid-1990s, rising from around 45 percent in the mid-1980s (Appendix 2). Finance, insurance and business services account for the biggest share in all countries. In general, growth in knowledge-based services has been consistent in the OECD area throughout the decade. Growth in high and medium-high technology manufacturing tends to be more cyclical in nature. In the United States, little growth occurred in this group of industries between 1988 and 1993: since then growth has been strong and sustained.

Investment in physical capital and in knowledge is a prerequisite for growth (Figure 2). Physical investment mainly covers expenditure for construction and machinery and equipment. It facilitates the diffusion of embodied new technology. Physical investment represents 20 percent of OECD-wide GDP, ranging from more than 30 percent of GDP for some countries (Korea, Czech Republic) to less than 15 percent for others (Sweden, Iceland). The U.S. is on the lower side of such investment, below the OECD average.

Investment in knowledge, including public spending on education, expenditures on R&D and investment in software, represents eight percent of OECD-wide GDP, a level similar to investment in equipment. This figure would exceed ten percent if private expenditure on education and training were also included. Investment in knowledge is highest in Nordic countries and in France (around ten percent of GDP), where such investment is more important than investment in equipment. Investment in knowledge is lowest in Italy, Japan and Australia (six to seven percent). With about nine percent, the U.S. is somewhat above the OECD average.[3]

Most OECD countries spend increasing amounts in the production of knowledge. Since the mid-1980s, investment in knowledge has grown by about 2.8 percent annually in the OECD area (slightly more rapidly than GDP), growth rates being highest in Nordic countries, Japan and the United States. With an aggregate expenditure of $206 billion in 1997, U.S. R&D investment far outstrips that of any other country (NSB 1998). It accounts for approximately 44 percent of the industrial world's R&D investment total. Indeed, the U.S. R&D expenditure in 1995 was more than the R&D expenditures of the next five countries combined (Japan, Germany, France, United Kingdom, Italy).

About two-thirds of the U.S. R&D investment originated in industry which also performed three-fourths of the R&D activity. Both proportions have been edging upward during the past quarter century. Less than one-third of the national R&D expenditure was provided by the Federal government, which has been steadily losing ground to industry as a source of R&D funds. Universities have also increased both their expenditure and performance of R&D significantly during the past few decades.

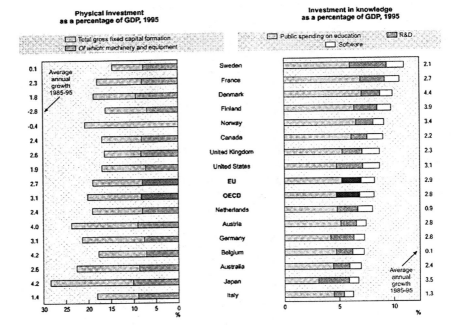

Figure 2. Investment in Tangibles and in Knowledge
Source: OECD 1999a: 17.

   Together with Japan, the Republic of Korea, Finland, and Switzerland, the U.S. registers the highest share of GDP devoted to R&D (2.7 percent, a percentage that trails only that of Sweden with three percent.) The United States also has one of the highest percentages of researchers in the labor force and by far the largest absolute number of researchers of any G7 country.[4] The percentage of researchers has been surpassed by Japan's rate of one researcher per 100 working people. Some of these trends are shown in Figures 3 and 4 below.

   Most of the officially registered R&D expenditures included in the figures above is spent and performed by relatively small numbers of large firms. Yet, much of the dynamism in the "new economy" is located in new, technology-based firms (NTBFs) where one of the greatest strengths of the American economy is said to reside. The success the United States in fostering the creation of large numbers of NTBFs rests in large measure on the ability of its financial system to underwrite ideas, hunches, and hopes and thus help turn them into innovations. The vehicle has been the venture-capital industry.

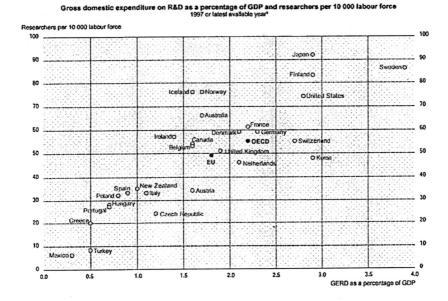

Figure 3. Recent Trends in Total R&D Efforts
Source: OECD 1999a: 29.

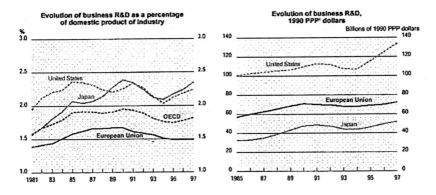

Figure 4. Business R&D
Source: OECD 1999a: 45.

Venture capital, defined as equity or equity-linked investments in young, privately held companies, where the investor is a financial intermediary who is typically active as a director, an advisor, or even a manager of the firm, really began in the mid-1970s due to the maturation of many of the elements of the financial system. By the late 1970s, the stock-exchange system grew receptive to novel forms of finance such as whole classes of derivatives. It absorbed and proved itself capable of handling massive amounts of capital raised by pension funds. Conjointly the investment banking business was revolutionized, whereby previously unacceptable levels of risk and reward became commonplace, which in turned spurred a demand for ever more profitable, that is ever higher risk ventures.

The decision that brought about the meteoric rise of venture capital was the 1979 Department of Labor's decision that explicitly allowed pension managers to invest in high-risk assets. In 1978, $424 million was invested in new venture capital funds. Eight years later more than $4 billion was invested. In the years 1996 and 1997, there was another leap in venture capital activity so that by 1997 venture capital in the U.S. market totaled over $8.7 billion.

These funds do not just underpin additional innovation, but support more efficient innovation than funds invested in traditional R&D vehicles. Samuel Kortum and Josh Lerner (1998) have scrutinized the positive relationship between venture capital and innovation in a survey of twenty industries covering the U.S. manufacturing sector over a three-decade period. They find that while venture disbursements account for only three percent of all R&D expenditures, they produce 15 percent of industrial innovations.

The U.S. venture capital industry is by far the largest and arguably most successful in the world. During the last available year (1997), venture capital expended in the United States was double that of the fifteen member countries of the European Union combined. Officially registered venture capital in Japan was, and remains, very small indeed. More than half of the U.S. venture capital funds in 1997 was invested in the areas of information technology and communications (Figure 5).

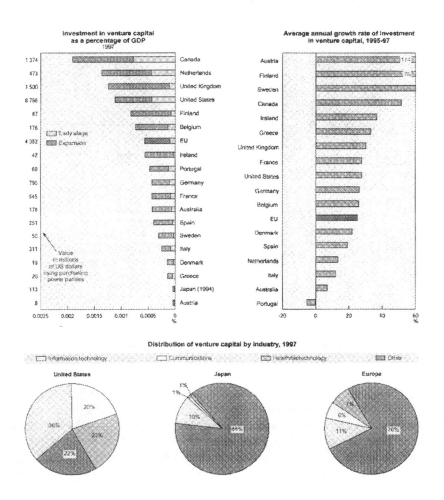

Figure 5. Venture Capital
Source: OECD 1999a: 55.

International trade is of relatively lesser importance to the United States than in many other OECD countries (Japan excepted). This trade, however, has risen significantly during the past few decades. The United States is the largest trading nation in the world. In 1997-1998, merchandise trade amounted to about 18 percent of GDP; trade in services amounted to an additional five percent of GDP. Trade in goods and services have become more important for OECD countries during the 1990s trade in services increased faster for most countries, including the United States. Services accounted for approximately 22 percent of the U.S. international trade of about 2 trillion dollars in 1997, resulting in a surplus of $88 billion compared to a deficit of $198 billion in merchandise trade (Table 1).

Table 1: U.S. GDP and International Trade

Components of U.S. gross domestic product (GDP) and trade as a share of GDP, 1994-98

Component	1994	1995	1996	1997	1998
	------------------ *Value (billion current dollars)* ------------------				
Personal consumption expenditures					
Goods	2,007.0	2,084.3	2,169.2	2,273.6	2,387.1
Services	2,709.1	2,873.4	3,038.4	3,220.1	3,420.8
Gross private domestic investment	1,007.9	1,038.2	1,116.5	1,256.0	1,367.1
Exports	721.2	818.4	870.9	920.3	912.9
Goods	481.9	546.5	582.1	643.2	634.7
Services	239.3	271.9	288.8	277.1	278.2
Imports (-)	-812.1	-904.5	-965.7	-1,032.8	-1,085.4
Goods (-)	-657.9	-740.0	-790.5	-862.4	-907.6
Services (-)	-154.2	-164.5	-175.2	-170.4	-177.8
Government consumption expenditures					
and gross investment	1,313.0	1,355.5	1,406.7	1,454.6	1,487.1
Gross Domestic Product	**6,947.0**	**7,265.4**	**7,636.0**	**8,110.9**	**8,511.0**
	------------------ *Percentage* ------------------				
Exports as a share of GDP	10.4	11.3	11.4	11.3	10.7
Goods	6.9	7.5	7.6	7.9	7.5
Services	3.4	3.7	3.8	3.4	3.3
Imports (-) as a share of GDP	-11.7	-12.4	-12.6	-12.7	-12.8
Goods (-)	-9.5	-10.2	-10.4	-10.6	-10.7
Services (-)	-2.2	-2.3	-2.3	-2.1	-2.1

Note.--Calculations based on unrounded data.

Source: USITC 1999b, p. 2-12.

High-technology industries play an increasingly important role in the international trade of manufactured goods. While high technology industries still account for a relatively small share of total OECD trade, their annual growth rate outstrips by far the average growth for manufactured goods. The three industries with the highest growth rates in OECD manufacturing trade between 1990 and 1996 are all high-technology industries: pharmaceuticals, electronic equipment and computers. When put together with medium-high-technology industries (especially motor vehicles, chemicals and machinery and equipment), high technology industries already account for the main share of OECD manufacturing trade (slightly more than 60 percent). If the trend of the 1990s continues high technology trade will overtake in importance low technology trade within the next five years (Figure 6).

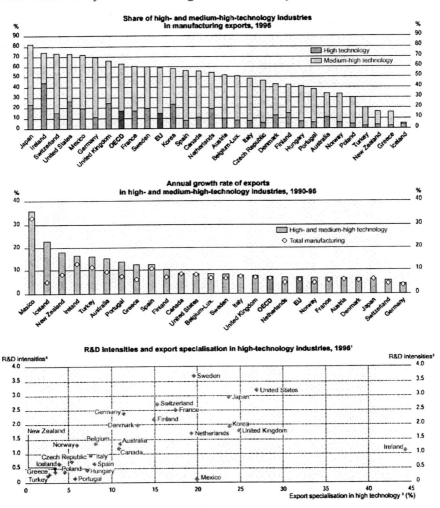

1. Or latest available year. Greece: 1993; Belgium, Hungary, Iceland, Ireland, Mexico, New Zealand, Portugal: 1995.
2. High-technology exports/Manufacturing exports.
3. Manufacturing R&D expenditures/Manufacturing production.

Figure 6. High Tech Industries in International Trade
Source: OECD 1999a: 61.

The merchandise exports of the United States are relatively concentrated in high and medium-high technology industries (Figure 7). A measure of revealed comparative advantage taking into consideration both exports and imports also shows that the country's relative strengths in manufacturing lie in high and medium-high technology industries (Figure 8).

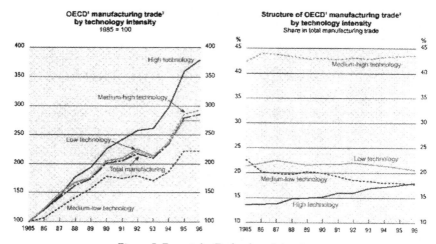

Figure 7. Exports by Technology Intensity
Source: OECD 1999a: 99.

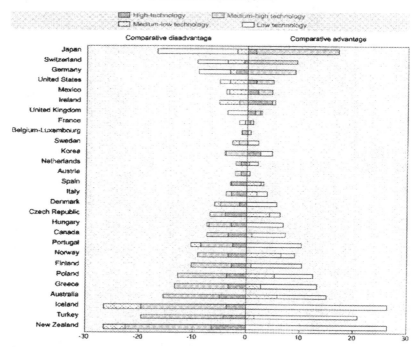

Figure 8. Revealed Comparative Advantage by Technology Intensity
Source: OECD 1999a: 101.

The United States remains the world's largest exporter of disembodied technology (licenses, patents, know-how and research, technical assistance), as indicated by a large, positive technology balance of payments (Figure 9).

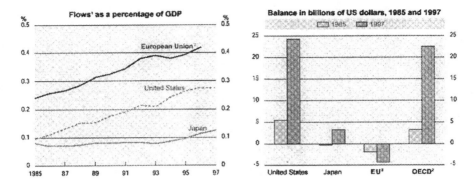

Figure 9. Technology Balance of Payments
Source: OECD 1999a: 97.

Finally, the United States features quite prominently in terms of various other measures of scientific prowess, inventiveness, and innovation. For example, U.S. scientists and engineers account for 36 percent of total scientific publications in the OECD area (compared to 37 percent for the EU and nine percent for Japan). U.S. organizations and individuals accounted for almost 30 percent of the applications to the European Patent Office in 1996. U.S. organizations and individuals have arrested the relative decline and solidified their position in terms of shares of patents issued by the U.S. Patent and Trademark Office. Citizens in the U.S. still enjoy the highest standard of (material) living—more than 30 percent above the OECD average (Figure 10). In addition, although growth in labor productivity had been lower than in other large OECD countries during the past few decades until the mid-1990s, this has not necessarily been true with manufacturing productivity (Figure 11). The pace of U.S. productivity growth has picked up significantly the past few years.

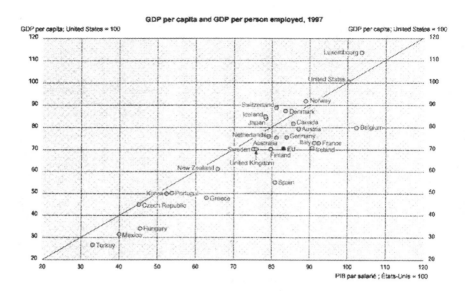

Figure 10. Productivity and Income Levels
Source: OECD 1999a: 83.

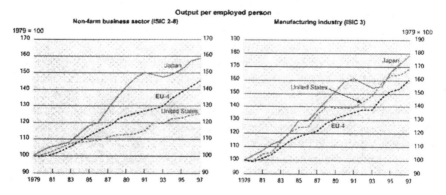

Figure 11. Productivity Growth
Source: OECD 1999a: 85.

2.2   Information and Communication Technology

While still accounting for a small, although increasing, percentage of
GDP (4.4 percent)[5] information and communication technology (ICT) is at

the core of the knowledge-based economy. The enormous and continuous technological advances in this area have decreased the cost and increased the speed of storing, processing, and disseminating information (voice, picture, data) by many orders of magnitude.[6] The omnipresence of ICT technologies contributes significantly to productivity growth by allowing firms to operate more efficiently while creating new markets for products and services. Firms, households and governments in the OECD area are investing large amounts in ICT, averaging seven percent of GDP in 1997, rising from 5.9 percent five years earlier. Two-fifths of this expenditure is for telecommunications equipment, two-fifths for software, and one-fifth for hardware. More than 50 percent of white-collar workers in OECD countries already have access to computers. This statistic masks wide differences, with Sweden at the top with more than 105 computers per 100 white-collar employees in 1997, followed by the United States with 82 computers, and tailed by Mexico with 12.

The United States and Japan dominate world production of ICT goods, the former accounting for approximately 30 percent and the latter for 25 percent of total OECD production of such goods in 1997 (Figure 12). The next largest producer is Korea accounting for approximately 6.5 percent (OECD 2000: 24). The United States also has the largest domestic ICT market (36 percent of the global market in 1997). Japan's domestic market, approximately half as large as that of the United States, also grew at a rate faster than average rate (Figure 13).

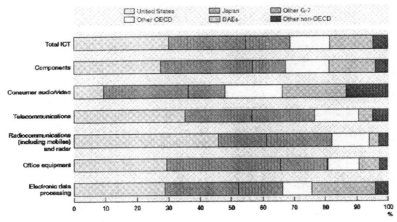

1. DAEs (Dynamic Asian economies) are: Chinese Taipei, Hong Kong (China), Malaysia, Singapore and Thailand.

Figure12. Global Production of ICT Goods
Source: OECD 2000: 25.

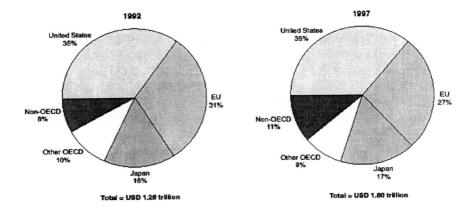

Figure 13. Global markets for ICT
Source: OECD 2000: 33.

ICT has become the dominant item in private equipment investment in the United States. IT equipment contributed more than half of the annual growth in real capital equipment spending between 1995 and 1998. While employment in ICT industries still represents a modest share of total U.S. employment (4.9 percent), forecasts expect almost half of the U.S. workforce to be working in industries that are either major producers or intensive users of ICT by the end of the first decade of the 21st century. Between 1990 and 1998, ICT industries created over 1.1 million jobs compared to about 14.8 million for the entirety of private sector employment. When IT-related occupations in non-ICT sectors are added the share of direct and indirect ICT employment is estimated to have reached 7.3 percent of total U.S. employment in 1996.[7]

The Internet is the fastest-growing segment of ICT. As access prices dropped over the past decade, the number of firms and households linking to it has increased dramatically. Electronic commerce is also developing rapidly developing, though from a very low base largely located in the United States.

R&D expenditure is rising fastest in ICT industries and services. Almost one in five U.S. patents was ICT related in the late 1990s compared to one in ten earlier in the decade, with U.S. organizations and individuals holding about 60 percent of those. The United States and Japan have a comparative advantage in ICT industries. A number of other countries such as Ireland, Korea, and Mexico have also developed significant strengths in hardware (electronic components, consumer electronics) in recent years, attributable largely to the operation of multinational corporations in those countries.

The United States has led global ICT investment. U.S. ICT intensity (ICT expenditure as a percentage of GDP) is two percentage points higher than that of the European Union. ICT intensity has risen strongly in Japan, climbing close to that of the United States (Figure 14).[8] ICT intensity has risen in virtually all OECD countries since 1992 at an annual average of almost 2.2 percent. For many countries, the increase in ICT intensity is mostly driven by investment in the modernization of telecommunications infrastructure.

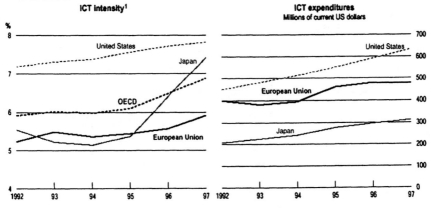

Figure 14. ICT Expenditures
Source: OECD 1999a: 21.

The sharp drop in hardware prices has resulted in a rapid increase of computer penetration rates in businesses and households. In many industries, the number of workers who use a computer at their job now ranges from 50 to 85 percent. In the manufacturing sector, U.S. Census data indicate that by the late 1980s, 83 percent of firms with 500 or more employees in the metals, machinery, electronics, transportation, and instrument industries used computer-aided design; 70 percent used numerically controlled machine tools (Berman, Bound, and Griliches 1994). These numbers have not only continued to grow in recent years but computer penetration has spilled over from manufacturing to the services and the computer is a ubiquitous feature of all aspects of American life (Figure 15). With the rise of Internet penetration due to drastically falling access costs, information technology is reshaping the way Americans work, study, shop, play and date.

On the basis of numbers of Internet hosts, the Nordic countries, the United States, and Canada are among the most wired with seven to eleven Internet hosts per 100 inhabitants, compared to an OECD average of less than four (Figure 16). There seems to be an inverse relationship between communication costs and Internet use—relative content availability in languages other than English may also be a factor (footnote 8).

In the United States, diffusion of computers and Internet access have also increased dramatically not only at workplaces but at public schools and libraries. In public schools, the average number of students per computer fell from 63.5 in 1984/85 to 6.3 in 1997/98. Internet access has more than doubled in four years: nine out of ten public schools had access to the internet at the end of 1998; one instruction room in two was connected to the internet. That same year four-fifths of college and university professors regularly used computers on the job. Sixty percent of other teachers did so as well.

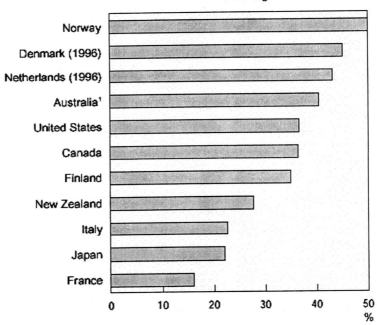

Household PC penetration rates, 1997
Percentages

Figure 15. Computer Penetration
Source: OECD 1999a: 23.

Internet access cost and Internet host density, 1998-99

Number of Internet hosts per 1 000 inhabitants, January 1999

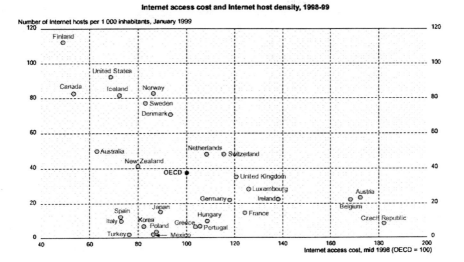

Figure 16. Internet Host Density
Source: OECD 1999a: 23.

In summary, the United States has been the leading force behind the intensifying transformation of the global economy into an information-based, and further, a knowledge-based one. The fact that the United States has been at the forefront of the knowledge-based economy in terms of the production and application of key technologies combined with the sheer weight of economy and internal market make the United States the engine leading the rest of the world toward a new era.

3. U.S. INNOVATION POLICY

The gradual emergence of the knowledge-based economy, in combination with mounting competitive pressures and a better understanding of the innovation process, has led to a very significant shift in the science and technology (S&T) policy orientation of most industrialized countries over the course of the past few decades. In both the United States and the European Union, for example, government attention has gradually shifted in the past decade from heavily supply-oriented S&T policies to innovation policies seeking a better balance with demand-oriented (technology-user-oriented) factors (Vonortas, forthcoming). Starting with robust macroeconomics, a generally liberal microeconomic environment, and a formidable S&T system, the U.S. government first paid attention in the

1980s to the introduction of extensive changes in the regulatory infrastructure affecting industrial competition and incentives to change (e.g., competition and intellectual property rights regulations). Only when these goals were largely achieved did the government move to implement programs providing active (yet selective) support to industrial research and development and technological innovation.

3.1   A Dramatic Shift in Policy Orientation

The old orientation of U.S. science and technology policy stood on twin pillars. First, a very active basic science policy, based on a consensus built around the suggestions of Vannevar Bush's report to the U.S. President at the closing phase of World War II (Bush 1945). Second, advanced technology was developed by several federal agencies in pursuit of their statutory missions. The most important of these missions has been national defense, resulting in large R&D expenditures by the Department of Defense—accounting until recently for more in expenses than all other government agencies combined—and extensive military procurement.

In the post war period, U.S. science and technology policy was based on the following principles (Branscomb 1993). Basic science is a public good. Federal agencies aggressively pursued the development of new technology for specific missions; the federal government refrains from picking winners through R&D investments; and the federal government creates the appropriate regulatory environment to enable efficient markets.

This was essentially a supply-side approach. The mechanisms through which government R&D investments assisted industrial innovation were in accordance with a linear model. Scientific discoveries (and mission technology spin-offs) would inevitably lead to new commercial technologies. The selection of technologies and the timing of commercial innovation were left to market forces.

In contrast, the policy orientation of the early 1990s had the objectives of strengthening America's industrial competitiveness and creating jobs; creating a business environment where technical innovation can flourish and where investment is attracted to new ideas; ensuring the coordinated management of technology across all agencies of the government; forging a closer working partnership between industry, the federal and state governments, workers, and universities; redirecting the focus of national efforts toward technologies crucial to today's businesses and a growing economy, such as information and communication, flexible manufacturing, and environmental technologies; and, reaffirming our commitment to basic science (White House 1993a: 1).

These objectives point to a radical shift in the traditional policies of the U.S. government. The basic principles of this new policy include (Branscomb 1993): shifting its priorities from large government missions toward assisting the technological prowess and international competitiveness of the private sector;[9] balancing the supply and demand sides of technology policy;[10] a more action role for state government;[11] increased public/private cooperative R&D projects; more relaxed antitrust environment allowing firms to enter multiple strategic alliances; the system of national laboratories should increase interaction with the private sector; research universities should interact regularly with the private sector; and large international science projects should be undertaken.

Greater attention to the demand side of technology policy indicates that innovation, rather than just technology, has become the government's policy target. A large number of programs were introduced during 1993-1994 to implement the new policy principles. In addition, existing initiatives relating to civilian technologies were given significant boost. Well-known examples of new or enhanced programs include the Advanced Technology Program (ATP), the Technology Reinvestment Program (TRP), the Environmental Technology Initiative (ETI), the Manufacturing Extension Partnership (MEP), the Partnership for a New Generation of Vehicles (PNGV), and the Small Business Innovation and Research (SBIR) program. Information technologies, advanced manufacturing technologies, and environmental technologies were considered areas of strategic importance needing government intervention due to significant infrastructural requirements and frequent market failure. The National Information Infrastructure (NII) initiative was put in place. The Defense Advanced Research Projects Agency (DARPA) was renamed the Advanced Research Projects Agency (ARPA) and its mission was refocused on dual use technologies. Government laboratories (many of them part of the Department of Energy's research system) were strongly induced to set up Cooperative R&D Agreements (CRADAs) with industry. Manufacturing R&D was promoted through collaborative agreements with the private sector made possible by an increasingly relaxed antitrust regulatory system. There were also efforts to make the Research and Experimentation (R&E) tax credit permanent.

3.2   Policy Continuity

The first Clinton Administration arrived with a grand vision that turned technology policy into a front-runner (White House 1993b. The new policy orientation reflected issues and solutions that had been debated for years. A significant number of high-visibility reports were produced during the 1980s stressing the need for radical policy change.[12] Even as far back as the late

1970s, President Carter's science advisor had considered several similar ideas.

The current position is that a more balanced supply-side/demand-side technology policy is more appropriate today for the U.S. than, say, twenty years ago. As mentioned in the introduction, the obvious justification for this relates to a change in society's basic perception of high technology from the output of R&D-intensive manufacturing industries to a style of work applicable to almost every industry (Branscomb and Florida 1998). This change is said to have revolutionized the features of successful technology policy, focusing it more on the distribution of knowledge, skill, entrepreneurship, and the facilitation of new forms of collaborating between firms, universities, and the government.

The S&T policy community in the United States had observed such changes taking place gradually since the late 1970s, and slowly but steadily had moved towards a position of extensive S&T policy modifications. The arguments often drew strength from the signs of declining American competitiveness from the mid-1970s to the mid-1980s in vital industries such as consumer electronics, automobiles, machine tools, and computers. The signs were strong enough to even move the Reagan administration—in principle hostile to anything that can be labeled microeconomic management—into action.

Two major steps taken in the 1980s need special mention. One was the discontinuation of the long-term policies of the United States related to competition and intellectual property rights. The other was the initiation of an extensive public debate on economic competitiveness, exemplified by the creation of the President's Commission on Industrial Competitiveness and its report in the mid-1980s (PCIC 1985).

The activities centered about the first step culminated in two concrete actions. First, there was a radical change in the philosophy of antitrust (competition) regulations, commencing with the new Merger Guidelines issued by the Antitrust Division of the Department of Justice and the Federal Trade Commission in 1982.[13] Second was the creation of the 11th Circuit Court in the District of Columbia, the first Court dedicated to the adjudication of issues related to intellectual property, also in 1982. Essentially, long-standing U.S. policy was reversed. A strict enforcement of antimonopoly regulations (based on a per se approach) and lax enforcement of intellectual property rights laws were reoriented toward a more relaxed enforcement of antimonopoly regulations (based on a rule of reason approach) and much stricter enforcement of intellectual property rights laws (Vonortas 1997).

These actions were perfectly in line with the Administration's philosophy that besides big missions like national defense, the role of the government should be limited to the general economic and regulatory environment in which businesses operate. Three successive Republican Administrations in the 1980s became increasingly convinced that the world had changed for American business and that this necessitated policy changes. They were willing to take the necessary steps to help strengthen what the S&T policy community claimed was the foundation of the competitiveness of American business: its ability to create and deploy technological innovations. They were willing to push for the aforementioned changes in antitrust and intellectual property rights policies. Nudged by a Democratic Party-dominated Congress, these administrations were also willing to introduce the Research and Experimentation (R&E) tax credit, to maintain government support of basic research, and to go along with supporting R&D in small businesses through the SBIR program (requiring all agencies with R&D budget to allocate part of it to small businesses). They were, however, much less willing to offer direct assistance to civilian technology development that many S&T experts had hoped.

The public debate on competitiveness culminated in the passing of the Omnibus Trade and Competitiveness Act in 1988 by the U.S. Congress. This was an important piece of legislation that the Bush Administration was forced to accept. Among many other provisions, it radically changed the nature of a little known agency known as the National Bureau of Standards (NBS). It renamed NBS into National Institute of Standards and Technology (NIST) and transformed it into a much more formidable agency absorbing the newly established Advanced Technology Program, Manufacturing Extension Program, and Baldridge Quality Award as additions to its long-standing laboratories for industrial standards.

Taking office in the early 1990s, the Clinton Administration reinforced the policies of its predecessors and added some new, more interventionist, policy instruments. It also added a strong vision of a more balanced supply-side/demand-side technology-cum-innovation policy. Perhaps the Clinton administration's most significant contribution has been its strong signal to American industry of a government seriously concerned with the need to foster technology for economic growth.

Unfortunately for the Administration, an extensively renewed 104th Congress quickly got busy unraveling its technology policy objectives. The 105th Congress, sworn in office in 1996, continued in the unfavorable direction set by its predecessor. The report of the House of Representatives' Science Committee of the 105th Congress indicated the desired limits of government involvement (US Congress 1998). The extended set of programs pushed forward in the first 4-year term of the Clinton Administration did not survive the turbulence period intact. Some were eliminated (e.g., TRP), others were weakened or neutralized (e.g., ATP), and still others lost their direction and became ineffective (e.g., PNGV). Even though the 106th Congress, taking office in 1998, was much more willing to negotiate, the enthusiasm of the second Clinton Administration for technology policy has seemed permanently curtailed. The phenomenal success of the American economy has also undermined the sense of urgency that prevailed a decade earlier.

Irrespective of what has happened to specific programs and policy measures, however, one thing is abundantly clear: there is much more awareness in all government strata today of the changing international environment of industrial technology and innovation, and the place of U.S. business in it, than ever before. The manifestations and effects of technology, the emergence of the knowledge-based economy, and the powerful effects of globalization are on the minds of policy decision-makers.

4.   COLLABORATION POTENTIAL ACROSS APEC

The United States has certainly left its mark on the last decade of a largely American-dominated 20th century. The only super power left standing after the Soviet Union crumbled, it has regained its status as the largest and strongest economy in the world, has been going through the longest continuous period of growth in its history, has led a sweeping wave of deregulation and privatization around the globe, has led the way to increasing openness in international trade and investment, and has taken bold steps to turn the knowledge-based economy into reality. On the eve of the 21st century, the U.S. aspires to build upon and extend its accomplishments.

The previous century brought us the computer and, together with ubiquitous and inexpensive telecommunications and transportation, the information society. The U.S. led the way into that phase of development. It is quite possible that it will also lead into the next phase, the knowledge-based economy. The reason has largely to do with the disproportionate size and vitality of its economy vis-à-vis its international partners. Other countries have been phenomenally successful in certain areas (e.g., exposure to Internet and mobile telephony by Nordic countries, IT hardware manufacturing by Japan and Korea). Yet, only the U.S. currently has the necessary pull to serve as the global engine for the emerging knowledge-based economy.

This process can take two basic paths. One way this can happen is by the United States first putting in place domestically the basic elements of a knowledge-based economy and then using its economic weight to spread it around the world. In doing so, the United States would act as a central hub where various visions, ideas, policies and methods in fields as diverse as manufacturing and education, voting systems and the environment are tested. The danger of this path is that the U.S. would acquire a substantial advantage in the infrastructure and know how of the new economy. Another path would be for other developed and developing nations, including those in the European Union and in APEC, to make substantive progress in adopting and adapting the structures of the knowledge-based economy, thereby offering their economies and societies as viable alternative models to the U.S. model of economic, cultural and social forms of organization. This path, while more difficult at first, certainly offers greater rewards for all, including the United States that would be challenged to ask itself some of the fundamental and provocative questions concerning the new economy it has succeeded in sidestepping in its recent period of success.

Globalization will increasingly reflect the features and requirements of the knowledge-based economy. As the United States is currently at the forefront both in terms of supporting and participating in the process of economic globalization and also in terms of establishing the basic building blocks of the knowledge economy, it is expected to play a leading role in the new world currently under construction. A particularly important position in this new world will be reserved for the countries of the Pacific Basin, particularly those in the Northern American hemisphere, East and South East Asia, and Australia/New Zealand. This region includes three of the G7 countries (including the top two), most of the fastest developers of the past half-century, and a significant number of the hitherto most successful participants in the global economy.

Much potential for collaboration exists between the United States and its APEC partners. On the one hand, the sheer weight of its economy and its success in moving toward a knowledge-based economy—as well as its defense importance for the region—makes the United States an indispensable central player in APEC. On the other hand, the past development success and further economic and defense potential renders the APEC countries of vital importance to the United States. Put simply, all sides have a vital stake in continued co-evolution. This is, of course, a basic prerequisite for success in any partnership. For this partnership to be sustainable in the longer term, APEC nations need to be able to offer themselves as more than markets and low-cost laborers. They need to be able to offer viable alternatives to the U.S. model of economic and social organization. To this end, APEC countries will need to take fundamental steps in transforming their industrial age economies into increasingly knowledge-based ones. In this the East Asian nations' traditional focus on education and social cohesion will be vitally important and may provide many APEC nations with the fundamentals necessary to undertake the difficult transformations required.

The transition from the traditional, manufacture-based economy to the new, knowledge-based economy will not be an easy one to make. While knowledge has always been the main source of long-term economic growth, the difference now is one of speed—IT is speeding up the shift toward a knowledge-based economy by lowering the costs of knowledge codification and transmission. Similarly the changing nature of production from tangibles toward intangibles is shifting the center of gravity of production from heavy manufactured products such as steel, copper wire and vacuum tubes to microprocessors, fiber optics and transistors, and services, thus making the economy lighter and less visible (*Economist* 1996).

Therefore and above all, individual countries will need to develop capabilities to introduce, nurture, and manage change. Economic prosperity will very much depend in the future on an economy's ability to innovate and its ability to adjust to change. Accommodating radical change is something America has tended to be good at (see Sections 2 & 3), as have the APEC nations in their 20th century histories. Experience with policies to accommodate change is one important contribution the United States can offer to its partners. When examining American policies, attention must be placed not on isolated policy instruments but on how several of them may be combined to introduce, nurture, and manage change. This is not to say that change is planned and managed perfectly in the United States. It is not. However, the U.S. has been successful at providing the appropriate policy infrastructure to sustain change as a more or less permanent state of affairs. This will be a core capability of that will need to be developed by governments of knowledge-based economies.

What can governments do to encourage the creation, diffusion, and speedy application of knowledge to production? It would appear that widespread spillover benefits to the rest of the economy from increased knowledge underwrite direct government support for R&D. While there are good arguments for it—particularly when it comes to science and the more generic kinds of technology—it can also be overdone. The effectiveness of widespread government direct involvement in stimulating innovation has yet to be proven. On the other hand, much the best thing that can be done is to provide an economic environment conducive to innovation. The way to do this in developed or developing countries is by deregulating markets, by encouraging competition, by removing barriers to the development of new products, and by letting entrepreneurs explore the possibilities. Governments also need to raise the standards of education and skills in order to allow their economies take full advantage of IT and the expansion of knowledge industries. Obviously, government policies must be much broader than those included in the traditional tool kit of science and technology policy.

We believe that the distinction between the three sets of policy proposed by Lundvall and Borras (1999) helps clarify the policy decision-making process in the new knowledge-based economy. While different countries will adopt different policy mixes to suit their specific circumstances, at a general level they will all be confronted with the following questions:

1) How to affect the pressure for change (or how to create the appropriate incentives to economic agents to innovate). The policies here include:
- General economic policy, macroeconomic policy more specifically, and sector level policies that affect relative prices, thus affecting relative expected rewards to investors;
- Trade policy which affects competition levels;
- Competition policy which affects domestic competition;
- Intellectual property rights policy, which affects competition levels, incentives to invent, rates of technology diffusion;and
- Regulatory and institutional infrastructure, which define the basic rules of the game and allow markets to function under the utmost transparency (to decrease certain kinds of uncertainty).

2) How to affect the ability to absorb change (or how to increase the ability to innovate). Policies here include:
- Science and technology policy, which affects the ability to create and disseminate scientific and technological knowledge;
- Innovation policy, which focuses on the introduction of new technologies and, more than S&T policy, addresses the demand side of the technology equation (technology user);and
- Human resource policies (including education, training etc.), which create the ability to create and deploy effectively the most important resource in the knowledge-based economy.

3) How to assist the losers from change (or how to partly redistribute the wealth from the winners to the losers). Policies here include:
- Social policies for income redistribution, unemployment compensation, pension financing for failing industries, etc.;
- Regional policies assisting structural change in regions locked into the wrong industries and technologies.

Reacting to a widely perceived faltering competitiveness of strategic industries, the U.S. government embarked in the early 1980s on a wide-ranging effort to fine-tune policies in the first set above. The second set of policies received much more attention in the late 1980s and the 1990s. Taken as a whole, the policies of the last twenty years have undeniably produced indisputable successes for this country. The failures have primarily been associated with a lack of attention to the third set of policies that has resulted in a widening income disparity between skilled, mobile, knowledge-based workers and lower skilled, less mobile workers.

Different countries will learn different lessons from the American experience but they will together need to set the basic rules under which an ever more interdependent global economic system must operate. While the basic rules of economics need not be rewritten, the truth is that traditional economic analysis has difficulties dealing with knowledge. Economists are currently addressing these difficulties. As far as governments are concerned, however, policy makers will need to understand economics better to be able to promote rapid change and greater uncertainty in the most appropriate ways. There are strong arguments against the use of protectionism and subsidies to shield workers and companies from change (besides temporary corrective measures). Doing so may seem less painful in the short and medium terms but also imprudent in the longer term for it would also shield economies from powerful sources of growth. Instead, the task of government in the new economy is to give people the tools they need to cope better with change.

Overall, we believe that the ongoing process of economic globalization is the only practicable route leading to a global knowledge-based economy. Pacific Basin countries have an historic opportunity to play leading roles and to offer alternative forms of economic and social forms of organization in a nascent knowledge-based setting. They must actively participate in the debate of some fundamental questions of the early 21st century: Is business-driven globalization the best way to arrive to the knowledge-based economy? To what extent are the experiences of one country with information technology and the information society transferable to another? Which is the form of globalization that best suits all players? To what extent can interdependence among countries expand without the institution of a formal and collective policy decision-making processes?[14]At what stage of globalization do losers stop being the responsibility of individual countries and become the collective responsibility of all partners? Can there be an equitable global economic system?

Appendix 1

Manufacturing industries on the basis of R&D intensity

Period 1970-80[1]	Period 1980-95[2]
High technology	**High technology**
1. Aerospace	1. Aerospace
2. Computers, office machinery	2. Computers, office machinery
3. Pharmaceuticals	3. Electronics-communications
4. Electronics-communications	4. Pharmaceuticals
5. Scientific instruments	**Medium-high technology**
6. Electrical machinery	5. Scientific instruments
Medium technology	6. Electronic machinery
7. Motor vehicles	7. Motor vehicles
8. Chemicals	8. Chemicals
9. Non-electrical machinery	9. Non-electrical machinery
10. Rubber and plastic equipment	**Medium-low technology**
11. Other manufacturing	10. Shipbuilding
Low technology	11. Rubber and plastic equipment
12. Other transport equipment	12. Other transport equipment
13. Stone, clay and glass	13. Stone, clay and glass
14. Petroleum refining	14. Non-ferrous metals
15. Shipbuilding	15. Other manufacturing
16. Non-ferrous metals	16. Fabricated metal products
17. Ferrous metals	**Low technology**
18. Fabricated metal products	17. Petroleum refining
19. Paper, printing	18. Ferrous metals
20. Food, beverages	19. Paper, printing
21. Wood and furniture	20. Textiles and clothing
22. Textiles and clothing	21. Wood and furniture

1. Based on direct R&D intensity: ratio of R&D expenditures to output in 22 manufacturing sectors in 11 OECD countries.
2. Based on direct and indirect R&D intensity: ratio of R&D expenditures and embodied technology flows per unit of output in 22 manufacturing sectors in 10 OECD countries.

Source: OECD 1996: 36.

Appendix 2

Value Added of Knowledge-Based Industries.

Percentages

		Share in business sector value added, current prices						Real value added growth Average annual growth rate		
		Total knowledge-based industries	High-technology industries	Medium-high-technology industries	Communications services	Finance, insurance and other business services	Community, social and personal services		Knowledge-based industries	Business sector
Canada	1996	51.0	2.2	6.1	3.3 [1]	24.1 [1]	15.4 [1]	1985-96	3.2	2.3
Mexico	1996	41.6	1.8	6.4	1.6	17.8	14.0	1988-96	3.8	2.9
United States	1996	55.3	3.0	6.1	2.9	30.8	12.4	1985-96	3.1	3.0
Australia	1996	48.0	0.9	3.2	2.9	26.1	14.9	1985-96	4.3	3.4
Japan	1996	53.0	3.7	8.6	3.6 [1]	37.7 [4] →		1988-96	4.0 [1]	3.3
Korea	1996	40.3	5.4	8.4	2.4 [1]	19.5	4.7	1985-96	12.5 [1]	9.1
New Zealand	1995	39.9	0.5	3.9	3.6	26.4	5.5	-	..	..
Austria	1996	43.8	9.6 [3] →		2.9	25.2	6.0	1985-96	3.7	2.9
Belgium	1996	46.3	8.7 [3d] →		2.2	35.4 [2]		1985-96	3.0	2.4
Denmark	1995	42.1	1.8	6.9	2.5	23.9	7.9	1985-95	1.4	2.0
Finland	1996	42.1	3.9	8.2	3.0	24.5	3.4	1985-96	4.9	2.0
France	1996	50.0	3.9	7.0	2.9	29.1	8.0	1985-96	2.8	2.0
Germany [5]	1996	58.6	2.9	11.1	2.6	42.1 [2] →		1985-96	3.7	2.5
Greece	1995	38.9	0.9	2.0	2.4 [1]	33.6 [2] →		1985-95	2.9 [1]	1.8
Iceland	1995	31.4	0.9	0.7	2.3	21.8	6.6	-	..	..
Italy	1996	41.3	1.4	6.4	2.1	31.4 [2] →		1985-96	2.8	2.2
Netherlands	1995	50.2	2.7	5.0	2.5	27.5	12.5	1986-95	2.9	2.7
Norway	1996	35.3	0.9	4.1	2.5	21.1	6.6	1985-96	1.7	3.2
Portugal	1993	33.9	1.4	4.0	2.8	16.4	9.3	1986-93	6.9	4.6
Spain	1994	37.9	1.6	7.2	2.5	20.4	6.3	1986-94	2.9	2.5
Sweden	1994	50.7	2.6	9.1	3.0	30.3	5.7	1986-94	2.4	1.7
United Kingdom	1995	51.5	3.3	7.2	3.3	28.3	9.4	1985-96	4.1	2.9
European Union [6]	1994	48.4	2.5	7.7	2.7	35.5 [4] →		1986-94	3.1	2.4
Total OECD [7]	1994	50.9	2.9	6.9	2.8	38.2 [2] →		1986-94	3.5	2.9

1. Secretariat estimate.
2. Includes Community, social and personal services.
3. Includes medium-high-technology industries.
4. Includes Shipbuilding.
5. Germany refers to western Germany.
6. Calculated with above EU countries, excluding Austria, Belgium and Portugal for shares; excluding Portugal for growth.
7. Calculated with above countries, excluding Austria, Belgium and Portugal for shares; excluding Mexico, New Zealand, Iceland and Portugal for growth.
Source: OECD, STAN database and Main Industrial Indicators, 1999.

Source: OECD 1999a: 115.

REFERENCES

Baumol, W. J., S. A. Batey Blackman, and E. N. Wolff. (1994). *Productivity and American Leadership: The Long View*. Boston, MA: The MIT Press (4th printing).

Berman, E., J. Bound, and Z. Griliches. (1994). "Changes in the Demand for Skilled Labor within U.S. Manufacturing: Evidence from the Annual Survey of Manufacturers." *The Quarterly Journal of Economics* (May): 367-98.

Branscomb, L.M., ed. (1993). *Empowering Technology*. Cambridge, MA: The MIT Press.

Branscomb, L.M. and R. Florida. (1998). "Challenges in Technology Policy in a Changing World Economy," in L.M. Branscomb and J.H. Keller, eds., *Investing in Innovation*. Cambridge, MA: The MIT Press.

Buckley, P. J. and M. C. Casson. (1998). "Models of the Multinational Enterprise," *Journal of International Business Studies*. 29(1): 21-44.

Bush, V. (1945). *Science:the Endless Frontier: A Report to the President on a Program for Postwar Scientific Research*. 40th Anniversary Publication by the National Science Foundation (1990).

Caves, R. E. (1982). *Multinational Enterprise and Economic Analysis*. New York: Cambridge University Press.

Caves, R. E. (1996). *Multinational Enterprise and Economic Analysis*. Cambridge: Cambridge University Press (2nd ed.).

Committee on Science, Engineering and Public Policy. (1992). *The Government Role in Civilian Technology: Building a New Alliance*. Washington, DC: National Academy Press.

Committee on Science, Engineering and Public Policy. (1993). *Science, Technology, and the Federal Government: National Goals for a New Era*, Washington, DC: National Academy Press.

Committee on Technology Policy Options in a Global Economy. (1993). *Mastering a New Role: Shaping Technology Policy Options in a Global Economy*, Washington, DC: National Academy Press.

Competitiveness Policy Council. (1993). *Technology Policy for a Competitive America, Subcouncil on Critical Technologies*, Washington, DC.

Council on Competitiveness. (1991). *Gaining New Ground: Technology Priorities for America's Future*, Washington, DC.

Dunning, J. H. (1998). "Location and the Multinational Enterprise: A Neglected Factor?" *Journal of International Business Studies*, 29(1): 45-66.

Economist. (1996). "The Hitchhiker's Guide to Cybernomics," A Survey of the World Economy, September 28.

Information Technology Advisory Group and Ernst & Young. (ITAG) (1999). "The Knowledge Economy", *Report to the New Zealand Minister of Information Technology*, August (http://www.moc.govt.nz/pbt/infotech/itag/publications.html).

Kodama, F. (1991). *Analyzing Japanese High Technologies: The Techno-Paradigm Shift*, New York: Pinter Publishers.

Kodama, F. (1995*). Emerging Patterns of Innovation: Sources of Japan's Technological Edge*, Boston, MA: Harvard Business School Press.

Kortum, S. and J. Lerner. (1998). "Does Venture Capital Spur Innovation?" *NBER Working Paper No. 6846*, Cambridge, MA: National Bureau of Economic Research.

Lundvall, B.A. and S. Borras. (1999). *The Globalising Learning Economy: Implications for Innovation Policy*, European Commission, Directorate-General XII (Science, Research and Development), Luxembourg: Office of the Official Publications of the European Communities (EUR 18307 EN).

Meares, C. A. and J. F. Sargent, Jr. (1999). *The Digital Workforce: Building Infotech Skills at the Speed of Innovation*, Report, Office of Technology Policy, Technology Administration, U.S. Department of Commerce, Washington, DC.

National Science Board. (1998). *Science and Engineering Indicators—1998*, Arlington, VA: National Science Foundation.

Organization for Economic Cooperation and Development. (1996). "The Knowledge-Based Economy," OCDE/GD (96) 102, Paris: OECD.

Organization for Economic Cooperation and Development. (1998). *Science, Technology and Industry Outlook*, Paris: OECD.

Organization for Economic Cooperation and Development. (1999a). *Science, Technology and Industry Scoreboard: Benchmarking Knowledge-Based Economies*, Paris: OECD.

Organization for Economic Cooperation and Development. (1999b). "The Knowledge-Based Economy: A Set of Facts and Figures," background paper for the 1999 meeting of the Committee for Scientific and Technological Policy at Ministerial level, Paris: OECD.

Organization for Economic Cooperation and Development. (2000). *Information Technology Outlook*, Paris: OECD.

United States Congress. (1998). "Unlocking Our Future: Toward a New National Science Policy," Report, House of Representatives, House Committee on Science (September 24).

United States International Trade Commission. (1999a). *Recent Trends in IS Services Trade*, Publication 3198, Washington: USITC.

United States International Trade Commission. (1999b). *Shifts in U.S. Merchandise Trade in 1998*, Publication 3220, Washington: USITC.

United States President's Commission on Industrial Competitiveness. (1985). *The Report of the President's Commission on Industrial Technology*, Washington, DC: GPO.

Vonortas, N. S. (forthcoming). "Technology policy in the United States and the European Union: Shifting orientation towards technology-users," *Science and Public Policy*.

Vonortas, N. S. (1997) *Cooperative Research and Development*, Kluwer Academic Publishers.

Vonortas, N. S. (1995) "New directions for US science and technology policy: The view from the R&D assessment front," *Science and Public Policy*, 22(1): 19-28.

White House. (1993a). "Technology for America's Economic Growth, A New Direction to Build Economic Strength," Washington, DC, February.

White House. (1993b) ."Technology for Economic Growth: President's Progress Report," Washington, DC, November.

---

[1] A large number of publications and reports with indicators relating to various aspects of the issue have appeared during the past few years, since the OECD championed the idea of the knowledge-based economy (OECD 1996). For this Section, we consulted primarily the following: OECD (1998, 1999a, 1999b, 2000) and United States International Trade Commission (1999a, 1999b).

[2] Of course, other factors have arguably created and reinforced this performance, including non-inflationary, stable macroeconomic environment; long streams of heavy business investment in information technology; the largest "technical enterprise" on the globe, based on continuous, extensive efforts in science, technology and innovation in government, industry, and universities; relatively deregulated, flexible, and competitive economy that facilitates rapid adjustment to changing economic environments; and, globalization has played to the American strengths of mounting competition, rapid structural change, increasing technological content of traded goods and services, and the rise of the importance of services, particularly finance and business services in international trade.

[3] It is possible that the exclusion of private investments in education and training, quite significant in the case of the United States, seriously underestimates the country's overall investment in knowledge. Other important omissions from this definition of investment in knowledge include expenditures on product design and organizational change.

[4] Almost 3.2 million people with a bachelor's degree or higher were employed in a scientists or engineer occupation in 1995. Of these, 42 percent were engineers and 30 percent computer and math scientists. The growth of S&E degree production has slowed down in more recent years. In 1995, 700,000 bachelor's and 146,000 master's S&E degrees were awarded in the United States (NSB 1998)

[5] Value added in ICT industries accounted for 4.4 percent of US GDP — which is the highest among countries in North America and the European Union. This definition includes ISIC Rev. 2 classes 3825 (office and computing equipment), 3832 (radio, television and communications equipment) and 72 (communication services).

[6] ICT industries account for a much larger proportion of business enterprise expenditure on R&D (BERD) than their share of GDP would imply. In 1997, ICT share of US BERD was

22 percent, compared to 26 percent for Japan, 28 percent for Canada, and 41 percent for Finland.

[7] By definition, the knowledge economy is based on a highly skilled, versatile workforce. IT workers are at the forefront of very significant changes taking place at the workplace due to time-based competition, shortening product lives, product and service proliferation, outsourcing, and so forth. For an excellent discussion of the main challenges confronting the US "core IT work force", and the progress in meeting those challenges, see Meares and Sargent (1999). For a very interesting summary of the discussion of IT, work, employment, different types of labor, and comparative advantage see the Economist (1996).

[8] It is an interesting phenomenon that ICT intensity is higher in English-speaking countries, in Sweden, Switzerland, and, to a lesser extent, in Japan and the Netherlands. There is some speculation that this is a temporary phenomenon related, at least in part, to the availability of Internet content (and more obviously to Internet access costs).

[9] National defense cannot any longer drive technologies in many cutting-edge fields. Government agencies are encouraged to buy off-the-shelf, state-of-the-art technologies from the private sector. Agencies with significant S&T budgets should try to develop, to the extent possible, dual-use technologies.

[10] That is, in addition to the creation of new technologies, significant effort is directed toward technology dissemination. The government starts paying attention to the ability of firms to locate, access, adapt and use new technologies.

[11] State governments are urged to be prepared to assist smaller firms, attract capital, and diffuse innovation-related knowledge (e.g., manufacturing extension services).

[12] See various reports by committees organized under the aegis of the National Academy of Sciences, National Academy of Engineering, and the Institute of Medicine — for instance, Committee on Science, Engineering and Public Policy (1992, 1993); and Committee on Technology Policy Options in a Global Economy (1993). See also Council on Competitiveness (1991), and Competitiveness Policy Council (1993).

[13] Subsequent versions of these guidelines have followed in the same direction.

[14] The experience of the European Union could be very valuable here. Europeans, of course, noticed that increasing economic interdependence brings increased dangers of foul play among partners as well as increased social interdependence. They opted for closer political and monetary union to deal with some of these difficulties.

Chapter 18

R&D Policy in Israel
An Overview and Reassessment

MANUEL TRAJTENBERG
Tel Aviv University and National Bureau of Economic Research

1.   INTRODUCTION

The high tech sector in Israel has turned in the course of the last decade into a striking economic success story, both by local and by international standards. In fact, Israel stands as one of the most prolific innovating economies, and as one of the few Silicon Valley types of technology centers in the world. There is no doubt that government policy was key to the emergence and early success of the sector, a policy embedded for the most part in the programs and budgetary resources of the Office of the Chief Scientist (OCS) at the Ministry of Industry and Trade. However, the very success of the sector and its relentless dynamism call for the periodic revision and reexamination of those policies. Moreover, the policy impasse of the late 1990s (due to tight government funding at a time of growing demand for Research and Development (R&D) funding) brought to the surface basic tensions that were built into the policies, and that could no longer be ignored.

Interest in R&D Policy as an area of research has experienced recently a marked upsurge within mainstream economics (see for example Klette, Moan and Griliches 1999; David and Hall 2000; Jones and Williams 1998, etc.). This probably reflects the perception that technical advances in Information Technologies (IT) and related areas have had a noticeable and sustained impact on productivity growth in recent years (contrary to the previous uneasiness in that respect vividly articulated in Solow's Paradox). Since R&D is driving the relentless flow of innovations that fuel IT and the New Economy, policies that affect R&D have thus become an attractive field of inquiry. Moreover, advanced economies other than the U.S., and in particular European countries, see it as a major goal to partake in the processes associated with the current wave of innovations, and therefore their interest in R&D Policy is immediate and pragmatic. So it is for Israel, where early recognition that its comparative advantage resides in its highly skilled labor and world-class academic resources (contrasted to its relatively poor endowment in natural resources) led the government to actively promote commercial R&D for the past three decades.

The main goal of this chapter is to provide the basic ingredients for the understanding of R&D policy in Israel, and to critically assess it in light of recent developments. It consists of a descriptive first part, whereby the various programs of the OCS are laid out in some detail, and a second section where we examine the outstanding policy issues. Following a brief account of the functioning and history of the OCS, we review in section 2.2 the OCS main programs, including their mission, mode of operation, budget and composition. Section 2.2.1 describes the standard R&D Grants Program, followed by the Magnet Program, and the Incubators Program; section 2.2.4 touches on International Cooperation, including the BIRD Program. Section 2.3 presents quantitative indicators of OCS activities over time, including budgets and projects by size of firms, followed in section 2.4 by a review of econometric studies on the contribution of the OCS, and an overview of the rise of the high tech sector in Israel with the aid patent data.

Part II opens with a discussion of allocation schemes for the regular OCS Grants Program in view of a rigid budget constraint, followed by an examination of possible ways of departing from the principle of neutrality. Section 3.2 deals with a host of related issues, such as the payback system, the conditionality of production in Israel, and the need for ongoing economic assessment of the various programs. Section 3.3 attempts to assess the Magnet program for the support of consortia engaged in generic R&D, and raises the question of the desirability of supporting it versus the regular commercial R&D projects. In section 3.4 we review the difficulties in setting a policy target for R&D spending, and lastly we ask in section 3.5 whether government policy should be aimed also at the supply side (of the market for R&D personnel), thus shifting away from the present exclusive focus on the demand side.

It should be emphasized once again that this chapter is meant to be first and foremost a *descriptive account* of ongoing R&D government programs in Israel, with the goal of providing a suitable framework for a much needed discussion on outstanding policy issues. These issues are of relevance not just for Israel but also for any economy contemplating active government involvement in R&D.

2. GOVERNMENT SUPPORT FOR INDUSTRIAL R&D IN ISRAEL: AN OVERVIEW[1]

The beginning of government support for industrial (civilian) R&D in Israel dates back to 1968: a government commission, headed by Prof. Kachalsky, recommended the creation of the Office of the Chief Scientist (OCS) at the Ministry of Industry and Commerce, with the mandate to subsidize commercial R&D projects undertaken by private firms. Support previously was confined to National Labs, and to academic R&D, in addition to the weighty resources that were devoted to defense and to agricultural research. And indeed, industrial R&D rose rapidly following the establishment of the OCS. Between 1969 and 1987 industrial R&D expenditures grew at 14 percent per year, and high tech exports grew from a mere $422 million in 1969 (in 1987 dollars), to $3,316 million in 1987 (Toren 1990).

The next key development was the passing of the *Law for the Encouragement of Industrial R&D* in 1985. This is the main piece of legislation that has defined the parameters of government policy towards industrial R&D. The stated goals of the legislation, to be implemented by the OCS, are to develop science-based, export-oriented industries, which will promote employment and improve the balance of payments. In order to do this, the legislation attempted to provide the means to expand and exploit the country's technological and scientific infrastructure, and leverage its high-skilled human resources.[2]

At the heart of the law is a program of financial incentives. Any company that meets certain eligibility criteria is entitled to receive matching funds for the development of innovative, export-targeted products. The OCS funds up to 50 percent of R&D expenses in established companies, and up to 66 percent for startups. The OCS supports and administers a wide range of additional programs, the main ones being: Magnet, a program to encourage pre-competitive generic research conducted by consortia; a program of technological incubators; and, various programs involving bilateral and multilateral international R&D collaboration. We review these programs here. Other, relatively minor programs aimed at specific stages along the innovation cycle or at particular segments in the progression from an innovative idea to a full-fledged commercial enterprise are described in Appendix 1.

2.1 A Review of OCS Programs[3]

This is by far the largest program, and administering it constitutes the main activity of the OCS. The way it works is as follows. Qualifying firms submit grant applications for specific R&D projects, these are reviewed by a Research Committee, and if approved (about 70 percent are) the applicants receive a grant of up to 50 percent of the stated R&D budget for the project. Successful projects (i.e., those leading to sales) are required to repay the grant, by paying back to the OCS royalties of three percent of annual sales,[4] up to the dollar-linked amount of the grant. Recipients of the R&D grants have to abide by the following conditions: (1) the R&D project must be executed by the applicant firm itself; (2) the product(s) that emerge from the R&D project must be manufactured in Israel; (3) know-how acquired in the course of the R&D may not be transferred to third parties.[5]

The Research Committee, chaired by the Chief Scientist, is responsible for defining the conditions for granting aid (within the confines of the 1985 Law), and for reviewing the applications and selecting the recipients. The committee is staffed both by qualified government officials and by public representatives, but it relies on (outside) professional referees and advisers to review the applications. Decisions of the Research Committee can be heard before an Appeals Committee.

Grants of (up to) 50 percent of the total R&D costs are given to projects that lead to know-how, processes or systems for manufacturing a new product/process or substantially improving existing ones.[6] Grants covering 30 percent of R&D costs are available for projects leading to *improvements* in existing civilian products, and 20 percent for improvements of military products. Startup companies qualify for grants of up to two-thirds of R&D costs, with a ceiling of $250,000 a year for two years. Products aimed at the military (export) market qualify for grants of up to 30 percent.

Israel has a long-standing policy of encouraging the development of an industrial base in peripheral areas (away from the main urban centers), which is reflected also in the R&D support programs. Thus, R&D projects performed in the preferential peripheral areas (Grade A Development Areas) are entitled to additional 10 percent grants: for civilian projects that means grants of up to 60 percent (rather then 50 percent for the others), and military projects are entitled to grants of up to 40 percent (rather than 30 percent for the others).

2.1.1   The Magnet Program

Notwithstanding the rapid growth of the high tech sector in Israel from the late 1960s onwards, it became clear by the early 1990s that the industrial landscape in Israel was too fragmented, and Israeli industrial companies were too small to be able to shoulder the escalating costs of developing new technologies in innovative fields. Moreover, Israel boosted excellent research universities, but they operated largely in isolation from surrounding industrial developments and needs, and hence the vast economic potential embedded both in the highly qualified academic manpower and in university research remained largely untapped.[7]

Table 1: Active Magnet Consortia as of December 1999

1.	Ground Stations for Satellite Communications
2.	Digital Wireless Communications
3.	Broad-Wide Band Communication (BISDN)
4.	Multimedia On-Line Services
5.	Diode Pumped Lasers
6.	Multi Chip Module (MCM)
7.	Magnesium Technologies
8.	Hybrid Seeds and Blossom Control
9.	Algae Cultivation Biotechnology
10.	DNA Markers
11.	Drug and Kits Design and Development (Daa't)
12.	MMIC/GaAs components
13.	0.25 micron/300 mm devices
14.	Ultra Concentrated Solar Energy (Consular)
15.	Network Management Systems
16.	Digital Printing
17.	Image Guided Therapy (Izmel)
18.	Computerized Industrial Processes
User Associations:	
1.	Users of Advanced Technologies in Electronics
2.	Users of Advanced Technologies in Metal

Against this background, the OCS established in 1993 the Magnet Program[8], to support the formation of consortia made of industrial firms and academic institutions in order to develop *generic, pre-competitive* technologies.[9] These consortia are entitled to multi-year R&D support (usually three to five years), consisting of grants of 66 percent of the total approved R&D budget, with no recoupment requirement. The consortia must be comprised of the widest possible group of industrial members operating in the field,[10] jointly with Israeli academic institutions doing research in scientific areas relevant to the technological goals of the consortia.

Mindful of possible conflict with anti-trust provisions, consortia members must pledge to make the products or services resulting from the joint project available to any interested local party, at prices that do not reflect the exercise of monopoly power. Keeping with the mandate to encourage pre-competitive technologies, support to the consortia ceases once the equivalent of the pilot plant stage is reached. That is, the additional R&D required for the actual commercialization of the products is not supported by Magnet, but the member companies may then apply for regular grants from the OCS. Contrary to the regular OCS support to industrial R&D projects, the Magnet program operates on a competitive basis, that is, it is open to any number of proposals for the formation of new consortia, and it selects only those that merit support on the basis of a ranking system.

By the end of 1999, there were 18 consortia in operation, commanding a budget of about $60 million, and four additional consortia in various stages of gestation. These consortia span a wide range of technologies, primarily in communications, micro- electronics, biotechnology, and energy. Table 1 shows the complete list.

2.1.2   The Incubators Program[11]

Technological incubators are support organizations that give fledgling entrepreneurs an opportunity to develop their innovative technological ideas and set up new businesses in order to commercialize them. The program was introduced in the early 1990s, when immigration from the former Soviet Union had reached its peak. Many of these immigrants were scientists and skilled professionals that came to Israel with highly valuable human capital as well as with plenty of ideas for innovative products. However, they were lacking in virtually all other dimensions required for commercial success, from knowledge of the relevant languages (e.g. Hebrew and English) and of commercial practices in western economies, to managerial skills and access to capital. Even though it targeted new immigrants, the program is open to all.

The goal of the incubators is thus to support novice entrepreneurs at the *earliest* stage of technological entrepreneurship, and help them implement ideas and form new business ventures. The premise is that the incubator would significantly enhance the entrepreneur's prospects of raising further capital, finding strategic partners, and emerging from the incubator as a going concern. Of course, this initial stage is the riskiest, and there were virtually no other sources of finance in Israel for such ventures. Since the mid-1990s, there has been a growing influx of venture capital, and hence the purely risk-sharing function undertaken by this program may be less critical at present than what it was at its inception.

Each incubator is structured so as to handle 10–15 projects simultaneously, and provides assistance in the following areas: determining the technological and marketing applicability of the idea, drawing up an R&D plan and organizing the R&D team, raising capital and preparing for marketing, provision of secretarial and administrative services, maintenance, procurements, accounting, and legal advice.[12]

To qualify, projects must be aimed at developing an innovative idea with export potential. The R&D team is to be made of three to six workers, and the stay at the incubator is of up to two years. The expectation is that there would be a prototype and an orderly business plan, and the project should be ready for further commercial investment and/or the involvement of a strategic partner. The budget for each project is of about $150,000 per year, for two years at most.[13] As with the regular OCS program, the ensuing products have to be manufactured in Israel, and if successful, the entrepreneur has to eventually repay the grant through royalties on sales.

Since its inception in 1991 and up to end of 1998, the incubators have managed close to 700 projects, of which about 200 were still running as of December 1998 in 27 incubators across the country. Current projects employ about 900 professionals, 70 percent of them recent immigrants, all with academic training and many with high degrees. Of the 500 graduating projects, the success rate was about 50 percent (i.e., half managed to continue on their own, the remaining half were discontinued). About 200 projects managed to attract additional investment, ranging from a mere $50K, to several $ million. There are no pre-determined technological areas for the submission of projects. The actual distribution of projects by fields has been as follows: electronics 27 percent, software 20 percent, medical instrumentation 17 percent, chemistry 27 percent, miscellaneous nine percent.

2.1.3   International Cooperation

The relative advantage of Israel's high tech sector manifests itself primarily in its technological prowess in the R&D stages. However, Israeli high tech companies suffer from serious difficulties in marketing abroad, primarily because of geographic distance from the target markets, and their relatively small size. Thus, cooperation with foreign companies active in the target markets is likely to increase the ability of Israeli technology and products to penetrate global markets. In that spirit, the Israeli government has signed in recent years a number of bilateral R&D cooperation agreements with foreign governments. These are meant to encourage contacts between Israeli and foreign companies leading to joint R&D, manufacturing and marketing. Foreign companies are expected to benefit by gaining access to advanced Israeli technology, and they are likely to derive commercial advantages from Israel's simultaneous free trade agreements with the U.S. and the European Union (few countries enjoy both).

Joint ventures between Israeli and foreign companies, authorized by the relevant authorities in the respective countries, are entitled to aid from both governments according to the regulations prevailing in each. Bilateral agreements exist already with a number of countries, including the U.S., Canada, France, Holland and Spain; their implementation is the responsibility of the Chief Scientist, assisted by MATIMOP, The Israeli Industry Center for R&D.

The BIRD Program

The Israel-U.S. Bi-national Industrial Research and Development Foundation (BIRD) was founded in the early 1980s under a convention signed by both governments. Its objective was to promote and support joint, non-defense industrial research and development activities of mutual benefit to the (private sectors of the) two countries. The Foundation has an independent legal status and its main office is in Israel. Its Board of Governors is comprised of representatives of the U.S. and Israeli governments.

BIRD participates in the funding of joint R&D via conditional grants amounting to 50 percent of the project costs, up to a maximum of $1.5 million per project. If a project succeeds, BIRD receives royalties, a pre-tax expense to the payer up to a maximum of 150 percent of the conditional grant. Only in cases where a project fails and there are no sales are the companies exempted from repaying the grants. BIRD also helps Israeli or American companies identify partners in order to enable them to submit joint R&D programs for funding by the Foundation.

Table 2: The OCS Budget 1988–2000 (in current $ million)

Year	(1) R&D Grants	(2) Paybacks	(3) Paybacks/Grants	(4) Net Grants*	(5) Magnet	(6) Incubators
1988	120	8	0.07	112	-	-
1989	125	10	0.08	115	-	-
1990	136	14	0.10	122	-	-
1991	179	20	0.11	159	0.3	3.6
1992	199	25	0.13	174	3.7	16
1993	231	33	0.14	198	4.6	23
1994	316	42	0.13	274	10	28
1995	346	56	0.16	290	15	31
1996	348	79	0.23	269	36	30
1997	397	102	0.26	295	53	30
1998	400	117	0.29	283	61	30
1999	428	139	0.32	289	60	30
2000**	395	128	0.32	267	70	30

* R&D Grants minus Paybacks. ** Estimates

2.2   Quantitative Indicators of OCS Support Programs

Systematic data on the OCS are hard to obtain, and there are no official statistics on the OCS activities and budgets. The lack of data has been detrimental to the functioning of the OCS and has surely impaired the formulation of R&D policy at all levels. The OCS has long been aware of the problem, and efforts are being made to remedy it in a fundamental way. The data presented here are based on reports supplied to us by the OCS in January 2000,[14] but there still remain question marks regarding some of the figures, and hence these should be seen as tentative data, which require further scrutiny.

The dollar figures in Tables 2, 5 and 6 are all in current dollars. To transform them into *constant* dollars one would have to construct an appropriate R&D deflator, of which the main component would be the wages of R&D personnel (see section 2.4.2 for a detailed discussion of deflators in the Israeli context). Lacking at present a reliable deflator, and rather than using ready-made but potentially misleading price indices, we opt here to leave the figures in current dollars.[15] Thus, all statements henceforth implying comparisons of dollar figures across time need to be qualified.

Table 2 shows the OCS budget since 1988, as well as paybacks, and the amounts allocated to the Magnet and Incubators program. Total R&D grants administered by the OCS increased steeply up to the mid-1990s, then increased slightly until 1997, and have remained constant since. Paybacks rose very fast throughout the whole period,[16] and in fact their weight in the OCS budget has increased dramatically from a mere 7 percent in 1988 to 32 percent by the late 1990s. What this means is that about 1/3 of the present OCS budget just constitutes *recycling of funds within the high tech sector, and not government subsidy to R&D*. The net subsidy is given in column 4 under Net Grants: these peaked in 1995, and have since declined slightly (certainly more so in real terms). Furthermore, if we subtract the funds allocated to the Magnet and the Incubators programs, we can see that the *net* subsidy to the *regular* OCS Grants program has declined very substantially since 1995 (by about 25 percent up to 1999, in nominal terms).

Table 3 shows the number of firms applying to the OCS for grants, total as well as first timers. Both peaked in 1994 and have declined substantially since. The decline includes, quite surprisingly, also startups that applied for the first time.[17] Given the rapid growth in the overall number of startups throughout the economy,[18] the decline in the number of first-time applicants may reflect a change in funding strategy. More start-ups may prefer to rely on venture capital funds rather than on the OCS (without strings attached in terms of production in Israel or the eventual sale of the firm to foreign corporations).[19] In the 1990s, 2,380 firms applied for support from the OCS for the first time. This is a large number by any standard, and offers further indication of the prominent role that the OCS has played in fostering the high tech sector.

Table 3: Number of Firms Applying for R&D Grants

Year	No. of Firms Applying	First-Time Applicants	
		Total	Startups
1990	451	216	34
1991	576	264	109
1992	626	241	165
1993	661	245	179
1994	777	291	218
1995	715	236	146
1996	705	257	200
1997	643	200	170
1998	629	222	165
1999	598	208	138
Total		2380	1524

Table 4:. Number of Projects Approved (by size of firms) [20.]

Year	Large	Small & Medium	of which Startups*	Total
1995	219	1303	357	1522
1996	212	1170	314	1382
1997	207	1045	270	1252
1998	266	1009	285	1275
1999	202	960	245	1162
Total	1106	5487	1471	6593

Table 5. Grants (in current $Millions) (by size of firms)

Year	Large	Small & Medium	of which Startups*	Total
1995	144	202	62	346
1996	149	199	66	348
1997	161	236	67	397
1998	157	243	60	400
1999	99	329	68	428
Total	710	1209	323	1919

Tables 4-6 show the distribution of projects and grants by size of firms.[21] The annual number of projects supported averaged 1,300 for the past five years, declining from a high of 1,500 in 1995 to 1,200 in 1999.[22] On the other hand, the average dollar amount per project increased from $227,000 in 1995 to $368,000 in 1999 (in nominal terms). Notice though that the average size of projects for *large* firms declined quite steeply, whereas that of small and medium firms increased a great deal. Large firms commanded about 40 percent of grants (in dollar terms) for most of the period, but their share of the budget declined steeply in 1999, to 23 percent.[23,]

Table 6:. Average Grant/Project (in $thousands) (by size of firms)

Year	Large	Small & Medium	of which Startups*	Overall Mean
1995	658	322	*174*	227
1996	703	366	*210*	252
1997	778	466	*248*	317
1998	590	463	*211*	314
1999	490	643	*278*	368
Mean	642	440	*220*	291

*Not including incubator projects

2.3   The OCS and the Rise of the High Tech Sector

The natural questions that one would like to pose now are those related to the *impact* of the OCS (e.g., To what extent has the OCS fulfilled the goals envision by the 1985 Law?) What effect have the various OCS programs had on the high tech sector and on the economy at large? We review first existing econometric studies, we then discuss some economic indicators contrasting R&D-intensive sectors to traditional ones, and lastly we present an overview of the rise of the high tech sector in Israel with the aid patent data.

2.3.1   Review of Econometric Studies

The consensual view in Israel is that the OCS played indeed a key role in the emergence and development of the high tech sector, a role that went beyond the mere administration of grants. There have been various studies in Israel examining *inter alia* the impact of R&D expenditures on productivity at the firm level (Bregman, Fuss, and Regev 1991; Griliches and Regev 1995; Bregman and Merom 1998). They all find that the returns to R&D have been high and in particular significantly higher than investments in physical capital. However, these studies do not address the effect of government support per se.

If one could assume that OCS grants brought about higher *total* R&D outlays (this is commonly referred to as additionality), then the findings of high returns to R&D would imply also positive returns to government support. Capital markets were extremely limited in Israel during the early stages of development of the high tech sector in Israel in the 1970s and

1980s and it is very unlikely that R&D grants supplied by the OCS would have crowded out private R&D funds back then. Later on though internal reform as well as international openness greatly increased the availability of funds to industry, bringing back to the forefront the additionality issue for the 1990s.

The basic conundrum posed by additionality is the obvious lack of counterfactuals (i.e. what would the recipient firm have done had it not received an R&D subsidy?), which effectively means the lack of appropriate controls (i.e. data on non-recipients that are otherwise similar to the recipients). Several recent papers have tried a variety of approaches to deal with it (see for example Busom 2000 and Wallsten 2000), but the jury is still out both on method and on stylized facts.[24] Feldman and Kelley (2000) come closest to having an appropriate control group: they followed both winners of ATP grants, and applicants that failed to receive grants. Surveying both types of firms, they find *prima facie* evidence of additionality (e.g., non-awardees tend *not* to pursue the proposed projects by themselves, awardees are more successful in seeking additional funding for the projects, etc).

Lach (2000) carefully examines this issue for a sample of Israeli manufacturing firms that performed R&D during the period 1991-95, and finds that the R&D subsidies granted by the OCS in fact stimulated long-run company-financed R&D expenditures. According to his estimates, an extra dollar of R&D subsidies increases long run company-financed R&D by 41 cents (evaluating the effect at the mean of the data). Thus, total R&D outlays increase at the margin by 1.41 dollars: the full amount of the subsidy, plus the additional, induced effect of 41 cents. However, it is not clear to what extent those results are robust, both to the choice of specification and of instruments; in fact, in other specifications Lach finds little or no additionality. The problem resides mostly in the paucity of the data (i.e. there are not many firms with any given set of characteristics at any point in time that can serve as controls for those receiving subsidies), and in the difficulty in finding appropriate instruments.

Taking a different track, Griliches and Regev (1999) examine whether the source of R&D funds per se (private vs. OCS grants) makes a difference on productivity (once again in a panel of firms), regardless of additionality. They find that it does: government-funded R&D appears to be significantly more productive than privately-financed R&D, by a surprisingly large margin. The reason may be rooted in the ability of the OCS to pick winners, and/or in the fact that the very process of applying for grants may compel firms to self-select projects, use more structured pre-assessment and planning techniques, etc. Finally, an unpublished study commissioned by the OCS itself examined the contribution of OCS grants to sales, exports, and the like, relying on detailed data from the OCS and on an extensive survey of firms (Michlol 1999). The study finds very high multipliers per dollar of OCS support, higher for small firms than for large ones; however, the study is careful to point out to its limitations, particularly given the lack of a suitable control group.

The evidence thus far available from these studies provide then econometric support, albeit limited, to the presumption that OCS grants have had a positive and significant impact on productivity in R&D-intensive sectors, and through them on the economy as a whole. Still, there is a long way to go in that respect, if only because a major ingredient of the rationale for government support to R&D, namely spillovers, has not been investigated at all. Beyond the aforementioned studies, we present now some evidence on the development of the high tech sector itself, with the implicit understanding that the OCS was one of the main drivers behind the raise of this sector. We do that in two ways: first, we briefly recount reports from the Bank of Israel on the performance of technological advanced sectors vis-à-vis traditional ones; second, we present an overall view of innovation in Israel, relying on comprehensive and highly detailed information on Israeli patenting in the United States.

Table 7. Performance Indicators by Type of Sector: Annualized rates of change, 1995-98

		Sector		
Indicator	Period	Advanced	Mixed	Traditional
Production	*1995-96*	8.0	6.3	5.9
	1997-98	6.0	0.3	-1.8
Labor Productivity	*1995-96*	3.5	2.4	4.2
	1997-98	4.5	0.6	2.2
Capital Stock	*1995-96*	10.7	6.4	9.7
	1997-98	10.0	6.1	6.8
Exports	*1995-96*	9.0	10.5	2.7
	1997-98	18.5	3.0	-1.4

Source: Bank of Israel, Annual Report for 1998, table B 10 (page 56).

2.3.2 Aggregate Sectorial Indicators[25]

Responding to the rapid changes in the composition of industry, and in particular the raise of the high tech sector, the Research Department of the Bank of Israel introduced a new classification in the mid 1990s which divided manufacturing into advanced, traditional and mixed sectors, according to the quality and composition of the labor force (e.g. the percentage of scientists and engineers), the quality of the capital stock, and the relative size of the R&D stock.[26] Table 7 presents selected indicators according to this classification.

The advanced sectors outperformed the two other categories in virtually all dimensions during the reported period (1995–98). The differences between them increased substantially in 1997 and 1998, a period characterized by a rather severe recession. During those years, the advanced sectors grew at a rate of six percent per year, whereas the others remained stagnant or declined. Similarly, exports from advanced sectors grew at a stunning 18.5 percent per year, whereas the mixed sectors exhibited an anemic three percent growth, and the traditional sectors *declined* 1.4 percent. Thus, Israeli manufacturing is shifting away from traditional industries and into technological advanced export oriented sectors.

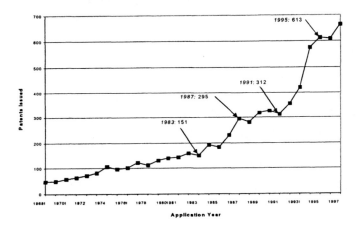

Figure 1. Israeli Patents in the U.S. - 1968-97

2.3.3   Innovation in Israel: Patent Indicators[27]

Patent-based statistics are often used as indicators of innovative activity. Indeed, their very wide coverage, long time series and richness of detail make them a unique and compelling data source for the study of technical change. There are also limitations: not all innovations are patented, both because of failure to meet patenting requirements, and because of strategic considerations. We present in this section an overview of innovation in Israel based on all patents awarded to Israeli inventors in the U.S., during the period 1968- to 1997 (over 7,000 patents), as well as patents of comparison countries. Given that the high tech sector in Israel is overwhelmingly export-oriented, and that the U.S. is a prime destination for those exports, there is reason to believe that Israeli patents issued in the U.S. are representative of the main technological trends and patterns in Israel.

Figure 1 shows the number of successful Israeli patent applications in the U.S. over time, starting in 1968. The growth in the annual number of patents has been very impressive, starting from about 50 in the late sixties, to over 600 in the late 1990s. However, the process was not smooth, but rather it was characterized by big swings in growth rates. Particularly striking are the two big jumps that occurred in the second half of the period: from 1983 to 1987, the number of patents doubled, and then they doubled again from 1991 to 1995.[28] Figure 2 shows industrial R&D expenditures (in constant 1990 dollars) along with patents.[29] There is clearly a (lagged) co-movement of the two series, as manifested for example in the following simple Pearson correlations:[30]

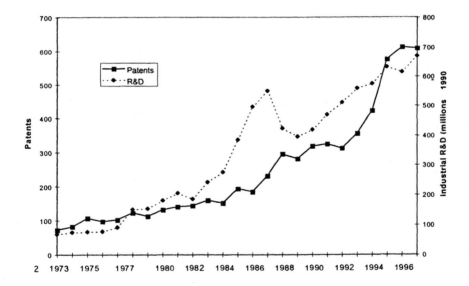

Figure 2. Israeli Patents and Industrial R&D

Thus, patents lead R&D by 2-3 years, and the correlation is stronger in rates (i.e., when using logs) than in levels. Looking in more detail, there is a striking run up in R&D from 1981 to 1986 (in particular, R&D expenditures more than doubled between 1980/81 and 1984/85), followed by the doubling of patents between 1983 and 1987. This is the period that saw the emergence of the high tech sector, and that is well reflected in both series. In 1986-88 we see a decline in the level of R&D spending, and the concomitant flattening of patenting in 1987 to 1991, and then again a sustained increase through the early-mid nineties that anticipates the second big jump in patenting.

Table 8: Pearson Correlation Coefficients for Patents and R&D, with lags

	R&D	R&D (-1)	R&D (-2)	R&D (-3)
Patents	0.850	0.877	0.884	0.883
Log (patents) with Log(R&D)	0.890	0.901	0.922	0.928

Although we do not have official figures for R&D grants from the OCS prior to 1988, available figures indicate that the behavior of the time series for grants move very closely to that of total R&D industrial spending (see for example Griliches and Regev 1999, table 6). In particular, from 1981 through 1986 OCS grants also doubled, they flattened during 1986 to 1988, and they grew fast again up to the mid 1990s (see Table 2 for the latter). It appears clear that industrial R&D expenditures are closely linked, with some reasonable lag, to patents, and so are R&D grants awarded by the OCS. Further research is needed to unravel the joint dynamics.

2.3.3.1   International Comparisons

We resort to international comparisons in order to put in perspective the overall level and trend over time in Israeli patenting. We do that with respect to three different groups of countries: (1) The G7: Canada, France, Germany, Italy, Japan, UK and USA; (2) a Reference Group: Finland, Ireland, New Zealand and Spain;[31] and (3) the Asian Tigers: Hong Kong, Singapore, South Korea and Taiwan.

(patents per 100,000 population)

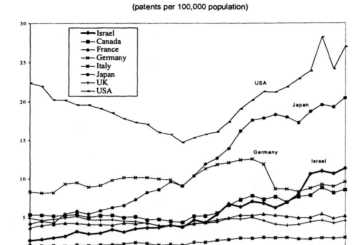

Figure3. Patents Per Capita: Israel vs. the G7

Figures 3-5 show the time patterns of patents per capita for Israel versus each of the above groups of countries. We normalize the number of patents by population, simply because this is a widely available and accurate statistic that provides a consistent scale factor.[32] Figure 3 reveals that Israel started virtually at the bottom of the G7 (together with Italy), but by 1987, it had climbed ahead of Italy, UK, and France and was on par with Canada. In the early-mid nineties it moved ahead of Canada and (the unified) Germany, thus becoming 3d after the USA and Japan. Using civilian R&D as deflator for these countries show a similar result. Thus, there is no question that Israel had surged forward and placed itself in the forefront of technological advanced countries, at least in terms of (normalized) numbers of patents.

(patents per 100,000 population)

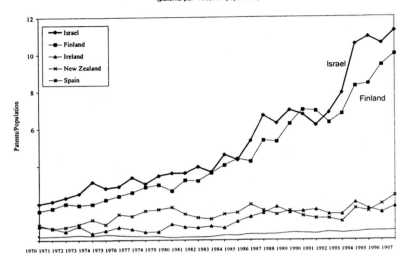

Figure 4:. Patents Per Capita: Israel vs. the Reference Group

The comparison with the Reference Group reveals that the only country that is game is Finland, which has followed a pattern virtually identical to Israel. The other three countries are well behind, and have remained at the bottom without any significant changes over time. As to the Asian Tigers, we can see immediately that Taiwan has grown extremely rapidly since the early eighties, actually surpassing Israel as of 1997. Moreover, indeed, Taiwan is widely regarded today as a high tech powerhouse, after being associated with low-tech, imitative behavior for a long time. South Korea seems to be embarked on a similar path. By contrast, Hong Kong and Singapore remain well behind.

Comparisons based on *normalized* patent counts notwithstanding, many aspects of the innovation process require a critical mass. For those purposes, the *absolute* size of the innovative sector counts, as proxied here by the (absolute) number of patents. Israel has still a long way to go in those terms: it stands well below all of the G7 countries, and is about ¼ the size of Taiwan and South Korea. The question is whether there are forces in the Israeli economy capable of keeping the momentum going for the high tech sector, bringing it up to the size required and ensuring its long-term viability. The stagnant budgets awarded in recent years to the OCS are not a good omen in that respect.

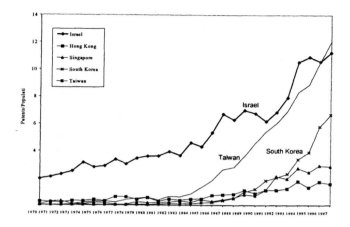

Figure 5:. Patents Per Capita: Israel vs. the NIC

2.3.4   The Technological Composition of Israeli Patented Innovations

The U.S. Patent Office has developed over the years an elaborate classification system by which it assigns patents to some 400 main patent classes, and over 150,000 patent subclasses. We have developed recently a new classification scheme, aggregating these 400 patent classes into six main categories: Computers and Communications, Electrical and Electronics, Drugs and Medicine, Chemical, Mechanical and Other. Figure 6 shows the shares of these categories over the decade 1985-94, for Israel and for the U.S. Up until the early 1980s the picture was quite stable in the U.S.: the shares of Mechanical and Other were highest (over 25 percent each), whereas Drugs and Medicine and Computers and Communications accounted just for a tiny fraction, up to five percent each. Starting in the early 1980s this static picture starts to change: the three top fields decline, whereas the bottom two surge forward, with Computers and Communications accounting by 1994 for over 15 percent of all patents.

The pattern for Israel is similar, except that the changes are more abrupt. The most striking development is the surge of Computers and Communications from about five percent in the 1970s (as in the U.S.), to a full 25 percent by 1994 and beyond. Likewise, Drugs and Medicine doubles its share from ten percent to 20 percent. The flip side is the much more pronounced decline in the traditional categories, with Chemicals exhibiting by far the sharpest drop, from 40 percent at the beginning of the period, to less than ten percent by 1996. The composition of innovations has thus changed dramatically in Israel, and seemingly in a healthy way, in the sense that they are in tandem with worldwide changes in technology, except that Israel is experiencing them at an accelerated rate.

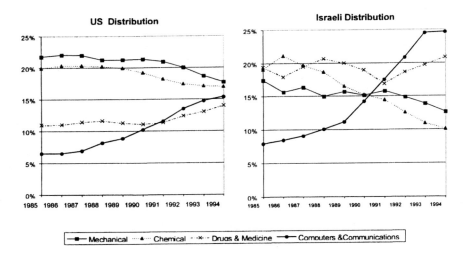

Figure 6:. U.S. vs. Israel Tech Categories - 1985-94

2.3.4.1   Who Owns, and Who Benefits from Israeli Patented Innovations?

The patent-based indicators mentioned so far suggest that Israel's innovative performance has been quite impressive. However, the question arises as to whether the Israeli economy can take full advantage of the innovations generated by Israeli inventors, in view of the composition of the patent assignees, i.e. of the owners of the intellectual property rights to those innovations. In fact, just about half of all Israeli patents granted in the last 30 years are owned by Israeli assignees (corporations, universities or government): the rest belongs to private inventors (unassigned patents) or to foreign assignees. This percentage is lower than most of the comparison countries, certainly much lower than the corresponding figure for the G7 countries except Canada (local assignees made 74 percent of patents in the U.S., 96 percent in Japan). The presumption is that (local) economic gains from innovation are correlated with this figure, and furthermore, that they are correlated with the percentage of patents owned by local *corporations* (just 35 percent in Israel). The trend is encouraging though: the percentage of patents that belong to Israeli corporations has been raising steadily, and stands now at close to 50 percent.

The overall picture that emerges from these patent indicators is thus mixed: on the one hand, Israel exhibits a rapidly growing and vibrant innovative sector that has achieved an impressive international standing. On the other hand, the Israeli economy has still a way to go in order to achieve critical mass and to realize the economic benefits embedded in those innovations.

3.   R&D POLICY IN ISRAEL - A REASSESSMENT[33]

After having described the programs and basic ingredients of R&D policy in Israel towards the industrial sector, we now undertake to examine the contents of such policy. Unfortunately, the lack of rigorous empirical research in this area hampers the formulation of sound, long term and well-grounded policies. Nevertheless, we shall scrutinize the policies currently in place and their implementation mechanisms, and evaluate proposals for changes in them that are called forth by recent developments. This should be seen just as an opening salvo, aimed primarily at fostering public debate in this area (see also Teubal (1999) for a detailed proposal for an R&D strategy for Israel).

First, we look at the system by which grants are allocated: with the recent imposition of a rigid budget constraint on the OCS, the present system is untenable, and hence we examine various alternatives that will incorporate this new reality. Second, we examine a series of policy issues that go beyond the allocation of funds: the payback system, the conditionality on production in Israel, etc. Third, we look in detail into the Magnet program, and the rationale for supporting it versus the regular OCS grants. Forth, we review the difficulties in setting a policy target for R&D spending, and lastly we ask whether government policy should be aimed also at the supply side (of the market for R&D personnel), rather than just keep subsidizing the demand side.

3.1   Rethinking the Rules of the Game in View of a Rigid Budget Constraint

The R&D Law in Israel does not address the thorny issue of how to allocate a (rigid) budget for R&D support if the demand for such support exceeds the budget provision. That is, the OCS support program was not meant to be competitive, and in principle, it should provide with R&D

subsidies to *all* projects that pass the eligibility criteria. The latter are based on technological and commercial feasibility, and other procedural considerations. Projects are judged one by one, and there is no attempt to rank them or establish otherwise a funding priority. The paramount principle of neutrality that has been a cornerstone of R&D Policy in Israel since the late 1960s precludes also picking projects according to fields or any other such consideration.

In 1997, the projected demand for R&D support greatly exceeded the budget provision (by about 50 percent, i.e. some $200 million), and the Treasury refused to consider any substantial increase to the OCS budget to accommodate such demand.[34]   An impasse ensued, bringing a great deal of uncertainty to the working of the OCS and to the high tech sector as a whole. A committee was formed to try to find a way out of the crisis. After months of deliberations the committee could not reconcile the conflicting forces at play: the imperatives of the existing law, the expectations of the high tech sector, and the perceived need to expand the R&D budget to foster the success of the high tech sector against the sudden imposition of a rigid budget constraint, that did not allow for any growth of demand.

The result has been ad hoc tinkering with both the OCS budget and its way of operation, in order to keep the system running without solving the underlying issues. More importantly, this protracted crisis made clear that the R&D law and the implementation mechanisms in place, are in need of extensive revision in view of the explosive growth of the high tech sector (as well as the rapid changes that took place within the sector), and the pressure that puts on the R&D support budget in an era of fiscal restraint.[35] Following is a discussion of the set of policy issues that lie at the core of this conundrum. The basic premise underlying the discussion is that, if current procedures are left unchanged, demand for R&D support will exceed present level budgets by wide margins, and hence there is an urgent need to design a suitable allocation mechanism.[36]

There are essentially two ways to go about allocating a fixed budget to projects that request support in excess of available resources. The first is to depart from the principle of neutrality in some dimension, the second to design an allocation mechanism that would do the job. Of course, the two are not mutually exclusive, and one could have a combination of both. We consider each in turn, starting from the latter.

3.1.1   Allocation Schemes for the Regular OCS Program of R&D Grants

Until now, the system has been such whereby all eligible projects are supposed to be supported, and in principle, the support should be equal across projects (in percentage terms). The eligibility criteria entail checks of technological and commercial feasibility (or viability), the good standing of the applicants, and other administrative criteria. There are three main options to move away from such system: (i) to adjust every time the support rates or the eligibility criteria to meet the budget constraint; (ii) to implement a competitive/ranking system; (iii) randomization.

The first option entails adjusting the support *rates* or the eligibility criteria with every new budget to meet the budget constraint. The major drawback is of course the uncertainty that such a policy shift will introduce, greatly impairing the ability of firms to plan ahead (certainly long term). In addition, this would make the whole support system vulnerable to political manipulation.

The second option simply means that projects would have to compete against each other for scarce support funds (as happens with the Magnet program). There will be a ranking system, and the funds will be allocated from the top down until the budget is exhausted. A serious issue that will almost certainly arise in such context is whether or not such system is compatible with neutrality, in view of the fact that any ranking system will be extremely hard to implement *across* fields, and the ranking would have to be done primarily *within* fields.[37] However, it may be that in any case the system will have to move away from neutrality.

The last option is some sort of randomization, that is, to chose at random from the set of projects that pass some eligibility threshold (as in the present system), up to the point where the budget constraint is met. We shall not analyze this option in any detail, simply because it would seem that it is (at least at present) politically unfeasible.[38] Thus, it seems that the only viable alternative at this point is to implement some sort of ranking/competitive system, as suggested above, and tie it with a conscious departure from neutrality.

3.1.2 Departures from Neutrality

As already mentioned, one of the hallmarks and basic premises of the OCS support programs has been all along *neutrality*, that is, the OCS does not select projects according to preferred fields or any such criteria, but responds to demand that arises spontaneously from industry. It is fair to say that such policy has been successful, since it reinforced existing competencies and emerging comparative advantage. Moreover, it avoided one of the main potential dangers of any industrial policy, namely, the picking of winners by government officials.

However, the fiscal constraint on the overall support budget implies that the OCS may have to depart from neutrality in any case, in which case it is certainly better to do it explicitly as a result of serious analysis, and not by default. There are at least two dimensions that the OCS could opt for non-neutral allocation policies: according to fields, and according to type (or rather size) of firms.[39] As already suggested, such departures could be made part of a revamped allocation scheme (e.g., adopting a ranking/ competitive system).

Departing from neutrality in terms technological fields is always dangerous, since it implies outguessing future technological and/or market developments, and deciding by committee what is better left to the market. Thus, one should avoid it except if there are some glaring market failures that need to be remedied. There is room to believe that may be the case at present in Israel with the field of biotechnology. Israel has a very talented and plentiful scientific workforce in Life Sciences. Yet, this pool of human capital in one of the most dynamic technological areas at present, and potentially one of the most important *future* growth areas, has yet to make a mark on industry (i.e. in biotech). Thus, there is room to consider taking a more active and entrepreneurial attitude towards this sector (not necessarily by channeling more funds to it) but that requires further study. The second possible departure from neutrality is differential support to firms of different sizes. We discuss this option now in more detail.

3.1.3   Departing from Neutrality: Large vs. Small Firms

In principle, the support policies of the OCS do not make any distinction among types of firms in terms of eligibility for the existing flat rate of support (50 percent of the approved R&D budget).[40] In practice though and as described in Part I, the support for large firms during the past two years has been reduced, reversing the previous trend whereby a handful of very large firms (large by Israeli standards) accounted for a large proportion of the total support dispensed. However, this *de facto* change has been essentially an ad hoc response to budgetary pressures (and hence is likely to be temporary), and not a well formulated policy reassessment. Thus, we still have to examine whether the principle of equal support to all firms regardless of size is a reasonable policy. In other words, the question is whether the rationale for R&D support (in terms of market failures etc.) holds equally for small and large firms. A brief review of the basic economic rationale for support to R&D reveals that indeed there is room to (re)consider the prevailing policy, and reduce the rate of support to large firms versus smaller ones.

First, the larger the firm, the more it is able to internalize the spillovers that it generates, and hence the smaller would be the divergence between the social and the private rate of return on the R&D that it performs. One of the main goals of government support to private R&D is precisely to bridge the gap between the two rates of return: absent that support firms will do too little R&D (relative to the *socially* desirable level), and hence the support is meant to encourage them to increase that amount, pass what is profitable according to the *private* rate of return on it. However, the more a firm manages to capture the spillovers that stem from its R&D projects, the less there is room to subsidize it on that basis. Size matters in that respect: small firms are hardly able to capture the externalities that they generate, but that ability increases as they grow larger.

A further rationale for government support of R&D has to do with risk and risk taking. First, the degree of risk of an R&D project from an economy-wide point of view may be lower than that perceived by private firms; or, closely related, the risk premium demanded by private investors may be higher than warranted because of asymmetric information. Second, the degree of risk aversion by private investors may be higher than the social rate. As a result, the market may provide for too little risk taking in R&D, and hence government support would encourage firms to move in the socially desirable direction.

The point in the present context is that there might be substantial differences in this respect between small and large firms. First, problems of asymmetric information are usually more acute for younger/smaller firms, and hence the risk premium that smaller firms are required to pay is often much higher. Second, R&D projects undertaken by small firms are, ceteris paribus, riskier than if done by larger firms, even if they are exactly the same in terms of technological goals. This is so because younger/smaller firms are disadvantaged relative to large firms in terms of a wide range of competencies and experience that are *complementary* to R&D, be it in marketing, pure management, access to complementary know how, etc. Thus, there is more room to subsidize risk taking by small firms than by larger ones.

Lastly, imperfections in capital markets usually affect small firms more than large firms. First, the availability of internal financing, which has been shown to be important in the context of R&D, is normally less constraining for older/larger firms than for smaller ones. Second, access to global capital markets is easier/cheaper for larger firms. Thus, government support to R&D meant to bridge over those imperfections ought to be channeled more towards small firms than to larger ones.

These considerations suggest that there is room to consider supporting small firms at higher rates than larger firms. One could envision the following support structure: Going startups (up to $5 M sales):[41] 66 percent; small to medium-sized firms ($5–$100 M sales): 50 percent (as at present); large firms (over $100 M): 33 percent. This is of course just an example – a serious proposal would have to pay a great deal of thought to the cut-off levels, the implications for the budget, etc.

3.2   Further Policy Issues

3.2.1   The Payback Scheme (Recoupment)

At present the policy is that successful projects (i.e. projects that eventually lead to sales) are required to pay back to the OCS the amount of support received, but the payback cannot account for more than a small percentage of annual sales.[42] The idea is that the OCS shares the risk of the R&D projects (effectively lowering the risk premium that private firms have to pay), and overcomes possible imperfections in capital markets by offering easily accessible finance. Moreover, it subsidizes R&D both in that it demands zero interest on the conditional loan, and in the sense already mentioned of lowering the risk premium. There are, however, serious drawbacks to such a system:

- Since the payback obligation applies to sales that stem directly from the projects supported, this immediately creates moral hazard problems in terms of how projects are defined, and all sort of pernicious incentives as to how to relate products/sales to projects.

- The previous issue implies that the OCS and the firms supported find themselves engaged in an antagonistic/confrontational situation that is detrimental to the efficient functioning of both.

- As we have seen in Part I, the weight of payback funds in the overall OCS budget is growing steeply over time, and there is a real danger of political opportunism in this respect, namely, that the commitment to R&D support may diminish but in the short run that could be disguised by the increased reliance on payback funds in order to support new projects.

Beyond those issues, the payback scheme may have had the unintended consequence of blurring the real intent of the R&D law, obscuring the true extent of the support budget, and hence the commitment of the government to R&D. As we have seen, such support is warranted for good economic reasons that call indeed for a subsidy to R&D. Contrary to some widely held perceptions, the intent and rationale of the R&D law is not for the government to assume just a financing role, in view of imperfections in existing financial markets in Israel. The main intent is to bridge the gap between the social and the private rate of return to R&D, and that calls for a straight subsidy. The recent availability of venture capital and the opening of the Israeli economy to foreign capital markets may reduce the effective cost of capital and perhaps the risk premiums to Israeli high tech firms. However, that has nothing to do with the fact that these same firms generate spillovers to the Israeli economy that they can only partially appropriate, a fact that calls for subsidizing R&D.

Thus, there is room to consider the phasing out of the payback scheme, or at least the offering of an alternative track consisting of a lower subsidy rate but without a payback proviso. If the payback scheme is eliminated, the R&D grants given by the OCS would become strictly and overtly what they were set out to be, namely, a straight subsidy, hence doing away with the hazards of political opportunism.

3.2.2 The Conditionality of Production in Israel

The R&D Law stipulates that if the OCS extends support to an R&D project, the innovation resulting from it should be produced in Israel. In fact, the Law states as one of its goals to increase employment in such a way. It should be clear that such conditionality might lead to serious allocational inefficiencies. Denoted by c_I the costs of producing in Israel, by c_A the costs of producing abroad, and by S the R&D subsidy. It is trivial to show that, if $c_I - c_A < S$, the firm will choose to take the R&D subsidy, execute the project in Israel and produce there even though production in Israel is more costly than abroad. If the inequality is reversed then the project will be carried out abroad altogether (including the R&D). Denote the cost disadvantage by $S' = c_I - c_A$. In the case where $c_I - c_A < S$, we can see that the R&D subsidy is in fact composed of two parts: $S = S' + (S - S')$. The first part, S', is then a subsidy to *production*, not to R&D, and only the second part is a true R&D subsidy. The larger is the gap between production costs in Israel versus those abroad, the more the R&D grants are in fact subsidizing inefficient production, that quite likely would not be otherwise located in Israel.

Thus, there is room to consider the elimination of this provision of the law: there is no strict economic rationale for it, and it leads, as said, to production inefficiencies. Israel presumably has a comparative advantage in R&D, not in the assembly of boxes containing the sophisticated innovations produced there. It should be clear also that if this conditionality is repealed, then the *effective* R&D subsidy could be increased without increasing the actual amount of funds disbursed. Denote by S_N the new subsidy, then one could have $(S - S') < S_N < S$. Of course, the government can legitimately try to encourage local employment, and see the R&D Law as one of the means to do so. In that case, though, it should be clear that part of the grants constitute in fact an *employment subsidy*, and should not be counted as R&D support.

3.2.3   Policy Changes and Support to Large Firms

We suggested above that the rate of support to large firms could be set a lower level than that to smaller firms. However, we envision the implementation of these policy changes as a comprehensive package. In that case, while lowering the rate of nominal support to large firms, the effective rate may actually increase, both because of the phasing out of recoupment, and of the conditionality to produce in Israel. This latter provision is likely to affect larger firms more than smaller ones, since for larger firms the options and opportunities to produce abroad are much more extensive. As to the payback scheme, it is also likely that the percentage of successful R&D is higher for them, and hence that the payback burden is also disproportionally higher for larger firms. On both accounts then larger firms stand to gain from the repeal of these provisions, thus compensating for the lower support rate.

3.2.4   Ongoing Economic Assessment and Policy Making

The drawing of sound economic policies towards R&D, innovation and the high tech sector is of paramount importance for the Israeli economy. At present, though there is no body in charge of setting such policies, and hence things happen in a rather haphazard way, in response to specific pressures and developments. What is needed is an economic policy unit, probably at the OCS, with the following mandate: (1) to collect and organize in a comprehensive and coherent way the data needed for policy making; (2) to set procedures for the ongoing evaluation of the effectiveness of the OCS policies; (3) to evaluate, research and discuss long term policies. It is interesting to note that the Advanced Technology Program in the U.S., which is the closest to the OCS in terms of intent, has such a unit as integral part of its mission and mandate.

3.3   The Magnet Program versus the Regular OCS Fund

As already mentioned, the Magnet program supports consortia of industrial firms and academia, aimed at developing generic, pre-competitive technologies common to the members of the consortia. The program finances two-thirds of the R&D consortia budgets with straight grants, and there is no payback obligation. Contrary to the regular program of the OCS, Magnet selects consortia on a *competitive* basis, and allocates in this manner a budget of about 60 million dollars per year to the winning consortia.

One of the phenomena that underlie the need for the Magnet program is the fact that R&D efforts in the Israeli high tech sector have been rather fragmented. That is, this sector is characterized by the existence of a very large number of small to medium firms, a handful of large ones (but none with sales of over one billion dollars), and a great deal of turnover.[43] There is no question that the vitality, daring and some spectacular successes of the sector owes in no small measure to these features, that provide favorable conditions for an accelerated Darwinian process. On the other hand, these same features call into question the ability of the sector, and of the Israeli economy as a whole, to reap the long term economic benefits from its own success. The recent sales of a series of highly successful Israeli companies to foreign corporations is just one of the manifestations of this syndrome.

Fragmentation was perhaps unavoidable, certainly in the initial stages of development of the high tech sector, since the overwhelming majority of high tech firms grow out of startups established by single technological entrepreneurs. Moreover, most of them aim (at least initially) at narrowly defined market niches. As the sector moves on though size matters: in order to tackle larger markets and contemplate accordingly longer term projects, there is need for larger entities, and that in turn calls for various forms of cooperation, joint ventures, mergers and acquisitions. However, for reasons that we do not profess to understand, too little seems to be happening in that respect *internally* (i.e., within Israel). In fact, we witness repeatedly not only failures of cooperation, but also even serious informational failures, in the sense that potential partners are unaware of the existence of each other, and/or of the potential for mutually beneficial cooperation.[44]

Given this background, the importance of Magnet may lie not so much in its formally stated mission (i.e., supporting *generic* R&D), but in the fact that it fosters cooperation, it facilitates the creation of larger (sometimes virtual) entities, it disseminates information about possibilities for joint ventures, and it encourages individual firms to seek such information. Contrary to deeply rooted belief; one cannot just *assume* that if there are profitable opportunities for cooperation they will necessarily be realized - the institutional framework definitely has an impact in that sense.

It is therefore quite certain that the economic rationale for government support to R&D is stronger for a program such as Magnet, both because of the aforementioned reasons, and because of more traditional (but equally important) motives, namely, that it deals with generic projects and strongly emphasizes the sharing and dissemination of information. Thus, there is room to consider the expansion of Magnet as a policy instrument, perhaps increasing the share of the overall R&D support budget that it administers. There are a host of specific issues having to do with the way the Magnet Program is implemented, but that is beyond the scope of this chapter.

3.4   How Much Support to R&D: Is There a Basis for Setting a Policy Target?

As we have seen in section 2.3, the budget of the OCS has stabilized since 1997 at a level of about $400 million per year, following a decade of rapid growth. The high tech sector has been lobbying for further increases, claiming that OCS grants play a key role in lowering R&D costs and hence in fueling innovation, in making Israeli companies more attractive to foreign investors, and in compensating for geo-political disadvantages.[45] The government has refused, arguing that the massive influx of Venture Capital and other forms of financing in recent years (primarily IPO's in Nasdaq) prove that there is hardly a need for further R&D subsidies, and that in fact there may be room to reduce them. The result has been an impasse in policy making towards this sector, and the concomitant uncertainty has probably had a detrimental effect on it.

Stepping out from the political economy aspects of the issue, the question is, how should we think about setting a desirable level of R&D support? Is the current level of $400 million appropriate, and if not, what sort of policy gradient should the government pursue? As we shall see, these questions pose serious conceptual and empirical difficulties that are well beyond the scope of this chapter. Thus, we shall content ourselves just with outlining these difficulties, in the hope that they will soberly inform the policy debate and prompt further, much needed research.

The basic premise underlying the sort of neutral, across-the-board R&D subsidies that the OCS dispenses is that, left to its own, the market will undertake too little R&D. If so, the question of how much R&D subsidies should the government give out amounts to asking how much of its resources should a country (in this case Israel) allocate to R&D? If this optimal R&D allocation exceeds the actual one, the R&D support budget should then be set to close the gap between them. Thus, there are two distinct problems to tackle: assessing the presumed gap between actual and optimal R&D spending in the economy, and devising ways to bring the economy to the desired level (and perhaps mix) of R&D spending through a subsidy program such as that of the OCS. Notice that the latter necessitates first a reliable estimate of the additionality factor.

Unfortunately, existing literature provides little guidance regarding the assessment of the gap, be it in modeling or in empirical implementation. Jones and Williams (1998) provides a notable exception. They take estimates of the social rates of return to R&D by Griliches and others (e.g. Griliches 1994; Scherer 1982), and uses them (as well as their own estimate) in the context of a Romer (1990) growth model to derive the optimal R&D to Gross Domestic Product (GDP) ratio. Jones and Williams find that the

U.S. devotes far too little resources to R&D, and that even taking a lower bound of 30 percent for the social rate of return to R&D, the optimal R&D/GDP ratio may be *2 to 4 times higher* than the present one of about 2.2 percent.

It is not clear though whether the results of Jones and Williams and the concomitant policy implications can be readily extended to other countries. First, the optimal R&D/GDP ratio depends critically on the ratio of the social rate of return to R&D, to the economy-wide real rate of return (e.g. the long term return on the stock market). On both accounts a country such as Israel may differ substantially from the U.S. Second, Jones and Williams consider R&D in the context of a close economy; in an open economy, whereby some of the benefits from own R&D spill over to other countries (see for example Coe and Helpman 1995), the notion of a social rate of return is far less clear.

Eaton, Gutierrez and Kortum (1998) provide further support to the notion that countries may be under investing in R&D. They laid out a detailed model of the R&D process and of the transmission of research outcomes across countries (based on Eaton and Kortum 1996), and proceed to calibrate it for the European Union (EU) countries, and to simulate its responsiveness to various policy levers. One of their conclusions is that increasing research activity in most European countries could make a substantial contribution to productivity levels not only in the EU but also throughout the Organization for Economic Co-operation and Development (OECD). However, Eaton, Gutierrez and Kortum stop short of endorsing the channeling of additional resources into R&D, and they certainly do not attempt to compute an optimal R&D/GDP ratio that could serve as an actual target for policy in any specific country. Still, their conclusions are congruent with a policy gradient of increasing R&D/GDP ratios, at least for most European countries.

3.4.1 R&D Ratios as Yardsticks for Policy

Much of the discussion in the literature on R&D policy is cast in terms of various R&D ratios, particularly in terms of the ratio of total civilian expenditures on R&D to GDP (in short, R&D/GDP). Countries compare each other in terms of these ratios, and often set targets based on averages for various reference groups (e.g. the European Union, the OECD, etc.) This is so not only because the amount of resources devoted to R&D obviously cannot be divorced from total resources available, but also because there is indeed a great deal of uncertainty in this respect, and hence political feasibility and expedience often requires such linkages.[46] Israel is no exception, and indeed Israel's standing vis-à-vis other countries in terms of R&D/GDP ratios figures prominently in the current debate. While they surely may play a useful role in informing policy making, we would like to argue that these ratios should be considered with great caution as yardsticks for policy, both because of measurement problems, and because of the importance of critical mass in the R&D context.

The measurement of R&D expenditures poses serious challenges to statistical agencies, both because it is very difficult to delimit the scope of what counts as R&D, and because of difficulties in computing appropriate deflators. Ever since the publication and widespread adoption of the Frascati Manual in the 1980s, there has been remarkable progress in achieving international harmonization in terms of what constitutes R&D. However, the changing nature of innovative activities poses renewed problems at every turn, as is the case for example with many types of software development and Internet-related innovations.[47] Prompted by the sense that existing data collection procedures failed to account for substantial portions of R&D activities, the Israeli Central Bureau of Statistics (CBS) introduced in the late nineties a new and much more detailed survey of Business Sector R&D (BSRD), that resulted in drastic revisions of previously available estimates. Thus, for example, the newly computed BSRD for 1997 was 44 percent higher than the previous estimate, and consequently the R&D/GDP ratio jumped up by about half a percentage point to 3.1 for that year, reaching 3.5 in 1999.[48]

The revision that the CBS has undertaken exemplifies the difficulties of setting policy according to these ratios: until the publication of the revised figures, existing estimates indicated that Israel's R&D/GDP was about average relative to the OECD, and moreover, that Israel's BSRD constituted a significantly smaller proportion of total R&D than in other countries (about 50-55 percent, compared to a median of 62 percent for the OECD). Thus, if these ratios were used as yardsticks for policy, it would have been reasonable to advocate further support to BSRD to increase its share, a move that would have resulted also in a moderate increase in the R&D/GDP ratio.[49] The current figures put Israel at the upper end of OECD countries in terms of R&D/GDP ratios, and about average in terms of BSRD/R&D. Thus, international comparisons of this sort would render at present very different policy recommendations.

The second measurement problem is that of devising appropriate deflators for R&D expenditures. The practice at the CBS has been to compute for each R&D-performing sector an index based on the average wages in the sector on the one hand, and the costs of materials and capital outlays on the other hand (each component weighted by its appropriate share in R&D). However, a survey of wages conducted separately by the CBS (as part of its general survey of labor and wages), indicates that wages for *R&D personnel* in the business sector rose much faster than average wages in the sector. Thus, computing a deflator based on these wages renders a very different picture, as can be seen in the following comparison (see below for further discussion on the new index):

Table 9: Annual Average Rate of Growth of BSRD: 1994–1999
(using revised figures based on new CBS survey[50]

In nominal Israeli Shekels	21%
Deflated by the CPI	12%
Deflated by the CBS R&D deflator (1994-98, prior to revision)	7%
Deflated by new index based on wages of R&D personnel in business sector*	~ 3%

*Provisional computations, hence figure is approximate only

    The impressive growth of BSRD in the past half-decade (12 percent per year, CPI-adjusted) is thus greatly attenuated when deflating it by the new and still provisional index, i.e. just about three percent per year. Of course, the R&D/GDP ratio would be significantly lower as well, if we were to compute it based on these real magnitudes. Once again, these disparities are just meant to illustrate the extent to which the figures that might serve us as guideposts for policy are sensitive to the way we treat these measurement issues.

    The second problem with international comparisons of R&D ratios for policy is that of critical mass. Contrary to other areas where the *relative* amount of resources may constitute a good enough yardstick (such as in health or education), what determines the impact of R&D on the economic performance of the economy is in many cases the *absolute* and not the relative amount invested because there are substantial indivisibilities in R&D both at the micro and macro levels. At the level of individual projects and/or firms, a wide range of technological areas require the commitment of relatively large amounts of R&D in order to make these projects at all feasible (in other words, the minimum efficient scale of projects in such areas is large). Thus, the development of communication satellites requires R&D budgets of hundreds of millions of dollars, and so do new ethical drugs.

    At the economy-wide level, the conduct of R&D requires a vast array of supporting infrastructure and services, the availability of adequate manpower (not only scientists and engineers but also supporting personnel of various sorts), and of financial institutions and markets. All of these would come into being only if enough R&D is being carried out to justify the emergence of the required infrastructure, venture capital institutions, etc. Moreover, the ability of firms conducting R&D to capture the spillovers generated by others in the same region/country depend as well on the existence of a sufficiently large nearby R&D sector. This latter factor can be critical for the chances of the high sector in the country to become a Silicon Valley. Thus, it is hard to compare R&D/GDP ratios for countries that vary a great deal in size, particularly when the differences are so extreme as between the U.S. or Japan and Israel.[51]

Table 10: The 15 Leading Industrial R&D Companies in the USA, and Israel: R&D Expenditures in 1997

1997 Rank	Company	R&D Expenditures	
		Millions $	R&D/Sales %
1	General Motors	8,200	4.9
2	Ford Motor	6,327	4.1
3	IBM	4,307	5.5
Israel's Total Civilian R&D		*3,129*	
4	Lucent Technologies	3,100	11.8
5	Hewlett-Packard	3,078	7.2
6	Motorola	2,748	9.2
7	Intel	2,347	9.4
8	Johnson & Johnson	2,140	9.5
Israel's Business Sector R&D		*2,006*	
9	Pfizer	1,928	15.4
10	Microsoft	1,925	16.9
11	Boeing	1,924	4.2
12	Chrysler	1,700	2.9
13	Merck	1,684	7.1
14	American Home Products	1,558	11.0
15	General Electric	1,480	1.7

Source: NSF Science and Engineering Indicators - Top 500 Firms in R&D by Industry Category,1999. http://www.nsf.gov/sbe/srs/nsf00301

Furthermore, the extent to which comparisons of R&D ratios are informative (and potentially telling from a normative point of view) depend *inter alia* on the growth strategy that the countries being compared have chosen. Israel has embarked long ago in a growth path that relies heavily upon the promotion of high tech, export-oriented sectors, reflecting its perceived comparative advantage in high-skilled labor. By contrast, countries such as Spain or New Zealand, while comparable to Israel in terms of current GPD per capita, have chosen a very different path (recall Part I, and Figure 4). Thus, while a R&D/GDP ratio of about one percent for Spain might be adequate given *its* growth strategy, Israel's much higher ratio may still be below mark.

In order to gain further perspective on the issue of absolute versus relative size of expenditures in R&D, consider Table 10, where we list the leading industrial R&D performers in the United States, and compare them to Israel as a whole. Thus, in 1997 the absolute amount of resources allocated to civilian R&D in Israel was $3,129 million, of which $2,006 million was business sector R&D.[52] That same year eight of the leading industrial R&D performers in the U.S. spent *over 2 billion dollars* in R&D, *each of them* more than Israel's industrial sector as a whole. To put it differently, *all* of Israel's business sector R&D amounted to the R&D done by Pfizer, and was slightly less than the R&D done by Johnson and Johnson. If we took instead Israel's total civilian R&D, that would place Israel as number 4, just in between IBM and Lucent. These gaps are well reflected also in patent statistics (see Trajtenberg 1999): Israeli inventors were granted in 1997 a total of 653 patents, of which slightly less than half went to Israeli corporations, i.e. about 320 patents. By contrast, that same year IBM was granted 1,758 patents, Motorola 1,151, Intel 407, Hewlett-Packard 537, General Electric 667, and so forth.

3.5 Prop up Demand, or Stimulate Supply?

As mentioned in Part I, the basic premise underlying Israeli R&D Policy has been all along that Israel enjoys a comparative advantage in high tech, science-based industries, because of the abundance of high-skilled labor and scientific personnel. This, coupled with the presumption that the market is likely to under invest in R&D, provides the rationale for the direct subsidization of industrial R&D, as done through the OCS programs. Viewed from the vantage point of the market for scientists and engineers, such policy is one that stimulates demand, implicitly if supply is sufficiently elastic to provide the additional personnel called forth by the government supported R&D.

Figure 7 casts serious doubts on this set of premises: wages of R&D personnel in the business sector have risen extremely fast in the second half of the 1990s, much faster than economy-wide wages (by 1999 the index of wages in R&D had risen 54 percent more than all wages). Clearly, the dramatic increase in R&D outlays by the Business Sector during the same period fueled the inflation in wages of R&D workers.[53] Mirroring these developments, there is circumstantial evidence of severe shortages in computer scientists and engineers, software developers, and related personnel.[54] The picture that emerges is thus of a very *inelastic* supply curve for qualified R&D workers in recent years. This implies that any additional financial resources channeled into BSRD would achieve little increase in real R&D in the short run, and instead would keep fueling wage inflation (see Goolsbee 1998, for a similar argument regarding the effect of government-supported R&D in the United States).

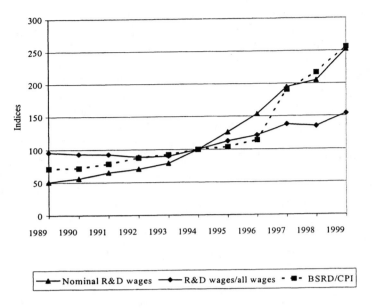

Figure 7:. Indices of Wages in R&D and Business Sector R&D (*1994:100*)

Shortages of highly skilled personnel seem to be a pervasive, worldwide phenomenon in recent years, certainly in the U.S. as well as in leading European countries.[55] Romer (2000) suggests that existing institutional arrangements in the U.S. higher education system limit the supply response to these market signals, and hence necessitate corrective policy changes. In essence, the incentive system within universities is not necessarily conducive to the timely supply of graduates in fields of high demand, both in terms of the number of students admitted to different fields, the mix of courses offered, and the channeling of graduate students into lengthy, often dead-end post-doc positions.[56] Thus, Romer advocates a shift of focus in government policy towards R&D, from the traditional subsidization of R&D itself that stimulates the *demand* for scientists and engineers, to programs that would directly encourage the *supply* of newly trained qualified manpower. In light of the trends depicted in Figure 7, government policy ought to address *both* sides of the market: the relative abundance of qualified manpower is no longer to be taken for granted, and there are plenty of institutional rigidities and frictions in the educational system to cast doubt on its ability to respond by itself in a timely fashion to market needs.

One specific problem in Israel in this respect, is that there are relatively large groups of the population that have acquired significant levels of general human capital, but not the skills that are required for the high tech sector, and that essentially do not participate in the relevant labor markets. These are primarily ultra-orthodox Jews, Israeli Arabs, and residents in the development towns located in the geographically more distant areas. The impediments to their partaking in the job opportunities offered by the New Economy are numerous, ranging from cultural barriers to geographical isolation. It is clear that tapping their potential could alleviate the shortages alluded to, and at the same time improve the economic standing of these groups.[57] This would involve providing the appropriate training, setting up an institutional framework that would allow their employment in the high tech sector without violating their cultural sensitivities and investing in infrastructure to bring them closer to the centers of economic activity.

The case of Bangalore in India exemplifies the wide range of possibilities opened in terms of employing skilled labor in R&D-related activities from the distance, without the workers having to migrate and adapt to the environment of the employer. Indeed, as documented in Arora and Arunachalam (2000), a large part of the burgeoning software sector in India does subcontracting development work for U.S.-based firms. It would seem that a similar model could be applied *within* Israel vis-à-vis the population groups mentioned above, that is, provide them with training *in situ*, and employ them in *their* communities via subcontracting employment relationships. There seem to be a host of coordination failures that prevent that from happening without intervention, and hence there is room for the government to undertake a facilitating role.

Developments in the labor markets associated with high tech have of course wider implications. In fact, one of the most striking trends in the Israeli economy of the past two decades has been the rapid rise in pre-tax income inequality. Attempts by the government to keep a lid on after-tax inequality have necessitated a dramatic increase in the share of the budget (and of GDP) going to welfare, a trend that seems unsustainable. The rapid rise in the relative wages of workers in the high tech sector has undoubtedly contributed to the growing income gap in recent years. Clearly, policies that shift up the demand for these workers would further increase inequality, at least in the short run, whereas policies that stimulate the supply response would presumably do the opposite. This is obviously a normative issue, and hence it lies well beyond the scope of this chapter. However, what is becoming increasingly clear is that, as the sectors and activities associated with advanced technologies gain in importance throughout the economy, policies towards them would have to be guided by a wider set of considerations, including their distributive implications.

Appendix 1:

ADDITIONAL SUPPORT PROGRAMS OF THE OCS

Beyond the main programs described above (the regular R&D Grants, Magnet, and the Incubator Centers), the OCS offers a variety of additional assistance programs, aimed at specific stages along the innovation cycle or at particular segments in the progression from a innovative idea to a full-fledged commercial enterprise. Although much smaller in terms of budget, these programs may play an important role in making sure that potentially viable projects don't fall in between the cracks along the hazardous way towards successful commercial implementation. Following is a concise description of some of these programs.

1. Bridging Aid

This program offers support for the transition between R&D and manufacturing and marketing. The intention is to enable companies that have completed the R&D stage to manufacture a number of prototypes for installation on the premises of potential clients, especially abroad. In the case of chemical innovations, the program supports the setting up of a pilot plant, enabling the manufacturer to obtain feedback on the performance of the new product or process.

Companies with sales of up to six million dollars may receive a grant of 50 percent for these purposes, whereas larger ones (with annual sales of up to $30 million) are eligible for 30 percent grants. Total approved spending may not exceed $600,000 over a 30-month period. Recognized transition period expenses generally include:

- Construction of prototypes;
- Adaptation to standards in foreign countries;
- Registration of the product for marketing abroad;
- Operation of a pilot plant, not including construction costs;
- Patent registration fees.

2. Aid in Establishing Industrial Incubators

The goal of this program is to encourage *established* companies to develop cooperative startups in new technological areas, taking advantage of the companies' existing infrastructure, finance and management. The OCS grants 66 percent of the approved R&D outlay, up to a ceiling of $300,000 annually for a maximum of two years. Thereafter the projects would qualify for standard R&D grants. The program is aimed at scientific entrepreneurs (including new immigrants), who are required to create a cooperative framework with an established Israeli industrial company, having previous R&D experience and annual sales of at least $5 million.

3. Sub-contracting Industrial R&D

This program supports the carrying out of civilian R&D projects for foreign companies, by Israeli enterprises acting as subcontractors. The goal is to initiate joint ventures with foreign partners, to help Israeli companies market their technologically advanced products abroad. The OCS grants up to 20 percent of the approved R&D costs. The Israeli subcontractor must be an industrial company with annual sales of up to $100 million, and the R&D project must be in a new area for the Israeli company.

4. Exploratory Studies for Industrial R&D Projects

This program supports studies of the market potential for new technologies, before the investment of large sums in the R&D stage. It is intended primarily for startup companies, or those with limited R&D experience. However, established companies interested in exploring new subjects not included in their current areas of activity are eligible as well. The program extends grants of 50 percent of approved costs, up to $30,000. The studies are to be carried out by experienced, external consulting companies, authorized by the OCS.

ACKNOWLEDGEMENTS

Prepared for and supported by the Advanced Technology Program (ATP). I wish to thank Ariel Ben-Porat and Guy Michaels for research assistance, and the Office of the Chief Scientist at the Ministry of Industry and Trade, Israel, for data and helpful discussions. In particular, I wish to thank Dr. Orna Beri, the outgoing Chief Scientist, for having brought me (through her gentle, continuous prodding) into the realm of R&D Policy, and for her dedication to the high tech sector, that has certainly been a source of inspiration to all.

REFERENCES

Arora, A. and V. S. Arunachalam. (2000). "The Globalization of Software: The Case of the Indian Software Industry." A report submitted to the Sloan Foundation, Carnegie Mellon University.

Bregman, A and A. Merom. (1998). "Productivity and its Causes in Israeli Industry, 1960 – 1996". Bank of Israel, Research Department, Discussion Paper Series 98.03, February.

Bregman, A., M. Fuss, and H. Regev. (1991). "High Tech and Productivity: Evidence from Israeli Industrial Firms." *European Economic Review 35*: 1199-1221.

Busom, I. (2000). "An Empirical Evaluation of the Effects of R&D Subsidies." *Economics of Innovation and New Technology.*

Coe, D. T and E. Helpman. (1995). "International R&D Spillovers." *European Economic Review.* 39 (5): 859-87. May.

David, P. A. and B. Hall. (2000). "Heart of Darkness: Modeling Public-Private Funding Interactions Inside the R&D Black Box." *NBER* Working Paper W753, February.

David, P. A., B. Hall, and A. A. Toole. (1999). "Is Public R&D a Complement or Substitute for Private R&D? A Review of the Econometric Evidence." *NBER* Working Paper W7373, October.

David, P., B. Hall and A. Tool. (1999). "Is Public R&D a Complement or a Substitute for Private R&D?" *NBER* Working Paper # 7373, October.

Eaton, J. and S. Kortum. (1996). "Trade in Ideas: Patenting and Productivity in the OCED." *Journal of International Economics* 40: 251-278.

Eaton, J., E. Gutierrez, and S. Kortum. (1998). "European Technology Policy: Research Efforts in Europe Matter." *Economic Policy* 0 (27): 403-430, October.

Feldman, M. P. and M. R. Kelley. (2000). "Winning an Award from the Advanced Technology Program: Economic Potential, Quality, and Risk." *Advanced Technology Program, NIST*, forthcoming as a NISTIR.

Goolsbee, A. (1998). "Does Government R&D Policy Mainly Benefit Scientists and Engineers?" *American Economic Review* 88 (2): 298-302. May.

Griliches, Z. and H. Regev. (1995). "Firm Productivity in Israeli Industry 1979 – 1988." *Journal of Econometrics* 65: 175-203.

Griliches, Z. and H. Regev. (1999). "R&D, Government Support and Productivity in Manufacturing in Israel, 1975-94." *The Economic Quarterly* 46: 335-356 November (in Hebrew).

Griliches, Z. (1994). "Productivity, R&D, and the Data Constraint." *American Economic Review* 84: 1-23.

Guellec, D. and B. van Pottelsberghe, (2000). "The Impact of Public R&D Expenditure on Business R&D." *Organization for Economic Cooperation and Development,* STI Working Paper 2000/4, Paris.

Hunt, J. and J. Tybout. (1998). "Does Promoting High Tech Products Spur Development?" Mimeo, March.

Israel Central Bureau of Statistics (CBS). (1998). "National Expenditure on Civilian Research and Development 1989-1997." *CBS Publication* No. 1086. Jerusalem, May.

Israel Central Bureau of Statistics (CBS). (1999a). "Survey of Structure of Labor Force, Patterns of Work and Innovation in Manufacturing - 1997." *CBS,* August

Israel Central Bureau of Statistics (CBS). (1999b). "National Expenditure on Civilian Research and Development 1989-1998." *CBS Publication* No. 1121. Jerusalem, October.

Israel Ministry of Industry and Trade, Office of the Chief Scientist (OCS). (1994). "Israeli Innovations and Technologies 1994." Jerusalem.

Israel Ministry of Industry and Trade, Office of the Chief Scientist (OCS). (1999a). "Encouragement of Industrial R&D in Israel". Jerusalem, September.

Israel Ministry of Industry and Trade, Office of the Chief Scientist (OCS) (1999b). "Magnet Program 1998 – Drawing Potential for Progress". Jerusalem.

Israel Ministry of Industry and Trade, Office of the Chief Scientist (OCS). (1999c). "Startups & Innovations – A Guide to Israeli Startups and High Tech Projects. Jerusalem.

Jones, C. I. and J. C. Williams. (1998). "Measuring the Social Returns to R&D." *Quarterly Journal of Economics,* pp.1119-1135, November.

Klette, T. J., and J. Moen. (1998a). "From Growth Theory to Technology Policy – Coordination Problems in Theory and Practice." *Statistics Norway, Research Department,* Discussion Paper No. 219, April.

Klette, T. J., and J. Moen. (1998b). "R&D Investment Responses to R&D Subsidies: A Theoretical Analysis and a Microeconometric Study." Oslo, Mimeo, June.

Klette, T. J., Moen, J., and Z. Griliches. (1999). "Do Subsidies to Commercial R&D Reduce Market Failures? Microeconomic Evaluation Studies." *NBER* Working Paper W6947, February.

Lach, S. (2000). "Do R&D Subsidies Stimulate or Displace Private R&D? Evidence from Israel." Hebrew University of Jerusalem, mimeo, June.

Michlol Consultancy. (1999). "Research on the Contributions of the OCS – Final Report." Unpublished mimeo. April.

National Science Foundation. (1998). *Science and Engineering Indicators 1998*. Washington, DC: U.S. Government Printing Office.

Romer, P. M. (1990). "Endogenous Technological Change." *Journal of Political Economy* 98: S71-S102, October.

Rosenberg, N. (1999). "American Universities as Endogenous Institutions." Mimeo. Department of Economics, Stanford University,.

Rosenberg, N. (forthcoming). "America's University/Industry Interfaces, 1945–2000." in G. Törnqvist and S. Sörlin, eds., *The Wealth of Knowledge. Universities in the New Economy*.

Scherer, F. M. (1982). "Inter-Industry Technology Flows and Productivity Growth." *Review of Economic and Statistics* 64: 627-634.

Teubal, M. (1999). "Towards an R&D Strategy for Israel". *The Economic Quarterly* 46: 359-383 (in Hebrew), November.

Toren, B. (1990). "R&D in Industry" in D. Brodet, M. Justman and M. Teubal, eds., *Industrial Technological Policy for Israel*. The Jerusalem Institute for Israeli Studies.

Trajtenberg, M. (forthcoming). "Innovation in Israel 1968-97: A Comparative Analysis Using Patent Data." *Research Policy*.

Trajtenberg, M. (2000). "R&D Policy in Israel: An Overview and Reassessment". *Foerder Institute for Economic Research*, Working Paper No. 7-2000, February.

Wallsten, S. J. (2000). "The Effects of Government-Industry R&D Programs on Private R&D: The Case of the Small Business Innovation Research Program." *Rand Journal of Economics* 31 (1): 82-100, Spring.

---

[1] As the title indicates, we confine ourselves to *civilian, industrial* R&D. Both defense R&D and academic R&D have played all along a pivotal role in Israel's overall research enterprise, and fueled to some extent the growth of high tech via a variety of spillovers, but these are beyond the scope of this chapter.

[2] The 1985 Law may soon undergo a significant revision, in view of the changes undergone by the high tech sector in the course of the last decade, and the budgetary restraint of the late 1990s that has resulted in excess demand for R&D grants under the present system.

[3] We draw for this section from a variety of material from the OCS (see Israel Ministry of Industry and Trade, 1994, 1999a, 1999b and 1999c), as well as from personal involvement with the OCS, in particular with the Magnet Program.

[4] Actually the original payback schedule was as follows: three percent of revenues from sales of the products developed for the first three years; four percent in the next three years, and five percent from the seventh year onwards. This schedule has been revised a few times, and the Treasury has long been pressuring the OCS to increase these percentages, and even impose interest payments.

[5] The Research Committee may grant exemptions to requirements (2) and (3), but as far as I have been able to establish, this has happened rarely.

[6] The 1985 Law was amended to place the software industry on an equal footing with other industrial sectors, so that software development projects qualify for the same type of aid.

[7] Israeli universities have proved also to be highly capable of generating innovations having economic potential (as manifested, for example, in the large number of U.S. patents assigned to them – see Trajtenberg 1999), but once again weak links with industry have prevented the extensive exploitation of such potential.

[8] "Magnet" is the acronym (in Hebrew) for "Generic, Pre-Competitive Research".

[9] Magnet supports also the integration of advanced technologies into industry via users' associations, but that is a secondary activity.

[10] Participation is limited to Israeli-based companies, or Israeli subsidiaries of foreign companies.

[11] In addition to the sources already mentioned, we drew material for this section from the internet site of the program, www.incubators.org.il

[12] Each incubator is an autonomous not-for-profit organization. Day to day operations are run by a professional (salaried) manager, and next to her operates a projects committee that selects and monitors the projects. These committees are composed of professionals from industry and academia, e.g. corporate executives, R&D managers, professors, etc. Committee members volunteer their time and expertise and do not receive any financial compensation.

[13] The budget for the incubator's administration is of $175,000 per year. This includes the incubator manager's salary, administrative expenses, outlays for sorting and studying of ideas, and organizational expenses for project commercialization and marketing.

[14] The data comes from the office of Lidia Lazens of the OCS, and was supplied by Shai Goldberg.

[15] A common practice is to deflate just by the rate of inflation in the U.S., but such deflator is in fact irrelevant for the case at hand.

[16] The projections for 2000 indicate that paybacks may have stabilized by now.

[17] The OCS defines startups as firms of up to three years of age.

[18] There are no official figures in that respect, but all indications are that startups have mushroomed in Israel since the mid-1990s. In fact, a recent newspaper report based on the number of startups that hired the services of accounting firms claimed that in 1999 alone 1,500 new startups were formed.

[19] This might also reflect a change in the technology mix of the newcomers, with more of them in Internet applications that represent novel business models rather than novel technology, and hence that may not qualify for support from the OCS.

[20] "Large firms" are defined with over $100 million in sales; startups refer to firms of up to three years of age.

[21] In table 4 some dollar series are aggregated into 5-year totals: these sums obviously don't mean much since the figures are in *nominal* dollars, but may still be useful as ballparks to compare across firms of different sizes.

[22] This figure refers to projects *approved*. In fact, the average number of projects applied for is about 1,800.

[23] This was a conscious policy decision by the OCS, meant to cope with the excess demand for support in view of the budget cap imposed by the Treasury.
A report prepared for the OCS in 1999 claimed that large firms commanded 56 percent of the OCS budget during the period 1985-94. If so there is a declining trend, beyond the one-time policy shift in 1999. However, the figures are not strictly comparable, and hence we cannot assert this with certainty.

---

[24] David, Hall and Tool (1999) survey a body of recent empirical studies, but do not find robust patterns that could be generalized. On the other hand, using a cross-country, macro economic model, Guellec and Van Pottelsberghe (2000) find evidence of significant additionality effects for 17 OECD countries.

[25] See also Israel CBS (1999a) for further detailed statistics on "advanced" versus traditional sectors.

[26] Thus the advanced sectors include, for example, electronics and electrical, the mixed sectors construction - related industries, and the traditional ones, textiles and apparel.

[27] This section consists of excerpts from Trajtenberg (1999).

[28] The in-between "flat" period of 1987-91 (which represents R&D activity done *circa* 1985-89) presumably reflects the big macro adjustment and micro restructuring that followed the stabilization program of 1985.

[29] The R&D figures are from Griliches and Regev (1999), table 1. Since these refer to *industrial* R&D, it may be more appropriate to relate them to Israeli *corporate* patents than to total patents. In practice, the two patent series move pretty much in tandem, and hence the correlations with R&D of either series are virtually the same.

[30] Patent applications reflect (successful) R&D conducted *before* the filing date, with lags varying by sector. Thus, the number of patents in a particular year should be attributed to investments in R&D carried out in the previous one to two years at least, and in some sectors further back.

[31] The Reference Group was chosen according to their GDP per capita in the early 1990s, that is, we chose the four countries that had at that time a level of GDP per capita closest to that of Israel (in ppp terms). Notice that, except for Spain, the other three countries in this group are very similar to Israel also in terms of population.

[32] Another normalization of interest would be R&D expenditures, but except for the G7, the figures for the other countries are far from satisfactory

[33] As mentioned in the Introduction, a great deal of research on R&D policy has been done recently. Aside from the references mentioned there, see also David et al 1999, Hunt and Tybout 1998, Klette and Moen 1998a, b.

[34] Apparently, this was the first time in the history of the OCS that demand exceeded the budget provision by a substantial amount.

[35] Indeed, in January 2000 the government initiated a move aimed at revising the R&D Law, in view of this fundamental conflict, as well as of the dramatic changes that have taken place in the high tech sector.

[36] Some projections indicate that would be true even if the budget were increased substantially.

[37] It is quite likely that the present system in actuality is not neutral either, but the lack of neutrality is disguised. In a ranking system, the issue rises to the surface and will have to be addressed head on.

[38] It is interesting to note that there is a great deal of interest in this policy both in the U.S. and in Europe, and it would seem that at some point some version of randomization will be implemented. One of the great advantages (in the long run) of such a policy is that it allows for methodologically sound assessment studies of the efficacy of government support (since the "control sample" is built in).

[39] In fact, it would seem that, while formally neutral, actual support policies favored particular technological areas, primarily electronics, and until the mid-1990s large firms over smaller ones (see below).

[40] Except for the incubators program, as described in Part I.

[41] Startups are defined here as young, small ongoing firms, not those that are in the "incubator" phase.

[42] The percentage was set at three percent, but there have been several attempts by the Treasury to raise it further (to 4.5 percent), and even to charge interest on the principal. In fact, the Treasury has been promoting the idea that the grants should turn into a conditional loan, which will serve as a way of overcoming financial constraints by R&D firms, but not as a straight R&D subsidy.

[43] Consider that the OCS have dealt with R&D projects of about 3,000 firms in the past 15 years, and keep in mind that, as said before, the whole industrial R&D of Israel amounts to that done by the number 28th R&D spender in the U.S., 3M (see Table 8).

[44] As a member of the Board of Directors of Magnet, I have witnessed many times this sort of "failures," not only between firms but also between firms and academia. One of the most striking was the case of the digital printing consortium: the main players involved were unaware until the formation of the consortium of crucial research on properties of ink that was being conducted at some academic institutions in Israel (virtually "next doors").

[45] The high tech sector is actually split in this respect: on the one hand the traditional electronics sector demands bigger budgets for the OCS; on the other hand, Internet-related ventures and some of the new software developers lobby instead for favorable tax breaks, particularly with regard to capital gains.

[46] Thus, advocating a move towards the mean R&D/GDP ratio of a "relevant" group of countries is politically easier to justify than persistent divergence from such reference ratios.

[47] Regarding the Internet, it is often hard to distinguish between developments that are purely the result of entrepreneurship as opposed to being the outcome of R&D as traditionally defined.

[48] These are the latest (and still preliminary) ratios computed by CBS for international comparisons. CBS (1999) reports a R&D/GDP ratio of 2.3 for 1996, the latest such official figure there. The revisions put the figure for that year at 2.8, so the increase in the ratio due to the new survey is at least of half a percentage point.

[49] See for example an earlier version of this chapter, Trajtenberg (2000).

[50] We inflated the old 1996 figure by a factor of 1.44 (recall that the new estimate for BSRD 1997 was 44 percent higher than the previous one) in order to compute the rate of change for 1996-97. From then on, we used the new figures.

[51] If one could compute an optimal R&D/GDP ratio for different countries, chances are that it would be a concave, decreasing function of size.

[52] These figures are based on the revised estimates produced by the CBS based on their new survey. The previous estimates placed Israel much lower in that scale: 16th in terms of BSRD, and seventh in terms of total R&D.

[53] The series for BSRD depicted in Figure 7 is not entirely consistent, in that the figures for 1997 onwards are those of the new survey of R&D in the Business Sector, which, as said, showed a large increase in the scope of R&D done by the sector. Thus, while the increase from 1993-94 to 1997-98 is plausible, the path of the series in between is not necessarily accurate.

[54] As reflected, for example, in statistics of job openings, as well as the frequent reports of increasing difficulties of existing companies in retaining R&D personnel.

[55] One of the related, hotly debated policy issues in many countries is the extent to which foreign high tech workers should be allowed in. This has become also a highly controversial issue in Israel.

---

[56] Romer's view would seem to contradict Rosenberg's (1999, 2000), who has persuasively argued that one of the key sources of strength underlying the technological and scientific prowess of the U.S. has been the responsiveness of universities to market needs and new technological developments. However, it could well be that what had characterized universities throughout most of the 20th century does not quite hold in recent years, and/or that the pace of change has accelerated, and hence the response of universities seems more sluggish now.

[57] These are mostly in the lowest income brackets, and account for a large fraction of the unemployed.

Index

Economics of Science, Technology and Innovation

1. A. Phillips, A.P. Phillips and T.R. Phillips:
   *Biz Jets. Technology and Market Structure in
   the Corporate Jet Aircraft Industry.* 1994   ISBN 0-7923-2660-1
2. M.P. Feldman:
   The Geography of Innovation. 1994   ISBN 0-7923-2698-9
3. C. Antonelli:
   *The Economics of Localized Technological
   Change and Industrial Dynamics.* 1995   ISBN 0-7923-2910-4
4. G. Becher and S. Kuhlmann (eds.):
   *Evaluation of Technology Policy Programmes
   in Germany.* 1995   ISBN 0-7923-3115-X
5. B. Carlsson (ed.): *Technological Systems and Economic
   Performance: The Case of Factory Automation.* 1995   ISBN 0-7923-3512-0
6. G.E. Flueckiger: *Control, Information, and
   Technological Change.* 1995   ISBN 0-7923-3667-4
7. M. Teubal, D. Foray, M. Justman and E. Zuscovitch (eds.):
   *Technological Infrastructure Policy. An International
   Perspective.* 1996   ISBN 0-7923-3835-9
8. G. Eliasson:
   *Firm Objectives, Controls and Organization. The Use
   of Information and the Transfer of Knowledge within
   the Firm.* 1996   ISBN 0-7923-3870-7
9. X. Vence-Deza and J.S. Metcalfe (eds.):
   *Wealth from Diversity. Innovation, Structural Change and
   Finance for Regional Development in Europe.* 1996   ISBN 0-7923-4115-5
10. B. Carlsson (ed.):
    Technological Systems and Industrial Dynamics. 1997   ISBN 0-7923-9940-4
11. N.S. Vonortas:
    Cooperation in Research and Development. 1997   ISBN 0-7923-8042-8
12. P. Braunerhjelm and K. Ekholm (eds.):
    The Geography of Multinational Firms. 1998   ISBN 0-7923-8133-5
13. A. Varga:
    *University Research and Regional Innovation: A Spatial
    Econometric Analysis of Academic Technology Transfers.*
    1998   ISBN 0-7923-8248-X
14. J. de la Mothe and G. Paquet (eds.):
    Local and Regional Systems of Innovation   ISBN 0-7923-8287-0
15. D. Gerbarg (ed.):
    The Economics, Technology and Content of Digital T V   ISBN 0-7923-8325-7
16. C. Edquist, L. Hommen and L. Tsipouri
    Public Technology Procurement and Innovation   ISBN 0-7923-8685-X
17. J. de la Mothe and G. Paquet (eds.):
    Information, Innovation and Impacts   ISBN 0-7923-8692-2

18. J. S. Metcalfe and I. Miles (eds.):
   Innovation Systems in the Service Economy:
   Measurement and Case Study Analysis   ISBN 0-7923-7730-3
19. R. Svensson:
   Success Strategies and Knowledge Transfer in
   Cross-Border Consulting Operations   ISBN 0-7923-7776-1
20. P. Braunerhjelm:
   Knowledge Capital and the "New Economy":
   Firm Size, Performance and Network Production   ISBN 0-7923-7801-6
21. J. de la Mothe and J. Niosi (eds):
   The Economic and Social Dynamics of Biotechnology   ISBN 0-7923-7922-5
22. B. Guilhon, (ed):
   Technology and Markets for Knowledge:
   Knowledge Creation, Diffusion and Exchange within
   a Growing Economy   ISBN 0-7923-7202-6
23. M. Feldman and A. Link (eds.):
   Innovation Policy in the Knowledge-Based Economy   ISBN 0-7923-7296-4

KLUWER ACADEMIC PUBLISHERS — BOSTON / DORDRECHT / LONDON

Printed in the United States
70627LV00001B/66